THE COMPLETE IDIOT'S GUIDE® TO

Understanding North Korea

by Dr. C. Kenneth Quinones and Joseph Tragert

ALPHA

A member of Penguin Group (USA) Inc.

—Ken's Dedication—To Julie, Nancy, and Cathy, my loves; Ed Wagner, my mentor; and Chuck Kartman, Bob Carlin, and Frank Metersky, my friends
—Joe's Dedication—To Berni and little Joe

International Standard Book Number: 1-59257-169-7
Library of Congress Catalog Card Number: 2003113809

06 05 04   8 7 6 5 4 3 2 1

Interpretation of the printing code: The rightmost number of the first series of numbers is the year of the book's printing; the rightmost number of the second series of numbers is the number of the book's printing. For example, a printing code of 04-1 shows that the first printing occurred in 2004.

Printed in the United States of America

Note: This publication contains the opinions and ideas of its authors. It is intended to provide helpful and informative material on the subject matter covered. It is sold with the understanding that the authors and publisher are not engaged in rendering professional services in the book. If the reader requires personal assistance or advice, a competent professional should be consulted.

The authors and publisher specifically disclaim any responsibility for any liability, loss, or risk, personal or otherwise, which is incurred as a consequence, directly or indirectly, of the use and application of any of the contents of this book.

Most Alpha books are available at special quantity discounts for bulk purchases for sales promotions, premiums, fund-raising, or educational use. Special books, or book excerpts, can also be created to fit specific needs.

For details, write: Special Markets, Alpha Books, 375 Hudson Street, New York, NY 10014.

Publisher: *Marie Butler-Knight*
Product Manager: *Phil Kitchel*
Senior Managing Editor: *Jennifer Chisholm*
Acquisitions Editor: *Mikal Belicove*
Development Editor: *Michael Koch*
Production Editor: *Megan Douglass*
Copy Editor: *Michael Dietsch*
Illustrator: *Chris Eliopoulos*
Cover/Book Designer: *Trina Wurst*
Indexer: *Julie Bess*
Layout/Proofreading: *Angela Calvert, Kathy Bidwell*

Contents at a Glance

Part 1:   **The Basics**   1

  1 North Korea—Roaring Mouse or Raving Maniac?   3
What all the fuss is about.

  2 Common Questions About North Korea   17
Answers to the most common questions about North Korea today.

  3 North Korea by the Numbers   31
A snapshot of the Democratic People's Republic of Korea.

Part 2:   **North Korea Yesterday**   **43**

  4 From Korean Myths to Kingdoms   45
Korea's emergence as a distinct culture.

  5 Enter the Dragon—The Chinese Legacy   59
The impact of the enormous neighbor on tiny Korea.

  6 Shrimp Among Whales (1864–1910)   75
Korea struggles to survive among the regional powers: China, Japan, and Russia.

  7 In Due Course (1910–1945)   89
Japan's colonization of Korea, and the Korean independence movement prior to World War II.

  8 The Rise of Kim Il Sung, the "Great Leader"   103
From communist guerrilla to Soviet-backed leader, Kim becomes his own man.

  9 The Korean War   117
Korea's division and Kim Il Sung's failed attempt to reunite Korea.

Part 3:   **North Korea Today**   **133**

  10 The Great Leader's Paradise   135
Juche and three pillars of bureaucracy, party, and army.

  11 North Korean Society   149
Cultural remnants, internal controls, and societal structures in the communist regime.

12 Education: Managing the Minds of the People   163
    Revising reality, and the tools to teach the masses.

13 The Economy: Supporting the Military   175
    *North Koreans focus on food and survival while supporting an
    enormous military machine.*

Part 4:   North Korea's Relationship with the World   189

14 North Korea and Russia: A Marriage of Convenience   191
    *Post-communist Moscow ends its alliance with Pyongyang,
    but Putin repairs the relationship.*

15 North Korea and China: A Love-Hate Relationship   203
    *Despite serious friction, the Beijing-Pyongyang alliance
    endures and prospers.*

16 North Korea and South Korea: The North-South
    Courtship   217
    Reconciliation has begun, but reunification remains elusive.

17 North Korea and Japan: Old Animosities Die Hard   231
    *Mutual animosity persists despite repeated efforts to normal-
    ize relations, and continuing trade.*

18 North Korea and the United States: A Dangerous Tango 245
    *From smile diplomacy and the Agreed Framework to the
    "axis of evil," relations with the United States remain icy.*

Part 5:   North Korea Tomorrow   259

19 North and South Korea: An Estranged Relationship   261
    *The legacy of the Korean War and the mutual distrust work
    against reconciliation.*

20 Conventional Forces—How Will They Be Used?   275
    *The forward-deployed, million-man army on the edge of the
    DMZ, with Seoul in the cross hairs.*

21 North Korea's Weapons of Mass Destruction   289
    *Missiles and nukes threaten stability in East Asia and far
    beyond.*

22 Terrorism—War Without Battles   305
    A legacy of past misdeeds and lingering mistrust.

23 Human Rights and Refugees   317
    No rights, only obligations.

24 Where Is North Korea Heading—War or Peace?   331
Containment or engagement, enforcement or inducement ...
the dialog begins.

Appendixes

A A North Korean Timeline   343

B Treaties, Declarations, and Joint Statements   359

C For More Information   375

D Glossary   385

   Index   399

Contents

Part I: The Basics   1

1 North Korea—Roaring Mouse or Raving Maniac?   3

Superpower or Starving Nation? 4
   War or Peace? 4
   Hawks and Doves 5
What Do the North Koreans See? 6
   Pay Me Not to Play 6
   Member of the Axis of Evil 6
   Pyongyang Picks Up the Gauntlet 7
The Great Proliferator 7
   Proliferation Security Initiative 8
   North Korea's Dynamic Duo 8
   Death and Despair 9
   Kim Jong Il: His Public Image 10
   Personal Relationships 10
   Richest in an Impoverished Land 10
Crazy Like a Fox? 11
   The Great Manipulator 11
   Kim's Geeky Side 12
Inside North Korea: The Military Matters Most 12
The Issue—Nukes or Not? 13
   Déjà Vu 14
   The New Nuclear Non-Crisis 14
   No to Nuclear "Blackmail" 14
   Spring in Beijing 15
   Multilateral Talks 15

2 Common Questions About North Korea   17

Where Is North Korea? 17
How Big Is North Korea's Army? 19
Does North Korea Have Nuclear Weapons? 21
How Far Can North Korea's Missiles Go? 22
Does North Korea Support International Terrorism? 23
Are the North Korean People Starving? 25
How Many North Korean Refugees Are in China? 27

Will Kim Jong Il's Regime Collapse? 27

Can I Travel to North Korea? 29

3 North Korea by the Numbers   31

The Korean Peninsula 31

North Korea's Turf 33

Climate *33*

Terrain *33*

Rivers and Borders *34*

Natural Resources 35

Transportation 36

Population 37

Religions 38

Political Nuts and Bolts 38

Government Divisions *38*

Government Structure *39*

Leadership *39*

Political Parties *39*

The Means of Production 39

Economy *40*

Currency *40*

GDP *40*

Industries *41*

Part 2: North Korea Yesterday   43

4 From Korean Myths to Kingdoms   45

History Is Power 45

Korea Through Korean Eyes 46

What's in a Name? *47*

Big Bird Meets the Bear *48*

Once a Korean, Always a Korean *49*

From Myth to History 50

The First "North" Korea—Koguryo (37 B.C.E.-668 C.E.) 51

Koguryo's Legacy—China's Little Korea *52*

Living History *52*

The First "South" Korea—Shilla (57 B.C.E.–935 c.e.) 53

Common Ground—Korean Culture 54

Korea Emerges from China's Shadow 54

Buddhism Flavors Korean Culture *54*

Korean Rugged Individualism *55*

Spreading the Faith *55*

Links to Modern Times *56*

Korea's Social Straitjacket *56*

Where Is Confucius? *57*

History Is Power! *57*

5 Enter the Dragon—The Chinese Legacy **59**

Kim Il Sung's Preferences 60

Mismatch with Marxism 60

Medieval and Early Modern Korea (935–1598) 61

King to Everybody, "This Is My Land" 62

Mandate of Heaven *63*

Let's Make a Deal *64*

Public Welfare for Noblemen *65*

The Best and the Brightest 66

Korea's Closing Door 67

Networking in Early Modern Korea 67

Genes and Success *67*

Brides and Success *68*

Out of Sight, Out of Mind *69*

The Social Pyramid *70*

Less Was Best *70*

Medieval Korea's Big Spenders 71

Those Damn Yankees 71

Mongol Hordes *72*

Japanese Pirates *72*

Enter the Europeans *72*

6 Shrimp Among Whales, 1864–1910 **75**

Calm Before the Storm 76

Yankee Go Away *77*

China's World Order *78*

The Gathering Storm on the Horizon 79

Opium Dealers at China's Door *80*

There Goes the Neighborhood *80*

Catholicism and Gunboats *80*

The Hermit Nation *81*

American "Yankees" Arrive *81*

The French "Yankees" Arrive *82*

Uncle Sam Returns with a Bang *82*

Japan Rattles Its Sabers 83
Whales Scramble for the Shrimp 83
   The China-Japan Rivalry Over Korea 84
   The Military Mutiny of 1882 (imo kullan) 84
   The 1882 Treaty of Chemulpo (Inchon) 84
   Korea's "Unequal" Treaties 85
   The Coup d'Etat *of 1884 (Kapsin Chongbyon)* 85
   The Americans Return 86
   The Sino-Japanese War of 1894–1895 86
   The Russo-Japanese War, 1904–1905 87
   The Protectorate Treaty of 1905 (Ulsa Convention) 87

7 In Due Course, 1910–1945   **89**
Prelude to Conquest 90
   The Distrusted Eagle—U.S. Complacency 90
   Japan's Iron Fist 91
   Korea's "Righteous Armies" 92
Independence Lost 92
   Japan as Number One 93
   Korea's Landlord 93
   Japan's Fortress Against Russia 94
   Korea's New Economy 94
   Winners and Losers 94
Erasing Korea 94
   The Dark Period (1910–1919) 95
   The March 1 Movement 95
   Good Cop, Bad Cop (1920–1930) 96
   Forced Assimilation (1930–1945) 97
Unkept Promises, Frustrated Hopes (1943–1945) 97
   Cairo Declaration 98
   Yalta Superpower Summit 98
   Growing Doubts 99
   The Superpowers Take Over 99
   Potsdam Conference 100
   Korea Divided 100

8 The Rise of Kim Il Sung, the "Great Leader"   **103**
The Struggle for Independence 104
   Rhee Syngman—Father of Korea's Political Right Wing 105
   Kim Ku—Father of Korea's Moderate Left Wing 106
   Lee Tong-hwi—Father of Korea's Left Wing 106

Kim Il Sung's Formative Years (1912–1934) 108
    Kim Il Sung's Family *108*
    Grandfather Takes on the American "Imperialists" *108*
    Father Clashes with the Japanese "Imperialists" *109*
    Kim Il Sung's "Arduous" March *110*
    Kim Il Sung Discovers Lenin *111*
    From Student to Guerilla *111*
    Kim Il Sung Sees "Red" *112*
    Life in the USSR (1941–1945) *113*
Korea Occupied (1945–1948) 113
    Kim Who? *114*
    The Korean Cold War *114*
    Korea Divided *115*

9 The Korean War   117
    The Never-Ending War 118
    Pre-War Chest Pounding (1948–1950) 120
        The Lineup *121*
        Kim Lunges South *121*
        On the Edge of Victory *123*
        MacArthur's End Run *125*
    Round Two—November 1950 125
        MacArthur's Waterloo *126*
        MacArthur Fired *128*
        Never-Ending Negotiations Begin *128*
        The Never-Ending War Begins *129*
        The Cost *131*

North Korea Today   133

10 The Great Leader's Paradise   135
    Paradise or Prison 136
        Double Dipping *137*
        Goodbye Marxism, Hello "KimIlSungism" *139*
        "Serving the Great" *139*
        Marx Versus Kim *140*
    North Korea's Political System 142
        North Korea's Self Image *142*
        North Korean–Style "Democracy" *143*
        The Korean Workers' Party (KWP) *144*

The Kim Dynasty 145
Token Parties 145
The Government 145
National Defense Commission 145
The Supreme People's Assembly 146
The Cabinet 146
The Judiciary 147

11   North Korean Society   149

Keeping Order 150
Kim Il Sung's "Ten Commandments" 150
Rank's Privileges 151
Sex as Status 151
City Versus Farm 152
From Black to Blue: Uniform Attire 152
At the Bottom 154
Big Wheels, Little Wheels 154
Traditional Despotism 155
Nepotism in the Kim Dynasty 155
Kim Jong Il's Family 156
The Former Heir Apparent 157
North Korea's New Aristocracy 157
Traces of Imperial Japan 158
Where's Stalin? 159
Keeping the Masses Faithful 160
Cracking the Whip 161
State Security Agency 161
Ministry of Public Security 161

12   Education: Managing the Minds of the People   163

Manipulating Reality 164
The Fiction of Armed Personnel 164
Confucius in a Juche Jacket 165
"Brainwashing" and "Reeducation" 165
Mind-Molding Mission 166
The Party as Teacher 167
Compulsory and Special Education 167
Basic Curriculum 168
Textbooks 169
Higher Education 169

University Curriculum *170*

Military Training *170*

Labor Education *171*

Graduation *171*

Models to Emulate 171

The Media—Mind-Numbing News 174

13 The Economy: Supporting the Military   **175**

The View From Pyongyang 176

Nature's Whim *176*

The Good Old Days *177*

Human Folly 178

Old Friend's Passing *179*

1990 Oil Shock *180*

Fertilizer—A Double-Edged Sword *180*

The Environmental Disaster *181*

Irrigation *181*

Where Have All the Tractors Gone? *181*

Monuments to Dad *182*

Sports Facilities *183*

Projects for the Masses *183*

Bullets and Bunkers *184*

Food Production *184*

Decline in Trade *185*

The Missing Link 185

Economic Remodeling *186*

The Ultimate Dilemma 187

North Korea's Relationship with the World   **189**

14 North Korea and Russia: A Marriage of Convenience   **191**

Ambitions in Northeast Asia 192

Keeping Imperial Japan Preoccupied *192*

Stiff-Arming the United States *193*

Squeezing Stalin and His Successors *193*

Pyongyang's Clinging Act 195

Radical Makeover *195*

Hard Times in Paradise *197*

Moscow Gives Pyongyang the Cold Shoulder *198*

Putin to the Rescue 199

Friendship Redefined 200
Nuclear Fallout 201
Moscow's Multilateral Solution 201
The New Korean Nuclear Crisis 201

15 North Korea and China: A Love-Hate Relationship   203
The "Lips and Teeth" Alliance 204
The "Blood-Bonded" Partnership 205
Yo-Yo Diplomacy (1960–1991) 206
Seesaw Diplomacy Since 1992 208
No More Free Ride 208
Trading Places 209
Investment 209
Border Crossings 210
The Warming Trend 210
Playing Hard to Get 210
The First Korean Nuclear Crisis 211
Fueling Relations 211
Nurturing Relations 211
Courting Pyongyang 212
Making Up 212
Finding Common Ground 213
"Illegal Immigrants" or "Refugees"? 213
Nukes and Yankees Keep Out 214
Direct Talks—Yes 214
Multilateral Talks—Yes; Sanctions—No 215

16 North Korea and South Korea: The North-South Courtship   217
Halfway There? 218
Distrust One's Kinsman 219
Containment 219
Deterrence's Double-Edged Sword 219
Confrontation 220
Mirror Imaging One Another 220
Spies and Subversives 221
Can We Talk? 222
Round One 222
Return to Rivalry 223
Soul Searching in Seoul 223
Olympic Strategy 224
Trading Places 224

After the Cold War 225
    The First Nuclear Crisis (1992–1997) 226
    The Agreed Framework 226
    Four Party Talks 227
Sunshine Diplomacy 227

17   North Korea and Japan: Old Animosities Die Hard   231

Pyongyang to Tokyo—You Owe Me! 232
    Talking the Talk 232
    Tokyo Tries It Alone 233
    Beating the "Four Dragons" 233
    Japan's North Korea "Lobby" 234
    Cashing In 235
Japan and North Korea—Round One (1990) 235
    Roadmap to the "Yellow Brick Road" 235
    The Never-Ending Talks 236
    Pipe Dreaming on the Tumen River 236
    Pyongyang's Radical Makeover 237
    The High Cost of Friendship 238
    Let's Not Make a Deal 238
Japan and North Korea—Round Two (1997) 239
    North Korea Blinks 239
    Behind the Blink 239
    Kim Jong Il Pops Off 240
    Outrage in Japan 241
    Jump Start Summit 242
    Bleak Prospects 243

18   North Korea and the United States: A Dangerous Tango   245

Gathering Storm 246
    Pyongyang's Coercive Diplomacy 246
    Rogue Nation 247
    Squabbling in Washington 248
    The Ticking Clock 248
    Containment 248
    Reagan's Modest Initiative 249
    Bush's "Carrot and Stick" Strategy 250
The Agreed Framework 251
    Uncertain Beginning 251
    "Suspended Withdrawal" 253

Wish Lists *253*

Beyond the "Red Line" *253*

Saving Face *254*

Kim Il Sung Is Mortal! *254*

Devil in the Details *255*

Helicopter Down! *257*

Making Nice with Congress—The Perry Report *257*

Flourishing Finish *258*

North Korea Tomorrow   259

19 North and South Korea: An Estranged Relationship   261

The Possibilities for Unification 262

War *262*

Regime Change *264*

Collapse *265*

Economic Sanctions *266*

Carrots and Sticks *267*

Opposition to Sanctions *267*

Sanctions' Impact *268*

Peaceful Co-existence and Reconciliation *268*

Renewed Dreams *268*

The Positive Side *269*

Remaining Hurdles 271

Future Prospects 272

20 Conventional Forces: How Will They Be Used?   275

Spying on North Korea 276

Super Snoopers *276*

Bean Counting *277*

The Intelligence Community *278*

National Intelligence Estimates *278*

Military Objectives 279

Forcing the Issue *280*

Changing Posture *280*

Playing Catch Up *281*

National Strategy *281*

Pyongyang's War Machine 282

Heavy Metal *282*

Special Operation Forces *282*

American-Supplied Helicopters 283
The "Back Benchers" 283
Antique Air Power 283
Fast Attack Navy 284
Command and Control 284
Blitzkrieg! 285
If North Korea Attacks: South Across the Border 285
Deterrence 285
North Korea's Achilles' Heel 286
Beyond the Facade 286

21 North Korea's Weapons of Mass Destruction 289

Pyongyang's Paranoia 290
The South Korean "Threat" 291
The U.S. "Imperialist" Threat 291
The Threat of a "Remilitarized" Japan 291
Faltering Friends 292
Pyongyang's Options 292
Deterring the United States 293
Ballistic Missiles 294
Technology Genealogy 294
Hwasong—*North Korea's Scud* 295
The Medium-Range Nodong 296
Nodongs *in Disguise* 296
The Taepodong *Missile* 296
Missile Exports 297
Target Countries 297
U.S.–North Korea Missile Talks 298
Making Nukes 298
In the Beginning 299
The Plutonium Program 300
Highly Enriched Uranium 300
Gas and Germs 301
Japan's Imperial Legacy 302
How Dangerous Are Pyongyang's WMDs? 303

22 Terrorism—War Without Battles 305

Joining the Big Leagues 306
Covert Espionage 306
Birds of Feather 307

Shoot-Out in Seoul 307

Remember the Pueblo! 308

Assassination of a Lady 308

Death by Hatchet 309

Murder in Rangoon 310

North Korea Makes the List 311

Japan's Abducted Citizens 312

Language Teachers 313

Normalization Talks Stalled 313

"Comfort Women" 313

Japan Responds 314

Japan Judged 314

Kim Jong Il Confesses 315

More Sanctions 315

Trying to Make Nice 316

23 Human Rights and Refugees   **317**

Far-Out Ideas 318

Obligations Versus Rights 318

Legalized Tyranny 319

Give Me a Break 320

Survival First 321

The Bottom Line 322

The Push for Change 322

Soft Versus Hard Landings 323

Repair or Revamp? 324

Big Brother Is Listening 324

The Ancestors Have Spoken 324

A Flood of Foreigners 325

The Flow of Refugees 326

Monitoring the Flow 327

Refugees or Migrants? 327

Continuity or Change? 328

24 Where Is North Korea Heading—War or Peace?   **331**

Ending the Cold War 331

About Face! 333

Kim Jong Il's Dilemma 333

Clinging to the Past 334

The United States's Dilemma 334
  Soft Landing *335*
  Hard Landing *335*
  Another Agreed Framework? *336*
  Living With Danger *336*
Stalemate 336
  The Dragon Puffs *337*
  North Korea's Wish List *337*
  Washington's Wish List *337*
  Shall We Talk or What ...? *338*
  "Ball" or "Gun" Bomb *338*
  Future Escalation *339*
  Six Party Talks *339*
It's in the Hands of the United States 341

Appendixes

A **A North Korean Timeline**   **343**

B **Treaties, Declarations, and Joint Statements**   **359**

C **For More Information**   **375**

D **Glossary**   **385**

   Index   **399**

Foreword

For years, sad to say, the dominant image of Korea in Americans' minds was from reruns of *M.A.S.H.* Nowadays, even with Korea in the news with some regularity, there remains a vast amount of confusion. The astonishing progress, both economically and democratically, of South Korea is still very much unacknowledged in the United States, and North Korea is known only as a sinister mischief-maker, albeit one with nuclear ambitions. The images that remain in our minds from TV, replayed over and over, show goosestepping troops, rows of missiles, and occasionally a picture of a chubby, impassive face belonging to the Dear Leader.

Sadly, not just the public, but many in government know little beyond these stereotypes. It is to meet the glaring need for authoritative, in-depth information that Dr. Kenneth Quinones and Joseph Tragert have written this book, *The Complete Idiot's Guide to Understanding North Korea.* I have been acquainted with Korea personally for well over 50 years, most recently as U.S. Ambassador to South Korea. I can say unequivocally that such a book, had it been available to me at the time, would have proven a godsend. It is replete with history, statistics, and an analysis of North Korea as it is today, both internally and with respect to the region and the world. It provides an overview of its military forces and capabilities, an assessment of its nuclear program, and a frank review of its human rights violations and its refugee problem. It offers a clear perspective on its dismal economic record and makes some projections about the future and the possibility of resolving the nuclear issue short of war. In sum, it is the best volume for reference one could ask for.

The authors are eminently qualified for taking on this task. Dr. Quinones has a Ph.D. in History and East Asian Languages from Harvard, has spent considerable time in both North and South Korea, speaks Korean fluently, and has served with distinction as point man for the U.S. State Department in matters relating to North Korea. He accompanied the first American recovery team into North Korea searching for remains from the Korean War. He has spent time at the principal nuclear facility there, and has had many opportunities to engage North Korean citizens and officials in conversation. In short, his knowledge is first-hand. Joseph Tragert is well versed in making this kind of knowledge readily available to the general public, having authored similar guides for Iraq and Iran.

This book is a fascinating read in itself, in addition to being an authoritative reference work. I predict there will be many copies sold to our government. We will all be well served if that is the case.

Dr. James T. Laney
U.S. Ambassador to South Korea (1993–1997)
President, Emory University (1977–1993)

Introduction

North Korea is grabbing its share of the news, again. Images of the grinning "Great Leader," his strutting son and heir, and their marching armies are our indelible impressions of North Korea. Winston Churchill once said that Russia was "a riddle inside an enigma, wrapped in a conundrum." The same can be said of North Korea today. However, conundrum or not, North Korea is a complex country that poses a significant challenge to peace and the existing world order. People would do well to better understand it.

How This Book Is Organized

We have organized this book into five parts, to help you learn more about the people of North Korea, the country's history, and its unique position in the world today.

Part 1, "The Basics," introduces you to North Korea. You'll find here much basic information about this puzzling place.

Part 2, "North Korea Yesterday," traces Korea's development as an independent nation with a unique culture, its place in China's traditional world order, how and why Japan colonized Korea, and its struggle to regain independence only to be divided.

Part 3, "North Korea Today," is a "how and why" of the Democratic People's Republic of Korea. We'll take a look at what keeps this totalitarian, virtually bankrupt state from collapsing.

Part 4, "North Korea's Relationship with the World," explores why North Korea, which claims to be "self reliant," actually is very dependent for its survival on its relations with old friends, China and Russia, and even its old enemies, South Korea, Japan, and the United States.

Part 5, "North Korea Tomorrow," sizes up why North Korea is such a threat to peace and the options we have for dealing with it and its threats.

At the end of the book, you'll find a number of helpful appendixes.

Extras

As you make your way through the book, you'll notice little pieces of information scattered throughout the pages. They are meant to help you gain an immediate understanding of a specific aspect of the topic at hand. Here's how you can recognize them:

Korean Concepts

These boxes provide definitions of concepts, terms, and terminology.

North Korea Fact

These boxes provide, as the name suggests, facts about North Korea.

Increase Your North Korea IQ

These boxes contain background details or supporting information that can accelerate or streamline your learning process. Jump in and out of these boxes—you'll enjoy what you find there.

Personal Recollections

Dr. C. Kenneth Quinones served as a Foreign Service officer in South and North Korea during the Reagan, Bush, and Clinton administrations. He was the first U.S. diplomat to enter North Korea and the first to live at its nuclear research center, and he helped the U.S. Army begin the recovery of U.S. Korean War MIAs. Dr. Quinones shares his first-hand insights and experiences on North Korea in these boxes.

Acknowledgments

We would like to thank those who helped, especially our wives, Julie Quinones and Bernadine Tragert; our agents, Jessica Faust and Gene Brissie; and our editor, Mikal Belicove.

Note on Romanization of the Korean Language

The McCune-Reischauer system for converting the Korean phonetic script into the Roman alphabet is used in this book.

Korea's 600-year-old phonetic alphabet has 14 consonants and 10 vowels. Unlike written Chinese, the Korean script is an alphabet. Each letter represents a sound without conveying meaning. Written Chinese, on the other hand, consists of several thousand pictographs. Each has a distinct sound and multiple possible meanings depending upon context and which other pictographs they are paired with.

Despite the Korean script's simplicity, written Chinese remained Korea's dominant written language until the civil and military service examination systems were discontinued in 1894.

In 1939, the royal Asiatic Society of Korea asked professors at Harvard University to establish a system to Romanize the Korean alphabet. The authors described their system as a "compromise between scientific accuracy and practical simplicity."

The McCune-Reischauer system was selected for use in this book because of its wide usage in English-speaking countries, its simplicity, and its relative political neutrality. The academic communities in the United States, United Kingdom, Canada, and Australia have long relied on the system, and continue to do so.

The governments of English-speaking nations also used the system, but the United States discontinued its use in 1995.

The governments of North and South Korea have their own official systems. Each system, however, differs significantly. Also, in South Korea, several official systems have been developed but later discarded.

Occasionally, prominent Koreans' preferred Roman spelling of their names has not been converted according to the McCune-Reischauer system. For example, the preferred spelling for the first leaders of North and South Korea, Kim Il Sung and Syngman Rhee, have been retained. The same is true for South Korea's capital, Seoul.

Trademarks

All terms mentioned in this book that are known to be or are suspected of being trademarks or service marks have been appropriately capitalized. Alpha Books and Penguin Group (USA) Inc. cannot attest to the accuracy of this information. Use of a term in this book should not be regarded as affecting the validity of any trademark or service mark.

Part 1

The Basics

You know that North Korea is a threat to peace in Northeast Asia and the United States because of its ballistic missiles and ambition to become a nuclear power. But where can you learn what North Koreans think about you? What makes them so hostile toward the United States? How can North Korea be a threat to world peace and at the same time be bankrupt and starving?

Well, this book is the place to start getting some answers. The guiding principle for the chapters in this part is "just the facts." You'll find out all you need to know to put this complex country into perspective.

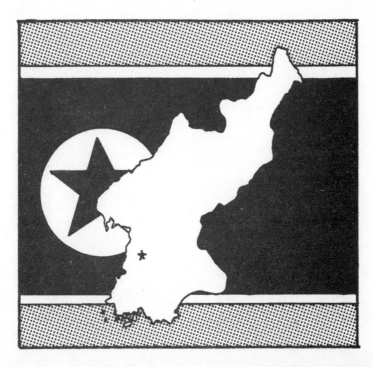

Chapter 1

North Korea—Roaring Mouse or Raving Maniac?

In This Chapter

- ◆ Why does North Korea act the way it does?
- ◆ Kim Jong Il—madman or manipulator?
- ◆ North Korea's threat to peace in Northeast Asia
- ◆ Options for resolving the nuclear impasse: diplomacy or war

In this chapter, we will introduce you to some of the more common concerns that North Korea raises in the minds of outside observers. A primary concern is the continuing dispute between the United States and North Korea over its weapons of mass destruction, concern that North Korea's leader is a person prone to irrational behavior, and the impoverished state of North Korea's population. This concern prompts others to wonder what kind of people rule North Korea and do they really pose a threat to the United States?

Superpower or Starving Nation?

To the Western observer, the news out of Pyongyang is always bad, and the rhetoric arrogant and threatening. The headlines in Western newspapers are bewildering. They proclaim either that the country is a mini-superpower armed with nuclear weapons and ballistic missiles aimed at the United States and its allies, or that its people are starving and need food aid. On the other hand, one day, North Korea's government-controlled press is accusing the United States of being an "imperialist" and a "warmonger," and the next day is pleading for understanding and food aid.

Increase Your North Korea IQ

Pyongyang is the capital of North Korea (its official name is the Democratic People's Republic of Korea or DPRK). With a population of about three million, it is the largest city in the country, and the center for political power and main entry point to the country.

War or Peace?

The United States and North Korea have been enemies since 1950 when North Korea invaded South Korea. The United States countered by leading a United Nations effort to preserve South Korea (the Republic of Korea or ROK). The Korean War Armistice signed in 1953 ended the hostilities. But Korea remained divided. Ever since, Washington and Pyongyang have maintained hostile postures toward one another. Failure to resolve their continuing impasse through diplomacy risks making the Korean Peninsula the flashpoint for another Korean War.

Pyongyang looking southwest from the Koryo Hotel. Note Pyongyang Central Railroad Station in the foreground.

The United States, its allies South Korea and Japan, and quite possibly others, would be drawn into that war. Eventually, China might even clash with the United States again (as it did during the Korean War). The cause would be North Korean leader Kim Jong Il's determined effort to build his own nuclear arsenal. President George W. Bush is equally determined to block Kim's ambitions. Both nations are clearly on a collision course.

Personal Recollections

Kim Il Sung's huge, brightly lit portrait glared down at me from atop Pyongyang's International Airport. The night sky was black, the air bitterly cold. My mind rushed back to Christmas Eve, 1963.

Thirty years earlier, just before midnight, I stepped from an airplane into the black, frigid night at Kimpo Airport near Seoul, South Korea. Shivering in my green Army dress uniform, I walked briskly toward a brightly lighted sign that spanned the path to the terminal. It proclaimed in bold black letters on a pale yellow background, "Welcome to Freedom's Frontier."

Now, on that December evening in 1992, I found myself on the other side of "Freedom's Frontier" in North Korea. I was the first American diplomat to arrive in North Korea since the Korean War ended in 1953. Inside the terminal, a uniformed North Korean soldier demanded to see my passport. He grimaced as he read the gold letters on its black cover. Tossing it back at me, he bluntly proclaimed, "We do not admit American imperialist diplomats!" I eventually was admitted with the help of North Korean diplomats. But I never got used to being called an "imperialist."

Hawks and Doves

People in the United States, and other concerned countries, are deeply divided on how to deal with North Korea. One group urges negotiations. It claims North Korea is too small and too poor to threaten world peace. It believes North Korea is acting like the small nation in the classic Peter Sellers comedy of the early 1960s, *The Mouse That Roared*. (In the movie, a tiny make-believe European nation decides the only way to get the United States's attention and receive U.S. foreign aid is to invade New York.) Give North Korea aid, the pro-negotiations group believes, and North Korea can be induced to calm down and join the world community

The other group sees North Korea as a real threat. It argues that the only way to deal with North Korea is to compel its leader Kim Jong Il to either discard his weapons of mass destruction and his million-man army or face the consequences—including war.

What Do the North Koreans See?

According to the experts, North Korea's leader, Kim Jong Il, believes the United States is out to "strangle" and topple his regime. Kim is determined to prevent this by keeping the "imperialists" from invading his domain while keeping his subjects submissive to his authority. By "imperialists," Kim means the United States, South Korea (or the Republic of Korea which North Korea has long considered a "puppet" of the United States) and Japan.

He has some big sticks for this purpose. They include a million-man army, thousands of tanks and artillery pieces, and an arsenal of several hundred ballistic missiles. But his biggest stick may be nuclear weapons. If it marries nukes to missiles, North Korea can terrorize and wreak havoc on its neighbors, particularly U.S. allies South Korea and Japan. It can also bombard the U.S. Army, Navy, and Air Force bases in these, countries, possibly killing thousands of U.S. citizens.

Pay Me Not to Play

A recurring tactic of North Korea's leaders since 1992 has been to threaten to develop weapons of mass destruction in the hope that other nations will give North Korea the aid it needs to perpetuate its totalitarian regime.

Former president George H. W. Bush and his foreign policy advisers initiated a strategy in 1988 aimed at "inducing" North Korea to trade its isolation and hostility for the diplomatic and economic benefits of engaging the international community and acting according to international law and norms.

Former president Bill Clinton essentially continued this strategy of "engagement" and negotiation. The effort yielded the first ever diplomatic agreement between the United States and North Korea, the Agreed Framework of 1994. In exchange for very significant economic benefits, and the promise of the eventual normalization of diplomatic relations, Pyongyang agreed to "freeze" all its nuclear weapons development and related nuclear activities. Both sides dragged their feet when it came to implementing the agreement. The actions of the two countries after they signed the agreement help define their current relationship. We will elaborate about this very significant and complex matter in Chapters 18 and 21.

Member of the Axis of Evil

When President George W. Bush took office in 2001, he decided to draw the line on Kim Jong Il. He ruled out further negotiations and concessions until North Korea had fulfilled its previous promises. The president also demanded that Kim give up his weapons of mass destruction before negotiations could commence. In short, the president offered to "talk anytime, anywhere," but also offered no negotiations and no concessions.

President George W. Bush identified North Korea, Iraq, and Iran as the "axis of evil" in a speech before Congress on January 2002. These three countries were singled out for their development of weapons of mass destruction, sponsorship of terrorism, and disregard for human rights.

President Bush may have coined the phrase "axis of evil," but he was not the first U.S. president to single out North Korea as a threat to the United States. In fact, North Korea bashing has been a bipartisan practice for some time. President Bush's father, former president George H. W. Bush, and his successor, Bill Clinton, labeled these same three nations plus Libya "rogue" nations and international "outlaws." They both cited similar reasons that President Bush used in 2002. As far back as the early 1980s, Libya and North Korea had earned their "rogue" badges for acts of international terrorism.

Pyongyang Picks Up the Gauntlet

The North Koreans reacted negatively to this apparent shift in U.S. policy. As the United States learned in October 2002, Kim also had started a second, secret nuclear weapons development program. He may have intended this to be a negotiating card. Nevertheless, it broke all of North Korea's previous promises that it would not develop nuclear weapons.

North Korea's reaction to Bush's strategy has been a series of blunders. None of North Korea's neighbors, especially South Korea and Japan, but also old supporters Russia and China, want it to have nuclear weapons. Furthermore, by breaking all of their previous promises not to develop nuclear weapons, the North Koreans have convinced the Bush administration that negotiating another agreement would only be futile. Simply put, the U.S. administration feels that the North Korean government cannot be trusted to keep its promises.

The Great Proliferator

The threat of North Korea's weapons extends far beyond its immediate neighborhood. It is very expensive to perpetuate the loyalty of the North Korean generals and other officials, who are the guardians of the regime. The North Korean war machine requires lots of oil, but North Korea has none of its own so the country must buy it. To earn *hard currency*, the North Korean leader can either let his people make goods to sell on the international market, or he can sell weapons of mass destruction.

North Korea's biggest export is weaponry. Among its biggest customers are some of the world's really bad guys like Iran, Syria, Libya, and Yemen. Pakistan, a U.S. ally in the war on terrorism, also likes North Korean missiles and related hardware. From these buyers, the North Koreans get hard currency and oil, whereas the buyers get ballistic missiles and spare parts.

Proliferation Security Initiative

The United States and some of its allies, are concerned that Kim Jong Il might add plutonium to his exports. To prevent this, President Bush in June 2003 announced the Proliferation Security Initiative (PSI). Several allies, including the United Kingdom and Japan, joined with the United States to monitor North Korea's exports. Interdiction of suspected North Korean plutonium shipments on the high seas, however, is not supported by international law.

North Korea's Dynamic Duo

Kim Il Sung was, like his son, a ruthless dictator. But he nurtured his subjects' respect by looking after their needs. During his reign, from 1948 to 1994, North Korea rebuilt itself after the Korean War, achieved impressive economic gains, and had ample food. But Kim Il Sung was ruthless when it came to dealing with South Koreans and their ally, the United States. He was responsible for starting the Korean War in 1950 and used terrorism against South Korea, but he was less a threat to world peace than his son.

Kim Jong Il inherited his father's position, an abnormality for a communist dictatorship. Thus Kim views himself as a king. He thinks North Korea is his personal domain, and the North Korean people his subjects. So long as they submit to his will, he will think for them and supply them their essential needs. At least that's what he claims.

Death and Despair

After Kim Il Sung's death in 1994, insiders noted that his son became depressed and turned to heavy drinking. Torrential rains and massive flooding in August 1995 wreaked havoc on crops and ushered in starvation in many areas of North Korea. This human tragedy seems to have shaken Kim Jong Il out of his stupor. Finally, four years after his father's death, Kim Jong Il declared himself his father's successor but many experts feel that Kim has yet to show equal concern for his people's welfare.

The younger Kim must impress his primary supporters, North Korea's powerful generals and the leaders of its communist party. In their eyes, Kim Il Sung earned the right to declare himself the "Great Leader" because he stood up to the "imperialists." In their view, he first expelled the Japanese "imperialists" at the end of World War II and then the American "imperialists" during the Korean War.

Increase Your North Korea IQ

Each Korean name has three parts: clan seat, family surname, and an individual's given name.

Clan seats rarely are mentioned with a surname, but all Koreans know their clan's identity. Surnames are distinguished by a clan's geographical origin. North Korea's leaders Kim Il Sung and Kim Jong Il are from the Chonju Kim clan. This tells us their ancestors came from an area that is now part of South Korea.

Korean names usually have three syllables. The first, like Kim, is the family name. The last two syllables are an individual's given name. One of the two syllables is usually shared with all other male members of their generation.

Conscious of his father's deeds, Kim Jong Il now seems determined to demonstrate that he is equal to his father. To do this, the younger Kim has taken on the United States and vowed to prevent it from "strangling" North Korea. Consequently, Kim Jong Il must avoid any appearance of bowing to the United States. If he were to do so, North Korea's generals and party leaders are certain to criticize him. This could severely erode domestic political support for Kim's regime. (See Chapter 10 for the political dynamics of North Korea.)

Kim Jong Il has also sought to cultivate North Koreans' respect for him by clinging to his father's legacy. He also sought to impress them by acting as a filial son, still a revered traditional Confucian value in North Korea. The younger Kim thus proclaimed his father president forever. He also reserved for his father the title "the Great Leader." Instead, Kim Jong Il prefers to be addressed as the "Supreme Commander." North Koreans commonly refer to him as the "Dear Leader."

Kim Jong Il: His Public Image

Kim Jong Il is famous for his appearance. A short, stocky fellow, Kim tries to make himself appear taller by brushing his hair up rather than back. To get this great "lift," he relies on hair permanents. Since taking his father's place, the younger Kim has traded his once very curly locks for a straighter, more mature look. But the 60-year-old Kim's hair is thinning, making it more difficult to create the lift his hairdresser once achieved. This shortcoming is partially compensated for with thick-soled shoes.

North Korea observers are familiar with the distinctive sunglasses Kim Jong Il usually wears. But he probably wore large, dark sunglasses because of eye problems. Kim is a diabetic and probably has cataracts. He wore the sunglasses to protect his eyes from bright sunshine. But he may have had the cataracts removed during his 2001 trip to Moscow. Ever since that trip, which took him across Siberia by train, he has appeared less frequently wearing sunglasses.

Personal Relationships

Kim has been married several times and has several children. Eventually, he is expected to designate officially one of them his heir. (See Chapter 11 regarding Kim's family.) During his youth, Kim is rumored to have been a playboy. He is believed to have invited attractive young women from around the world to his kingdom. In the 1970s and 1980s, some observers believe Kim Jong Il collected a large library of pornographic films, but this inclination appears to have subsided with age.

Richest in an Impoverished Land

No one outside North Korea can know the extent of the Kim dynasty's wealth, but it far exceeds the needs of the ruler of one of the world's most impoverished nations. Kim's father was a smart investor whose Taesong Investment company, a firm registered in the United Kingdom, deals in stocks on the London Exchange and trades precious metals, especially gold, in Europe's markets. The Kim family is believed to maintain large secret accounts in Swiss banks.

Kim inherited several large country estates from his father. He enjoys fine wine and liquor, but is not a fashionable dresser. In public, Kim usually appears in a drab green suit. He is famous for giving away Rolex watches and luxury cars to trusted generals and officials, but he apparently does not relish such status symbols.

Personal Recollections

In 1995 and 1996, I was responsible for leasing North Korean cargo flights; we transported U.S. Defense and Energy Department equipment to North Korea in connection with work at North Korea's nuclear research center and we recovered Korean War U.S. servicemen's remains. North Korean officials in Beijing managed to include on each flight a few cases of expensive European liquor and wine bound for the "highest level of government." Obviously, these officials were not shipping this booze to their buddies. It was bound for their "Dear Leader" and his buddies.

Crazy Like a Fox?

"Kim Jong Il is not crazy." Some experts contend that he has a great deal in common with the villains in James Bond movies. Kim, like most dictators, is a complex person of sharp personality contrasts. He is a crafty, arrogant, sometimes secretive, other times flamboyant, and ruthless fellow who is easy to despise. But at the same time, his occasional brash impulsiveness reveals a keen sense of insecurity.

The Great Manipulator

Some Pyongyang watchers describe Kim as being "irrational" and "unpredictable." Actually, just the opposite is true. He is a highly intelligent manipulator of human emotions. This ability, plus his willingness to do anything to perpetuate his regime, make him predictable, calculating, and dangerous.

Personal Recollections

A friend was visiting Seoul in 1994 when one of Kim Il Sung's representatives to talks with South Korea threatened to turn the city into a "sea of fire." He asked what his Korean host thought of this. The host answered that if Kim wanted to do this, Kim could order some of the thousands of North Korean artillery pieces arrayed near the DMZ to fire on the city. Seoul is only about 30 kilometers south of the Demilitarized Zone (DMZ) that divides the two Koreas. Well within artillery range. Seoul would be ablaze in minutes, and with little warning.

If he cannot get his way using diplomacy and negotiations, he often reverts to threats, something diplomats commonly refer to as "saber rattling." He excites fear by threatening to use sophisticated weapons against his neighbors. President Bush has accused him of "nuclear blackmail." One of Kim's favorite threats is to claim that he will unleash the devastating fury of his enormous war machine on highly vulnerable South Korea. This puts at risk the lives and prosperity of our 45 million South Korean allies. It also places in harm's way the 35,000 U.S. troops stationed there, plus about 100,000 American citizens who live and work in South Korea.

Kim's Geeky Side

Modern technology apparently fascinates Kim Jong Il, but it is more than just a hobby. He uses it to empower his nation's military might. The only outdoor monument to Kim Jong Il stands at the entrance to the Yongbyon Nuclear Research Center where North Korea has produced plutonium for nuclear weapons. The 50-foot-high centerpiece of the monument depicts a boyish looking but confident Kim Jong Il. Behind him stand scientists, technicians, and soldiers. Flanking Kim's image on both sides are huge, bright-red concrete flags. Inscribed on each are Kim Jong Il's words that encourage the nation's scientists and technicians to use their knowledge to promote the nation's defense and prosperity.

Kim Jong Il is also credited with promoting North Korea's linking into the Internet. According to a Russian friend, the train car he rode from North Korea to Moscow in 2001 was equipped with an elaborate bank of computers and monitoring screens. With a click of his mouse, Kim could call up the daily weather forecast, get detailed data about any town in Russia, and track his gold transactions at the London and Zurich gold exchanges.

North Korea has installed a nationwide network of advanced fiber optic telephone lines. These link him and his commanders to all areas of the nation. Buried underground, their transmissions are safe from being intercepted by electronic "eavesdropping" by U.S. intelligence aircraft. The secure fiber optic network also carries North Korea's secure "intranet," an internal computer network that feeds information via computer link from all areas of the country to the capital.

Inside North Korea: The Military Matters Most

Kim relies more on psychology than coercion to keep his army in line. He keeps the million-man army subordinate by keeping the generals loyal to him. He strokes the generals' egos with shiny medals and promotions. He bestows BMWs and Lexus cars on them and stuffs their pockets full of hard currency. They have access to the best apartments in the capital, villas in the countryside, and ample supplies of the best European booze. They and their visitors from abroad can also visit so-called "happy houses" where they can enjoy karaoke and the favors of young ladies.

The North Korean army remains subordinate to the generals because soldiers and their immediate family members are assured the first cut at all of life's basic necessities—food, medical care, clothing, and housing.

Despite popular impressions, Kim's political power does not grow out of a gun barrel. The 23 million North Koreans not in uniform still must rely upon him, his loyal soldiers, and the Communist Party cadre for everything they need. Kim keeps these humble masses subdued by rationing their food. His bureaucracy decides where the majority of North Koreans may live and work and even the level of education they can achieve.

The military controls the production of most machines, leaving few for the people to use to grow food and to build homes, schools, and offices. This compels most people to endure constant exhausting manual labor while consuming minimal amounts of food.

The Issue—Nukes or Not?

So long as the Kim regime persists, so, too, will its capacity to threaten peace and prosperity on the Korean Peninsula and far beyond.

A second Korean War would wreak havoc on both North and South Korea. Japan would not escape because U.S. military bases there would be targets of North Korean ballistic missiles. U.S. soldiers, of course, would be caught in the middle of the war because most of them are thinly stretched across the main invasion route to Seoul, South Korea's capital.

The United States and South Korea agreed in July 2003 to reposition all U.S. combat units south of Seoul. But this redeployment is not scheduled to begin for several years, and will not be completed until 2011.

Increase Your North Korea IQ

The Korean Peninsula is the land mass where North and South Korea are located. It is situated between China and Japan.

Most frightening, however, would be the possibility of another clash between the United States and China, like the one that occurred during the first Korean War of 1950–1953. China maintains its defense treaty with North Korea. In the event of a foreign attack on North Korea, China is obligated to come to North Korea's aid. If another clash does take place, it is possible for that war to escalate to a nuclear level because China today has a nuclear arsenal, something it lacked in 1950.

Déjà Vu

A persistent source of friction between the United States and North Korea is Kim Jong Il's determination to build a nuclear arsenal. North Korea's declaration in October 2002, that it had resumed its nuclear weapons development program sparked escalating tensions with the United States. This ignited the second nuclear crisis on the Korean Peninsula during the past decade.

In 1992, the International Atomic Energy Agency (IAEA, the United Nations nuclear watch dog agency) found evidence that North Korea might be hiding how much plutonium (the core element of a nuclear bomb) it had produced. As a member of the Treaty on the Non-proliferation of Nuclear Weapons (NPT), North Korea was required to report this to the IAEA.

Instead, North Korea declared in March 1993, that it would withdraw from the NPT. The international community promptly condemned North Korea for its declaration. Urged by the United Nations and its close ally South Korea, the United States agreed to negotiate with North Korea. In October 1994, Washington and Pyongyang signed the Agreed Framework. In it, the United States promised to form an international consortium to construct two nuclear reactors in North Korea, among other things (see Chapter 18 for details). In exchange, North Korea agreed to remain in the NPT, and to "freeze" its various nuclear programs, and to allow IAEA inspections to resume.

The New Nuclear Non-Crisis

Suspicions persisted that North Korea might be secretly continuing its nuclear weapons program. When Pyongyang confirmed these suspicions to U.S. diplomats in October 2002, tensions quickly mounted. North Korea renounced the Agreed Framework, expelled the IAEA's inspectors, and withdrew from the NPT.

No to Nuclear "Blackmail"

President Bush has repeatedly emphasized that he will not reward North Korea's past misdeeds and breaking of its promises by negotiating with it or offering it any concessions. Instead, he demands that Kim Jong Il concede his past misdeeds and disarm. If he does so, President Bush in January 2003 suggested he would reward Kim with a "bold initiative" that would include food and fuel for North Koreans. Kim Jong Il's foreign ministry spokesman promptly dismissed Bush's offer as "pie in the sky."

President Bush then offered to engage North Korea in multilateral talks. When a State Department official was asked what this meant, he explained such talks would resemble an academic roundtable discussion. Ten parties (the United States, Russia, China, France, the United Kingdom, South and North Korea, Japan, and Australia, plus the European Union) would be invited to participate. Each would take a turn telling North Korea how it could regain international respect and enjoy the economic benefits of membership in the international community. However, the North Koreans rejected the offer and continued to insist on having direct bilateral talks only with the United States.

> **Personal Recollections**
>
> Late in 2002, I traveled to New York to meet with my former North Korean colleague who is now one of North Korea's ambassadors to the United Nations. He greeted me with the words, "Déjà vu, here we go again with another crisis." When I later asked him about President Bush's multilateral roundtable offer, he dismissed it as completely "unacceptable."

Spring in Beijing

In April 2003, China intervened and invited Washington and Pyongyang to diplomatic talks in Beijing. The meeting only confirmed the deep divide between the two antagonists. The United States demanded that first, North Korea had to dismantle its nuclear weapons programs and allow international inspections to verify this had been done. Only then would the United States consider engaging North Korea in diplomatic negotiations. North Korea adamantly responded that it would do as the United States demands, but only if the United States discontinues its "hostile" policy toward it and agrees to engage in diplomatic negotiations. North Korea's chief delegate bragged that his nation was on the verge of becoming a nuclear power.

Multilateral Talks

The United States, in close consultation with China, South Korea, and Japan, then called for multilateral talks to address the impasse. After considerable pressure from China, North Korea reluctantly agreed to participate in such talks.

At the end of August 2003, the six nations most concerned about North Korea met in Beijing to exchange views on how to defuse the impending nuclear crisis. These so-called "Six Party Talks" brought together the United States, Japan, North and South Korea, China, and Russia. The nations agreed that the Korean Peninsula should remain free of nuclear weapons. They also urged the United States and North

Korea to resolve their impasse through peaceful, diplomatic dialogue. But the meeting ended with the United States and North Korea still at odds over how to reach a resolution.

So at the outset of the new century, the North Koreans are rattling their sabers and threatening dire consequences to all who resist them. The world has been down this dangerous road before, but each trip is more risky than the one before. The international community firmly opposes North Korea's acquisition of nuclear weapons. But at the same time, there is an equally solid consensus that the best course of action is for the United States to negotiate with North Korea.

Assessing the pros and cons of the U.S.-North Korea dispute will better enable citizens living in democratic societies to reach their own conclusions and to express their views confidently and freely to their colleagues and their governments. We hope the following chapters will be of value in this regard.

The Least You Need to Know

- North Korea's military muscle and technology make it a formidable adversary and a credible threat to world peace.

- North Korea's current leader Kim Jong Il is viewed by many as a ruthless despot whom it is feared will stop at nothing to perpetuate his regime.

- President George W. Bush refuses to negotiate directly with Kim Jong Il, but expresses confidence that a "peaceful, diplomatic" solution is possible.

- The longer the impasse persists, the greater the risk of war.

Common Questions About North Korea

In This Chapter

- Where is North Korea?
- North Korea—military threat or mighty mouse?
- Flood, famine, and refugees
- What's keeping Kim Jong Il in power

In this chapter, we will answer some of the more frequently asked questions about North Korea, including where it is; whether its weapons of mass destruction really threaten its regional neighbors, the United States, and its allies; how many North Koreans are starving and fleeing their homeland; and how this regime manages to stay in power.

Where Is North Korea?

North Korea occupies the northern half of the Korean Peninsula. This peninsula is strategically located between China and Japan, with Russia close by.

The Korean Peninsula is the only place in the world where the interests of all the world's superpowers— the United States, Japan, Russia, and China—come together.

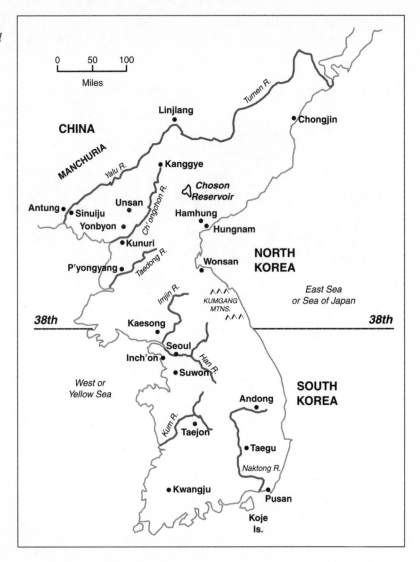

If you happen to be in Seoul, jump in your car and drive north along the Han River. You will reach North Korea's southern border with South Korea in about 45 minutes, depending on traffic. But you cannot cross into North Korea. The two halves of the Korean Peninsula are divided by the Demilitarized Zone (DMZ). This narrow "no man's land" is one of the most dangerous places in the world. It is lined with barbed wire on both sides and filled with hundreds of thousands of land mines. Beneath and beyond the DMZ's gently rolling hills, 1,500,000 heavily armed North and South Korean and U.S. soldiers man bunkers and trenches waiting to kill anyone who tries to cross the DMZ. Warning—taking a stroll into the DMZ could be hazardous to your health. We recommend you stay south of the border in South Korea. It is a much safer place.

Author Quinones (then deputy director, U.S. Embassy Tokyo's Mutual Defense Assistance Office, June 1992) "pilots" the nuclear attack submarine USS Indianapolis.

How Big Is North Korea's Army?

No Western observer can say for sure, but the North Korean army is huge. Generals control much that goes on in North Korea. They try to hide the reality of North Korea beneath a thick layer of camouflage. All the best experts can do is guess. Probably North Korea has one million or more men and women in its army, navy, and air force. Some estimates range as high as 1,200,000 personnel. Backing them are another 7,450,000 reservists. If these numbers are true, the Korean People's Army (KPA), as it is called in North Korea, is the fifth largest land force in the world behind the People's Republic of China, the United States, Russia, and India.

Size and surprise make the KPA a fearsome force. Seventy percent of its manpower is concentrated along the northern edge of the DMZ ready to lunge south with little warning. All ground units are fully *mechanized*. They are hunkered down inside camouflaged or underground concrete bunkers. Similar underground

> **Increase Your North Korea IQ**
>
> South Korea has 690,000 soldiers, marines, sailors and airmen. U.S. forces in Korea (USFK) number 35,000 soldiers and airmen. Backing them are the U.S. forces in Japan (USFJ) which number 60,000 marines, soldiers, airmen, and sailors.

bunkers are packed full of ammunition, food, and fuel. You cannot see these fortifications from the air. But when it rains hard, the bunkers flood, flushing the troops outside and ruining the stores inside.

Big is not better. The KPA has a huge inventory of hardware: tanks, armored fighting vehicles, artillery, multiple rocket launchers, and antiaircraft guns and missiles. However, North Korea's heavy metal is outdated. It is old Soviet-designed stuff the U.S. military handily defeated during the Gulf War in 1991 and Operation Iraqi Freedom in 2003. South Korean and American equipment is better by far, except for one thing: North Korea's 10,000-plus artillery, especially its accurate, rapid firing, long-range guns, is concentrated just north of Seoul and U.S. troops. Protected in concrete bunkers, it can rain havoc on both targets at a moment's notice.

Korean Concepts

Mechanized units have tanks and armored vehicles. They are more mobile because of their vehicles, and are able to move more quickly.

North Korea's air force and navy cannot measure up to the high tech muscle of U.S. and South Korean forces. North Korea's air force is a paper airplane. Its bombers are 50 years old. Except for a couple dozen modern, Soviet-designed fighters, most of its airplanes are Model-Ts compared to the U.S. and South Korean computer-loaded, smart bomb–carrying F-15s and F-16s.

But then there is the matter of weapons of mass destruction.

Yongbyon Nuclear Research Center—Kim Jong Il, father of North Korea's nuclear program, guards the entrance.

Does North Korea Have Nuclear Weapons?

Again we must guess. The best guessers are the United States intelligence community. This includes the Central Intelligence Agency (CIA), Defense Intelligence Agency (DIA), National Security Agency (NSA), and the Energy and State Departments' nuclear and political analysts. They have the best information available in the *National Intelligence Estimate.*

Korean Concepts

A **National Intelligence Estimate (NIE)** is a special study commissioned by the nation's leaders to assess an adversary's potential to threaten the security and interests of the United States. It reflects the U.S. intelligence community's best thinking, both its consenting and dissenting perspectives. Depending on the topic, participants in NIE's usually testy discussions often include the National Security Council (NSC), the Central Intelligence Agency (CIA), Defense Intelligence Agency (DIA), Joint Chiefs of Staff (JCS), State Department Bureau of Intelligence and Research (State INR), Department of Energy, and National Security Agency (NSA).

According to official U.S. government statements, North Korea may not yet have any nuclear weapons. But experts believe North Korea probably has enough highly radioactive plutonium to make several atomic bombs. North Korea has claimed since April 2003 that it has several nuclear weapons and is prepared to "demonstrate" that they work.

North Korea also has everything it needs to make more plutonium. At its top secret Yongbyon Nuclear Research Center, 8,000 nuclear spent fuel rods have been removed from storage. North Korean diplomats claimed in July 2003 that their country had completed extracting plutonium from these rods. If this is true, then North Korea has enough plutonium to make upward of eight nuclear weapons.

North Korea Fact

Nuclear weapons get their bang from plutonium or highly enriched uranium. Nuclear power plants run on uranium **fuel rods.** As atomic particles bombard the rods, some of the uranium is changed into plutonium. Once the energy in the uranium rods has been used up, the rods are replaced. The depleted uranium in the old rods can then be "reprocessed" in a chemical process that separates the plutonium from the old uranium. The plutonium can then be formed into a bomb using sophisticated equipment.

One thing is certain. If North Korea has in fact made nuclear weapons, as it has repeatedly claimed, it is well equipped to do so. The question over the total number of weapons is somewhat irrelevant. It would take only one nuclear weapon to destroy much of the city of Seoul (home for about 15 million people) or Tokyo (20 million people).

Then there are the questions of whether North Korea has developed a trigger mechanism to set off a nuclear bomb. Before a nuclear weapon will explode, it must have a trigger that ignites a nuclear reaction. This is a sophisticated piece of equipment. North Korea has yet to test a nuclear device, but again, it claimed several times in 2003 that it was prepared to test one of its nuclear bombs. This would be the only why to find out whether its "trigger" will cause a nuclear explosion.

Finally, there is the question of how it would deliver a nuclear weapon.

How Far Can North Korea's Missiles Go?

North Korea's arsenal includes missiles with various ranges. These missiles cannot reach the United States yet, but they can reach South Korea and Japan.

The souped-up Scud C (its North Korean name is *Hwasong 6)* can put a 1,500 pound conventional bomb on a target 500 kilometers (or 300 miles) from its launch site. This is North Korea's most reliable and accurate ballistic missile. It has been in production since the early 1980s and successfully tested several times.

While the Scud C cannot reach the United States, it can hit any one of the many U.S. military bases in South Korea. Also, if it were targeted on a South Korean city, chances are many U.S. citizens would also die. At least 50,000 U.S. citizens live and work in South Korea.

Then there is the Scud D, better known around the world as the *Nodong*. This ballistic missile can deliver a 1,000 to 1,500 kilogram (1 to 1.5 ton) warhead to a target 1,000 to 1,500 kilometers (600 to 900 miles) from its launch pad. This range is great enough to hit any place in Japan—and thus threatens all Japanese citizens—and any of the several U.S. military bases, including the aircraft carrier battle group stationed near Tokyo and the U.S. Marine Corps and Air Force bases on Okinawa.

Finally, there is the much feared, but greatly over-rated *Taepodong*. When talking about this missile, experts must revert to guessing. Theoretically, this three-stage ballistic missile is designed to deliver a several hundred kilogram (half-ton) weapon a distance of 10,000 kilometers or 6,000 miles. This would be far enough to hit the Western United States, including Alaska, Hawaii, and the West Coast. But the first

Taepodong launching was a flop. The missile sailed out over the Sea of Japan on August 31, 1998, but according to the DIA, the second stage misfired and the missile dropped into the sea. It has not been tested since.

Of course, the North Koreans have not given up. The DIA believes they are working on *Taepodong II*. This is believed to be a two-stage missile. The first stage is a cluster of Nodong rocket engines strapped together to give it more boost. The second stage is a single Nodong missile attached to the first stage. The arrangement has yet to be tested. If the *Taepodong II* does fly, it would increase the urgency of the debate in the United States over deploying an antiballistic missile system.

None of these missiles, however, can deliver a nuclear warhead. The U.S. intelligence community agrees that North Korea needs much more time and sophisticated technology to accomplish this task. North Korea also lacks bombers capable of delivering a nuclear weapon. At the present time, and for some years to come, the only reliable way for North Korea to attack another country with a nuclear weapon is to purchase a nuclear tipped ballistic missile, or deliver one via ship.

North Korea Fact

All of North Korea's ballistic missiles trace their ancestry to 40-year-old Soviet rocket technology obtained via Egypt:

- ◆ *Hwasong 6* (Scud C)   A reliable short-range, single-stage, liquid-fuel rocket with a 500 kilometer (300 mile) range carrying a 770 kilogram (three quarter ton) payload.
- ◆ *Nodong*   A fairly reliable medium-range, single-stage, liquid-fuel rocket with a 1,500 kilometer (780 mile) maximum range carrying a 1,000 kilogram (one ton) payload.
- ◆ *Taepodong I, II*   An untested, multistage rocket with an estimated range of 10,000 kilometers (6,000 miles) carrying a several hundred kilogram (half ton) payload.

Does North Korea Support International Terrorism?

No, not since 1987 has it sponsored or been known to be involved in terrorist acts. But North Korea remains under economic sanctions because it has not yet cleaned up its act entirely. Pyongyang still gives aid and comfort to some aging members of the Japanese Red Army (JRA). Early in the 1970s, this Japanese terrorist gang massacred people at an Israeli airport and hijacked two Japanese airliners. In 1988, a member was arrested with a bundle of explosives while speeding on the New Jersey Turnpike. He is serving a life sentence. Also in 1988, some of his comrades are suspected of having killed five people, including a U.S. servicewoman, at a club in Naples, Italy. Since 1996, eight other JRA members have been imprisoned, but the leader remains at large. Antiterrorism experts believe that at least a couple of the suspects live in North Korea.

North Korea in the 1970s and 1980s had a bizarre way of recruiting Japanese-language teachers. Its agents kidnapped more than a dozen young Japanese and hauled them off to Pyongyang. In one instance, a couple of young Japanese women were dragged off Japan's beaches, dumped into a submarine, and taken to North Korea. Not until September 2002 did North Korea accept responsibility for these outrageous misdeeds. North Korea's leader apologized to the Japanese people, but he still has not revealed all the facts surrounding the abductions.

Several of the victims died at suspiciously young ages. The Japanese people are convinced these young people were murdered, possibly tortured to death. In an effort to make some sort of amends, Kim Jong Il allowed some of the kidnapped victims to visit Japan, but without their spouses and children. Once in Japan, the victims still refused to return to North Korea. Ever since, the Japanese government has demanded that North Korea allow their spouses and children to leave North Korea.

North Korea Fact

One of the Japanese kidnap victims is married to a former American soldier, Charles Jenkins. He defected to North Korea in 1965 while stationed with the U.S. Army in South Korea. In North Korea, he often played the role of the American villain in movies. He met his Japanese wife while teaching English at the Pyongyang University of Foreign Languages. Their two children remain in North Korea with their father. Jenkins has told the Japanese press that he would not leave North Korea until 2004 when the statute of limitations runs out on his desertion.

South Koreans have been the main targets of North Korean terrorism. In 1968, a heavily armed platoon of North Korean soldiers infiltrated South Korea. Their target was the South Korean president. Police discovered them a few hundred yards from the president's residence. All the North Korean soldiers died in the ensuing shootout.

Undaunted, the North Koreans tried again in August 1974. This time it was a lone gunman, a young pro-Pyongyang Korean resident from Japan. He missed his target, the president, but tragically shot dead the first lady.

Even with that disaster, Pyongyang persisted in its efforts to kill the South Korean president. In October 1983, North Korean agents planted a bomb in the ceiling of the national memorial building in Rangoon, Myanmar (Burma). Fortunately for South Korea's president, his motorcade was delayed and the bomb exploded before he arrived. Still, half his cabinet was brutally murdered. The entire episode was filmed in bloody color, but the film has never been shown in South Korea.

North Korea's last known terrorist activity occurred in 1987. Two of its secret agents, a young woman and an elderly man, planted a bomb on a Korean Air flight bound for Seoul from the Middle East. After the couple had gotten off the flight and the plane was hundreds of miles away, it exploded in flight near Thailand, killing almost two hundred people. As the couple was being arrested, the old fellow popped a cyanide tablet and died on the spot. The young woman lived to tell the story, and also to explain how she had learned Japanese from a young Japanese woman who had been kidnapped by North Korean agents.

Since the 1987 bombing, North Korea has been under U.S. economic sanctions mandated for nations that support or commit acts of terrorism. The sanctions will not be lifted until North Korea releases the surviving members of the Japanese Red Army to Japanese authorities and satisfies Japan's demands concerning the kidnapping of its citizens.

Are the North Korean People Starving?

Very few, if any, North Koreans are now starving, although this was not always the case. Still, many go to bed hungry every night. Getting enough food remains a struggle, particularly for those who farm the land, or work and study in the frigid, poorly lighted factories and schools.

The United Nation's World Food Program reported in February 2002 that the proportion of underweight children had dropped from 61 percent in 1998 to 21 percent in 2002. The rate of acute malnutrition (wasting) had fallen during the same period from 16 percent to 9 percent. The UN study also discovered that the farther one traveled from the capital, Pyongyang, the higher the rate of malnutrition among children.

Near famine conditions, and a public health crisis, spread across the nation during the winter of 1995. North Koreans became the focus of a global humanitarian effort. From September 1995 to the end of October 2001, the world gave North Korea 6,000,000 metric tons of food worth about one billion U.S. dollars. More aid for public health, agricultural recovery, sanitation, and education steadily increased in recent years. Despite the economic sanctions imposed in 1987, the United States and South Korea have given the most food aid, about half the entire total. Other leading donors have been the European Union, China, and Japan.

Korean Concepts

Nature created conditions in both North and South Korea that make **self sufficiency in food** virtually impossible. South Korea today imports about 70 percent of its food, but its prosperous economy enables it to pay its food bill. North Korea is on the verge of bankruptcy. Modernizing its chemical fertilizer plants and using more of its crude oil imports from China to increase chemical fertilizer and pesticides production would also increase food production, but this would reduce the hard currency and fuel available for its huge war machine.

Food production has improved considerably since 1998, but still North Korea depends on several hundred thousand tons of imported food annually. South Korea and China continue to supply annually several hundred thousand tons of food aid. Japan has stopped sending food aid in 2001, and U.S. food aid has declined significantly since 2001. Meanwhile, Pyongyang has begun to purchase some grain from its few friends.

Personal Recollections

I was in North Korea in August, September, and October 1995. Torrential rains in August caused devastating floods. The corn and rice harvests were destroyed. I saw women and children dressed in rags wandering in the fields looking for leaves, grass, anything they could eat.

For months I never heard birds nor saw squirrels. They had all been eaten. One frigid day in January 1996, I saw thousands of people ice fishing on the Taedong River and nearby lakes. In July 1996, I visited the zoo in Pyongyang. Most of the animals had starved to death. The few remaining animals like the elephants and monkeys were too feeble to stand.

Just as severe was the lack of fuel to cook food or heat homes and water for washing. The floods had filled the coal mines, making it impossible to continue mining for the nation's basic fuel for heating. Deforestation had already stripped the hills of wood. Rice straw, a common substitute for wood, had all been burned by mid-winter in 1995. By January 1996, smoke coming from chimneys of homes and factories was a rare sight. People appeared in the streets and in the offices in dirty clothes, and themselves unwashed. Only after I had become repeatedly ill did I learn to stop shaking hands because there was no warm water or soap for washing.

Secrecy makes it impossible to know exactly how many people died from hunger and related illness between 1995 and 1999. Estimates of deaths range from 200,000 to 3,000,000 people. A generally accepted figure is about 10 percent of the population, or 2–2.5 million persons. Not all these deaths were from starvation alone. Illness killed many people because chronic hunger had weakened them. Cold killed others in the winters of 1995 and 1996 when the country suffered severe shortages of coal and other materials.

One can only imagine the extent of human suffering the people of North Korea have endured over the past half-century. The quality of life has not improved over the years despite the population's superhuman frugality and intense labor. We will have more to say about the causes and consequences of this continuing saga in future chapters.

How Many North Korean Refugees Are in China?

Hunger, illness, unemployment, and oppression have compelled tens of thousands of North Koreans to leave their homeland since 1995. Most have risked imprisonment, even execution by crossing into China. Their exact number is impossible to know. Estimates have ranged from a high of 50,000–300,000 in 1996 and 1997, to 15,000–50,000 in 2000. More recent estimates fall somewhere between these two numbers. The office of the United Nations High Commissioner on Refugees (UNHCR) appears comfortable with the 15,000–50,000 estimate.

The North Korean refugee crisis, like the food shortage, has become a contentious political and international issue. China, siding with North Korea, refuses to recognize the North Korean transients to be bona fide refugees. Instead, Beijing labels them "illegal migrants" and expels many back to North Korea.

The international humanitarian community is split over how to deal with the situation. Some groups prefer a low-profile effort that accents providing the refugees with food and medicine after they have arrived in China. Other humanitarian groups take an activist approach. They urge the North Korean migrants to seek asylum inside diplomatic compounds or to flee to Mongolia, from where they can pressure the South Korean government to arrange their safe passage to South Korea. The United States continues to prefer a low-profile approach that accents providing humanitarian relief to the refugees via United Nations relief agencies. See Chapter 23 for additional details and discussion about North Korean refugees.

Will Kim Jong Il's Regime Collapse?

Given the horrendous conditions North Koreans must endure, why don't they rise up and overthrow their "Dear Leader"? Are they afraid of him, or do they really respect him? We can only guess at the reasons for the staying power of Kim Jong Il's regime.

A keen sense of nationalism, a pervasive fear of foreigners, and a strong desire for national reunification and for individual survival, plus some respect for their leader, combine to sustain Kim's regime. First and foremost, all Koreans, North and South Koreans alike, are nationalistic. They love their nation and are intensely proud of its 2,000-year-old distinctive cultural heritage. Their encounter with Japanese imperialism between 1910 and 1945 taught them to love their nation ardently, and they came to respect those leaders who opposed the Japanese and fought for Korea's independence.

Kim Il Sung was one of many such patriots. But since the 1940s, he manipulated modern Korean history to promote his political fortunes. Then he proclaimed himself, with the Soviet Union's help, the foremost champion of Korea's struggle for independence from Japanese imperialism. This enabled him to become North Korea's founding leader in 1948. The elder Kim then declared that he would reunify Korea. With Soviet backing, he invaded South Korea in June 1950 to expel the "American imperialists" from Korea's southern half. When the Armistice was signed three years later, an estimated 3 million Koreans and 50,000 Americans lay dead. An unknown, but certainly significant, number of Chinese and North Korean soldiers also were killed.

Nevertheless, Kim declared victory in 1953. Thereafter, all North Korean school children were taught that he was their great defender and the United States replaced Japan as their worst enemy. These teachings, plus the United States's extensive bombing during the Korean War, convinced most North Koreans that they preferred Kim's authoritarian leadership to that of the alleged "imperialists."

Ever since 1953, most North Koreans have known only what they have experienced first hand or what their government has taught them about the outside world. The government-controlled mass media daily tells them that their tiny nation is under constant threat of invasion by the hostile and "imperialistic" superpowers, specifically the United States and Japan. As for South Korea, North Koreans are told that it is a U.S.-dominated puppet regime.

Unable to know any better, North Koreans accept what their government tells them. Thus North Koreans revere Kim Il Sung as their "Great Leader" because they believe he restored Korea's independence and then defended it against the "American imperialists." Anyone who questions what the North Korean authorities preach, or criticize the nation's leadership, is promptly labeled an unpatriotic enemy of the state.

Often the North Korean people's reverence for their "Great Leader" is compared by outsiders to that of a religious cult. This is somewhat misleading. Kim Il Sung, like

Japan's emperor, came to personify Korean nationalism and the Korean nation, at least in the minds of North Koreans. They do not distinguish between love of nation and respect for their "Great Leader." Rather than propagating a personality cult, Kim used history to fuse himself with the Korean nation and its independence. Any who attacks him is seen as assaulting the beloved nation. All patriotic North Koreans immediately rally against such critics, especially foreign enemies like the United States.

Kim Jong Il has benefited greatly from his father's legacy. It is the sole basis of his political legitimacy. Chances are North Koreans will continue to submit into the foreseeable future to his authority out of a combination of respect for his father and fear of foreigners and of the North Korean secret police. North Korea's current regime probably will endure, at least until Kim Jong Il's death. But at that point its fate becomes quite uncertain. Kim Jong Il's appointed heir is not guaranteed a smooth transition to power in the event of his father's death.

Can I Travel to North Korea?

Yes, Westerners are free to travel to North Korea and the United States government does not block travel there for its citizens. U.S. economic sanctions limit how much hard currency you can bring to and spend in North Korea, and what you can take there on your travel.

But don't book your flight yet. The bigger problem is getting admitted to North Korea. North Korea does not issue visas to the casual traveler. And U.S. tourists are not welcomed. You're considered a security risk, especially since you will want to take pictures of everything in sight.

Only special categories of people are admitted. Most U.S. journalists are denied entry. They tend to ask too many questions and insist upon taking photographs that would document the negative side of life in North Korea. Korean Americans are as carefully screened as journalists. After all, Korean Americans are hard to control. They speak Korean and can blend into the crowd on the sidewalk. Humanitarian workers do relatively well when it comes to getting a visa. After all, they have the knowledge, skills, and material aid Kim Jong Il so desperately needs to sustain his regime.

The Least You Need to Know

- ◆ North Korea is a military power armed with a huge army and ballistic missiles and may be close to developing several nuclear weapons.

- ◆ North Korea's military might does not pose a threat to North America yet, but it is a very real threat to U.S. allies, South Korea and Japan, and U.S. citizens living in those nations.

- ◆ The North Korean people continue to endure a severe shortage of food and medicine, and a significant number have fled to China in the hope of improving their quality of life.

- ◆ Despite all the problems, Kim Jong Il's regime does not appear now to be on the verge of collapse; but he is aging, and his regime is unlikely to endure long after his death.

Chapter 3

North Korea by the Numbers

In This Chapter

- ♦ North Korea's geography
- ♦ Land and people
- ♦ Government and politics
- ♦ Industry and agriculture

North Korea obviously is a big headache for a lot of people. In this chapter, we will answer some of the more frequently asked questions about the country, its population and resources. To help you get oriented, we locate it for you, describe its geography, and size up its infrastructure and natural resources.

The Korean Peninsula

Nature was not generous to the Korean Peninsula. It is a small, crowded strip of granite with few valuable minerals and other natural resources. Yet during the past half century, the Korean people's accomplishments have captured world attention. While South Korea emerged as a dynamic player in the world economy, North Korea became a potent threat to world peace and the security of the United States and its allies in the region. How Kim Il Sung, North Korea's former "Great Leader," managed to do this with so little is the essence of understanding North Korea.

Statistics about North Korea are notoriously unreliable, particularly if they come from official sources in Pyongyang. The data presented here was collected from publications of the United Nations, the governments of South and North Korea, and the United States.

North and South Korea share the Korean Peninsula, which covers 85,563 square miles (222,154 square kilometers). The entire area is equal in size to the British Isles, or the state of Minnesota. The trip from the southern tip to the border with China is about 600 miles (1,000 kilometers). This distance is about the same as between Boston and Washington, D.C. Seoul, Korea's traditional capital and the modern capital of South Korea, is about mid-point, just as New York is halfway between Boston and Washington, D.C. At its waist, the peninsula measures a short 130 miles. The following table provides an overview of how the area that is covered by this short distance breaks down into North and South Korea, including population figures.

North and South Korea at a Glance

	North Korea	South Korea
Geography		
Land area	47,000 square miles	38,563 square miles
Mountains	80 percent	70 percent
Arable land	14 percent	21 percent
Irrigated land	14,600 square kilometers	13,530 square kilometers
Forests	74 percent	67 percent
Coast line	1,497 miles	1,448 miles
Land borders	1,004 miles	143 miles
Population*		
Population	24 million	48 million
Population density	195 per square kilometers	485 per square kilometers
Median age	27 years	31 years
Age 0–14	28 percent	23 percent
Age 15–64	67 percent	71 percent
Sex ratio (males per 100 females)	95	101
Urban population	70 percent	81 percent

*Population figures based on South Korean government estimates.

> **North Korea Fact**
>
> North Korea's really touchy about people entering its turf. It claims a 12 nautical mile territorial sea limit and a 200 nautical mile "exclusive economic zone." Plus it claims a 50 nautical mile "military boundary zone" in the East and West Seas where all foreign vessels and aircraft without permission are banned.

North Korea's Turf

North Korea covers 55 percent of the peninsula or 47,000 square miles (120,410 square kilometers). It is about the size of New York State or Louisiana.

Climate

North Korea is a land of four distinct seasons. Summers are hot and humid. In the lowlands, temperatures range between 70 to near 100 degrees Fahrenheit (20–29 degrees Celsius). Temperatures peak in August. Fall is short. It begins in mid-September and continues till the end of October. Winters are long and bitterly cold. Temperatures can dip below minus 20 degrees Fahrenheit (minus 13 degrees Celsius). Frigid winds sweep south from Siberia in January and February. Winter temperatures can get much colder in North Korea's northeast mountains. Spring, like fall, tends to be a short, mild, dry season.

Sixty percent of the 43 inches of average annual precipitation falls between June and September. Much of it arrives during the annual monsoon which begins in late June and continues until mid-July. Typhoons in August and September may bring damaging torrential rains and winds.

Terrain

Rugged mountains cover about 80 percent of the land area. They are the Korean Peninsula's most striking geographic feature. These ranges run the entire length of the peninsula from north to south, through the peninsula's center, and along its east coast. They are not as tall as the Rocky Mountains, but they are just as steep. Dense forests, mostly various kinds of pine, still cover much of the northeastern mountains.

Some of North Korea's most scenic mountains are as follows:

◆ The Chilbo, or "Seven Treasures," Mountains' jagged peaks decorate an area on the northeast shore.

- The Kumgang, or "Diamond," Mountains' steep, saw-toothed peaks are the most famous. They form a national park in North Korea's southeast corner, and are bordered by the East Sea and South Korea. South Korean tourists began visiting the area in 1998.

- The Myohyang, or "Fragrant," Mountains are one hundred miles northeast of Pyongyang. Kim Il Sung built here his favorite hide-a-way and the "International Friendship Exhibition," two enormous underground bunkers filled with gifts from foreign governments and visitors.

- Paektu-san, or "White Head," Mountain is an enormous extinct volcano, rising 8,300 feet (2,744 meters) high. Some Koreans believe this was the birthplace of their nation's legendary founder, Tangun (see Chapter 4). Kim Il Sung claimed his son Kim Jong Il was born at the massive mountain's southern base in a log cabin. The claim suggests a parallel between Koreas' legendary founder and North Korea's current ruler. One thing is certain, the younger Kim never had to study by firelight or split rails.

- Yak-san, or "Medicine," Mountain is named for its abundant medicinal herbs and spring-blooming azaleas. At the mountain's northern base we find the Yongbyon Nuclear Research Center.

Broad fertile plains cover the area west of the mountain ranges. Long ago the forests here were chopped down for firewood or timber. In the northwest, the rolling hills are devoid of trees and scrubs. There are endless corn fields with scattered rice paddies flanking rivers and stream.

Each spring, the brown paddies are slowly converted into lime green carpets of rice and corn. By August, the fields have become emerald green. Autumn's cooling temperatures and shorter days paint the fields a smooth gold. Brown reclaims the land after the fall harvest.

Rivers and Borders

Rivers and streams tend to flow westward from the mountain ranges in the east through the plains to the west as they carry melted snow and rainwater to the West Sea. From north to south, you will find the following rivers on a map:

- Yalu (in Chinese) or Amnok (in Korean) River forms the northwest border with China.

- Tumen River forms the northeast border with China.

- Kuryong (Nine Dragon) River drains the northwest plain and supplies cooling water to the Yongbyon Nuclear Research Center.

- Ch'ongchon River drains the north central region and waters the corn fields of the northwest plain.

- Taedong River cuts through the central plains and Pyongyang, the capital.

- Imjin River drains the south central plain and waters the southwest region, North Korea's rice bowl.

Rivers form Korea's border with China. Just to the east of the border's midpoint is the huge extinct volcano, Paektu-san, which literally means "white head mountain." Inside its massive crater is a crystal-clear lake. Each spring, melting snow replenishes the lake's calm waters. As they spill from the crater, the waters flow in opposite directions, forming the two rivers that separate Korea from China. The Yalu River (or Amnok in Korean) flows west toward the West Sea (the Korean name for the Yellow Sea). The Tumen River trickles east toward the East Sea (the Korean name for the Sea of Japan).

Increase Your North Korea IQ

The West or Yellow Sea (dyed yellow by the sands blown from China's Gobi Desert) borders Korea's west coast. Along this west coast are some of the world's most extreme tides. The scenic, rocky east coast is bordered by the East Sea or Sea of Japan. Koreans, north or south, don't like their seas being called "Yellow" or "Japan." They insist on "East" and "West," and are jointly pushing the issue in the United Nations.

Natural Resources

Deposits of a few valuable minerals are scattered across North Korea's northern provinces. Minerals needed for making steel—iron ore, limestone, coal and magnetite—are the most abundant. Zinc is a major export, as are gold and silver. There is ample uranium ore to fill domestic demand. Based on South Korean government estimates, resources break down as follows (in metric tons):

Limestone	100.0 billion
Coal	14.7 billion
Magnetite	6.5 billion
Iron ore	3.0 billion
Zinc	12.0 million
Nickel	1.2 million

Manganese	0.2 million
Copper	75 thousand
Silver	5 thousand
Gold	1 thousand

Noticeably absent are any known oil reserves, although in recent years European drilling companies believe they have found potentially profitable oil deposits in the West Sea.

Transportation

Most goods are transported via train. There are an estimated 2,949 miles (4,915 kilometers) of track. About 63 percent is electrified.

North Korea has about 18,720 miles (31,200 kilometers) of roads, but less than 10 percent are paved. All roads naturally lead to Pyongyang. There are very few cars in private hands. People outside Pyongyang either walk or catch a ride in a tractor-pulled cart.

Increase Your North Korea IQ

Myohyang-Pyongyang Expressway is a four-lane, 160-kilometer highway that serves no purpose other than to carry officials and visiting dignitaries between the capital and the Fragrant Mountains.

Tongil-ro or Reunification Highway is a poorly paved, 160-kilometer, four-lane expressway between Pyongyang and Panmunjom in the DMZ where the Korean War Military Armistice Commission (MAC) used to meet. It was built to impress South Korean officials as they drove from Seoul to Pyongyang. Commercial traffic is banned.

Pyongyang-Nampo Expressway is a 60-kilometer, six-lane concrete road that carries commercial traffic between the capital and West Coast's main port.

Pyongyang-Wonsan Expressway carries commercial traffic over a two-lane concrete road between the capital and the east coast port of Wonsan.

Distances are relative to road conditions. The 60-mile trip from Pyongyang to the Yongbyon Nuclear Research Center via the old road takes three and one half hours in good weather, considerably longer if it is raining or snowing. Via the expressway the trip takes 90 minutes, even though half the trip is over an unpaved road. There are no "facilities" along the way.

Population

No one knows for certain how many people inhabit North Korea, not even its government. Because of continuing secrecy, experts can only make educated guesses. North Korea claims a population of about 22,224,195 people. But the pervasive starvation between 1995 and 1998 and the unknown mortality rate make an exact population count impossible.

Most of the urban population lives in cities of between 70,000 and 300,000 people. The rural population is concentrated south of the Ch'ongchon River and west of the central mountain ranges. The following table lists North Korea's top ten cities, the estimated population, and the type of city.

Top Ten Cities

City	Population	Type
Pyongyang	3,000,000	Capital
Nampo	900,000	Main west coast port
Hamhung	740,000	East coast industrial port
Ch'ongjin	540,000	East coast industrial port
Sunch'on	440,000	Central industrial city
Kaesong	410,000	Military command center
Kaechon	340,000	North central industrial city
Tanch'on	340,000	East coast industrial port
Wonsan	305,000	East coast port and naval base
Haeju	240,000	West coast port and naval base

An estimated 30 percent work in industry, 30 percent in services, and 5 percent on active military duty. Around 35 percent of the people are involved with agriculture, including a small percentage of soldiers.

Here is a list of some key facts about North Korea that summarize some important characteristics. Specific data should not be taken at face value, given the dubious nature of North Korean statistics. Nevertheless, it is provided for comparative purposes.

◆ **Life expectancy.** North Korea claims (and the U.S. government estimated in 2003) an average life expectancy of 71 years—74 years for females and 68 for males.

- ◆ **Ethnic groups.** North Korea is racially homogeneous. There is a small, fully assimilated Chinese community, and a few Japanese and other foreigners.

- ◆ **Language.** Korean is the official language. The most widely studied foreign languages are English, Japanese, and Chinese. According to South Korean educational professionals, Russian fell to the bottom of the favorite foreign language list in 1990.

Religions

"Freedom of religious belief" is promised in the North Korean Constitution, but the government bans organized worship as "counterrevolutionary." Government-controlled Buddhist and Christian organizations exist. Some three hundred Buddhist temples are preserved as museums. Paying respect to Buddha as a philosopher is permitted but is not widespread. The Confucian practice of paying respect to one's ancestors also is allowed, but not for members of the Korean Worker's (Communist) Party.

Sunday Christian church services are performed at three Christian (two Protestant and one Catholic) churches in Pyongyang. These services are held primarily for the benefit of foreign visitors. An underground Christian movement is believed to be active, particularly in the northernmost provinces.

Political Nuts and Bolts

North Korea's relative small population inhabits a small geographical area, but a relatively huge bureaucracy administers the country. Actually there are three bureaucracies: the Communist Party, the army, and the governmental administration. Here we outline the governmental structure. See Chapters 10 through 13 for discussions about the other bureaucracies, plus a discussion about how these three bureaucracies relate to one another.

Government Divisions

North Korea is nominally a republic with a constitution, president, and nine provinces, plus four special administrative districts. These special districts are the capital of Pyongyang, the main west coast port of Nampo, the northeast port of Ch'ongjin, and the south-central city of Kaesong. We say "nominally" since North Korea certainly is not a republic in the same way the United States uses the term.

Government Structure

Kim Jong Il rules the so-called Democratic People's Republic of Korea (DPRK). He chairs the National Defense Commission (NDC), a council of his top nine civilian and military officials plus himself as chairman. They are all members of the nation's ruling political party, the Korean Workers (Communist) Party (KWP). Many are ranking generals in the (North) Korean People's Army (KPA). The State Administrative Council reports to the NDC and oversees the nation's civil administration.

Each year the 687-member Supreme People's Assembly (SPA) loyally rubber-stamps the national budget. The legal term of office is five years. Suffrage is universal beginning at age 17, but elections are not held regularly.

The judicial system reflects German and Japanese legal practices prior to World War II. The Central Court stands at the judiciary's apex. Subordinate to it are provincial, municipal, People's, and Special Courts. There are three kinds of Special Courts: Military, Traffic, and Transportation. Each specializes in handling military personnel and transportation workers. All judges are appointed. The SPA elects a prosecutor-general who heads the Central Procurators' Office in Pyongyang.

Leadership

Kim Jong Il assumed power in July 1994 and inherited all political power from his father Kim Il Sung. He named his father president for eternity but accepted the titles of general secretary of the KWP, supreme commander of the KPA, and chairman of the NDC. About 75 officials staff the government's top civil and military positions.

Political Parties

The dominant political party is the communist KWP. The national constitution designates the KWP the nation's ruling party. The KWP has an estimated membership of three million. The Politburo of the Party Central Committee oversees the party and was once considered the most powerful government organ. The NDC displaced it after Kim Jong Il's succession. The two token splinter political parties are the Korean Social Democratic and Chondoist Chongu Parties.

The Means of Production

North Korea's economy is often described as a "failed" socialist system and a "closed" economy. These are dated descriptions. True, North Korea perpetuates many characteristics of a socialist economy. But economic reforms are underway. North Korea has dispatched hundreds of experts abroad since 1996 to learn and to assess the economies of other nations. The apparent aim is to revitalize North Korea's economy by developing a synthesis of foreign practices and concepts with domestic political and economic priorities. One consequence is that North Korea is "opening" its economy to international trade. Whether the effort will ultimately succeed in restoring North Korea's former economic vitality remains to be seen. Since 2000, the influx of aid and investment from China, South Korea, the European Union, and the United Nations has halted the nation's economic decline and boosted agricultural production. Nevertheless, North Korea remains an impoverished nation. See Chapter 13 for a more in depth discussion of North Korea's economy.

Increase Your North Korea IQ

North Korea is believed to have one telephone for every 22 persons, one television for every 22 people, and three radios for every 22 people, but only one Internet service for the entire nation.

Economy

There are two economies: the secret military and the dilapidated civilian one. The military economy gets the best of everything available. The civilian economy hovers on the verge of bankruptcy. The civilian industrial sector produces few goods competitive in the international market. The agricultural sector has increased production in recent years but the nation remains heavily dependent on food aid to feed the population.

Currency

North Korea until June 2003 had two kinds of official currency. One was pegged to an artificially propped-up foreign exchange rate of about two North Korea won per one U.S. dollar. Only foreigners and privileged officials could use it. The other currency was legally available only to North Koreans and had no exchange rate. Reality caught up with both currencies in the summer of 2002. North Korea declared an end of its "foreign" currency and replaced it with U.S. dollars and other hard currencies.

GDP

No one really knows the true size of North Korea's real gross domestic product (GPD). The South Korean government estimated its value in 2002 to be $22 billion using a *purchasing power parity* methodology. This ranks North Korea among the poorest nations in the world.

Industries

The secret military economy's leading products and exports are conventional weapons (rifles, ammunition, artillery, and armored vehicles) and ballistic missiles. Civilian sector exports in 2001 consisted of minerals, metallurgical products, textiles, and fish products estimated to be worth $826 million. Its biggest trading partners are South Korea, China, and Japan.

Korean Concepts

When a country produces output in a currency that is not readily converted (like North Korea), economists can use the **purchasing power parity** method. In this method, the relative values of similar "baskets of goods" are compared. This gives a conversion factor for the total output of the economy in question.

The Least You Need to Know

- ◆ North Korea occupies the northern half of the Korean Peninsula, and is about the size of New York State.

- ◆ Rugged mountains dominated the east and northeast regions while fertile lowlands cover the nation's western half.

- ◆ Natural and mineral resources are limited, but there are small deposits of gold, coal, and uranium, and abundant timber.

- ◆ The population of North Korea is about half that of South Korea.

- ◆ The government is run by Kim Jong Il, a hereditary authoritarian ruler.

- ◆ The economy hovers on the edge of bankruptcy.

Part 2

North Korea Yesterday

Winston Churchill once said that Russia was a "riddle inside an enigma, wrapped in a conundrum." The same can be said for North Korea. In this section, we will attempt to peel back the layers of history that have created today's North Korea. We will trace Korea's development as an independent nation with a unique culture, its place in China's traditional world order, how and why Japan colonized Korea, and its struggle to regain independence only to be divided.

"From the past comes the present" is the theme of this part. You will get the background and insights that help you understand why North Korea has emerged as the country we know today.

Chapter 4

From Korean Myths to Kingdoms

In This Chapter

- ◆ How do the Korean people view themselves?
- ◆ Where did Koreans come from?
- ◆ The kingdoms before Korea
- ◆ North Korea's point of view: history or propaganda?

Winston Churchill once said that Russia was a "riddle inside an enigma, wrapped in a conundrum." The same can be said for North Korea. In this chapter, we peel back the layers of history that have created today's North Korea.

History Is Power

Let's begin peeling away the conundrum of North Korea by looking at it from the inside out.

Kim Il Sung climbed to power behind a gun. But once in power, he sought to control North Korea's population by gaining control of the people's minds. Like the despots Stalin in Moscow and Mao Zedong in China, Kim seized control of the mass media and education system. He and his closest colleagues then propagated their version of Korean history. It was designed to place Kim on a political pedestal as the "Great Leader" and to legitimize his authoritarian rule.

Kim Il Sung was an ardent nationalist and a crafty politician. Kim also wanted to be just as loyal to Marxism as he was to Korea, and craved the respect of his communist mentors Stalin in Moscow and Mao Zedong in China. Toward these ends, he ordered his historians to squeeze Korean history into the Marxist mold. But it did not fit. Koreans had done their own thing in history.

Nevertheless, Kim Il Sung persisted. He blended historical fact with myth, mixed in some Marxism, and presented this to the North Korean people as their historical legacy.

His goal was not truth, but rather the legitimization of his authoritarian rule. History, in other words, became a political tool. Knowing something about Korean history, and how North Koreans see themselves and their history, will help us to see through the illusions Kim Il Sung created and his son is using to perpetuate his power.

Marxism's father was Karl Marx, a nineteenth-century German scholar. He and another German friend, Friedrich Engels, wrote *The Communist Manifesto* in 1848. Their best-seller presented what they claimed to be a scientific theory of history.

According to them, economic forces propel history through distinct stages. Man, in short, is motivated by greed. In each historical stage, workers struggle with owners for control of the economy. In ancient times, land-owning nobles clashed with slaves. In the medieval era, feudal lords struggled with peasants. In modern times, ruthless and wealthy capitalists fought with impoverished factory workers. Ultimately, Marx claimed, the working classes would unite and gain the upper hand.

Beginning in this chapter, and continuing through Chapter 6, we will trace Korea's historical legacy. In the process, we will see the extent to which it does not conform to Marxism-Leninism.

Korea Through Korean Eyes

Most Koreans agree that there is only one Korean nation and one race of Korean people. North Koreans have long chanted the motto, "*han nara*," or "one country." In South Korea, the phrase was banned prior to 1988 during the decades of authoritarian rule. It was considered a "communist" term. But now South Korea's main opposition political party proudly wears the label, "*han nara dang*," or "the party of one country." This change in attitude came during the 1992 Olympiad when the two Koreas decided to field a single team. Their common flag depicted the entire Korean Peninsula on a white background.

All Koreans see their nation's division as a tragic consequence of superpower rivalry at the end of World War II. North Koreans have long considered the labels "northerners" and "southerners" to be artificial distinctions imposed by foreign governments, specifically the United States and Russia. Older South Koreans who survived the Korean War generally remain reluctant to be so candid. But younger Koreans in South Korea increasingly agree with their northern kinsmen's long-held view.

North Korea Fact
A way to anger Koreans is to suggest that they have something in common with either the Chinese or Japanese. Koreans view themselves as a culturally and genetically unique group of people.

Koreans living in northern Korea consider themselves Koreans, not "north" Koreans. They have been educated to call themselves "*Choson in*," or "people of Choson," the ancient name for Korea. They claim this label with intense pride. As for their southern kinsmen, the North Koreans call them "*nam Choson in*," or "southern Koreans." The designation is similar to the one Americans use when identifying regions within the United States. The label identifies a geographical area, not a separate political entity.

What's in a Name?

There is a lot of history behind Korea's name. Portuguese explorers in the sixteenth century derived "Korea" from "Kaorai," the Chinese pronunciation for the medieval Korean kingdom "Koryo."

Koreans living in North Korea, China, Japan, and Russia call their homeland "Choson." This is Korea's original name. It predates by a millennium the name "Korea." The last dynasty to rule the entire Korean Peninsula was "Yi Choson," or the "Choson of the Yi dynasty." Choson means "morning calm." American missionaries working in Korea in the late nineteenth century nicknamed Korea "land of morning calm."

South Koreans and Korean-Americans refer to Korea as "Hankuk," which means "nation of Han." Han was the name of a prehistoric tribe believed to have first settled the Korean Peninsula, but the name "Hankuk" was not coined until the end of the nineteenth century. It came into common use after the Republic of Korea was established in South Korea in 1948.

People in South Korea, however, were taught until recently to divide Koreans geographically into North Koreans (literally *pukhan saram*) or South Koreans (*Hankuk saram*). This changed when South Korea became a democratic country after 1988. Young Koreans born after the Korean War (1950–1953) began calling themselves and their northern kinsmen "*uri minjok*," or "our people."

Personal Recollections

In front of a North Korean solider, I called his beloved Korean language by its South Korean name (Hankuk), and luckily lived to tell the story. It was on my first visit to North Korea in December 1992. After a long wait, I was finally invited to present my passport for entry into North Korea. I had greeted the soldier in the Korean language and he asked where I had learned to speak it. I confidently responded in my best Korean, "I studied Hankuk mal in the United States." His face changed to an angry grimace and his eyes bulged as he lectured me, "There is only one Korea and its name is Choson, not Hankuk. There is only one Korean people and they call themselves Choson, not Hankuk saram. And there is only one Korean language and it is called Choson mal, not Hankuk mal." Outnumbered 24 million to one, I promptly concluded that it would be healthier not to disagree. I nodded my complete agreement. Tossing my passport toward me, he jerked his head to the left to indicate that I could enter his fatherland. I did not hesitate.

Big Bird Meets the Bear

All Koreans trace their nation's birth back 5,000 years and their ancestry to the legendary figure named Tangun. He is believed to have set up Korea's first dynasty, the Choson, in 2333 B.C.E. According to legend recorded in one of Korea's ancient historical texts, the *Samgukyusa* or *Memories of the Three Kingdoms*, Tangun's father was a bird deity and his mother a bear. (Koreans are quick to explain that they do not actually believe the story.) The bird and the bear got together on Paektu-san, the huge extinct volcano on the China-North Korea border. Tangun eventually grew up and made his capital near modern day Pyongyang. His descendants are credited with having ruled Choson for a millennium.

According to ancient records, Tangun was buried in the mountains about an hour's drive southeast of Pyongyang. Japanese archeologists claimed they found the tomb site in the 1920s. Kim Il Sung in the 1990s directed that his archeologists seek out the remains of Tangun. Amazingly, they claim they found them in 1993. A massive granite pyramid was erected at the site and the alleged remains of Tangun were placed inside.

Personal Recollections

The American Army returned to North Korea in July 1996 after a 43-year absence. Eight specialists from the Army's Central Identification Laboratory (CILHI) had come to locate and take home the remains of American soldiers who had died in the Korean War. As the State Department's representative with the group, my job was to keep them safe and to resolve any misunderstandings. When our North Korean army hosts offered to give us a guided tour of Tangun's grave, we eagerly agreed.

Soon we stood at the foot of a gray heap of granite. It looked more like a brand new Mayan pyramid than an ancient Korean king's tomb.

We entered a dark narrow passage way. Inside we gathered in a dimly lighted chamber at the tomb's center. Before us, a brown lacquered coffin rested on an elevated platform. A North Korean officer next to me, speaking in Korean, whispered in my ear, "You are fortunate. We will show your comrades Tangun's bones without cost. Usually we charge visiting Japanese tourists a lot of money to see the bones." I thank him but thought it best, not to translate his comment into English. Abruptly, the top of the coffin was lifted and set to one side, exposing a skeleton. A stunned American soldier whispered to his commanding officer, "Sir, them bones can't be 5,000 years old." His commander first ignored him. The disbelieving soldier could not suppress his dismay, and speaking louder said, "Sir! No way can those bones ..." His commander wisely cut him off and concluded the exchange with a curt, "Son, it's a political matter."

The commander was correct. In North Korea, myths and history are indeed political matters.

Once a Korean, Always a Korean

In Korean eyes, ancestry is the essence of being Korean. You are what your mother makes you. If she was Korean, you are a Korean regardless of your father's roots or your national citizenship.

Identification as a Korean gives one membership in the unique, extended Korean family. Being Korean is both a source of pride and obligation. The ancestors of this extended family have distinguished themselves for two millennia, Koreans believe, by sustaining their homeland's political independence and cultural uniqueness.

South Korean parents expect their offspring to learn, respect, and contribute to their cultural heritage. To do this, Koreans must learn the Korean language, eat Korean food (especially *Kimchi*), and make their parents proud. The last part is the most difficult. It usually requires that you get good grades and try to go to an elite university.

> **Korean Concepts** _____
>
> Kimchi is a staple of Korean meals. One of many kinds of side dishes, Kimchi is spicy hot, salty, and smelly, and contains chili peppers, scallions, garlic, chopped cabbage, radishes, cucumbers, or other green leafy vegetables. To qualify as a bona fide Korean, you should eat Kimchi morning, noon, and night. Others may limit themselves to the evening meal.

North Korean parents similarly motivate their children to aim high. In Pyongyang, this means joining either the Korean Workers Party or the Army, and attending Pyongyang's Kim Il Sung or Kimchaek Universities. Parents who live outside Pyongyang generally have to settle for much lower expectations.

From Myth to History

From a mix of myth and history, Korea began to emerge as a single nation some two thousand years ago. In prehistoric times, successive waves of nomadic tribes charged out of the broad plains of central Asia and swept across the Korean Peninsula. After countless centuries, tribes traded their horses and nomadic life for oxen and rice agriculture. From the legendary ancient Choson kingdom and the Chinese colonies, three kingdoms emerged on the peninsula: Koguryo, Paekche, and Shilla. A small domain named Kaya also appeared in the fourth century C.E.

The unique qualities of Korea's political and cultural traditions were forged during the Three Kingdoms Period (18 B.C.E.–935 C.E.). Buddhism nurtured creativity and defined aesthetic standards. Koreans' artistic achievements, particularly in the ceramic and metal-casting arts, are still revered today around the world. Shilla unified the Korean Peninsula. Its monarchs turned to China's Confucianism to assert their authority through a centralized bureaucracy and to temper the power of noble clans through a system of competitive civil service examinations. Linguistic dialects merged into the Korean language and a uniquely Korean literature developed. All Koreans, regardless of their political persuasion, point to this period as the golden age of Korean cultural accomplishment.

Tracking Korean history, especially the ups and downs of Korean kingdoms and dynasties, is confusing, to say the least. As an aid, we offer below, and in subsequent chapters, occasional time lines.

Ancient Kingdoms of Korea and Western Civilization

Korean Kingdom	Period	Western Time Line
Ancient Choson	1,000–200 B.C.E.	Greek Civilization
Han States and Han China's colony Lolang	200 B.C.E.–100 C.E.	Roman Empire
Three Kingdoms	18 B.C.E.–935 C.E.	Roman Empire Split (392)
Paekche	18 B.C.E.–660 C.E.	Spread of Christianity
Koguryo	37 B.C.E.–668 C.E.	Anglo-Saxons in Britain
Kaya	42 B.C.E.–562 C.E.	
Shilla	57 B.C.E.–935 C.E.	Mohammed (570–632)
Parhae	669–928 C.E.	First Holy Roman Emperor crowned
Unified Shilla	618–935 C.E.	in 800 C.E.

The First "North" Korea—Koguryo (37 B.C.E.-668 C.E.)

Koguryo (founded in 313 C.E.) dominated the northern two thirds of the Korean Peninsula for several centuries after its founder expelled imperial Chinese colonial governors from the peninsula's northwest corner. China's second unified dynasty, the Han, in 109 B.C.E. had established colonies in the Korean Peninsula's northwest corner to block nomadic tribes from raiding the region northeast of modern Beijing. The successors of Koguryo's founder extended their domain well north of the Yalu and Tumen Rivers into modern day China's southeast corner.

Korean Concepts

Yonbyon (in Korean) or **Yanbian** (in Chinese) is China's "little Korea." Located west of where the Chinese, Russian, and Korean borders intersect, Yonbyon is home of over two and one half million ethnic Koreans. Some of their ancestors settled here centuries ago, others migrated there during Japan's occupation of the Korean Peninsula (1910–1945); Kim Il Sung was one of them. Others now flee North Korea in search of food, work, and safe haven in Yonbyon.

Today, the archaeological remnants of the Koguryo Kingdom can still be found scattered across what was once called southern Manchuria. Now the region encompasses the modern Chinese provinces of Liaoning and Jilin. The southern area of Jilin

Province contains the Korean Autonomous Region of *Yanbian* (sometimes referred to as Yanji in Chinese, or *Yonbyon* in Korean). Yanbian shares its eastern border with Russia.

Koguryo's Legacy—China's Little Korea

The Yanbian region is now home to an estimated 2,500,000 ethnic Koreans. The Korean language has equal billing with the Chinese language. Ethnic Koreans, known in Chinese as *jiaoxen ren* (people of Choson) or *Choson chok* in Korean, dominate the provincial government, schools, and all the professions. China's central government remains sensitive to the area's Korean orientation and Koguryo legacy.

A calm concern persists in Beijing that some day Koreans might reclaim the area as part of their homeland. Since 1995, the flow of refugees from North Korea into the region has heightened Chinese government concerns that the Korean population in the area might eventually overwhelm that of the ethnic Chinese, both in terms of numbers and political clout. South Korean commercial investment and Christian missionary work in the region has further excited these concerns.

Living History

North Korea's founder Kim Il Sung identified himself and his domain with Koguryo and its monarchs. Like Koguryo, Kim's domain ruled the Korean Peninsula's northern half. Like Koguryo's founder, Kim expelled the "imperialist" from Korea. Koguryo's find was credited with having ended the Chinese colonies on the Korean Peninsula. Kim claimed credit for having ended Japan's modern colonization of Korea between 1910 and 1945.

China's first communist dictator, Mao Zedong, attempted to eradicate the remnants of China's archaic past, but Kim Il Sung worked to preserve Korea's historical legacy. In doing so, he sought to legitimize his rule by linking it to the Koguryo, Korea's earliest kingdom.

Koguryo's rulers, like Kim Il Sung, sanctioned a single system of thought. Buddhism filled the Koguryo's philosophical needs. This motivated Kim Il Sung to preserve Buddhism artistic legacy. Two excellent examples of early Koguryo Buddhist architecture and art survive, near Yongbyon in the form of the two temples on Yak-san, or Herbal Mountain (see Chapter 3). Another fine example of an early Buddhist Temple is the eleventh-century Pohyon-sa in the Fragrant Mountains (Myohyang-san) (see previous chapter).

Pyongyang served as Koguryo's capital in the fifth century C.E., just as it does today for North Korea. Heavy U.S. bombing of the city during the Korean War obliterated most of the ancient wooden structures. Under Kim Il Sung's direction, portions of ancient Pyongyang's fortress walls were restored. The city's famous gates also were reconstructed. Twenty-five kilometers east of Pyongyang, the tomb of Koguryo's first ruler, Tongmyong, was rebuilt per Kim's directions.

Koguryo was the largest and most powerful of Korea's ancient three kingdoms. Its authority extended well south of Seoul, South Korea's capital. Koguryo maintained an unsteady co-existence with the Paekche to its southwest and Shilla to its southeast. The small kingdom of Kaya was squeezed between the borders of Koguryo's southern neighbors.

The First "South" Korea—Shilla (57 B.C.E.–935 C.E.)

Koguryo's repeated clashes with China and its southern kinsmen slowly sapped its strength. Early in the seventh century, Koguryo's army destroyed the greatly superior forces of an invading Chinese army. But the Chinese eventually allied with Koguryo's competitor, Shilla, and overwhelmed it.

The Chinese-Shilla alliance first conquered the Paekche kingdom (18 B.C.E.–660 C.E.). This small kingdom ruled the Korean Peninsula's southwest corner. Buddhism dominated religion and politics. The kingdom prospered as the intermediary in trade between China and Japan. As Shilla's forces overwhelmed Paekche, its royalty and nobility fled to Japan. There, according to Japan's oldest historical record, the Korean Paekche nobility merged with Japan's newly emerging nobility to form the Japanese imperial family and aristocracy.

The combined forces of Shilla and China then crushed Koguryo in 668. The kingdom's last monarch, together with 200,000 prisoners, was taken to China. When Chinese generals took control of Koguryo's conquered domain, Shilla confronted its former ally in 671. Shilla in 735 finally reclaimed all of the Korean Peninsula south of the Taedong River.

China retained control of the Korean Peninsula north of Pyongyang until the early eighth century. To the northeast of China's colony a former Koguryo general established his own kingdom, Parhae (P'ohai in Chinese) north of the Tumen River in what is now modern China's Jilin Province. Most of this kingdom's aristocracy traced its ancestry to Koguryo's nobility. Parhae survived until the 935 when Shilla unified the entire Korean Peninsula. China at the time was consumed in political chaos and unable to counter Shilla's expansion.

Common Ground—Korean Culture

Buddhism was the most dominate belief in ancient Korea. Korean students of Buddhism carried it to Korea via China and travel by ship through the South China Sea. Art focused on Buddhist themes; the seated Buddha, brightly colored paintings of paradise and hell, and the decorations that cover the ceilings and eaves of Buddhist temples. Korean craftsmen over the centuries preserved the ancient Chinese architectural style in the sweeping roofs and ceramic roof titles first seen in temples, and then adapted to Korean palaces and official buildings. The memorization and chanting of Buddhist scriptures and the recording of detailed historical annals and travel journals set the stage for the subsequent introduction of Confucianism.

Korea Emerges from China's Shadow

China's impact weighs heavily on this cultural legacy and Korea's pre-modern political institutions, but much that is now considered uniquely Korean culture derives from Korea's Three Kingdoms Period (18 B.C.E.–935 C.E.).

Koreans defined themselves as a nation and people during this period. Political authority was centralized under the Shilla monarchs. Social distinctions came to be rooted in the pedigree of one's ancestors. A uniform social pyramid with rigidly defined social classes formed. A preoccupation with pedigree and status forged a hereditary nobility that competed with the monarchy for power, prestige, and wealth. This rivalry pitted monarchy against nobility, and Confucianism against Buddhism. Political power during the Three Kingdoms Period gradually shifted from the nobility, who preferred Buddhism, to the monarchs, who championed Confucianism.

A similar duel between ideologies is underway today on the Korean Peninsula. North Korea continues to favor authoritarianism and socialism while South Korea subscribes to democracy and capitalism. South Korea's preference now appears destined for victory in this duel.

Buddhism Flavors Korean Culture

Like frosting on a cake, Buddhism's legacy gives Korean culture its aesthetic appeal. It also fostered Koreans' original respect for learning and literature. Buddhism was the most dominate belief in ancient Korea, at least for the nobility.

Buddhism, like Christianity, has many sects. Each accents a different way to get to the same place, heaven or, as Buddhists prefer to call it, paradise. To get there, you have to get out of hell, or earth as Westerners prefer. Release from hell can come only after you realize that cravings for the pleasures of the body condemn one's soul to a vicious cycle of birth and rebirth in hell, or earth. To escape, one must reject their individual identity and selfish desires and merge with the universal "force beyond physical existence."

Few ancient Korean nobles found Buddhist aestheticism very appealing. They discovered Son Buddhism (the Korean name for Japan's Zen Buddhism). Son Buddhism requires that you occasionally climb a mountain, ponder the beauty of nature, and write poetry while drinking rice wine. You could get to paradise simply doing what aristocrats, and others, like to do best—kick back, chill out, and party.

Korean Rugged Individualism

Son Buddhism's anti-intellectual tendencies encouraged individualism. It encouraged pragmatism or "free thinking." But another Korean priority kicked in to determine who qualified to be a "free thinker." In ancient times, you had to be of noble blood, and have ample wealth if you wished to head for the hills to think freely and write poetry while getting drunk.

Fortunately for modern Korea, many talented men and women of ancient Korea rejected monastic life. They also refused to merely indulge in wine, women, and song. Instead, these blue blooded Buddhists defined ancient Korean culture, art, and philosophy. Some became Buddhist monks, and served as Korea's first bureaucrats. They served as political advisers, scribes, and fortune tellers in the royal court.

Spreading the Faith

Korea gave as good as it received. While some Korean Buddhist monks were refining Buddhism and China's arts, others carried Chinese and Korean culture to Japan. When Paekche's royal family, nobility, and Buddhist advisors and tutors fled the Chinese-Shilla forces in the ninth century, they made western Japan their new home. The craftsmen who accompanied them brought knowledge of paper making, printing with carved wooden blocks, and the making of lacquer ware and ceramics. Korean monks gathered in central Japan in Nara, Japan's oldest capital. They brought with them Paekche's symbols of royal authority. Japan's imperial family later adopted them as its own—the sword and curved jade jewel. Members of ancient Japan's nobility traced their ancestry to Korea. They also introduced the ancient Japanese to the Buddhist scriptures and Chinese writing system.

Links to Modern Times

In contemporary North Korean society, the new breed of nobility consists of those men, and a very small number of women, who have won admission into the Korean Workers Party, North Korea's communist party. This is North Korea's nobility. Unlike their ancient ancestors, however, they are preoccupied with statecraft and political power. But this politically protected, and economically pampered group, can afford to continue Korea's ancient tradition of "free thinking." Kim Il Sung's interpretation of Marxism-Leninism, as we will see in Chapter 10, puts most North Koreans in a mental straitjacket. But Korean Worker Party members are permitted to candidly criticize the implementation of policy, but only so long as they do not criticize the "Great Leader" or his son, Kim Jong Il.

Korea's Social Straitjacket

Another characteristic of Korea is its preference for rigid social and political hierarchy. This, too, can be traced back to ancient Korea. Shilla Koreans divided themselves according to birth. The closer one's lineage to royalty, the higher one ranked in society. With social status came access to wealth. Wealth equipped the individual to acquire knowledge. This enabled a man (women need not apply) for positions of power and prestige at court.

Shilla society was divided into royalty, nobility, commoners, and slaves. Status was hereditary and determined by one's mother's status. The nobility competed for access to the monarch by either serving at court or becoming monks in one of numerous powerful and wealthy Buddhist monasteries. This enables the individual to perpetuate his family's power and wealth by preserving ownership of land. A class of commoners, most of whom were involved in commerce and trade, facilitated commerce in urban cities and vigorous trade with China and Japan. Slaves, many believed to have been prisoners of war and their descendants, provided the manual labor in towns and on farms.

Present-day North Korean society maintains a similar rigid hierarchy. Kim Il Sung and his son are Korea's new monarch. Generals and communist party officials serve the same role of ancient Buddhist monks, and are similarly rewarded. Those outside this minority, North Korea's workers and farmers, form the commoner class. Modern North Koreans guilty of some political infraction or crime are banished to slave labor camps. We will revisit this theme in Chapters 11 and 12.

Where Is Confucius?

Using the Chinese script, Koreans began to record their myths and legends, history and interpretations of Buddhism. A primitive Korean phonetic script evolved to record the pronunciation of Chinese written characters. A single Korean language emerged, although the ancient languages of Koguryo and Paekche echo in the dialects of modern Korea. This set the stage for the spread of Confucian thought, as we will discuss in Chapter 5.

History Is Power!

Most experts agree that Kim Il Sung craved power, not the truth. He saw history as a political tool to extend his power and to legitimize his rule. He accented the unique-ness of the Korean people and intertwined himself with their historical and cultural legacy. He associated himself with Tangun, the "great" ancestor, and the Koguryo Kingdom's founder, Tongmyong. Massive monuments were erected in their honor. He drew parallels between their accomplishments and his. He highlighted Koguryo's expulsion of the ancient Chinese colonial rulers and the Korean kingdom's domina-tion of the Korean Peninsula's northern two thirds. He linked his capital to Koguryo by restoring its remnants.

Pyongyang today is a city of museums. Each portrays a chapter of Korean history in vivid color and convincing models. Kim Il Sung crafted the chronology, themes, and details of each display. After all, he saw himself not just as the "Great Leader," but also the "Great Teacher" and the "Great Defender" of Koreans, their nation and historical legacy.

Daily thousands of school children, college students, and young soldiers troop through the Central Museum of History. Tucked shyly away on the southeast corner of Kim Il Sung Plaza, this unappealing gray block of concrete houses displays of Korea's pre-modern history. Atop the capital's highest hill, the massive Museum of the Revolution documents Kim's version of his rise to power and the birth of his dynasty. Before it stands a towering bronze statue of the man himself. Down the hill to the north we come to the "Memorial Hall to Victory in the War to Liberate the Fatherland." Around the world, this war is better known as the Korean War. Here, in this massive gray mausoleum one finds Kim Il Sung's "evidence" for proclaiming that he and his army won the Korean War.

The Least You Need to Know

- ◆ Koreans consider themselves a race of people with a unique and highly refined cultural tradition that is distinct from China and Japan.

- ◆ All Koreans, whether living in North or South Korea, see their homeland as a single nation tragically divided by the United States and Soviet Union since the end of World War II.

- ◆ All Koreans look to Korea's ancient Three Kingdoms as the origin of their nation and culture.

- ◆ Kim Il Sung saw history as a tool to further his political ambitions and to legitimize his authority.

Chapter 5

Enter the Dragon— The Chinese Legacy

In This Chapter

◆ Does Marxism match Korea's history?

◆ Why did Confucius win out over Buddha?

◆ Mongol hordes and Japanese "Vikings"

◆ Europe discovers Korea

Many of contemporary Korea's political practices and institutions have their roots in medieval and early modern Korea. This is generally true of both Koreas since both halves of the Korean Peninsula first encountered modern Western society under Japanese colonial rule.

But South Korea has undergone a much more extensive transformation than North Korea. Since 1945, South Korea has been a much more open society than the communist north. The presence of large numbers of foreigners living and working in South Korea, combined with the exodus of South Koreans as students, merchants, and immigrants to foreign lands have eroded many traditional political preferences in South Korea.

Kim Il Sung's Preferences

North Korea's founder Kim Il Sung early on decided to perpetuate selected traditional Korean political preferences. These included a monarchy, centralized political authority and bureaucracy, a balance between ancestry and merit as established through education and examination, allegiance to a single political ideology, and conformity rather than diversity of political views. Toward this end, he closed North Korean society to all but a select few foreigners and most alien political thought, except for Marxism-Leninism. Consequently, contemporary North Korean political institutions and society have much in common with their medieval and early modern ancestors.

Here we assess North Koreans' interpretation of their pre-modern history and the roots of many political institutions and practices in modern North Korea.

Mismatch with Marxism

Korean history doesn't follow Karl Marx's rules. The Soviet Union's collapse dumped Marx's views into history's recycling bin, but not in North Korea. There the study of history, as molded by Marxism, remains mandatory (see Chapter 12).

To keep his buddy Stalin happy back in Moscow, Kim tried to squeeze Korean history into Marx's mold. It did not fit. Simply put, the Koreans lived their history their own way, not as Marx later theorized.

> **Increase Your North Korea IQ**
>
> Karl Marx's book *The Communist Manifesto* fascinated the young Kim Il Sung. Marx (1818–1883), a German-born scholar, co-authored it in 1848 with Friedrich Engels. The book became an all time best-seller. They claimed economic forces and greed propelled humanity through history toward a utopian paradise. Along the way, humanity encountered "class struggles" between the rich and poor. Each struggle defined a stage in human progress. The ancient struggle between land-owning aristocrats and slaves set the stage for the medieval struggle between armed feudal lords and their peasants and serfs. Then came the industrial revolution. Capitalists exploited urban workers. Marx predicted the workers' inevitable victory. They would set up a socialist economy in which there was social and economic equality. Utopia would inevitably follow. This has never happened anywhere.

Kim Il Sung, like East Asian kings and despots before him, used history to legitimize his rule and justify his actions. Kim sought to propagate a "scientific" interpretation of Korean history that accomplished several of his political goals.

Foremost, Kim wanted to consolidate his power at home. He decided to legitimize his supremacy over his competitors by propagating an interpretation of Korean history that cast him as the foremost champion of Korean nationalism. At the same time, Kim wanted to demonstrate to his Russian mentor Stalin and Chinese mentor Mao Zedong that he was their intellectual equal and ideological partner.

Kim found what he needed in Marxism. The German historian Marx had argued that history was an evolutionary process. Human development moved through a series of historical phases. Greed motivated man's actions. In each phase, the poor would rise up in "class struggle" and overthrow those who exploited them. In the final historical phase, urban workers would overthrow wealthy "capitalists," create a socialist state in which all wealth was equally distributed. Ultimately, Marx theorized, a classless utopia would form.

Kim seized on Marxism's inevitable utopia. Its theory of class struggle rationalized his push for political power. Marxism's claim to be "scientific" appealed to early modern Korean intellectuals and technocrats, people Kim would need to staff his government. Another magnate for popular appeal was Marxism's promise of equality and wealth for all.

Kim was interested in political power, not the pursuit of truth. His application of Marxism was highly selective. His blending of Marxism and Korean history ignored some aspects of its theory and distorted portions of Korean history. The outcome is an artificial and forced interpretation of Korean history that is best labeled propaganda. Yet this blend of failed theory and distorted fact remains mandatory learning for all North Koreans.

First we will quickly review Korea's medieval and early modern historical periods, and then contrast this with Kim's view of the same history.

Medieval and Early Modern Korea (935–1598)

Only two dynasties ruled Korea during the millennium between 935 to 1910. They were the Koryo (918–1392) and Yi Choson (1392–1910). Both were set up by generals. Kim Il Sung liked that precedence when legitimizing his own rule. The Koryo dynasty's first capital was in Seoul, but then was moved north about 30 miles to Kaesong. Kim Il Sung liked that precedent, too. The Yi Choson dynasty had only one capital—Seoul. Kim didn't find that as useful.

Koreans didn't live by Marx's guidelines. The recurring theme in Korean history is not a struggle over the economic means of production (which is Marx's theory for social evolution). In traditional Korean society, land was wealth. Early in Korean history it was decided that the king owned the land and reserved the right to "lend" it to his loyal followers. This meant politics, not economics, propelled history.

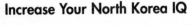

> ### Increase Your North Korea IQ _____
>
> In Europe, medieval feudalism and commerce gave rise to most cities. Unlike medieval Europe, Korea's early cities were the capitals of kingdoms and centers of administrative activity.
>
> Koguryo (37 B.C.E.–668 C.E.) Pyongyang
>
> Paekche (18 B.C.E.–660 C.E.) Kongju
>
> Shilla (57 B.C.E.–C.E. 935) Kyongju
>
> Parhae (669–928) Tunhua (China)
>
> Koryo (918–1392) Kaesong
>
> Choson (1392–1910) Seoul

There were plenty of struggles, to be sure. Most, however, were between squabbling members of the royalty, nobility, and gentry as each competed for the king's favor so they could grab more political power and prestige (and more land). If the noble lacked political clout, the king could reclaim that noble's turf. Examples of the Marxist class struggle are hard to find in Korean history.

King to Everybody, "This Is My Land"

The Koryo kings solved a lot of political problems. The first was who could wear the crown. Their Shilla forefathers had tried passing it around to a small circle of nobles. This had not worked well. But the Koryo kings decided the best way was to keep the crown in the family and pass it to their first born surviving son. Those who objected either became slaves or raised armies and overthrew the dynasty. That's what the Yi Choson dynasty's founder did to Koryo in 1392. Of course, this was not an original idea. The Koreans got it from China where dynasties dated back to 200 B.C.E.

North Korea Fact
Confucius had a profound and continuing impact on East Asia. He lived in China about 500 years before Christ. China was divided among many warring kingdoms. Confucius taught rulers and their advisers how to rule. He never wrote anything, but his students took good notes. Confucius taught that peace would come only after proper etiquette was practiced between ruler and subject, husband and wife, and so on. Kings liked Confucius because he taught that they deserved respect above all others.

Koryo's kings found benefit in adopting Chinese ideas. The king's challenge was how to get the powerful aristocracy to accept the king's claim to all the land. Buddha's ideas were great for telling people how to leave hell on earth and get to paradise. But Koryo's kings wanted to know how to calm the aristocrats' squabbling so they could find some peace on earth, and enjoy its pleasures before heading off to paradise.

Confucianism had the answers. China's ancient political philosopher Confucius and his disciple Mencius made their living telling Chinese monarchs how to rule. The Koryo monarchs were eager students of both the Chinese language, the key to reading what Confucius had said, and Confucian thought. In addition, since Chinese kings learned from Confucius, it was only fitting that the Koryo kings should also learn from Confucius.

Mandate of Heaven

According to Confucius, dynastic founders and their heirs had to earn their right to wear a crown. In East Asia, there was no tradition similar to Europe's "divine right" concept. According to Mencius, Confucius's disciple, the ancestors got really angry when a king fell into evil ways, ruled arbitrarily, exploited his subjects, and pocketed all the wealth for himself. When angered, the forefathers unleashed the forces of nature on the evil king's domain. Flood and famine fostered popular frustration and discontent. Rebellion followed. From the milling masses benevolent men would rise up and gather armies to overthrow the decadent dynasty. Victory went to the most benevolent fellow, or so the theory went. The idea caught on in China. Later Europeans translated the concept as the "Mandate of Heaven" because of the role ancestors played in the process.

Increase Your North Korea IQ

Chinese, Koreans, and Japanese do not "worship" their ancestors. Catholic Jesuit missionaries long ago fostered this myth. Confucianism is a political philosophy, not a religion. Its central theme is that people can minimize conflict between themselves by following proper etiquette. Within the family group, children should respect parents, even after they have passed away. Each year at the time of the lunar calendar's August full moon, East Asians visit their parents' gravesites. There they perform a ritual that resembles sharing a meal with their deceased parents. This is done to express gratitude to their parents for having given them life and for the harvest that has just been gathered. Not doing this could upset the ancestors who, East Asians believe, watch over Nature. This could result in calamity.

Well, if a person had just crowned himself king and set up a new dynasty, like the Koryo founder had done in 935, the idea was "heaven sent," so to speak. He (women were excluded from traditional politics) liked it because he could excuse his disloyalty to his former boss by claiming the old king was no good. All he had done was kick the old king out for everyone's benefit. Then, because he was such a nice guy, he deserved the Mandate of Heaven and to crown himself king.

Let's Make a Deal

The Mandate of Heaven was a great idea, but still rather academic. Kings, just like you and I, live and work in the real world. In China, the founder of the new dynasty declared his predecessors corrupt and punished them either by execution or banishment to repair the Great Wall or some other life long public works project.

Koryo's founder couldn't afford to anger medieval Korea's hereditary nobility, and did not have a Great Wall. Medieval Korean nobility still exerted more control over the land than the royal household. The transition from noble to royal control of the land was a gradual process.

Koryo's founder handled things the Korean way. He began by adopting another Chinese idea. He declared exclusive ownership of all the land. Land produced rice, which was wealth. As king, he could do what ever he wanted with his land. He could "lend" it to his royal kinsmen and loyal noble supporters, but it remained his.

North Korea Fact

Mandate of Heaven remains a potent political concept in East Asia. This ancient Chinese concept is rooted in the teachings of Confucius's most famous student, Mencius. He taught that a ruler's right to rule was tied to his conduct. So long as he looked after his subjects' welfare, he could retain the Mandate of Heaven. Otherwise, the ancestors who controlled the forces of nature would unleash natural calamities upon his kingdom. His subjects would rise up, and with the ancestors' help, reclaim the Mandate of Heaven and pass it to a new ruler. In 1995, floods inundated North Korea. Famine and disease followed. Many South Koreans saw this as indicating North Korean leader Kim Jong Il had lost the Mandate of Heaven. Many North Koreans probably thought the same, but were not free to say as much.

He offered Korea's medieval nobility a deal they could not afford to turn down. In exchange for their signing up to the Mandate of Heaven, plus letting him claim ownership of the land, the king would agree to share his power and wealth with them.

The next thousand years of Korean history is largely the tale of the dueling between Korea's medieval and early modern kings and noblemen to make the deal work. During the early Koryo Dynasty, politics were mainly competition between royalty and the nobility. As the dynasty matured, the dueling increasingly involved the monarchs and his officials versus some formidable and wealthy Buddhist monasteries. After a Koryo general had overthrown the dynasty in 1392 and crowned himself the first Yi Choson king, royalty and nobility resumed their squabbling. As Korea's last dynasty aged, politics shifted toward rivalry between powerful noble families.

Public Welfare for Noblemen

Koryo's kings borrowed another idea from China to get the nobles either to stop swinging swords at each other or living off their ancestral assets. The kings adopted a centralized bureaucracy. Again, Shilla's monarchs had tried the idea, but with limited success.

At the time, a centralized bureaucracy was on the cutting edge of political institutions. Rome had figured out how to administer a vast empire through a centralized bureaucracy, but this wisdom had not served the interests of medieval Europe. During the Dark Ages, Europe lingered as a patchwork quilt of splintered feudal domains.

Korea was a single cohesive political entity by 950. The king set himself up as the chief bureaucrat. Subordinate to him was a State Council of Ministers he appointed to manage his domain. Their jobs were specialized. He had a chief executive officer, then known as a prime minister, and ministers to handle internal and external affairs, war, taxation, public works, the royal house hold, even a government accounting office.

Beyond the capital, the Koryo dynasty divided itself first into circuits and two border regions, then into provinces. Provinces were further subdivided into counties, districts, and garrisons. The king appointed his representative, a governor, to each province.

The bureaucracy's main role was to ensure a steady flow of tax revenue to the king's treasury. It served the secondary purpose of making the nobility dependent on him for jobs and prestige. During each harvest, the king's officials oversaw the gathering, threshing, and weighing of rice. Other grains and food were cultivated, but rice was the same as cash. These officials watched as the rice was divided. A portion went to the king's granaries, another portion to the noble family commissioned to oversee the king's land, and a smaller portion went to the local officials and their subordinates as payment for their services.

The Best and the Brightest

After the idea of a bureaucracy had caught on, the next problem became how to manage the competition for jobs. In the beginning, there had been enough jobs to go around. But as the number of noblemen grew, so, too, did the competition for the limited number of jobs.

Again, the Chinese had the answer. They set up a system of examinations so that all the applicants have an equal opportunity to compete for a job. Now this was really on the cutting edge. The United States did not establish its civil service examination system until the 1880s. The Koreans did it in the eleventh century, and the Chinese a thousand years earlier.

Korea's adoption of the Chinese examination system changed the course of its history. Passage of the civil and military service examinations became the primary route to power, prestige, and wealth. Every nobleman's mother wanted her son to pass the test and enter the bureaucracy. After all, the pay was good, the work steady, and retirement benefits appealing.

North Korea Fact

Most people know about civil service examinations, but most do not know where they started. The Chinese came up with the idea about 2,000 years ago. From then until about 100 years ago, first the Chinese, then the Koreans, used written examinations to determine who was best qualified to staff the bureaucracy. The Chinese invention of paper more than 2,000 years ago made it possible to have such examinations. China had two levels of examination equivalent to a B.A. and M.A. The Koreans, always wanting to do their own thing, added a third level of competition.

In time, the best and the brightest of medieval and early modern Korea's noblemen prepared for the examinations. Teaching became the second most sought after occupation after civil service. A parallel military service examination system was used to staff the top echelons of the military. It also served as an alternate entry route into the civilian bureaucracy, if you were high born and had the right connections. No self-respecting nobleman wanted to humble their family, or themselves, by getting into commerce or working with their hands as artisans and craftsmen. Farming was fit only for commoners and slaves.

Korea's Closing Door

China became the fountain of all politically correct knowledge in early modern Korea. Aspiring bureaucrats had to master written Chinese, no small accomplishment. They also had to spend their youth memorizing the Confucian classics. Other sources of knowledge were deemed irrelevant because they did not prepare one for the examinations. Foreign ideas were seen as suspicious and irrelevant, along with science and mathematics, because they did not prepare you to pass the civil service examinations.

Koryo and Yi Choson era nobility excelled at politics, statecraft, scholarship, and calligraphy. The bureaucracy and examination systems promoted paper and ink making, as well as printing. Korea used the world's first movable metal type 100 years before the Gutenberg Bible was first printed in Germany.

But interest in science, technology, and philosophies other than Confucianism languished. Mental energy was invested in memorizing Chinese, ancient classics, and history. There was no reward in pondering why apples fell from trees (like Newton's discovery of gravity), technological innovations, or trying to make Korean and foreign systems of thinking mesh.

Buddhism, once the dominant philosophy, retreated to the mountain tops and became the pursuit of a few hermits and artists. This was particularly true after the early Yi Choson dynasty dismantled the late Koryo's large monasteries. The early Yi Choson monarchs did this to prevent the monasteries from contesting their authority to collect taxes from these establishments as well as the kings' preference for Confucius.

Networking in Early Modern Korea

The Koreans did not just roll over and become Chinese. More often than not, Koreans' Chinese intellectual imports fit Korea's social realities as well as a round peg in a square hole. Koreans had to tinker constantly with their imported Chinese ideas to make them fit. Eventually, what began as Chinese ended up having unique Korean characteristics.

Genes and Success

The Chinese style examination system eventually became the primary route to political power and prestige. But the Yi Choson nobility added their own style of affirmative action. Legally, anyone was eligible to take the examination. In China this happened on a regular basis. But in Korea, the examinations gradually became the exclusive business of noblemen. Applicants for the tests had to present ancestral and official government documents to establish their noble pedigree. This effectively eliminated commoners and slaves from the competition.

China's examination had two levels of tests, equivalent to B.A. and M.A. degrees. The Koreans added a third, Ph.D. level to their tests. You could win the Ph.D. without first getting an M.A., but everyone first had to win the B.A.

The owner of noble pedigree and a civil service examination degree still needed two more things for success. He (noble women dared not even think about doing anything other than having noblemen's babies and writing poetry) had to marry a well-born bride and have ties to the right people in the right areas of the country.

Brides and Success

The status of women in Korea declined considerably after the introduction of Confucian thought. In ancient times, women had been allowed to rule and own property. The ownership of property lingered on into the Koryo dynasty. But women were banished from the halls of government. Occasionally a queen projected herself into matters of government. Official historians later condemned them as squabbling, petty minded persons.

By time Yi Choson rulers reigned, noble families used their daughters to provide the king with spouses and concubines. Powerful noblemen emulated their monarchs by marrying a primary wife while keeping one or more concubines or secondary wives.

Legally, one's social class was determined by the social status of one's mother. The son born of a nobleman and his primary wife had preference over all others. His half brother, who was born to a concubine, even of noble lineage, was deemed illegitimate. During much of the Yi Choson dynasty, these illegitimate sons were banned from competing in the examinations. Their inheritance was significantly less than their legitimate brothers.

Arranged marriage was standard practice. Fathers wanted to ensure that their pedigree remained pure. Detailed genealogical records were maintained to trace one's ancestry. Official census and tax records recorded the names of one's parents, in-laws, and three generations of ancestors.

Politically powerful families sought to preserve and perpetuate their influence by marrying their sons and daughters into other similarly powerful kinship groups. Occasionally, the monarch would reach out to a declining noble family for a new concubine or bride for his son. The move would restore the declining family's political fortunes. It also served to maintain a balance of power between the royal family and the competing noble families.

Out of Sight, Out of Mind

Regionalism in Korean politics has its roots in early modern Korea. Being born into a noble clan or family was insufficient to guarantee appointment to civil or military office after success in the examination system. An ambitious and capable nobleman had to be born into a family located in a region of the country where other nobles congregated.

North Korea Fact

Regionalism is a recurring theme in Korean politics. During Yi Choson (1392–1910), northerners were excluded from high office. Southerners labeled them uncultured because their ancestry traced back to the ancient warrior kingdom of Koguryo. In modern times, South Koreans continue to see northerners as being more warlike than they. South Koreans also identify with one of three areas: the southeast (*Yongnam*), the southwest (*Honam*), and the central region around Seoul. The southeast corresponds with the ancient Shilla's domain, the southwest with ancient Paekche, and the central region with the Yi Choson dynasty's capital area. South Koreans tend to vote for a presidential candidate from their parents' home "region."

After crowning himself king, Yi Choson's first king enrolled his most loyal supporters in a new nobility. He awarded them official titles, positions in his centralized bureaucracy, and leases to land. This new nobility was supplemented by older noble families that pledged their allegiance to the king.

The entire group was split into civil and military officials. This gave rise to the Korean word for nobility, *yangban*, which translates as "two columns." Civil officials received land around the immediate vicinity of Seoul, the capital. The military officials, so they were more prone to defend the monarch's capital and his civilian officials, were granted leases to land that formed an outer circle around the capital.

As the population grew in subsequent centuries, branches of the original royal and noble families established themselves in areas beyond the capital region. The further removed from the capital, the less one's chances of success in gaining an appointment in the central bureaucracy.

During the Yi Choson's 500-year history, men from the northern half of the kingdom had virtually no chance of being appointed to a civil official position in Seoul, regardless of how successful they had been in the civil service examination.

The reasons for this geographic bias remain vague and largely unexplored. The pattern of exclusion only became evident in recent years after a systematic study of the more than 50,000 men who passed the dynasty's civil service examination. One possibility is that the dynasty's nobility sought to minimize competition for appointments by labeling "northerners" the descendants of "uncultured" nomads who had established the Koguryo kingdom.

The Social Pyramid

Yi Choson society was dramatically different from contemporary Chinese society. Korea had a rigid social pyramid. Members of the royal and noble families concentrated at its apex. They governed the kingdom. Commoners gathered in the middle class. They tended to live in cities and towns, and specialized in commerce. There were a few free-born farmers who cultivated small plots of land. The lowest social class consisted of slaves. Slaves formed a significant element of the population. They were legally bonded to their owner and available for sale or barter. But all indications are that Korea's slave system was relatively benign. Owners tended to treat slaves humanely, and to provide decent working conditions and all basic human needs.

Less Was Best

Koreans traditionally were a frugal people. Most manufacturing centered on carpentry, textiles, metal making and shaping, ceramics and paper production, and leather goods. Artistic decorations were usually limited to noblemen's homes. They preferred paintings and *celadon*, artistically refined ceramics best suited for decoration rather than daily use. Everyone needed furniture, tools, a roof over their head or an office, and carts and carriages. They also needed leather goods for shoes and to control their horses and oxen. Silk and cotton were needed for flowing official robes and to adorn high-born ladies. Most others wore plain white cotton clothing. Korea's growing centralized bureaucracy, mighty Buddhist monasteries, and private Confucian academies needed lots of ink and paper.

Increase Your North Korea IQ

Koryo celadon is world famous. Celadon refers to a highly artistic form of ceramic dishes. Celadon is formed from wet clay into a variety of decorative dishes. Cups, bowls, plates, water droppers (for mixing writing ink), incense burners, serving pitchers, and vases were popular shapes. Decorative designs were either cut into the wet clay or painted onto dry clay. The decorated dish was covered with a fluid called glaze and placed in an oven. The "firing" of the ceramic hardened the glaze and protected the user from the lead in the clay. Heat also caused a chemical reaction in the glaze that determined the dish's final color.

Medieval Korea's Big Spenders

Like elsewhere throughout history, Korea's royalty and nobility were the big spenders. Buddhist temples became big consumers in the medieval period. The aristocrats and monks aspired to emulate the luxuries that China's rich and powerful gathered. Competition with the "Kim's" down the road also drove the market for luxury goods.

Korea's traditional aristocrats collected small decorative items for their homes. This nurtured landscape painting, and the making of celadon, ceramics, and furniture. The relatively grandiose desires of the royal family and Buddhist monasteries fostered architecture, the painting of large decorative murals, the carving of large wooden figures, and the casting of Buddha's image and large bronze bells.

Commerce and trade never caught on in medieval and early modern Korea. Buddhism and Confucianism fostered frugality. Kings promulgated laws that limited the size of homes. Even the homes of nobles were kept relatively small. No massive stone castles or towering churches dotted the Korean landscape like those in Europe.

Those Damn Yankees

Koreans early on decided they did not like foreigners, whom they referred to as *yain* (*yanggui* in Chinese). Every time they showed up, there was trouble. First it was the invading Chinese in the seventh century. Then there were the Khitan people, a nomadic group who roamed from modern Manchuria into Central Asia. They frequently raided the Korean Peninsula from ancient times till the early Koryo period. Following the Chinese example, the Koreans tried to fence them out with their own "Long Wall." But like China's Great Wall, the nomadic hordes always found ways to get around and over walls.

Increase Your North Korea IQ

The southern Chinese referred to Europeans in the sixteenth century as **yanggui**. Literally it means "ocean spirits," and acquired a negative connotation. By then it was more accurately translated as "ocean devil" and applied to Europeans. The term "yaren" or "wild men" was applied to the uncivilized nomadic tribes of inner Asia. The Koreans adopted the Chinese usage. British seamen and soldiers corrupted the pronunciation to "yankee" and applied it to their upstart cousins during the American Revolution. Americans since gave it a benign spin, but modern Chinese and Koreans still use it in the old manner.

Mongol Hordes

The Mongols came thundering into the Korean Peninsula in the thirteenth century. First they plundered the cities and tore up the countryside. Then they forced Koreans to help them invade Japan. Twice the Koreans had to build huge fleets to carry the invasion forces. The 1274 effort with 25,000 soldiers failed. The Mongols tried again in 1281 with a combined force of 140,000 Mongol, Chinese, and Korean warriors.

Fortunately for Japan, a powerful typhoon blew up from the South China Sea. It struck the Mongol fleet just as it was preparing to land. The fleet was devastated. The Japanese were thrilled with the typhoon and named it the *"Kamikaze"* or literally "divine wind." By this point, the Japanese got really angry with their Korean cousins.

Japanese Pirates

The Japanese returned the favor in the form of marauders. There were pirate-traders who began plundering Korean trading ships and ports during the thirteenth and four-teenth centuries. They also raided China's coastal region. These were not typical pirate bands. Their numbers could reach 5,000 to 6,000 pirates per raid.

A Korean military expedition to the Japanese islands failed in 1419 to suppress the Japanese pirates. Afterward, the Koreans struck a deal with the Japanese feudal lords. The Japanese agreed to stop the raids in exchange for being able to set up permanent settlements in Korean ports and sending a specific number of trading ships to these ports each year.

But the Japanese returned with a vengeance at the end of the fourteenth century. Japan's unifying warlord sent a feudal army of 160,000 warriors to conquer Korea and fight its way to China. Despite China's massive intervention on Korea's side, the Japanese conquered the southern two third of the peninsula. The Koreans' use of the world's first iron clad war ships, combined with Chinese superior manpower, finally drove the Japanese from the peninsula in 1598.

Enter the Europeans

For good reason, the Koreans did not want anything to do with foreigners when the Europeans began showing up in the sixteenth century. The first Europeans entered Korea with the Japanese samurai army at the end of the century. These were Catholic missionaries who provided for the religious needs of Japanese Christian feudal lords and warriors.

After these first Europeans departed with the Japanese, a Dutch ship was blown onto a southern Korean island. The crew was taken prisoner and transported to Seoul. Gradually, some of the crew began to learn the Korean language and won the trust of the hosts. Eventually, this hand full of Europeans provided Korea's royal court its first insights into Europe. Based on what they had to say about Europe at the time, the Koreans decided they were much better off not getting involved with these new, red headed and bearded "barbarians."

By the seventeenth century, Korea had decided its interests were best served by becoming the "Hermit Nation." It closed its doors to all foreigners. Any who dared knock, except for the Chinese and Japanese, were referred to Beijing.

The Least You Need to Know

- ◆ Korean history does not conform to Marx's point of view of history.

- ◆ Korea's medieval and early monarchs found the teachings of Confucius valuable for asserting their authority over Korea's hereditary nobility.

- ◆ The Yi Choson dynasty (1392–1910) adopted the Chinese models for a centralized bureaucracy and a system of civil service examinations, but continued the Korean preference for a powerful hereditary nobility, which could check the king's authority.

- ◆ Korea's ancient and early modern encounters with foreigners from Central Asia and Japan convinced them the best foreign policy was to exclude all foreigners and to rely on China to defend the kingdom from them.

Chapter 6

Shrimp Among Whales, 1864–1910

In This Chapter

◆ Christianity's clash with Confucianism

◆ Korea as the "Hermit Nation"

◆ China's world order crumbles

◆ Japan's colonization of Korea

North Koreans have been taught to see their present problems with the United States through the eyes of Kim Il Sung. He taught, and his son continues to propagate, that the United States aims to conquer their homeland so it can exploit its people, resources, and strategic position. "The U.S. imperialists are trying to strangle us" is the preferred mantra in Pyongyang.

Kim Il Sung and his historians, all students of Lenin's interpretation of modern history, traced modern U.S. foreign policy directly back to Japan's early twentieth-century colonization of Korea. Then they drew a straight line back to Korea's encounter with the United States and Europe in the nineteenth century. Kim Il Sung topped this off with *Vladimir Lenin*'s views of nineteenth-century world history.

Increase Your North Korea IQ

Vladimir Lenin (1870–1924) was the father of the 1919 communist revolution in Russia. He also had a profound influence on Kim Il Sung. Lenin refined the theories set forth in Karl Marx and Friedrich Engels's *The Communist Manifesto*, including the "historical dialectic" which described the evolution of society to the final stage of communism (see Chapter 5). Lenin claimed imperialism would emerge on the eve of human history's transition from capitalism to socialism. European governments and the wealthy would team up to establish colonies around the world. The capitalists then would exploit local labor to gather raw materials for their industries back home. Lenin predicted these "imperialist" nations' greed would drive them to destroy one another, opening the way for the emergence of socialism and then communism in industrialized nations.

North Koreans have yet to be told that recent history proved Lenin wrong. Imperialism did emerge around the world in the nineteenth and early twentieth centuries. But capitalism has not collapsed. If anything, communism has collapsed after an 80-year run. However, the North Korean state-controlled media has not reported these recent events to their readership. Here we look at the historical record free of its Leninist distorts.

Calm Before the Storm

Before anyone was thinking about Lenin and the historical dialectic, the Yi Choson (1392–1910) people appeared to have been fairly comfortable with their situation, at least during the dynasty's first four centuries. The monarchy was stable until the mid-nineteenth century. Royal family members engaged in the occasional intrigues and betrayals against one another, but this had little effect beyond the capital. Nobles continued to squabble over official ranks and titles, appointments to office and marriages. They divided themselves into factions that endured for centuries, but again this had little if any effect on most Koreans living outside the capital.

Life was fairly tranquil until the dynasty's last century. Occasionally the failure of a crop or incident of official corruption sparked rumbles in the rice paddies, but clashes between the upper and lower classes tended to be sporadic and brief. In the nineteenth century, however, more than half dozen uprisings disrupted the traditional calm.

The Yi Choson era was a period of gradual but significant change. Agricultural technology was refined. Food production kept pace with population growth. For the most part, shortages of food were short lived and occasional. Regional patterns of commerce developed, linking farms to towns and towns to cities. Production centered on traditional goods: silk, paper, ceramics, processed sea foods, bamboo, and wood produces. Trade with China and Japan gradually increased, but not with other foreign countries.

Intellectual life revolved around Confucianism. The civil service examinations kept the nobility's energies focused on memorizing Chinese characters and what Confucius had said. Buddhism retreated to the mountain tops. Hermitages became the abode for the artistically inclined and those frustrated with the examination system. Painters of landscapes and portraits, and fashioners of ceramics emulated the work of their Chinese tutors.

A small school of Confucian-educated and intellectually pragmatic noblemen acquired a keen interest in the study of Korea's past and present. This group came to be known as the "Students of Reality," or *Sirhak* in Korean. Beginning in the eighteenth century, their curiosity opened the door for Catholicism to seep into Korea.

Yankee Go Away

Early (pre-nineteenth century) Yi Choson Koreans had reason to see foreigners as troublemakers, as we noted in the previous chapter. Over the centuries, Koreans, both high and low born, agreed the best way to deal with foreigners was to keep them out. Early on, Koguryo Koreans built walls for this purpose. When these failed to do the job, Koguryo expanded its borders northward. That angered the Chinese. Gradually, the Koryo (918–1392) decided the best barrier to nomadic hordes would be the Yalu and Tumen Rivers that make up the modern China–North Korea border (see Chapter 3).

Koryo's kings turned to appeasement when the Mongol hordes rode across the Yalu River into northern Korea in the thirteenth century. Koryo formally recognized the new dynasty the Mongols had set up in China. Korea's monarch complied with Mongol demands that Korea build and man two huge fleets for the Mongol invasions of Japan. However, this attempted appeasement backfired. The Japanese sought revenge against the Koreans for their assistance to the Mongols. First came the pirate raids on Korean trading ships and ports in the fourteenth and fifteenth centuries. Then, a full-scale effort to conquer Korea came at the end of the sixteenth century.

Faced with the alternatives, the Yi Choson monarchs decided in the fifteenth century that the best way to protect their domain from marauding horsemen and seafaring pirates was to join the Chinese world order.

North Korea Fact

The Chinese world order describes the international system China established in East Asia 2,000 years ago. China's size, population, wealth, superior political institutions, and technology enabled it to dominate East Asia. Nations that recognized China's supremacy sent it tribute and emulated its philosophy and institutions. In return, China deemed these nations "civilized" and protected them from the so-called "barbarians," people who rejected China's hegemony and refused to adopt its ways. China's military forces stood ready to defend Korea and Vietnam because they emulated and revered China. When Britain and Russia challenged China's supremacy after 1800, China designated them "barbarians." After a century of conflict, the Chinese world order collapsed and a period of colonization and political chaos followed.

China's World Order

China for centuries had been the ultimate superpower in East Asia. No nation in the region could rival its size, population, resources, states craft, and cultural refinement. All of this, however, had made its northern neighbors, the nomadic tribes of Central Asia, envious. Whenever they fell on hard times, the Mongols' ancestors jumped on their ponies and headed south into China to raid, plunder, rape, and pillage.

The emperors of China's second centralized dynasty, the Han (195 B.C.E.–220 C.E.), came up with a plan. Historians today refer to it as the "Chinese world order." The ancient Chinese classified people according to the extent to which they conducted their affairs according to the way of Confucius and the Chinese emperors. The Chinese naturally stood at the top of the pyramid. Their emperors bestowed upon themselves the silken robes of the "*Son of Heaven*." China was deemed paradise on earth and its inhabitants the guardians of civilization.

 Increase Your North Korea IQ

China's emperors claimed the title, "Emperor of Heaven." They saw themselves as the link between the ancestors, guardians of nature's forces, and human society. Armed with the "Mandate of Heaven" (see Chapter 5), China's emperors were responsible for maintaining harmony among men. Failure to do so could excite rebellion and cost the emperor his mandate.

Korea's late Koryo and Yi Choson monarchs demonstrated their recognition of the "Son of Heaven" by avoiding not calling themselves "emperor." Likewise, they restricted the size of their palaces to avoid any appearance of being rivals to their Chinese counterparts. The Japanese were not so deferential to the Chinese. From ancient times they referred to their monarch as emperor.

China's emperors bestowed the cloak of "civilized people" on non-Chinese people who subscribed to China's view of the world, recognized the supremacy of China's emperor and lived by the teachings of Confucius. There were some real benefits to being considered among the "civilized people" in addition to the "Son of Heaven's" complements.

China promised to help defend the domains of neighboring king who signed up to China's world order. China, in return, improved its defenses by surrounding itself with a ring of loyal buffer states. Korea and Vietnam were China's most reliable traditional allies. Taiwan eventually recognized China's supremacy, but Japan never did.

An elaborate set of diplomatic rules developed over the centuries. Diplomatic missions shuttled back and forth between the various capitals of the Chinese dynasties and Korean kingdoms. Each time a Chinese emperor died, had a birthday, or got married, Korea's monarch dispatched a tribute mission to China. China's monarchs responded in kind. Gradually, the exchange of tribute assumed the additional role of facilitating trade.

China's economic and military supremacy was essential to this world order. So long as China's hegemony was unrivaled, Korea willingly allowed China to manage its foreign affairs. Confident in Chinese ability to deter or deal with any invaders, Korea did not maintain any significant military forces after the 1598 expulsion of Japan's samurai invaders.

The Gathering Storm on the Horizon

The Chinese world order then faced a threat that it would eventually be unable to overcome. The Europeans arrived. Europe's threat to the Chinese world order dates from the end of the sixteenth century. A century after Columbus stumbled across North America, the Portuguese, Spanish, and Dutch found their way to East Asia. When these unshaved and unwashed strangers first began to appear along China's coast, the Chinese gave them the nickname, *yanggui*, which was adopted later into the English language as "yankee" (see Chapter 5). Originally this was a relatively benign term that meant "ocean spirits" since the first Europeans seemed to be blown across the ocean beneath "white clouds" (read sail boats). As their conduct became increasingly offensive, the term acquired a negative connotation.

By the eighteenth century, the Chinese and Koreans agreed these Europeans were no better than the uncivilized and unwashed nomadic "wild men" from Central Asia. Both groups, Chinese and Koreans concluded, were barbarians best excluded from their domains. The Portuguese were allowed access to a small sliver of land on China's southern coast that came to be known as Macau. A miniature Great Wall was built there and so as long as the Portuguese stayed behind it, they could trade with the Chinese. The Spaniards and Dutch had to settle for colonizing the Philippines and the Indonesia Archipelago, which the Dutch named the Dutch East Indies. The Dutch, less assertive and militarily threatening than the Spanish and Portuguese, convinced Japan's feudal rulers to grant them exclusive trading rights there.

Opium Dealers at China's Door

Following the Dutch and Portuguese, the British really stirred things up late in the eighteenth century. Having lost control of North America because of the upstart Americans, the British asserted themselves in East Asia. The British East India Company, hard pressed to turn a profit in its trade with China, turned to pushing opium on the Chinese people. After half a century of frustrating effort, the British Crown clashed with the Heavenly Ruler in Beijing during the Opium War of 1839–1842. China's long-closed door was forced open and the opium followed. The demise of the Chinese empire, as well as its world order was now a matter of time.

> **North Korea Fact**
>
> Britain was the biggest pusher of opium during the nineteenth century. After defeating China in the Opium War of 1840, British-owned opium grown in India poured through Hong Kong and Shanghai into China. This was a key factor in convincing the Koreans not to open their country to trade with western nations. This earned Korea the title of the "Hermit Kingdom."

There Goes the Neighborhood

The Koreans watched in horror as the British turned China into an opium den. Geography benefited Korea at the time. Located at East Asia's northern extreme, the British and other Europeans overlooked it, as they were preoccupied with trying to get into China and Japan. Occasionally, a Dutch seaman floated onto Korea's coast or a Catholic priest wandered into Seoul. They kept the Korean court informed about their European kinsmen's unsavory activities. This news convinced the Koreans they were better off staying behind the Heavenly Emperor's royal robes and referring all European peddlers to him.

Catholicism and Gunboats

Catholicism made a bad start in Korea. The first Catholic missionaries arrived in 1592 together with the invading armies of feudal Japan. They carried both Rome's Catholic cross and knowledge of Europe's military might. However, they had to pack up and leave when the Koreans and Chinese expelled the Japanese in 1598.

A second wave of missionaries began trickling into Korea in the early eighteenth century. Korea's nobility was more interested to learn about Europe than about Catholicism, but these missionaries were the nobility's only available source of information about Europeans. Nevertheless, a few noblemen and their servants converted. By the mid-nineteenth century, Korea had about 12 French priests and upward of 20,000 Korean Catholics.

But then the gunboats began to appear on Korea's coast. The British showed up in 1832 and again in 1845. The French arrived with three gunboats in 1846, followed by the Russians in 1854. All were referred to Beijing. Still, these comings and goings, plus the Opium War, made the Koreans nervous.

The Hermit Nation

In 1866, things got out of hand. A German adventurer seeking trade with Korea robbed the tomb of the royal regent's father, best known by his title the *Taewon'gun*. Obviously that was not the way for the German to endear himself to the throne and Koreans. The Taewon'gun slammed Korea's door shut and persecution of Catholics followed. Of the 12 Catholic priests active at the time, 9 were executed, as were several hundred of their followers.

North Korea Fact
Taewon'gun was the royal title given the father of Korea's last monarch Kojong. Kojong was adopted to the throne at a young age so his father served as regent until Kojong came of age. South Koreans are taught that the *Taewon'gun's* refusal to open Korea to trade retarded its modernization and contributed to its colonization by Japan. Kim Il Sung sidestepped the issue, but commended the Taewon'gun for resisting the "imperialists."

American "Yankees" Arrive

Americans' first appearance on Korea's door step could not have been more inappropriately timed. In September 1866, an American Protestant minister leased the USS *General Sherman* and sailed it up the Taedong River almost all the way to Pyongyang. His visit came just two months after the German blunder. He had the same aim of opening Korea to trade. Instead, the Taewon'gun ordered the ship destroyed. Some crafty Koreans floated burning barges into the ship, setting it on fire. All hands perished.

Increase Your North Korea IQ _____

In 1866, an American religious minister sailed the merchant ship USS *Sherman* up the Taedong River toward Pyongyang in the hope of opening Korea to trade. The Taewon'gun ordered the ship destroyed. Kim Il Sung claimed that his grandfather participated in setting the ship ablaze. North Koreans identify the incident, which occurred near Kim Il Sung's boyhood home, as the start of U.S. imperialism against Korea. There is no historical record to confirm or deny Kim's claim.

The French "Yankees" Arrive

It did not take long for the other shoe to drop. In October 1866, a French naval squadron arrived to revenge the execution of the Catholic priests. French troops raided Kanghwa Island, a large island at the mouth of the Han River that flows from Seoul. The French torched farm villages and *plundered* stocks of grain. Then they sailed off with one of the four archives of the Yi Choson's dynastic records plus some historically very significant artifacts. The raid made both the French and Catholicism most unwelcome in Korea for a long time.

Increase Your North Korea IQ _____

The **French plunder** of 1866 included examples of the world's first metal movable type. Koryo printers first experimented with metal type in the thirteenth century. By the fifteenth century, Koreans were using movable metal type routinely to publish books for the royal archives and for the use of royalty and nobility wishing to prepare for the civil service examinations. The French government is still negotiating the artifacts possible return to Seoul, South Korea—120 years later.

Uncle Sam Returns with a Bang

It took a little longer for the United States to put together a retaliatory attack. The U.S. Asiatic Squadron finally showed up in 1871. After bombarding Kanghwa Island's fortresses, the marines landed. Several sharp clashes followed. The Koreans claim victory because the marines eventually picked up their fallen comrades and sailed away. The Americans claim victory because they overran the Korean fortresses. Either way, Korea continued its policy of excluding foreigners and refusing to trade with them.

Japan Rattles Its Sabers

Just as things seemed to be settling down, the Japanese showed up. They presented themselves much as the United States had done in 1854 when U.S. Navy Commodore Perry sailed his big black gunboats into Tokyo Bay and declared "let me trade or else." The Japanese show of force worked. By this time the Taewon'gun had stepped aside. His son, the young and inexperienced King Kojong, signed the Treaty of Kanghwa in 1876.

The Kanghwa Treaty became known as Korea's first in a series of "unequal" treaties. Japan gained the same concessions the European powers had won in similar treaties with China. Korea's three most important ports at the time were opened to Japanese trade. These were: Pusan at Korea's southern tip, Wonsan on the central east coast, and Chemulpo or modern-day Inchon on the west coast near Seoul. Japanese citizens were granted exclusive areas in each port where they could reside and conduct their business unhindered by Korean laws. Such an arrangement was called extraterritoriality. Korea's subsequent treaties with other nations contained similar concessions.

Whales Scramble for the Shrimp

Koreans, both in North and South Korea, tend to see their nation as a hapless victim for foreign powers. Some times they compare their motherland to a shrimp because it is small and helpless. Also, the Korean Peninsula vaguely resembles the shape of a shrimp. On the other hand, foreign powers are compared to whales—large and powerful like the world's powerful nations. Koreans conclude the comparison by pointing out that the whale's favorite food is shrimp.

All Koreans also imagine that their nation is a rabbit. The Korean Peninsula appears to them to be a rabbit standing on its hind legs, face looking to the west toward its traditional benefactor China. Its alert, raised ears pointed toward the northeast and Russia. Behind the rabbit lurks Japan, Korea's traditional enemy.

Actually, these comparisons are fairly accurate summaries of the situation Korea found itself at the end of the nineteenth century. One fact Koreans generally overlook is that the crumbling of the Chinese empire, combined with Korea's own military impotency and quarreling political leadership, created a power vacuum in Northeast Asia that Japan felt compelled to fill to fend off the European powers. National security concerns, much more than greed, appears to have been Japan's primary motive.

> **North Korea Fact**
>
> At the end of the nineteenth century, one of Japans most powerful generals and accomplished senior statesman declared that Korea was "a dagger pointed at the heart of Japan." He was concerned that Russia was determined to colonize Korea. He was right because in 1904, the small Japanese empire challenged and defeated another huge empire because of Korea—the Russian Empire.

The China–Japan Rivalry Over Korea

Rivalry between Japan and China intensified after 1876. Japan feared that a Western imperialist nation like Russia might seize Korea and use it as a base to launch an assault on Japan. To counter such a possibility, Tokyo urged Korea to discard its traditional subordination to China, accept Japan's assistance to modernize the Korean government and army, and align its foreign policy more with that of Japan. China was equally intent upon preserving its traditional world order. Korea's young and inexperienced King Kojong found himself and his nation trapped in the middle.

The Military Mutiny of 1882 (*imo kullan*)

In 1882, Korean soldiers receiving modern military training mutinied, and killed Korean government officials and their Japanese military trainers. They also tried unsuccessfully to assassinate Queen Min, the bride of King Kojong, Korea's last sovereign monarch. China and Japan dispatched troops to restore order. The Chinese blamed the Taewon'gun, the king's father and champion of the exclusion policy, for the mutiny and took him to China. The incident intensified the rivalry between Japan and China over Korea even more.

> **Increase Your North Korea IQ**
>
> Like other queens, Queen Min sought to elevate her kinsmen to high office. This enabled her to exert influence on the king. Both Japan and China came to view her as an obstacle to their plans for Korea. She died a tragic death in 1895 when Japanese soldiers assassinated her in the palace, dismembered her body, and burned it.

The 1882 Treaty of Chemulpo (Inchon)

Japan demanded that the Korean king compensate it for the death of Japanese officials and dispatched an expeditionary force to Seoul to back up its claim. China reacted by asserting its traditional responsibility for Korea's foreign affairs.

The incident was resolved when the two nations signed the Treaty of Chemulpo, now South Korea's major west coast port of Inchon. Japan received an indemnity, a royal apology, expanded rights for Japanese to travel and trade in Korea, plus the right to post a guard detachment at its Seoul legation. But Japan recognized China's authority to manage Korea's foreign affairs. Two Chinese government representatives, one of German nationality named P.G. von Möllendorff, were sent to Seoul to oversee its foreign relations. China also maintained troops in the Korean capital.

> **Korean Concepts**
>
> "Unequal" was applied decades later to all the treaties East Asian nations signed with the European powers and Japan in the nineteenth century. These treaties all granted foreigners the right of "extraterritoriality." This meant local law and punishment did not apply to foreigners, and it gave them exclusive legal privileges. Thus the treaties came to be seen as "unequal" to local citizens.

Korea's "Unequal" Treaties

King Kojong, under China's influence, sought to counter Japan's assertiveness by allowing Western nations similar terms granted Japan under the 1875 Treaty of Kanghwa. Japan's influence, it was hoped, would be checked by competition with Western nations. A series of *"unequal" treaties* with the United States and several European nations ensued:

1882	Treaty of Chemulpo (Inchon) with Japan and China
1882	Treaties with the United States and Germany
1884	Treaties with Great Britain, Russia, and Italy
1885	Convention of Tientsin Between China and Japan
1886	Treaty with France
1888	Overland Trade Agreement with Russia

The *Coup d'Etat* of 1884 (*Kapsin Chongbyon*)

Japanese advocates of Korea's modernization concluded Korea's queen, Queen Min, and her powerful kinsmen had to be purged from court to end Korea's submission to China. Between 1882 and 1884, a group of ambitious Korean advocates of modernization had gathered in Tokyo. Led by the nobleman Kim Ok-kyun, they called themselves the Enlightenment Party (*kaehwadang*). With Japanese financial assistance and urging, they returned to Seoul. On the evening of December 4, 1884, they attacked the king's in-laws at the palace's entrance.

The coup failed. Chinese troops drove the surviving Korean coup members and their Japanese supporters from Korea. The incident was resolved by the 1885 Convention of Tientsin (China's main northeast port at the time). Japan paid Korea a fairly large indemnity as part of the agreement. Both Japan and China agreed to withdraw their troops from Korea, but China retained control of Korea's foreign relations. Japan's influence on the Korean Peninsula subsided temporarily.

The Americans Return

Americans' second arrival in Korea proved much more auspicious than the first. The second American Protestant missionary to arrive reached Seoul shortly before the 1884 coup attempt. He happened to be a medical doctor. The night of the coup, he was summoned to the palace to treat the king's in-laws who had suffered severe sword slashes. The American poured hot wax into the wounds, saving the lives of the king's in-laws, among others.

Benevolent deeds such as this, plus the Japan-based American Trading Company's honest and prompt servicing of the Korean court's purchases won Americans respect at the palace. Young Korean noblemen were dispatched on study tours to the United States, and American missionaries and businessmen were welcome in Korea over the next decade.

The American Trading Company in the late 1880s was granted a royal permit to prospect for precious metals near Unsan in north central Korea. "Unsan" literally means silver, but the Americans found gold there. Korea's modern postal system began when lonely Americans at Unsan sought to exchange letters with loved ones back home. As we will see shortly, Russian merchants soon became envious of the Americans' success at the court and in Unsan.

The Sino-Japanese War of 1894–1895

Japan's rivalry with China exploded into war in 1894. The immediate cause was the 1894 rebellion led by Korean advocates of *Tonghak* or "Eastern School." Disgruntled Korean scholars sought to counter the spread of "Western Learning" (including Catholicism) by formulating a new religion rooted in traditional East Asian philosophy. They rallied peasants in southwest Korea and tried to forcefully restore the Taewon'gun to power. Japan and China saw the rebellion as an opportunity to expand their influence on the Korean Peninsula. Both rushed troops to Korea.

The Sino-Japanese War of 1894–1895 soon ensued. Japan's quick victory exposed China to be a paper dragon. The 1895 Treaty of Shimonoseki (the westernmost port on Japan's main island of Honshu) ended the war. China recognized Korea's independence. Japan received a huge indemnity of about 400 million ounces of silver (which effectively bankrupted China), plus Taiwan, the Pescadores Islands, and the Liaotung Peninsula in southern Manchuria.

Japanese soldiers then snatched defeat from the jaws of victory. Believing Queen Min blocked Korea's modernization, and seeing her as an enemy of Japanese interests in Korea, they brutally hacked her to death in the royal palace and burned her remains. King Kojong soon after fled to the Russian diplomatic mission. Japan was briefly compelled to retreat from the peninsula while Russia asserted its influence. Kojong then declared himself emperor of Korea, formally ending Korea's subordination to the Chinese world order.

The Russo-Japanese War, 1904–1905

Japan feared Russia would use Korea as a stepping stone to invade its home island. Korea's monarch had also become suspicious of Russia's intentions. In February 1904, Japan convinced Emperor Kojong to grant Japan authority to handle Korea's foreign relations and to reform its government. When Russia contested this, the Japanese destroyed Russia's Far East fleet in a surprise attack. Japan's military might surprised both Europe and the United States. President Theodore Roosevelt brokered the 1905 Treaty of Portsmouth (named for the New Hampshire city) that handed victory to Japan and won him the Nobel Peace Prize.

The Protectorate Treaty of 1905 (*Ulsa* Convention)

For Korea, the Treaty of Portsmouth opened the way for Japan's annexation of Korea. Japan dispatched its most distinguished politician and diplomat at the time, Ito Hirobumi, to Seoul. With Japanese soldiers occupying the Korean palace, Ito compelled Korea's monarch to agree to a treaty that placed his kingdom under Japan's protection and advice.

Kojong contested the arrangement in 1907 by dispatching a U.S.-headed mission to the Second Hague Conference on World Peace. The effort failed when the Western powers preferred to sustain Japan's claims to Korea. The Japanese forced Kojong to step down and to pass the crown to his son, Sunjong. The 1910 Treaty of Annexation formally ended Korea's almost 2,000 years of independence and converted the nation into a colony of Imperial Japan.

The Least You Need to Know

◆ Yi Choson Korea (1392–1910) voluntarily participated in China's world order to protect itself from raiding Central Asian nomads, plundering Japanese pirates, and European traders.

◆ The European encroachment into the Chinese world order eroded China's supremacy in the latter half of the nineteenth century, exposing Korea to external pressure to break with tradition and to engage the international community.

◆ Japan, fearing foreign occupation of Korea could lead to an invasion of its home islands, fought China and Russia for domination of the Korean Peninsula.

◆ Korea ceased to exist as an independent nation when Imperial Japan annexed it in 1910.

Chapter 7

In Due Course, 1910–1945

In This Chapter

- Korea under Japan's colonial rule
- Korean independence movement
- Life under Japanese colonial rule
- World War II and Korea's fate
- Korea's division

Japan's 30-year effort to cajole, induce, and force Korea to break with the Chinese world order and Confucian tradition culminated with Korea becoming a Japanese colony. On August 22, 1910, Korea's reluctant leaders signed the Treaty of Annexation, ending Korea's 2,000 years of independence. The saga of Japan's annexation of Korea still haunts Japan's relations with the two Korean nations. Lingering Korean suspicion of Japan can be attributed to the following Japanese actions around the turn of the twentieth century:

- Japan's support for the coup of 1884
- Its attempt to compel the reform of Korea's government in 1895
- The brutal assassination of Korea's queen
- The forced abdication of the Yi Choson dynasty's last two monarchs, Kojong and his son Sunjong

In addition, the legacy of Japan's colonial rule of Korea from 1910 to 1945 has further intensified Koreans' distrust of Japan. Anti-Japanese sentiment remains the cornerstone of Korean nationalism. Nevertheless, Japan's harsh rule introduced a hesitant Korea to industrialization and modern commerce. But for Koreans, the most profound consequence of Japanese colonial rule has been their nation's division politically, ideologically, and economically into North and South Korea.

In this chapter, we explore why anti-Japanese sentiment and anti-imperialism became core ingredients of modern Korean nationalism. Kim Il Sung would capitalize upon this sentiment to propel himself to power after Korea achieved independence from Japan in 1945. Additionally, we will discuss why Koreans in both Koreas, but especially in North Korea, developed an intense distrust of the United States even though it helped restore Korea's independence.

Prelude to Conquest

Japan had moved cautiously to secure its influence on the Korean Peninsula. Prior to challenging Russia in 1904, Japan allied with Great Britain in 1902. When Japan was confident of victory in its 1904–1905 war with Russia, Tokyo responded positively to Washington's call for a negotiated peace treaty. Japan's leaders, despite popular dislike for the terms, accepted the Treaty of Portsmouth that was brokered by U.S. President Teddy Roosevelt. Tokyo's civilian prime minister and cabinet needed U.S. diplomatic support abroad more than popularity at home.

The Distrusted Eagle—U.S. Complacency

The subsequent *Taft-Katsura Accord* of July 27, 1905, has come to exemplify to Koreans the reason for their underlying distrust of the United States and other superpowers. After the Treaty of Portsmouth had been signed, then U.S. Secretary of War William Howard Taft (later president) met with Japan's diplomatic representative, Count Katsura. They agreed, in essence, that the United States would not interfere in Japan's "sphere of influence" in Korea and Japan would do likewise regarding the U.S. colonization of the Philippine Islands. President Teddy Roosevelt subsequently confirmed this understanding.

Later the prominent American diplomatic historian Tyler Dennett characterized the accord as a "secret pact." All Koreans have come to believe the Taft-Katsura Accord symbolizes superpower treachery, particularly that of the United States, regarding Korea's loss of independence.

Korean Concepts

As China's world order crumbled at the end of the nineteenth century, Britain, Russia, Germany, France, and Italy, plus the United States and Japan, scrambled to carve East Asia into spheres of influence. The United States declared its "Open Door Policy" for China, hoping to prevent China from being carved into colonies and thus being excluded from the China trade. Rather than jockey over creating colonies, the powers instead established "spheres," an area in which a single power declared dominant influence. The **Taft-Katsura Accord** recognized the Philippines as being the United States's sphere and the Korean Peninsula as Japan's sphere of influence. Despite the initial U.S. "Open Door" policy, both powers then converted their spheres into colonies.

Japan's Iron Fist

Japan's colonial rule actually commenced with the Protectorate Treaty of November 18, 1905. Korea's monarch, his palace occupied by Japanese soldiers, surrendered authority to handle Korea's foreign relations to Japan. The so-called treaty also allowed Japan's emperor to designate a Japanese "resident-general" to "advise" Korea's nominal ruler.

When Emperor Kojong proved uncooperative, the Japanese forced him to abdicate his crown to his son Sunjong. The Japanese resident general Ito Hirobumi then compelled the new monarch to accept a new treaty on August 1, 1907. The new treaty formalized Japanese oversight of Korea's internal affairs. Korea at that time ceased to exist as an independent political entity.

Increase Your North Korea IQ

Sunjong, Yi Choson Korea's last monarch, was the son of King Kojong and Queen Min. He was crowned when Japan forced his father to abdicate in 1907. Childhood illness left Sunjong mildly retarded. After Korea's 1910 annexation, the Japanese arranged his marriage to a Japanese princess and the couple lived in Tokyo. The Japanese believed the princess could not bear children, and hoped this would end the Korean monarchy. However, the couple had a daughter named Yi Pang-ja (Lee Pang-ja).

Despised in Japan and Korea, she married and had a son who was educated in the United States and who married an American woman. No claimants to the Yi Chosun throne survive.

Increase Your North Korea IQ

The late nineteenth-century Japanese politician Ito Hirobumi is revered in Japan as the father of its first constitution and its parliamentary democracy. In Korea, however, he is despised as the personification of Japan's colonization of Korea because of his role as Japan's first colonial administrator there. The Korean nationalist An Chung-gun (1879–1910) shot and killed Ito Hirobumi on October 26, 1909.

Korea's "Righteous Armies"

Korea's armed resistance to Japan dates from 1896 and peaked in 1908. Queen Min's assassination in October 1895 had sparked the formation of so-called Righteous Armies. Similar bands had sprung up to resist Japan's late sixteenth-century invasion of Korea.

When Japan disbanded the Korean army in 1905, new Righteous Army groups resumed guerrilla warfare against the Japanese troops in Korea. Japan dispatched 8,000 troops to Korea to suppress this resistance. Japanese official records list 2,819 clashes in which 17,600 Koreans were killed.

Japan was the ultimate victor. The remnants of the Righteous Army sought safe haven in the southeast corner of Manchuria, just north of the Korean border with China and near the Russian Maritime Provinces. Later this area became the home base for North Korean leader Kim Il Sung's band of anti-Japanese guerrillas, a story we will pursue in Chapter 8.

Independence Lost

The 1910 Treaty of Annexation ended Korea as an independent kingdom. Korea became Japan's second colony after Taiwan. The Korean monarch was not involved with the treaty. Instead, the hapless Korean prime minister, Yi Wan-yong, signed it. This earned him a Japanese title of nobility, but Koreans' perpetual condemnation.

An authoritarian colonial bureaucracy replaced the Yi Dynasty's 500-year-old monarchy and centralized Confucian bureaucracy. After Ito Hirobumi's assassination in 1909, Japan's imperial army assumed responsibility for Korea's rule. Japan's resident general, a military general, became Korea's new ruler. Appointed by the emperor, the resident general was responsible solely to his military superiors in Tokyo and, theoretically, to the emperor.

Japan's leaders believed their nation had replaced China as the dominant power in East Asia. The colonial philosophy of Japan's leaders declared Japanese racial, cultural, and military superiority over all other East Asian peoples. This attitude affected all aspects of Japan's colonial rule of Korea.

Japan as Number One

At this time Japan was in the early stages of developing a constitutional monarchy. The constitution ensured Japanese citizens political and basic human rights. These rights did not apply to Koreans. Although technically citizens of Japan, they did not enjoy any of the benefits of citizenship, only its obligations to revere the emperor, obey both Japanese laws and those the resident general promulgated, and pay taxes.

Japanese held the majority of positions in the government. It started with 10,000 officials in 1910. On the eve of World War II, about 87,000 people (52,000 Japanese and 35,000 Koreans) worked for the colonial administration. Another 190,000 Japanese worked for enterprises affiliated with the colonial administration. By comparison, France's colonial administration of Vietnam in 1937 required only about 2,900 French civil servants; 10,000 French soldiers; and 38,000 Vietnamese bureaucrats and soldiers.

Increase Your North Korea IQ

The Japanese government-general replaced Korea's monarchy in 1910, and the previous Japanese "adviser," the Resident General. Japan's emperor appointed Korea's rulers who had the title of resident general. Unlike European colonial administrations, Japan's rule of Korea relied on a large and intrusive civil service staffed mostly by Japanese and backed by a large police force. The government-general was disbanded after Japan surrendered at the end of World War II in 1945.

Korea's Landlord

Japan became Korea's largest landowner. The resident general claimed ownership of all the Yi Royal Household's land, about 21,756,000 acres or 40 percent of Korea's entire land area. The Japanese government owned the Oriental Development Company, established in 1907. This company's mission was to prevent the overcrowding of Japan's home islands at a time of rapid population increase and exclusion from migration to other nations (outside the empire). It hoped to encourage 30,000 Japanese to resettle annually in Korea. The Japanese hoped not just to administer Korea, but also to ingrain the Japanese culture and Japanese people there, and overwhelm the indigenous Korean culture. But by 1940, only 708,000 Japanese were living in Korea, just 3.2 percent of the population.

Japan's Fortress Against Russia

Japan's imperial army converted Korea into a fortress for defending the Japanese home islands from Russia. A Japanese-built railroad linked Pusan, Korea's southeastern port, to Uiju (modern name Sinuiju), a city on Korea's northwest border with China. The facilities of Korea's major ports were modernized. Roads were paved. All administrative and police offices across the peninsula were linked by telephone and telegraph. By 1945, Korea had some 6,100 kilometers of railroad track and 53,000 kilometers of improved roads.

Korea's New Economy

Japan's military used Korea as a supply base for its war with China and the United States. Korea supplied steel, tools, machines, and chemicals. Iron and pig-iron production jumped from about 60,000 tons in 1934 to 450,000 tons in 1943, plus another 100,000 tons of steel. Manufacturing leaped from 17.7 percent of the economy in 1931 to 40 percent by 1939. The number of Koreans working in industry climbed from 385,000 in 1932 to 1,322,000 in 1943.

Even with the rapid industrialization, agriculture remained the primary activity for most Koreans. The agricultural sector sustained significant change of its own. Colonial policies favored Japanese land ownership and rice production. Korea's farmers lost out. By 1945, almost 70 percent of them were tenant farmers. Rice exports to Japan increased steadily, causing prices to rise in Korea. Crop diversification declined as absentee landlords ordered more rice planted. Rice farming is heavily dependent on irrigation, but the system fell into disrepair as the burgeoning industrial sector absorbed most new capital investment.

Winners and Losers

The Japanese military and colonial administration, plus affiliated Japanese commercial enterprises, benefited while most Koreans endured poverty. Young Koreans left farms for low-paying jobs in the cities and outside of Korea. Between 1940 and 1945, more than one million young Koreans, mostly from the southeastern provinces, went to work in Japan. Others worked for the Japanese imperial army constructing fortifications across the Pacific and in Southeast Asia.

Erasing Korea

Japan sought to erase Korea as an independent nation. Toward this end, it pursued three distinct strategies: armed suppression, inducement, and education. Initially, it relied on the first method, but eventually came to practice all three simultaneously.

The Dark Period (1910–1919)

From 1910 to 1916 Resident General Terauchi Masatake concentrated on forcefully imposing his will on Korea. After the Righteous Armies were subdued, he established a colonial police force. In 1910, the colonial administration had 6,222 police, half of them Koreans. The number subsequently climbed to 60,000 by 1941. All Korean-led groups were forcefully disbanded. Thousands of Koreans were arrested, some were placed on blacklists that barred them from employment, and others were imprisoned.

The March 1 Movement

Anti-Japanese sentiment erupted on March 1, 1919, the birthday of modern Korean nationalism. The outburst of nationalistic sentiment has come to be known as the *Sam il* or *March 1 Movement.* "Sam il" is Korean for "three one," a reference to the third month's first day of 1919.

President Woodrow Wilson's January 8, 1919, issuance of his famous "Fourteen Points" excited hope among the Korean people around the world that their nation's independence would soon be restored. Wilson's points proposed "self determination" for colonized people. In response to Japan's objections, he later clarified that the Fourteen Points were not intended for people under Japanese colonial rule. He was more concerned keeping the European powers in check at the Versailles Peace Conference at the end of World War I.

Shortly after Wilson's announcement, Korea's monarch Kojong died on January 22, 1919. A loose coalition of anti-Japanese and pro-Christian Korean leaders in Korea, Japan, China, and the United States decided to use the date of the

Korean Concepts

Koreans everywhere, regardless of their political and ideological orientation, celebrate **March 1, 1919,** as the birthday of Korean nationalism and their nation's awareness of being a modern nation-state.

monarch's funeral in Seoul, March 1, to demonstrate to the world the Korean people's desire for independence from Japan.

On March 1, 1919, 29 self-appointed representatives of the Korean people gathered in Seoul to read a Korean declaration of independence. The timing of the declaration combined with rumors that Kojong had been poison sparked nationwide anti-Japanese demonstrations. An estimated one million people participated.

Taken by surprise, the colonial police reacted forcefully. Violent clashes continued from March to December 1919. Japanese authorities estimated 553 demonstrators and police died; 1,409 were injured; and 12,522 Koreans were arrested. Korean national-ists claimed 7,500 dead; 15,000 injured; and 45,000 arrested.

Suppression of the movement did not dispel Koreans' resentment of Japanese rule. On the contrary, anti-Japanese sentiment intensified. The colonial police tactics scattered the movement's leadership. As a result, Korean exile organizations sprang up in China, both in Manchuria and Shanghai, Russia (principally southeastern Siberia), and in Hawaii and Los Angeles in the United States. Korea's modern political leaders would eventually emerge from these hotbeds of Korean nationalism, away from the reach of the Japanese.

Good Cop, Bad Cop (1920–1930)

Trying to lower the cost of occupation, Japan then shifted from playing bad cop to trying to be a good cop. Initially, a number of measures assuaged Korean wrath. Harsh punishments for minor infractions were discontinued. Laws that regulated traditional funerals were made less intrusive. Salaries for Korean civil servants were adjusted upward, but remained significantly below those of their Japanese counter-parts. Koreans were appointed to judgeships and governmental advisory councils.

Public information and educational opportunities were opened to Koreans. Two Korean-owned newspapers were licensed. The number of Koreans enrolled in high school increased significantly. Also, a larger number of Koreans were allowed to attend colleges both in Korea and Japan. From 111,000 Koreans enrolled in school in 1910, Korean school enrollment climbed to 1,776,078 by 1941. Even with this increase in students, in 1945 more than half the Korean population remained illiter-ate. About 20 percent of Koreans had received some formal education, of whom only 5 percent advanced beyond primary school.

As these improvements were being put in place during the 1920s, Japan's colonial police became quite adroit in applying a system of "carrots and sticks." Koreans who complied with the rules and regulations were rewarded with opportunities to enter the civil service, to send their children to school, and to participate in commerce. Those who grumbled or resisted were excluded. The police also became quite accomplished in applying censorship, and physical and mental coercion.

Forced Assimilation (1930–1945)

The Kwangju Student Resistance Movement of 1929–1930 marked the end of the so-called Cultural Reforms and a return to military rule and coercive tactics. The immediate cause was Japanese male students' ridicule of female Korean students in the southwest city of Kwangju. The local population objected to this behavior. Again, the police responded with brutal force, sparking a nationwide outburst of anti-Japanese sentiment. For five months, an estimated 54,000 young Koreans demonstrated violently against the Japanese overlords. All the while, one of Korea's earliest socialist oriented organizations, the *Sin'ganhoe*, worked to coordinate the anti-Japanese movement.

> **Korean Concepts**
>
> The **Sin'ganhoe** was a national coalition of Korean patriotic groups formed in 1927 with the goal of undermining Japanese rule from within Korea. The founder was a widely respected Christian activist who died shortly after the group's formation. Korean socialists then gained control of it. They seized upon the Kwangju Student Resistance Movement of 1929–1930 to lash out violently at Japanese colonial rule. Japanese police arrested the leadership and compelled the organization to disband in 1931. Thereafter, the colonial police cracked down hard on any and all politically oriented Korean groups in the name of protecting the emperor empire from the Soviet Union and communism.

Japan's military attempted to coerce Koreans into submitting to the Japanese emperor's authority. Japanese became the standard language in government, business, and education. Koreans were eventually forced to adopt Japanese names and barred from performing ancestral rites.

Koreans responded pragmatically. For the sake of survival, they complied. But their resentment of Japanese rule only intensified Korean awareness of being culturally distinct, and made them all the more intent to reclaim their nation's independence.

Unkept Promises, Frustrated Hopes (1943–1945)

World War II for most Koreans in Korea was a time of hardship and virtual despair. The imperial Japanese army exploited Korea's population and resources to the maximum extent possible. Tens of thousands of young Koreans were taken to Japan to work in factories and mines. Young men were assigned to labor and police battalions and dispatched to the far corners of the Japanese empire. Young Korean women were induced to service the sexual desires of Japanese soldiers. Meanwhile, the Japanese government misled their citizens and colonial subjects about the empire's gradual demise.

Allied victories in the Pacific rekindled Korean hopes in the United States and China that Japan would be defeated and Korea's independence restored. (You will learn more about these Korean resistance groups in Chapter 8.)

Cairo Declaration

Korean hopes for independence soared after the Cairo Conference of 1943. Leaders of the Allied nations fighting the Axis powers (Germany, Italy, and Japan) gathered in Cairo, Egypt, at the end of November 1943. The attendees included British Prime Minister Winston Churchill, Chinese President Generalissimo Chiang Kai-shek, American President Franklin D. Roosevelt, and Soviet Premier Josef Stalin.

They jointly promised in the Cairo Declaration of December 1, 1943, that, "mindful of the enslavement of the people of Korea, [the Allies] are determined that in due course Korea shall become a free and independent nation." After the conference, the Allied leaders understandably refocused on their priority concern—defeating the Axis powers. Korean independence was thus shelved to a later date.

Ever since, all Koreans have pointed to the Cairo Declaration as further evidence for not trusting powerful nations.

Yalta Superpower Summit

The Allied leaders gathered again at the Russian resort of Yalta on February 8, 1945. Post-war Korea was a major concern. President Roosevelt's briefing paper recommended that "an interim international administration or trusteeship should be established for Korea." It was further suggested that the United Nations or, independent of it, the four powers (the U.S., Great Britain, China, and the Soviet Union) should jointly administer Korea after its liberation from Japan. President Roosevelt, according to U.S. State Department records, proposed to Stalin a three-member trusteeship that excluded Great Britain. Stalin agreed to the need for an internationally supervised trusteeship, but preferred that Great Britain be included.

Growing Doubts

On June 8, 1945, acting Secretary of State Joseph Grew issued a public statement to calm rumors then circulating among Koreans in the United States. Feeding the rumors was the fact that representatives of the Korean provisional government had not been invited to the San Francisco Conference where the United Nations was born.

Grew denied in his statement that a secret agreement had been reached at Yalta, which would contradict the Cairo Declaration. He drew a distinction between the "legally constituted authorities" invited to the San Francisco conference and the Korean provisional government that did not possess "qualifications requisite for obtaining recognition by the United States as a governing authority."

His statement concluded that U.S. policy aimed …

> to avoid taking action which might, when the victory of the United Nations is achieved, tend to compromise the right of the Korean people to choose the ultimate form and personnel of the government which they may wish to establish.

Increase Your North Korea IQ

Dr. Syngman Rhee (Yi Sung-man) (1875–1965) was a leader of Korea's independence movement and South Korea's first president from 1948–1960. Born in Seoul, he learned English and advocated Korea's modernization. This landed him in prison in 1889. Freed in 1904, Rhee fled to the United States where he earned a Ph.D. at Princeton University.

Rhee joined the delegation that sought to represent Korea at the 1919 Versailles Peace Conference. Denied access, the delegation established the provisional government of Korea in Shanghai. Disillusioned by politics, he returned to Hawaii to teach. In 1948, Rhee went to Seoul and was "elected" South Korea's president. Korean students toppled his corrupt regime in 1960, forcing him to flee back to Hawaii where he died.

The Superpowers Take Over

After Roosevelt's death, President Harry Truman on June 15, 1945, informed China's leader that the other Allied powers had agreed upon a four-power trusteeship of Korea. At the Berlin conference of July 22, 1945, Soviet Foreign Minister V. M. Molotov suggested discussion of the trusteeship for Korea, but none was conducted.

On July 24, 1945, the Korean Independence Movement leader in the United States, Dr. Syngman Rhee, sent a telegram to the Berlin Conference asking the leaders of the four powers to extend formal diplomatic recognition to the provisional government of Korea. He received no response.

Potsdam Conference

The U.S. and Soviet Chiefs of Staff met in Potsdam on July 26, 1945, and agreed on a boundary between their areas of military operation on the Korean Peninsula. This line ran across the peninsula from east to west and just south of the 41st parallel.

The Potsdam Proclamation was issued the same day. In it, the leaders of the four Allied powers called for Japan's unconditional surrender and affirmed that the "terms of the Cairo Declaration shall be carried out."

Korea Divided

Inadvertently, the superpowers' agreements had set the stage for Korea's division. The Soviet Union declared war on Japan on August 8, 1945, two days after the United States dropped the first atomic bomb on Hiroshima, Japan. By August 12, Soviet troops had entered Korea.

Japan's emperor declared the surrender on August 15. The same day, President Truman sent the other Allied leaders a draft general order for the supreme commander for Allied powers in East Asia, General Douglas MacArthur. The general was to have Japanese authorities issue the order. The draft set the 38th, not the 41st, parallel as the boundary between U.S. and Soviet occupation forces on the Korean Peninsula. Unaltered, the order was issued. Japanese forces north of the 38th parallel surrendered to Soviet forces. Those south of the 38th parallel began surrendering to U.S. forces when they arrived in Korea on September 8, 1945.

Ever since, Koreans have struggled to reunify their nation.

The following table summarizes the World War II Allied powers agreements on Korea.

World War II Allied Powers Agreements on Korea

Agreement	Date	Promise
Cairo Declaration	December 1, 1943	Promised Korean independence "in due course."
Yalta Conference	February 8, 1945	Proposal that an international trusteeship would temporarily rule Korea.

Agreement	Date	Promise
San Francisco Conference	June 1945	The Allied powers and supporting nations established the United Nations. The U.S. secretary of state denied representatives of the provincial government of Korea access to the conference.
Berlin Conference	July 22, 1945	Allies agreed to establish a trusteeship to temporarily rule post-liberation Korea.
Potsdam Conference	July 26, 1945	U.S. and Soviet commanders agreed to divide the Korean Peninsula along the 41st parallel into a Soviet zone of operation in the north and a U.S. zone south of the 41st parallel.
Potsdam Proclamation	July 26, 1945	The four Allied powers called for Japan's unconditional surrender and affirmed that the "terms of the Cairo Declaration shall be carried out."

The Least You Need to Know

- Korea became part of the Japanese empire in 1910.

- Japan's harsh and intrusive colonial rule of Korea made anti-Japanese sentiment a cornerstone of Korean nationalism.

- All Koreans commemorate March 1, 1919, as the birthday of modern Korean nationalism.

- The Japanese imperial army turned Korea into a supply base for its conquest of northeast China during World War II.

- The Allied powers (United States, Great Britain, China, and Soviet Union) in 1943 promised to restore Korea's independence "in due course."

- The Allied powers' defeat of Japan restored Korea's independence, but lingering disagreement between the United States and the Soviet Union contributed to Korea's division.

- Many Koreans harbor a distrust of major powers because of Korea's experience between 1904 and 1945.

Chapter 8

The Rise of Kim Il Sung, the "Great Leader"

In This Chapter

- ◆ Korea's splintered independence movement
- ◆ The young Kim Il Sung
- ◆ Guerilla war against Japan
- ◆ Kim's Soviet interlude
- ◆ Korea on the eve of division
- ◆ Kim Il Sung takes control

The history of twentieth-century Korea is the tale of two struggles. First came the effort to discard the yoke of Japanese colonialism and to restore Korea's independence. The effort dates from 1896 and the rise of the Righteous Army bands following Queen Min's brutal assassination (see Chapter 7). Japanese colonial police repression and factionalism among the Korean leadership splintered the independence movement after 1919. Unity was never restored. Ultimately, two groups emerged as competitors to rule an independent Korea.

The second struggle commenced in 1945. For more than a half century, this second struggle has centered on Korea's reunification. Two contending Korean factions emerged victorious from the Japanese colonial period, one ardently anticommunist and the other, led by Kim Il Sung, championing communism. The leaders of these contending camps ever since have linked their rivalry to the Korean people's desire for national unification. The U.S.-USSR Cold War rivalry has further complicated the situation. Even today, with the Soviet Union gone, the echoes of the Cold War continue to sound on the Korean peninsula.

In this chapter, we examine the rise of Kim Il Sung, a key Korean contender for control of a unified Korea. The Soviet Union aided Kim's rise to power. This alone, however, cannot explain his success in taking control of North Korea in 1948 and successful rule of it until his death in 1994. Here and in future chapters we will focus on understanding Kim's success, as it is vital for understanding the perspective of modern North Korea.

The Struggle for Independence

The Korean independence movement functioned in an uncoordinated and sporadic manner in its formative years. The Japanese colonial police were partly responsible. They discouraged and forcibly disbanded all Korean political coalitions. Disputes between Korean leaders over strategy and tactics also were to blame.

Increase Your North Korea IQ

Here is a short list of prominent leaders of Korea's early independence movement:

An Chung-gun (1879–1910) assassinated the Japanese statesman and first resident general of Korea, Ito Hirobumi, in 1909. An was executed, but his brother An Chang-ho continued his cause.

Kim Ku (1876–1949) was a founding member of the Korean provisional government. During World War II he formed a division of Korean soldiers in China's anticommunist Nationalist army headed by Chiang Kai-shek. A South Korean army officer assassinated Kim Ku in Seoul in 1949.

Lee Tong-hwi (Yi Tong-hui, ?–1928) also was a founding member of the Korean provisional government. In 1919 he established the first Korean communist party, the Koryo Communist Party, with funds from Lenin's Communist International.

Syngman Rhee (Yi Sung-man, 1875–1960) emigrated to the United States in 1904, received a Ph.D. from Princeton University, and joined the Korean provisional government in 1919. Rhee became the first president of the Republic of Korea in 1948.

The Japanese colonial police's heavy-handed suppression of the March 1, 1919, independence movement convinced a small group of political activists to form a cohesive Korean independence movement leadership. They gathered in Shanghai, China, on April 9, 1919, and established the provisional government of Korea. Their aim was to rally support from all Koreans and to win foreign governments' diplomatic recognition of their group as the Korean government in exile. Three of their members, Syngman Rhee, Kim Ku, and Yi Tong-hwi, represented the main currents in early modern Korean politics.

Rhee Syngman—Father of Korea's Political Right Wing

Rhee Syngman became the first president of the Republic of Korea (see Chapter 7). An ardent nationalist, Rhee was an equally devout Christian. He sought to focus international pressure on Japan as the best way to restore Korea's independence. He opposed unilateral, armed attempts to end Japan's rule and was an avid anticommunist.

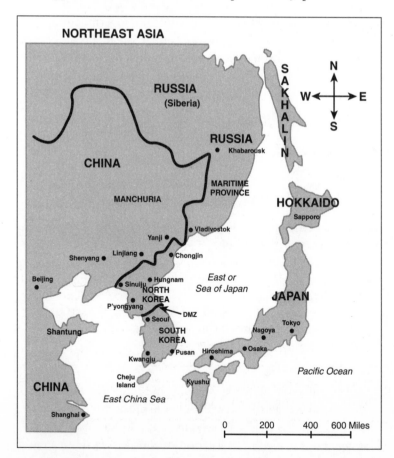

Map of Northeast Asia.

Kim Ku—Father of Korea's Moderate Left Wing

Kim Ku represented the independence movement's moderate left wing. Born in the northern province of Hwanghae, he joined the 1894 Tonghak Rebellion (see Chapter 5) to fight Chinese and Japanese troops who entered Korea to suppress the rebellion. Escaping from prison, he became a Christian in 1903. He was again imprisoned in 1911 for plotting the assassination of the Japanese resident general. Released in 1917, Kim Ku helped organize the March 1, 1919, independence movement.

After fleeing to Shanghai, Kim Ku joined the provisional government. Eventually he allied with China's Nationalist, anticommunist Chinese leader Generalissimo Chiang Kai-shek. Chiang helped Kim Ku establish a Korean military academy in southern China. The academy's graduates formed an army division that fought with Chiang's Nationalist army against the Japanese in World War II.

After the war ended in August 1945, Kim Ku returned to Korea as the president of the provisional government. His moderate coalition, the *Minjuuiwon* (Democratic League), included many socialists. But the U.S. Army occupation government disbanded Kim's coalition. He then ignored U.S. opposition and attended a reunification conference in the Soviet-controlled north in 1948. After his return to Seoul, Kim was sidelined politically. A South Korean army officer assassinated him in June 1949.

Lee Tong-hwi—Father of Korea's Left Wing

Lee Tong-hwi (Yi Tong-hui) was the father of the Korean communist movement. Russian communists helped Lee organize the Korean People's Socialist Party (*Hanin Sahoedang*) in June 1918, at Khabarovsk in southern Siberia. The group renamed itself the Koryo Communist Party (*Koryo Kongsandang*) in April 1919.

North Korea Fact
Kim Il Sung claimed that he formed the first genuinely communist revolutionary organization in Korea, the "Down-with-Imperialism Union," on October 17, 1926, ignoring Lee Tong-hwi's formation of the Koryo Communist Party in April 1919. Just before his death, however, Kim stated in his autobiography, "… the Korean Socialist Party headed by Ri Tong Hui (Yi Tong-hui) started to disseminate Marxism-Leninism as the first socialist group of Korea" (*Kim Il Sung Reminiscences*, Volume I, page 49).

Lee's opposition to Japanese rule dated from 1908 when he and other Korean patriots established a secret society in Seoul called the New People's Association (*Shinminhoe*). The predominately Christian group was falsely accused in 1911 of plotting to assassinate the Japanese resident general. Lee fled to southern Manchuria. Lee subsequently became a founding member of the Korean provisional government in Shanghai and was appointed its minister of military affairs.

Lee believed Koreans would have to form their own army to expel Japan. Given the ambivalence of the United States and European powers to Lee's plan, he turned to Russia's new communist rulers, the Bolsheviks. Eager to export their own revolution, the Bolsheviks helped Lee establish the first Korean communist party. He and other Korean nationalists also formed guerilla bands to harass the Japanese colonial administration in northern Korea.

By late 1919, Lee Tong-hwi was the premier of the provisional government. His emphasis on armed resistance, the diversion of funds from Moscow directly to his communist party rather than to the provincial government, and the desire to move the organization to Siberia, splintered this government. He resigned in January 1921 and returned to southern Manchuria to coordinate armed raids into his home province of Hamgyong in Korea's northeast corner. Lee fell ill and died in Siberia in 1928.

We cannot draw a straight line from Lee Tong-hwi to Kim Il Sung. But we can say that Lee, not Kim, was the father of the Korean communist movement. Also, Lee and his colleagues initiated the armed anti-Japanese movement in southern Manchuria, not Kim Il Sung.

But Kim Il Sung survived, unlike so many other early Korean anti-Japanese leaders who fell prey either Japan's suppression or to illness. Kim, not these others, got to write the early history of Korean communism. However, Japanese colonial police records and the recollections of other Koreans have enabled historians to begin reconstructing a more accurate account.

North Korea Fact

Confucianism emphasizes the historical record as an accounting of human virtue and vices. Court historians recorded a monarch's every deed hoping to keep him on the narrow path of virtue. Historical records acquired potent political significance. Those who wrote history could either praise or condemn their predecessors. Kim Il Sung raised this practice to an art form. He used history to glorify himself and his supporters while condemning his rivals. North Korea's historical record was crafted according to Kim's political agenda, not to record the truth.

Consequently, Kim Il Sung was able to declare himself the father of Korea's socialist anti-Japanese movement. According to the North Korean publication, *Brilliant Exploits* (Pyongyang: Foreign Languages Publishing House, 1988): "On October 17, 1926, General Kim Il Sung formed the Down-with-Imperialism Union, the first genuinely communist revolutionary organization in Korea." Adding insult to injury, Kim did not include Lee Tong-hwi in North Korea's pantheon of "heroes of the revolution." In short, survival (and erasing the record of rivals and predecessors) was one of the key reasons for Kim's eventual successful climb to power.

Kim Il Sung's Formative Years (1912–1934)

Despite Kim's claims, and those of North Korea's official history, he did not play a prominent role either in Korea's independence movement or its communist movement prior to 1934. He was only six years old when the March 1 movement exploded in 1919. Thereafter, he was preoccupied with getting an education, mostly in China. His father may have given him his first awareness of the Russian Revolution, Lenin, and communism. Not until 1929 did the 17-year-old Kim team up with Korean communist activists, which promptly landed him in jail.

Kim Il Sung's Family

Kim Il Sung (1912–1994) claimed descent from an impoverished tenant farm family. In his 1994 autobiography, *Kim Il Sung Reminiscences,* he traced his ancestors to the southern Korean city of Chonju (about one hundred miles south of Seoul). He claims they moved during Yi Choson to the small farm village of Mangyongdae, which is located a few miles west of Pyongyang. We have no way to confirm Kim's claim that his great-grandfather and grandfather (Kim Po-hyon, 1871–1955) "eked out a scanty living."

Grandfather Takes on the American "Imperialists"

Mangyongdae just happens to be about half a mile (one kilometer) from the spot where Koreans burned the USS *General Sherman* in 1866 (see Chapter 5). Kim claimed his great grandfather Kim Ung-u participated in the ship's destruction. The Yi Choson historical records recount the incident in detail, but there is no list of those who participated.

Kim Il Sung was born on April 15, 1912, in Mangyongdae, the eldest son of Kim Hyong-jik (1894–1926) and Kang Pan-sok (1892–1932). His father gave him the name Song-ju, which Kim eventually changed to Il-song.

> **Increase Your North Korea IQ**
>
> Korean women never take their husband's family name after marriage, a continuing tradition believed to trace back to ancient times before Korea's adoption of Confucianism lowered women's status.

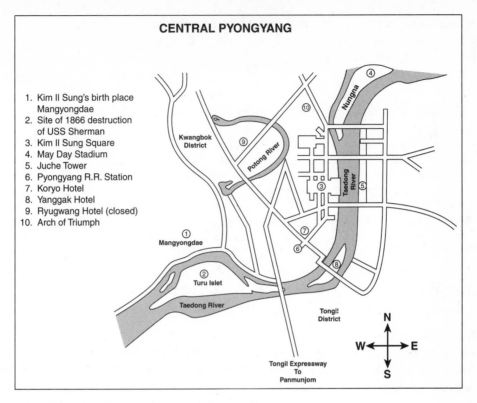

Map of area from Pyongyang west to Mangyongdae.

Kim admitted that his maternal grandfather, Kang Ton-uk, (1871–1943) taught at a private traditional rural school. Teachers in Korea, then and now, are esteemed. Acquiring an education in the Confucian classics required long years of study to master the written Chinese language. This suggests Kang's family was anything but impoverished. It also suggests that Kim's father's parents had acquired sufficient wealth to arrange their son's marriage to a woman from a relatively accomplished rural family. If so, this would help explain how Kim's father, Kim Hyong-jik, was able to enroll in 1911 in Sungsil Middle School, the first private American Christian school in Pyongyang.

Father Clashes with the Japanese "Imperialists"

Study at Sungsil Middle School introduced Kim's father to the strong anti-Japanese sentiment then prevailing throughout the Korean Christian community. His father left the school before graduation to begin teaching at a small rural Christian school southwest of Pyongyang.

Personal Recollections

During lunch with Kim Il Sung in October 1993, he confirmed that his mother Kang Pan-sok (1892–1932) had been a practicing Presbyterian. Later in his memoirs, Kim recalled occasionally attending church with his mother, "But I became tired of the tedious religious ceremony and the monotonous preaching of the minister ...." Kim's maternal family's involvement with American missionaries would help explain why Kim's father enrolled at Sungsil, a Christian school, instead of a traditional rural Confucian school.

Somehow, Kim recalls, his father was able to travel to China in 1916. There his father may have established contact with the Chinese nationalist anti-Japanese movement. After returning home, Japanese police arrested Kim's father in 1917. Released a year later, Kim's father may have traveled to Manchuria, Kim later recalled, to link up with early anti-Japanese groups near Yanji, Manchuria. At the time, about 20 patriotic Korean, anti-Japanese associations were active there. Some were the remnants of Righteous Army bands that had fled the Japanese colonial police.

Kim's father then resumed his studies, shifting from education to medicine. Participation in the March 1, 1919, demonstrations in Pyongyang again disrupted his formal education. Kim Il Sung, although only six years old, claims that he "joined the ranks of demonstrators in my worn out shoes."

In 1920, Kim's parents fled to southern Manchuria with him and his two younger brothers. For two years he attended a Chinese elementary school in Lianjiang. After his uncle's arrest in Pyongyang in April 1921, Kim's parents sent him back to their home village in Korea as a precaution since the Japanese police had resumed their hunt for his father.

Kim Il Sung's "Arduous" March

Kim claims he walked the 250 miles alone in 14 days, a possible feat. After returning to his home village, he studied at the Changdok School, a modern institution with 200 students headed by his maternal grandfather. Here he learned Korean history, language, and about Koreans' heroic anti-Japanese activities. But then the Japanese police arrested another uncle. Kim returned to his parents (no record of whether he walked this time) and completed his elementary education at the Chinese school in Fusong, about 60 miles northeast of Lianjiang.

Increase Your North Korea IQ

The Chinese city of Lianjiang was the main assembly area for the Chinese forces that overran advance elements of the U.S. Army and Marine Corps in November 1950 during the Korean War. It is located mid-point on the China-Korea border. Today it is a major transit point where North Korean gold and timber are exchanged for Chinese grain. An American company owns a mine east of Lianjiang that is about two miles north of the China–North Korea border.

Kim Il Sung began elementary school there. When Dr. Quinones visited Lianjiang's school in the winter of 1999, the students were "studying" English by watching an American basketball game. Michael Jordan was their hero.

Kim Il Sung Discovers Lenin

After his father's death in 1926, the 14-year-old Kim claims he began middle school in Fusong, Manchuria. There he says he learned about communism while reading the Chinese books *The Fundamentals of Socialism* and *The Biography of Lenin*. Japanese government documents next place Kim Il Sung at the Yuwen Middle School in 1929. He recalled that there he first read the works of Marx and Lenin.

His claims are dubious. To read Chinese translations of these books would have required the equivalent of a college education in the Chinese language. At the time, Kim had yet to graduate from high school. More likely he learned about communism while attending an underground communist study group.

By 1930, the Japanese army had established a continuous presence in southern Manchuria and had virtually eradicated the Korean communist movement there. No sooner had Kim Il Sung joined the underground communist youth group in May 1929 than he and his colleagues were arrested.

From Student to Guerilla

The North Korean People's Army proclaims Kim Il Sung as its founder and credits him with having formed the army on April 25, 1932. This is fiction. Japan's conquest of Manchuria and establishment of the puppet kingdom of Manchukuo in 1931 fused the Chinese and Korean anti-Japanese armed movements in southern Manchuria into a cohesive fighting force. Communist-trained Chinese warriors led numerous guerilla bands that included small groups of armed Koreans.

Kim Il Sung's greatest accomplishment between 1932 and 1940 was staying alive. After his release from prison, he apparently joined one of these Korean guerilla groups. His mentor during this period was an accomplished Chinese communist leader who had received training and some funding from Moscow.

Constant Japanese army suppression virtually wiped out the early leadership of the Korean communist movement. Hundreds of supporters died or were imprisoned. Others surrendered or defected to the Japanese. But, according to Japanese military police records, Kim's star rose steadily. The price on his head climbed from a lowly 20,000 yen ($10,000) in 1936 to 200,000 yen ($100,000) only three years later.

Kim Il Sung's huge bronze likeness faces southeast, arm extended, waiting to greet the rising sun.

Kim Il Sung Sees "Red"

Kim Il Sung's leadership and exploits on the battlefield, plus his continued survival, caught some high-ranking Soviet officers' attention. Some historians claim Kim traveled to Moscow. Others say the Japanese army forced him and his band to retreat into the Soviet Union's Maritime Province. We simply do not know which occurred, but we do know that Kim found himself inside the Soviet Union, with the blessings of the Soviet military.

The Soviet Union and Japan had clashed in 1937, but by 1940 an uneasy truce existed between them. Moscow was preoccupied with Hitler in Europe. Japan remained deeply suspicious of Stalin's intentions regarding Korea, and was also ardently anti-communist. But Tokyo's priority was the conquest of China.

Japan's suspicions were justified. The Soviet Union trained Chinese and Korean anti-Japanese guerilla fighters at three camps in its Maritime Province. Stalin probably hoped his forces could deflect Japan's army away from Siberia. Also, Soviet military officials, like their Imperial Russian predecessors, saw Korea as eventually providing strategically important access to East Asia and the Pacific Ocean.

Life in the USSR (1941–1945)

Middle-ranking Soviet officials apparently induced Kim Il Sung to accept training in the Soviet's Maritime Province. Kim's activities at this time remain obscure. His memoir provides some insight, but a more reliable picture must await future research in the Soviet archives.

We can say that while many of Kim Il Sung's potential rivals for power died fighting the Japanese, Soviet officials groomed him to play a leading political role in post-war Korea. Kim remained active in the guerilla movement along the China-Korea border, but he also enjoyed a relatively normal family life. In 1942, Kim's wife Chong-suk gave birth to their first son, Kim Jong Il (Kim Chong-il) on February 16, 1942.

> **Increase Your North Korea IQ**
>
> Kim Chong-suk (1919–1949) was Kim Il Sung's wife and the mother of North Korea's second ruler, Kim Jong Il. Born to a poor farm family, she became an orphan. In 1935, she joined Kim Il Sung's guerilla band as a kitchen helper and accompanied Kim to the Soviet Union where they apparently married. On February 16, 1942, she gave birth to their first son, Jong Il. Her second son, Pyong-il, was born in 1944 but drowned in 1947. Their daughter, Kyong-hui, was born in 1946 and graduated from Kim Il Sung University in 1984. She served on the Korean Workers Party Central Committee in 1988, and in the Supreme People's Assembly in 1990. Kim Chong-suk died in Pyongyang in 1949 while delivering a stillborn baby.

Kim claimed his future heir Jong Il was born at the so-called "secret camp" at the southern base of Paektu-san (White Head Mountain; see Chapter 3). The claim suggests a politically potent parallel with the mythical birth of Korea's first ruler on the mountain. Some Korean historians contest this. Instead, they say the birth occurred in the Soviet Union. At this point, we simply do not know.

Korea Occupied (1945–1948)

The Soviet Army entered northern Korea on August 26, 1945, and U.S. troops arrived in the south on September 8. Both armies followed the script prepared by the Allied powers' leaders at meetings earlier in the year (see Chapter 7). Both armies respected the 38th parallel as the line separating their zones of occupation, as set forth in Supreme Allied Commander General MacArthur's September 2 order.

Kim Who?

Kim Il Sung was not greeted as a hero when he returned to Pyongyang on September 19, 1945. To most Koreans, he was merely one among many obscure anti-Japanese guerilla fighters. But Kim had the support of local Soviet military commanders.

Stalin was preoccupied with Nazi Germany throughout World War II. To "Uncle Joe" the Far East was indeed far away. Korea was of marginal concern until the war's end. Stalin's government and the Soviet Communist Party relinquished responsibility to local military and Party officials in the Maritime Province to organize a pro-Soviet government for Korea. They, not necessarily Stalin, groomed Kim for power and backed his rise.

> **Increase Your North Korea IQ**
>
> On September 18, 10 days after U.S. troops occupied South Korea, President Truman confirmed the Cairo Declaration's promise (see Chapter 7) that Korea "shall become free and independent." But he also cautioned, "… the assumption by the Koreans themselves of the responsibilities and functions of a free and independent nation … will of necessity require time and patience."

Kim faced little competition in Pyongyang. Most prominent Korean independence leaders had flocked to Seoul, Korea's traditional capital. Kim's sole competitor in the north was Cho Man-sik, a Presbyterian deacon widely respected for his anti-Japanese activities. The large Korean Christian community in the north admired him.

In Seoul, the Japanese-educated Pak Hon-yong headed the Korean Communist Party. Socialism had attracted many of the young Koreans who attended college in Japan. They swelled the communist party's ranks once Japan's defeat seemed inevitable. Consequently, the number of communists and socialists in southern Korea at the end of World War II outnumbered those north of the 38th parallel.

The Korean Cold War

As had happened in many countries around the globe where the United States and Soviet Union initially agreed to share power, the Allied agreements concerning the transfer of power to Koreans quickly fell apart. The Soviets promptly put Kim Il Sung in charge of an interim Korean government. They then declared numerous Japanese factories built in northern Korea as war redemption and dismantled and shipped them home.

In the south, the Korean provisional government leadership returned to Korea and teamed up with their counterparts in the south. Many of these southern Koreans were socialists who had already formed the Korean People's Republic (*Choson Inmin konghwakuk)*. Korean provisional government leader Kim Ku took charge and declared this Korea's interim government. But the U.S. Army promptly moved to disband it. Instead, it formed the U.S. military government and staffed it with former Japanese colonial officials.

Koreans throughout the peninsula were disappointed and outraged with their superpower liberators. (This presents an interesting parallel for the U.S. military government rebuilding Iraq.)

The United States and Soviet Union struggled for months to establish a temporary multilateral trusteeship to rule Korea. The effort ultimately failed. On September 17, 1947, the United States took the issue of Korea's independence to the UN General Assembly. It adopted a U.S. proposal that a UN Temporary Commission on Korea be established. A second resolution called for elections to be held not later than "March 31, 1948 to choose representatives with whom the [UN Temporary] Commission may consult regarding the prompt attainment of the freedom and independence of the Korean people and which representatives, constituting a National Assembly, may establish a National Government of Korea."

Korea Divided

In February 1948, the U.S. military government alleged that "communists in South Korea, acting under instructions from Soviet-occupied North Korea," launched a "terrorist campaign" to block the May elections. Meanwhile, in April, Kim Il Sung's People's Council approved a draft constitution for the establishment of a Democratic People's Republic of Korea.

Because of opposition in the north, the elections were held only in the south on May 10. Before the votes had been counted, a national assembly was formed in South Korea and on May 31 it elected Syngman Rhee its chairman. On June 25, 1948, the UN Temporary Commission on Korea declared "that the results of the ballot of May 10, 1948, are a valid expression of the free will of the electorate in those parts of Korea which were accessible to the commission and in which the inhabitants constituted approximately two-thirds of the people of all Korea."

On July 17, the national assembly promulgated a constitution for the Republic of Korea (ROK), and on July 20, it elected Rhee the ROK's president. Washington promptly recognized the ROK and declared it the sole legitimate government of Korea. The ROK took over from the U.S. military government on August 15, 1948.

In the north, on August 25, a Supreme People's Council was "elected" with Kim Il Sung as its chairman. On September 9, this group proclaimed the establishment of the Democratic People's Republic of Korea (DPRK) and claimed jurisdiction over all Korea. Kim Il Sung was declared the DPRK's leader, and on October 12, the USSR extended formal diplomatic recognition to the DPRK. In the Soviet-controlled north, "elections" involved Soviet Communist Party representatives, in consultation with their military counterparts. They compiled a slate of unopposed, preapproved candidates for whom Korean Communist Party members then could either vote for or against. Usually the "nay" votes were token, at best.

By the fall of 1948, liberated Korea ceased to be a unified nation.

The Least You Need to Know

- Kim Il Sung claimed he was born into a poor farm family, but his father studied at an American Christian school in Pyongyang, which suggests he was not poor.

- Korea's communist movement began long before Kim Il Sung knew anything about communism, but Japanese suppression of the movement wiped out its early leaders, enabling Kim to emerge.

- Kim Il Sung led anti-Japanese guerilla bands along the China-Korea border, possibly beginning as early as 1935 and until 1945.

- Soviet military officials groomed Kim Il Sung to lead Korea after World War II, but then Kim had to defeat factions within the Korean Communist Party to consolidate his power.

- Kim Il Sung was not widely known to the Korean people when he returned home in September 1945, but Soviet backing propelled him to the presidency of the Democratic People's Republic of Korea when it was established in September 1948.

Chapter 9

The Korean War

In This Chapter

- ◆ Who started the Korean War?
- ◆ Why did the United States get involved?
- ◆ Why did China enter the war?
- ◆ The Korean War Armistice

North Korea's invasion of South Korea on June 25, 1950, like the Japanese attack on Pearl Harbor in 1941, has had a profound and lingering impact on U.S. politics and foreign policy. The attack came as a total surprise and caught the United States completely unprepared. At the time, Americans were preoccupied with the so-called Cold War in Europe. The Soviet Union since 1945 had asserted its influence over central Europe and appeared to be threatening to do the same in southern and western Europe.

But in East Asia, the "Communist menace" was making even more dramatic gains. The world's most populist nation, China, fell to communism in October 1949. The remnants of China's noncommunist forces, long supported by the United States, retreated to the small island of Taiwan. Meanwhile, communist-led bands of warriors had taken up arms against their colonial rulers, the British and French, in Southeast Asia. Then came the

North Korean invasion. The world seemed on the verge of being overwhelmed by the communist-dominated dictatorships of the Soviet Union and China.

President Harry S. Truman quickly decided to draw a line on communism. He ordered General Douglas MacArthur, commander of U.S. forces in Japan, to repel the communist invasion of South Korea. In doing so, the president risked engaging in a nuclear war with either the Soviet Union and China or both.

The Korean War compelled the United States to concentrate massive resources on countering communism's expansion around the world. U.S. foreign policy until the end of the Cold War in 1990 centered around the "containment" of communism.

The Soviet Union, China, and North Korea were labeled international outlaws and villains unworthy of international trust. China, North Korea, North Vietnam, and eventually Cuba were denied normal diplomatic and commercial relations and ex-cluded from international organizations such as the United Nations. Their misdeeds were punished with a multitude of economic sanctions that denied them access to the international and U.S. markets.

The United States spent billions of dollars in foreign aid to counter Soviet influence in the so-called third world of economically under developed nations. South Korea and South Vietnam became show cases for this American effort in East Asia.

To ensure its security, the United States turned to deterrence. This consisted of devel-oping and maintaining an arsenal of weapons of mass destruction so massive and destructive that no nation would attempt to attack the United States. The United States ringed the so-called Soviet bloc of nations with a network of military alliances. This enabled it to surround the Soviet Union and its allies with an awesome arsenal of nuclear equipped jet bombers, ballistic missiles, and submarines.

Ultimately, the United States and its allies proved victorious in this Cold War, except for one place—the Korean Peninsula. Here, the Cold War persists.

In this chapter, we look back now at the Korean War because its legacy still haunts the nations of Northeast Asia and the United States with the risk of a second Korean War.

The Never-Ending War

The United States is still at war with North Korea. The Korean War Armistice, signed in 1953, only quieted the guns. Technically, a state of war has persisted ever since. Nor did the armistice erase the war's cause. Korea remains divided, despite the deaths of an estimated three million civilians and soldiers from North and South Korea, China, the United States, and other members of the United Nations.

Personal Recollections

On Independence Day 1996, a U.S. Army major, a sergeant from Western Samoa and I, the State Department liaison officer, arrived at Pyongyang International Airport. We were the advance team for the first U.S. military personnel to return to North Korea since the Korean War. Colonel Li of the North Korean People's Army greeted us as soon as our feet touched the ground. Reading from a prepared statement, he informed us that we represented a "hostile military force." Our safety was guaranteed, but we should consider ourselves "under detention" during our stay in his "fatherland." After two days, I was able to use a letter promising U.S. visas for North Korea's team to participate in the Atlantic Olympiad as an excuse to contact the Foreign Ministry. That done, we subsequently were released to a downtown hotel.

The war's legacy still haunts. It has formed two schools of thought about how to deal with those who threaten the security of the United States and its allies. During the Korean War, the enemy was communism and the Soviet bloc. Today it is terrorism and the "axis of evil." Today's so-called "hard liners" and "soft liners" can trace their roots back to the Korean War, to either General MacArthur (a Republican) or President Truman (a Democrat).

The general wanted to use total war to defeat communism. He believed a joint invasion of communist "Red" China with the Nationalist Chinese forces of Generalissimo Chiang Kai-shek would end the communist threat and reunite Korea. MacArthur also wanted to drop atomic bombs along the Korea-China border to halt the flow of Chinese soldiers and war material.

Increase Your North Korea IQ

General Douglas MacArthur, a West Point graduate, commanded U.S. forces in the Pacific during World War II. After the war, he became the Supreme Allied Commander of the Far East and ruler of occupied Japan from 1945 to 1953. When the Korean War started, MacArthur took charge of UN forces. MacArthur wrote in the spring of 1951 to a congressman, "... here in Asia is where the communist conspirators have elected to make their play for global conquest. ... if we lose the war to Communism in Asia, the fall of Europe is inevitable ..." President Truman interpreted this letter, and MarArthur's similar public comments, as a challenge to presidential authority and fired him in April 1951.

Truman preferred "limited" war against communism. He was concerned that MacArthur's strategy would ignite World War III and a global nuclear holocaust.

So-called moderates won round one. Truman fired MacArthur, and the war remained conventional and limited to the Korean theater. Ever since, American politicians and foreign policy makers have argued over whether to emphasize armed "enforcement" or diplomatic inducement to achieve U.S. foreign policy objectives.

Pre-War Chest Pounding (1948–1950)

June 25, 1950, marks the official start of the Korean War. Actually, rumblings of war were heard much earlier. By 1949, the Cold War was heating up. President Truman initiated a policy of containment of communism in Europe that began in Greece. On June 24, 1949, the Soviet Union began the "Berlin Blockade" by closing land routes to the U.S., British, and French sectors of Berlin. The Allies responded with the Berlin Airlift. In September, the Soviet Union exploded its first atomic bomb. By October, however, Chinese communist leader Mao Zedong declared the establishment of the People's Republic of China. U.S.-backed anticommunist Nationalist leader Chiang Kai-shek retreated to Taiwan in December 1949.

All the while, North and South Korean leaders Kim Il Sung and Syngman Rhee were testing one another's armed strength along the 38th parallel. Both proclaimed their determination to forcefully reunify Korea. Rhee declared in March 1950 his intention to cross the 38th parallel despite U.S. opposition. Referring to the North Koreans, Rhee stated that he felt compelled to "respond to the cries of our brothers in distress." To his lobbyist in Washington he confided his desire to attach north "to the Tumen and the Yalu" rivers, and "mop up" Kim Il Sung's "guerillas" and "bandits."

Kim Il Sung was more discrete. First, he convinced Stalin in 1949 that he just "wanted to prod South Korea with the point of a bayonet" to collapse Rhee's shaky government. Soviet intelligence advised Stalin that the United States probably would not rush to South Korea's defense. Mao independently reached the same conclusion. U.S. Secretary of State Dean Acheson seemed to confirm this when he did not include Korea within the U.S. defensive perimeter in a January 1950 speech.

───── **Personal Recollections** ─────

After a two-hour discussion with Kim Il Sung, we never expected to have lunch with him. It was October 11, 1993. But there we were, a member of the U.S. Congress, his staff, and I, the State Department escort officer, munching six courses with North Korea's "Great Leader." When one of the Americans asked about Stalin and the Korean War, Kim pondered momentarily and then answered, "Stalin was my close friend. He is dead. Let's let him rest in peace." Subsequent research has shown that Stalin did not encourage Kim to invade the South, but once Kim had decided to do so, Stalin backed Kim's effort to forcefully reunify Korea.

The Lineup

Kim's army quickly became a formidable military force of 135,000 personnel. Former Korean anti-Japanese guerillas filled the upper ranks of the new Korean People's Army (KPA) with battle-hardened officers. Soviet troops had withdrawn from North Korea in 1948, but at least 350 Soviet advisers remained to train the KPA how to use state-of-the-art Soviet T-34 tanks, artillery, and automatic weapons. Moscow also supplied 180 new aircraft, including 40 fighters and 70 dive bombers.

South Korea lagged far behind. Korean graduates of the Imperial Japanese army academy filled the officer ranks of the new South Korean army. South Korea's 20 million citizens were more than double those of North Korea's 9 million, but the South's army was much smaller. Its nine army divisions totaled about 90,000 poorly trained and equipped soldiers. Washington had refused to supply it with heavy mortars and anti-tank weapons. U.S. Army officers believed rice paddies would render tanks useless, so no tanks were sent to South Korea. Yet the head of the U.S. Korean Military Advisory Group claimed five days before the war that "my forces could hold the Commies."

Kim Lunges South

Again it was a Sunday morning, just nine years after Pearl Harbor. On June 25, 1950, two tank-tipped KPA columns attacked across the 38th parallel. They headed for Seoul, the South's capital of about 1,250,000 people. Soviet military advisers directed the assault.

Personal Recollections

Sunday, June 25, 1995, I was at North Korea's Yongbyon Nuclear Research Center (in North Korea, the letter "n" is added to the front of the word to make it read "Nyongbyon"). watching a documentary about the Korean War on North Korean television. Watching with me was Atomic Bureau officer Mr. Han. I asked him who started the war. Looking perplexed, he answered, "You American imperialists!" How do you know that, I asked. Looking amazed, he responded adamantly, "Everyone knows that!" Well, I thought to myself, I could have argued the point, and risked restarting the war … or kept my peace and remained free to go home. I zipped my lip.

South Korean President Rhee called General MacArthur in Tokyo. At first his aides refused to wake him. When he answered the telephone, Rhee reportedly yelled, "We've warned you many times. Now you must save Korea!" MacArthur promised to send fighter aircraft, artillery, and antitank weapons.

A journalist later that day reportedly asked the general about the situation. Mac-Arthur was quoted to have answered that the invasion was just a "border incident," one that the South Koreans could handle. In Washington, where it was Saturday evening, the Pentagon learned of the situation from press inquiries.

Meanwhile, Kim Il Sung declared in a radio broadcast from Pyongyang that Seoul's "puppet regime" had declined "all methods for peaceful reunification proposed by the DPRK." He also accused South Korea of having committed "armed aggression."

President Truman learned of the invasion on Sunday morning, Washington time, after his flight from Missouri landed in Washington. Perhaps energized by the recent "loss" of China to the communists, Truman acted decisively. He directed MacArthur to assist South Korea by sending U.S. military aircraft and antitank weapons. He then ordered his staff to convene an emergency meeting of the UN Security Council.

The ragtag South Korean army stalled the KPA for two days, allowing tens of thousands of Koreans to flee south from Seoul. But on the third day, resistance crumbled. At Miari Pass on Seoul's northern edge, hundreds of civilians died in a murderous crossfire. Hundreds more were blown to their deaths when South Korean soldiers prematurely destroyed the only bridge across the Han River, which slices through the middle of Seoul from east to west.

As KPA tanks rolled into Seoul, the United States led the drive to get the UN Security Council to pass a resolution that called on UN members to rush to South Korea's defense. (At the time, there was no U.S.-South Korean defense treaty.) MacArthur was promptly named commander in chief of the UN command (CIN-CUNC). The Soviet UN representative was then boycotting Security Council meetings in protest over an unrelated diplomatic squabble. Caught completely off guard, he did not attend the Security Council meeting in which the resolution to defend South Korea was debated, and so he could not veto the Council's decisions.

Increase Your North Korea IQ

The five permanent members of the UN Security Council are the United States, United Kingdom, France, Russia (formerly the Soviet Union), and China (now the People's Republic of China, formerly Nationalist China [Taiwan]). Other UN members rotate membership in the Security Council on a revolving basis. Only the five permanent members can veto any proposed resolution before the Council. If no veto is exercised, the resolution passes or fails on a majority of the voting members present.

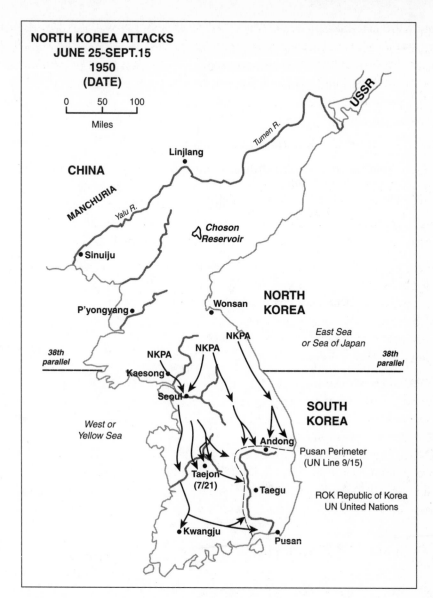

North Korea attacks South Korea—June 25–September 15, 1950.

On the Edge of Victory

The KPA continued to roll south over sporadic South Korean and U.S. resistance. One hundred miles south of Seoul, the KPA surrounded and defeated the first U.S. Army division to enter the war. Six weeks into the war, a North Korean victory seemed inevitable.

With their backs literally to the sea, South Korean and U.S. resistance stiffened at the famous "Pusan Perimeter" around the port of Pusan on Korea's southeastern tip. U.S. Air Force bombs began decimating the KPA's forward troop concentrations and supply lines. U.S. reinforcements from Japan and supplies filled Pusan and moved quickly to the front. By the end of August, the UN forces still clung to the Korean Peninsula's southeast tip, but the KPA's lunge south had stalled.

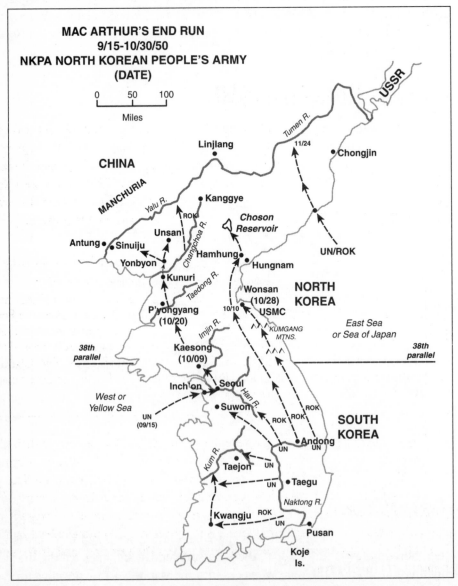

The Korean War—MacArthur's End Run—September 15–October 30, 1950.

MacArthur's End Run

General MacArthur's fabled military career reached both its high and low points during the Korean War. Against most of his advisers' better judgment, in early September he ordered an amphibious assault at Inchon on Korea's west coast, 200 miles behind the front lines. The KPA in the south was severed from its supply base in the north. Within three weeks, UN forces, spearheaded by U.S. and South Korean units, expelled the KPA from South Korea and crossed the 38th parallel into the north. By early October of that year, Kim Il Sung's once mighty war machine had been reduced to retreating rabble.

Round Two—November 1950

MacArthur turned cocky as Kim Il Sung fled north. The general formed two columns, one on each side of the Korean Peninsula and ordered them to march north to the Korea-China border. Meanwhile, an estimated 200,000 so-called Chinese People's "Volunteers" trickled into the central mountains of North Korea. Many were former soldiers in Chiang Kai-shek's anticommunist Nationalist army or ethnic Koreans from southern Manchuria. They joined Mao's army after Chiang fled to Taiwan.

Increase Your North Korea IQ

China's long and bloody civil war pitted the anticommunist forces of Generalissimo Chiang Kai-shek, president of the Republic of China (ROC) and leader of its Nationalist (KMT) political party, against Chinese Communist Party (CCP) leader Mao Zedong. In 1949, Mao forced Chiang to retreat to the island of Taiwan where Chiang reestablished his government. Mao in October 1949 declared the establishment of the People's Republic of China (PRC), or "Red China" as it was called in the United States. The United States continued to recognize Chiang's government as China's only legitimate government until 1974.

General MacArthur's public utterances about teaming the United States with China's anticommunist leader Chiang Kai-shek concerned China's new communist regime in Beijing. Mao Zedong, leader of the People's Republic of China, and his officials publicly cautioned the UN forces about unspecified consequences if they advanced to China's border with Korea. Mao's priority was to protect his regime. Saving Kim Il Sung and promoting communism were lesser concerns. UN commander MacArthur, urged on by South Korean President Rhee, ignored the warnings and drove north hoping to reunify Korea.

Late in October, South Korean advanced units captured some Chinese troops north of Yongbyon and near the Myohyang Mountains (see Chapter 3). MacArthur belatedly confirmed the U.S. intelligence reports' accuracy, but dismissed intelligence assessments that Red China was about to enter the Korean War. The worse defeat in U.S. military history ensued.

The lead units of the U.S. Eighth Army on the Korean Peninsula's west side halted their northward advance just southwest of the small town of Unsan. Shortly after the U.S. soldiers finished their Thanksgiving Day dinner, tens of thousands of China soldiers attacked. The U.S. soldiers were overrun. Hundreds died or were captured. Survivors retreated south, leaving behind an estimated 800 dead, wounded, or imprisoned.

> **Increase Your North Korea IQ**
>
> Unsan is a familiar place to Americans. They first took up residence there in the 1880s after the Korean king awarded the American Trading Company a license to prospect for precious metals in the area. Unsan literally means "silver mountain," but the Americans found gold. They operated the mines there until the Japanese took over in the 1930s. After the Korean War, the first Americans to Unsan were the U.S. Army's Central Identification Laboratory, Hawaii (CILHI), team when in July 1996, it began its search for U.S. Korean War dead remains. Each summer until 2002, CILHI teams returned and eventually recovered about 160 sets of remains. Given the continuing tensions between the United States and North Korean, the future of this effort remains uncertain.

On the east coast, Chinese troops also attempted to surround the second northward advancing UN column. But U.S. marines, U.S. army soldiers, and South Korean troops fought off the freezing and starving Chinese troops in intense fighting during some of the coldest weather ever recorded in Korea's northeast corner. Yet the UN forces were slowly forced to retreat southward. Meanwhile, to the west, the U.S. Eighth Army's retreat turned into a rout.

MacArthur's Waterloo

Kaechon (or Kyechon) today is a gray concrete city of 340,000 people. In December 1950, it was known as Kunuri and it was to become the site of one of the most disastrous defeats in the annals of the U.S. Army. After their defeat at Unsan, the U.S. Eighth Army fell back through Yongbyon to Kunuri. Remnants of South Korean, Turkish, and British units joined them there.

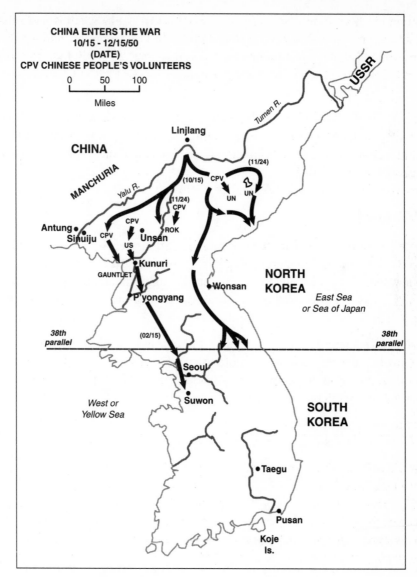

China enters the Korean War—October 15–December 15, 1950.

As the UN column began its retreat south out of Kunuri, it encountered the "Gauntlet." This was the American nickname for the stretch of narrow road where Chinese and North Korean forces ambushed the retreating UN column of tanks, trucks, and troops.

The U.S. First Cavalry Division led the way into the trap. Hundreds were killed, captured, and wounded. The British (including the actor Michael Caine) held their position on the column's west flank. But on the east flank, South Korean and Turkish resistance collapsed. Panic ensued as hundreds of UN troops abandoned their equipment and colleagues to flee south toward Pyongyang. The UN forces' retreat did not halt until they were 40 miles south of Seoul.

Hopes for Korea's unification were dashed. By early December 1950, all UN forces had fallen back south of the 38th parallel. Chinese and North Korean forces reoccupied Seoul. Three months of bloody combat at the beginning of 1951 enabled the UN to reclaim Seoul. Communist forces were slowly pushed north to the general area of the 38th parallel.

MacArthur Fired

General MacArthur, embarrassed by his tremendous defeat, but supported by South Korea's president and numerous Republican members of Congress, urged all-out war against Red China. He called for the dropping of atomic bombs on the northern side of the China–North Korea border to halt the flow of men and material from China into North Korea.

President Truman preferred "limited" war. He ruled out both the use of nuclear weapons and the resumption of an offensive across the 38th parallel. After a lengthy (and often public) political duel, the president on April 10, 1951, announced he would replace General MacArthur.

Echoing the president's policy, Secretary of State Acheson declared on April 30 that the UN's objectives were to stop aggression against South Korea, to prevent the conflict's spread, and to restore peace and security to Korea. He concluded that "[t]he UN never contemplated the use of force to … establish a unified … country [Korea]."

Never-Ending Negotiations Begin

One year after the war had begun, the Soviet Union suggested to the United States on June 27, 1951, that the opposing commands in Korea might broker a military armistice. The armistice negotiations began on July 10 near Kaesong (see Chapter 3). Fighting all along the front continued as the talks dragged on for months.

Retired World War II hero General Eisenhower in his bid for the presidency promised to go to Korea to end the war. He was elected and replaced Truman in January 1953. Still the talks continued.

Increase Your North Korea IQ

The United Nations Security Council on July 7, 1950, passed the U.S.-proposed resolution that established the United Nations Command (UNC) as the central command for all UN forces that fought under the UN flag during the Korean War. The U.S. president was designated to name the UNC commander. He chose General Douglas MacArthur as the first commander in chief, UN command (CINCUNC). Ever since, the commander in chief, U.S. Forces Korea (USFK) continues to wear the "CINCUNC" hat. The UN General Assembly voted in 1978 to discontinue the international body's affiliation with the UN Command after the United States and South Korea established their Combined Forces Command (CFC).

Neither Korean government did much to promote an armistice. Both hoped their superpower champions would promote their common priority—Korea's reunification. Meanwhile, the contending Korean sides combated fiercely for every inch of turf. South Korean forces gradually pushed several miles north across the 38th parallel. Both they and their North Korean foe suffered heavy casualties. UN forces on the western half of the peninsula, mostly U.S. units and small units from other UN member nations, held the line against largely Chinese forces.

Whether Soviet leader Josef Stalin's death on March 5, 1953, had a constructive impact on the stalled negotiations remains to be determined. But by the end of March, the communist side responded positively to a UN proposal regarding the exchange of prisoners. Abruptly, the impasse crumbled and negotiations moved promptly toward an armistice.

The Never-Ending War Begins

Representatives of all the combatants signed the Korean War Armistice on July 27, 1953, except for one. South Korea's President Rhee rejected the agreement and refused to sign it. In a letter to President Eisenhower, Rhee alleged that the UN seemed to be teaming up with the "enemy" and to accept the armistice was "to accept a death warrant." His priority remained Korea's reunification, not the ending of hostilities. Kim Il Sung, quite likely under pressure from Moscow and Beijing, had his representative sign the armistice.

On June 8, terms of the armistice had been virtually worked out. Negotiators on both sides signed an agreement regarding the exchange of prisoners of war to take effect the date of the armistice. This understanding became part of the armistice.

A Neutral Nations Repatriation Commission (NNRC) was set up. Staffing it were representatives from Sweden, Switzerland, Poland, Czechoslovakia, and India. They were to oversee the prisoner exchange. But on June 18, Rhee tried to undermine the agreement. He ordered South Korean guards to open the gates of prison camps to allow 25,000 anticommunist North Korean prisoners to escape into South Korean society. Only 8,600 North Korean prisoners remained for the prisoner exchange. Only the chief UN negotiator's written apology to the North Korean side put the armistice back together.

The Korean War Armistice was signed finally at the small village of Panmunjom on July 27, 1953. It was a truce, not a peace treaty. Hostilities were "suspended," not ended. A 4,000-meter-wide demilitarized zone (DMZ) was drawn 151 miles across the Korean Peninsula's waist. UN forces withdrew 2,000 meters to the south and Communist forces 2,000 to the north. The no man's land between became the DMZ. The military demarcation line (MDL) bisected the DMZ. Like the 38th parallel, it was to have been a temporary demarcation line. Ever since, it has been the *de facto* border between South and North Korea.

The armistice's implementation fell to the Military Armistice Commission (MAC). Originally, 10 officers staffed the MAC, 5 from the UN and 5 from the communist side. On the UN side, a general-rank U.S. officer headed the UN team. Accompanying him were two U.S. military officers plus one each from the United Kingdom and South Korea (ROK). Four North Korean and one Chinese "People's Volunteer" army officers staffed the other half of the MAC. Since 1994, however, the MAC has become dysfunctional. North Korea contested the MAC's authority when the U.S. designated a South Korean general as its commander. China subsequently withdrew from the MAC.

Five Joint Observer Teams were formed to investigate reported armistice violations that occur within the DMZ. Each team had six members, three each from the UN and communist sides. Joint duty officers, one from each side, manned a hotline telephone link between the opposing armies. These teams continue to monitor the situation along the DMZ but they consult only if there has been a major armed event in or near the DMZ.

Each side has a MAC secretary. Actually, this is a military command and administrative support group. The UN MAC reports to the UN Command in Seoul. The North Korean secretary reports to a general in Kaesong.

All MAC meetings used to convene at the joint security area (JSA), generally known as Panmunjom. MAC staff are still permitted free movement within the JSA. Tourists are also still allowed to visit the area, but they must remain on their side of the MDL.

Overseeing the Armistice and MAC activities was the Neutral Nations Supervisory Commission (NNSC). Originally, it consisted of four senior military officers, one each from Sweden, Switzerland, Czechoslovakia, and Poland. The UN designated Sweden and Switzerland, and North Korea the other members. (At the time, Poland and Czechoslovakia were part of the Soviet-controlled Communist Bloc.) Their job was to monitor, through inspection and investigation, both sides' compliance with the armistice. But the NNSC was disbanded in 1994 after Czechoslovakia divided into two nations, and North Korea compelled Poland to withdraw from the NNSC.

Originally, the armistice designated 10 ports, 5 each in the North and South Korea as authorized entry points for military replacement personnel and equipment. Neutral National Inspection Teams were assigned to each port to monitor compliance with the armistice. This provision ceased to be effective because of North Korea's refusal to allow the inspection teams freedom of movement. In 1956, the UN halted further access to ports in South Korea (largely in reaction to North Korea's move), rendering the provision defunct.

The Cost

No one knows how many people died during the Korean War. Estimates tend to approach three million deaths. An estimated two million Koreans died. This number includes both North and South Korean soldiers and civilians. Official UN estimates for South Korean casualties set the number at slightly more than one million people, but 330,000 persons are listed as "missing in action." The United States, according to official data, suffered 172,707 casualties: 54,246 dead (including those who died from injuries and illnesses not related to combat); 103,284 wounded; 8,177 missing in action; and 7,000 prisoners of war.

Neither North Korea nor China have issued official casualty numbers. Some historians estimate upward of 900,000 Chinese soldiers died.

In the end, the armistice stopped the killing but could not erase the war's cause—Korea's division. Tragically, the Korean War crystallized the existence of two rival regimes on the Korean Peninsula, each the beneficiary of a rival superpower.

The Least You Need to Know

◆ North Korea, with assistance from the Soviet Union, invaded South Korea on June 25, 1950.

◆ The United Nations Security Council urged UN members to help South Korea defend itself.

◆ The United States and South Korean forces fought together under the UNs flag. Fourteen other UN members sent troops.

◆ The People's Republic of China entered the war on North Korea's side as UN forces approached China's border.

◆ The Korean War Armistice, signed in July 1953, ended the fighting, but a state of war continues between the United States and North Korea, the primary negotiators of the armistice.

Part 3

North Korea Today

North Korea's leader Kim Jong Il faces a dilemma. His first priority is to perpetuate his regime, but at the same time he must open his society to the changes that are vital to economic revival. But change and foreign influence could undermine his authority.

This part focuses on the "how and why" of the Democratic People's Republic of Korea, and assess prospects for Kim Jong Il's future.

Chapter 10

The Great Leader's Paradise

In This Chapter

- ◆ Reality beyond the illusion
- ◆ Juche—Kim Il Sung's brand of communism
- ◆ The Korean Workers' Party
- ◆ The bureaucracy
- ◆ The National Defense Commission

After the Korean War, Kim Il Sung set out to achieve reconstruction, reunification, and his own brand of communist revolution. In this chapter, we will focus on two of Kim's three "R's," reconstruction and revolution. We will save reunification for Chapters 16 and 19.

Between 1953 and 1980, Kim made impressive progress toward reconstruction. Massive help from Moscow and Beijing proved invaluable to his efforts, but Kim's success was equally a result of his own abilities and the effort of the North Korean people. Kim's first step was to consolidate his power after the Korean War. He proved to be an adroit and ruthless despot.

Then, to mobilize and, whenever he deemed necessary, to coerce the population of North Korea to follow him, he forged his own interpretation of Marxism-Leninism. To ensure conformity to his rule and ideology, he closed

North Korea to the outside world, declared this the sole acceptable ideology of his domain, and installed a system of "carrots and sticks" to reward his followers and to punish any who dared grumble about his absolute rule.

Kim Il Sung's legacy continues to dominate political institutions and thought in his son Kim Jong Il's domain. But South Korea's own successful reconstruction and its alliance with the United States blunted Kim's plans to forcefully reunify Korea and to impose his brand of communist revolution on South Korea.

Paradise or Prison

North Korea since the Korean War has been a cloistered, secretive society. Even the diplomats of its closest allies, the Soviet Union and China, endured tight controls regarding whom they could meet and where they could travel.

As we saw in Chapter 6, pre-modern Korea had made itself the "Hermit Kingdom." Its rulers rejected contact with Western nations seeking diplomatic ties and trade. In this way, its rulers hoped to avoid clashing with the Europeans, particularly the British, and to keep out opium.

Kim Il Sung's closed door policy had very different reasons. His aim was to exclude foreign political and economic ideas inconsistent with the ideology he was propagating to strengthen his power. From the end of the Korean War until his death in 1994, North Korea remained his "Hermit Domain."

North Korea's preoccupation with secrecy does not trace back to Korea's earlier history. The Korean War appears to have intensified North Koreans' desire to hide their society from the outside world. Secrecy enabled North Korea's leaders, particularly its military, to hide the nation's strengths and weaknesses. This has kept the outside world guessing about North Korea's actual military might, and economic and political conditions.

Myths about North Korea multiplied. Pyongyang excelled in creating positive myths, whereas Seoul highlighted negative ones.

Kim Il Sung declared his domain a paradise. Magazines full of colorful pictures portrayed smiling, well-fed and well-dressed North Koreans in modern factories and emerald-green rice paddies. Occasionally a returning visitor or a defector offered a peek behind the veil of secrecy and propaganda. They revealed a despotic and regimented society that had more in common with Orwell's imagined society in his famous book, *1984*, than with any kind of paradise.

Another myth is that North Korea is a miniature model of Stalin's Soviet Union. As we shall see, this, too, is a lingering illusion fostered for political reasons during the

Cold War. Moscow wanted the world to see North Korea as being aligned with it, and not aligned with Beijing. Seoul and Washington wanted people to see Pyongyang as Moscow's puppet. Both illusions blurred the truth.

Only a handful of Americans were admitted before 1996. Merely visiting North Korea did not necessarily enhance their or our understanding of this secretive society. Their every move was restricted and monitored while in country. After returning home, a few made careers describing the society they had not seen. Some constructed theories using information that others deemed unreliable. Others, concerned that negative comments could adversely affect relatives in North Korea, said nothing or tended to exaggerate the positive.

But since 1996, North Korea has hesitantly opened itself. Access to people and places continues to expand. Need provided the impetus. North Koreans were starving in 1996. They urgently needed the world's humanitarian aid. First came representatives of the UN relief agencies. Members of European and American private voluntary organizations (PVO) followed. Soon a trickle of U.S. and European Union government officials began arriving. Since 1998, the number of South Korean visitors has increased to where it is in excess of several thousand annually.

Abruptly, the trickle of information turned into a swollen stream. Then, too, the number of self-proclaimed North Korea "experts" has exploded. We now must scramble to sort fact from fiction, while assessing the expertise of the so-called "experts." Like the blind men feeling the elephant, the struggle continues to accurately depict North Korea. The impending crisis in U.S.–North Korean relations demands, however, that we look beyond the illusions North Korea has projected to us. In this chapter we share with you our best effort to portray the real North Korea as it exists today.

Double Dipping

North Korea was anything but a paradise at the end of the Korean War. During the war's first year, Seoul and nearby cities like the port of Inchon had sustained the most damage. During the next two years, combat was limited to a 15- to 20-mile-wide strip of land across the peninsula's waist. Seoul and the remainder of South Korea were spared more damage.

But in the north, the United States eventually dropped more bombs on North Korea during the Korean War than it had around the world during World War II. Pyongyang and all North Korean industrial centers were smoldering rubble. The transportation system and power plants were destroyed. Production of everything, except some food, had come to a halt. North Korea was an economic wasteland.

Moscow and Beijing rushed to rebuild North Korea. They competed to turn war-torn Pyongyang into a showcase for their different approaches to communism. Pyongyang itself was not the prize. They were after the allegiance of so-called "third-world" nations that had won independence after the end of World War II and the collapse of Europe's empires. Economically underdeveloped, these nations wanted a quick solution to their economic woes.

Communism seemed to offer two different roadmaps. Moscow's approach followed an urban proletariat industrial road to Communism's utopia. Beijing's path led to an imaged rural agrarian peasant paradise.

Increase Your North Korea IQ

The **Sino-Soviet dispute** benefited North Korea for four decades. It smoldered during the late 1950s. Beijing felt Moscow was not fulfilling its promise to aid it economically and to help it develop nuclear weapons. The dispute erupted into the open in 1960 when the Soviet Communist Party condemned Mao Zedong for "dogmatism" and China accused the Soviet Union of "imperialism." Continued competition for the allegiance of unaligned, noncommunist governments of developing nations perpetuated the rivalry. In 1969, the situation escalated to the point where the two communist giants clashed militarily along China's northeast border. Bilateral relations were not normalized until the late 1990s, well after the demise of the Soviet Union.

Kim Il Sung saw opportunity in the rivalry and took full advantage of it. From Moscow he received heavy industrial equipment, power plants, hydroelectric dams, electrified railroads, and a massive electrified irrigation system. Beijing gave him crude oil to power the Soviet-made machines, food, and fertilizer. His communist benefactors provided markets for North Korea's exports of gold, zinc, steel, and fabric. Arms and munitions gradually became an increasing percentage of these exports, with most bound for socialist-leaning dictatorships in the Middle East and Africa.

Pyongyang's southwest suburbs; the banner reads, "Long Live the Great Leader Comrade Kim Il Sung."

Goodbye Marxism, Hello "KimIlSungism"

Double-dipping in the communist bloc's aid basket created political problems in Pyongyang. Rival factions soon formed. Some leading officials favored Moscow, others Beijing, and still others Kim Il Sung.

Kim worked cautiously during the decade after the Korean War to consolidate his power. Kim's motivation appears to have been political power. He used his nationalistic interpretation of Marxism-Leninism to discredit his rivals as being less loyal than he to North Korea. As the Sino-Soviet rivalry intensified in the late 1950s, Kim gradually purged the so-called pro-Soviet and pro-Chinese officials. By the time the Sino-Soviet dispute burst onto the world stage in the late 1950s, Kim held absolute power in Pyongyang.

Kim Il Sung's quest for power motivated his reinterpretation of Marxism-Leninism. His apparent intention was to legitimize his political ascendancy by establishing himself as the equal of Soviet champion Marx and communist China's leader Mao Zedong. He also accented nationalism and anti-imperialism as the cornerstones of his doctrine. This dual emphasis solidified his domestic support while also asserting North Korea's political independence from Moscow and Beijing. This differentiation is critical. One cannot understand North Korea without distinguishing between Marx and Kim Il Sung.

Kim called his interpretation juche. This Korean word is usually translated as "self reliance." Actually, this is quite misleading, as you will see in the following discussion. A better English rendering might be "self determination." But this phrase is normally associated with the ideals President Woodrow Wilson set forth on the eve of the Versailles Peace Conference in 1918 (see Chapter 7). Here we will stay with the orthodox translation to avoid confusion.

"Serving the Great"

Kim Il Sung's tendency to graft selected European concepts and practices onto some aspects of Korea's tradition is evident in his political philosophy. First and foremost, Kim was a nationalist. His patriotism motivated him to reject Korea's subjugation to any big power. At first, this meant Japan and China. Japan was despised because it colonized Korea. He held China accountable for Korea's haplessness at the end of the Yi Choson dynasty.

For hundreds of years, Yi Choson Korea had practiced a policy of "serving the great," or *sadae* in Korean. This practice was consistent with the traditional Chinese world order. In exchange for China's protection, Korea adopted China's primary political institutions. As discussed in Chapter 6, this included Confucian thought, a centralized

bureaucracy, and a civil service examination system. Korea's r   ent
tribute-bearing delegations to Beijing as expressions of gratit   of
China's superiority.

Kim Il Sung associated the practice of "serving the great" wi   ness
and inability to fend off Japanese imperialism at the end of t   ry.
On the one hand, he needed China's assistance, but at the sa   er-
mined not to allow Korea to again become Beijing's satellite   der-
lying distrust of China is the fact that all but a handful of Chinese troops   ew
from Korea soon after the Korean War had ended. We will have more to say about
Pyongyang's love-hate relationship with Beijing in Chapter 15.

The Soviet Union aroused similar concerns. Its predecessor, Imperial Russia, had
participated in the late nineteenth century scramble for "spheres of influence" in
Northeast Asia (see Chapter 7). Lenin's communist Revolution had replaced Russia's
monarchy. Kim Il Sung apparently detected in Stalin and his successors urges similar
to their imperialist predecessors. Moreover, having Moscow-leaning officials in his
regime could intensify the rivalry with Beijing. With post-war reconstruction well
underway, and his power consolidated in Pyongyang, Kim declared his ideological
independence from both countries.

Marx Versus Kim

Kim Il Sung is the father of *juche*, a doctrine that he systematized over several decades.
Kim's public speeches and essays in the late 1940s and well into the early 1960s are
sprinkled with the jargon of orthodox Marxism and Leninism. These references subsequently decline as his interpretation matured. By the 1970s, juche emerged as an
ideology distinct from European communism and the thoughts of Mao Zedong.

Korean Concepts

Juche is Kim Il Sung's interpretation of Marxism. The two ideologies are quite
different. Marx claimed universal validity. He made mechanical forces drive history
and concluded mankind would inevitably reach an egalitarian, utopian society free of
government. Kim emphasized nationalism, not obedience to a universal ideology. He
saw man as the prime mover of history. Utopia, in Kim's view, would be a reunified,
socialist Korea.

Kim's son, Kim Jong Il, and North Korean historians (with the help of some sympa-
thetic Japanese scholars), claimed juche's formulation dates from the beginning of

Kim Il Sung's anti-Japanese activities. This view, first put forth in the 1980s, is not substantiated by Kim Il Sung's early, unrevised writings and public speeches.

Juche is a paradox. In North Korea's rigid authoritarian political hierarchy, we would expect to find an ideology with similar features. After all, Marxism imposes an inflexible logic on its followers. However, juche is surprisingly pragmatic. Of course, political reality in North Korea rules out any opposition or alteration of the ideology. One either accepts the infallibility of North Korea's juche, or one is deemed worthless and treated accordingly.

Juche is a faint echo of Marxism. Kim Il Sung rejected Marx's claim of having come up with a scientific law to explain human conduct. Kim also rejected Engel's mechanical passage of humankind from one historical phase to another. Kim did retain the concept of class struggle between the owners and workers, but he favored Chinese communist leader Mao Zedong's clash between landlords and peasants over Marx's capitalists and urban workers. Kim also rejected Lenin's placement of workers in the vanguard of revolution. Kim assigned this role to soldiers and teachers.

Juche verges on being the opposite of Marxism. It is human-centered and nationalistic, and it rejects universal explanations for human conduct. Kim replaced Marx and Engel's universal and mechanical forces with human conduct as the driving force behind history. He argued solutions were best found in the analysis of local conditions, not the application of universal principles.

Kim and Marx had opposite goals. Marx urged urban workers to unite behind a global outcry against capitalism's perceived exploitation, overthrown their overlords, and launch the socialist phase of history. Marx envisions the eventual withering away of the state and the dissolution of all social and economic classes. Marx predicted that humanity was predetermined to achieve an egalitarian utopia without government or social and economic distinctions.

Kim favored the opposite viewpoint. He saw the state as the all-encompassing and benevolent defender of nationalism, the national character, and the masses. Revealing his preference for Korean tradition, Kim forged a centralized bureaucratic state. North Korean society was formed into a corresponding rigidly stratified hierarchy. Kim placed himself and his close kinsmen at the top of both the state and social pyramids.

Kim's totalitarian "democratic centralist" state became his machine for enforcing *collectivism*. Like the followers of Marx, Kim's disciples saw the sharing of profits and other benefits as vital to forging unity among workers. But Kim, unlike Marx, saw no need for equal distribution.

> **Korean Concepts**
>
> **Collectivism** is the essence of European socialism and North Korean juche, but they are different concepts. Europeans accent the equal sharing of obligations and benefits. Kim defined collectivism in the Confucian context. Society must collectively revere the ruler for the sake of social order. Kim Jong Il said in a 1991 speech, "The masses ... cannot be the masters of society unless they are united behind the Party and Suryong [the Korean word for "leader", which in North Korea is reserved for either Kim Il Sung or Kim Jong Il] because socialist society is based on collectivism. ... It is the monopolistic role of the Suryong to provide the masses with correct guidelines and with scientific strategies and tactics, converting the masses into an organized whole."

Kim Il Sung liked Lenin's view of imperialism. It conformed to his dislike of the Japanese colonialists. He applied the same assessment to the United States. But Kim broadened Lenin's definition of imperialism to include ideological and cultural imperialism.

North Korea's Political System

North Korea is often misperceived as a static, unchanging society. Pyongyang's leaders have fostered this illusion. They would have us believe that Kim Il Sung's leadership was always accepted, never contested, and that his interpretation of Marxism dates from his youth. As experts are now realizing, juche developed over nearly half a century of political factionalism and sometimes contentious relations with China and the Soviet Union.

There is a strong current of continuity in North Korea. But neither Kim Il Sung nor his followers could halt change. Gradual change within political institutions and practices is a continuing aspect of North Korea. Here we can mention briefly some of the more significant trends of continuity and change.

North Korea's Self Image

North Korea's constitution describes the nation as a socialist republic founded by President Kim Il Sung. The state's fundamental task is to "complete the victory of socialism in the northern half of the Republic, to expel foreign forces on a national scale, to reunify the country peacefully through great national unity, and to attain complete national independence."

These goals were significantly altered after 1990. Until that time, North Korea claimed as one of its national goals the communization of the entire Korean Penin-sula. But then the two Koreas signed on December 13, 1991, their "Agreement on Reconciliation, Nonaggression and Exchanges and Cooperation between the South and the North." They promised to "recognize and respect each other's system," and "not interfere in each other's internal affairs."

Neither side has been completely faithful to its promises.

But, by and large, North Korea appears to have given up the idea of Korea's forceful reunification. This appears to be more a recognition by Pyongyang of South Korea's military might and economic prowess than a lack of desire to fulfill its earlier objectives.

North Korean-Style "Democracy"

North Korea's political leaders also claim their nation is "democratic," as proclaimed in the nation's name, the Democratic People's Republic of Korea. The definition of "democracy" differs radically from the one common to democracies elsewhere in the world today.

In North Korea, the concept of democracy is consistent with that of Vladimir Lenin, the leader of the 1919 Russian communist revolution, and juche thought.

The government's ultimate goal, according to the North Korean constitution, is to model the entire society according to juche. This places Lenin's concepts of "democratic centralism" and "dictatorship of the proletariat" at the core of *North Korean-style democracy.* The "proletariat" are those whom the leader has admitted into his political party, the Korean Workers' Party (KWP), because of their loyal service to him and their comprehension of his juche thought.

Korean Concepts _____

North Korean–style democracy is modeled after the Russian communist version. Lenin mixed political activism with Marxist theory. He said urban workers, or the proletariat, once formed into the Communist Party, would overthrow the capitalists. Lenin then assigned the party two roles. First, it would staff the government and practice the "dictatorship of the proletariat." The Party also would monitor the masses. Knowledge of their concerns would be passed up through the party to the leadership. National policy could then reflect the "will of the masses." This process was "democratic centralism." It was "democratic" because it theoretically reflected the popular will, yet was "central" because the party controlled the flow of information and policy formulation.

Kim Il Sung, however, never seemed satisfied with his Russian communist mentors. He always added his own spin to their thought. Kim emulated Lenin's ideas about the communist Party's role, but placed scholars and teachers on an equal footing with Lenin's workers and farmers, and Mao's peasants. Lenin and Mao were anti-intellectual. Both assigned little value to scholarship. Mao went so far as to launch his "Great Proletarian Cultural Revolution" with which he tried to erase China's cultural legacy and Western cultural influence. During the Cultural Revolution, thousands of teachers, musicians, and anyone inclined toward traditional Chinese or Western culture were killed or sent to reeducation camps, for the "crime" of being a teacher.

Personal Recollections

> During a lunch on October 11, 1992, Kim Il Sung told a visiting U.S. Congressional delegation (I was the State Department escort officer) that he admired scholars. "Look at the symbol of the Korean Workers' Party," he told us. "Lenin made the hammer and sickle the symbol of his party." The aging Kim Il Sung, beaming with pride, claimed "I added the writing brush to the hammer and sickle. The Korean Workers' Party is the only communist party that reveres scholars."

Kim saw value in scholarship. He wanted his scholars to record the nation's history, preserve its cultural legacy, and teach this to future generations of Koreans. These activities, Kim believed, were of fundamental political value. Through approved scholarship and education, he would propagate nationalism and his juche thought.

The Korean Workers' Party (KWP)

Kim Il Sung and his son practice democratic centralism by controlling government and society through their political party, the Korean Workers' Party (KWP). The KWP is the leading political institution in the land. It controls the government and army. According to the KWP's charter, it "… is the vanguard organization of the working class and is the highest type of revolutionary body among all organizations of working masses."

The KWP claims three million members. Kim Jong Il was elected KWP general secretary in October 1997. Beneath him, the KWP has three principle levels: the Central Committee of the Politburo, the Politburo, and the Party Congress.

The Central Committee of the Politburo is the most powerful party organ. It elects the Party leadership, staffs its committees, and nominates candidates to fill top-ranking positions in the government. The Politburo—which Kim Sung Il's son, Kim Jong Il, chairs—is a council of policy advisers. The Party Congress has become defunct since none has been convened since 1980.

The Kim Dynasty

Kim Il Sung added his own twist to the Soviet brand of democratic centralism. Orthodox practice required that the communist Party elect its leader. Kim made succession hereditary, clearly a traditional Korean preference. His heir, Kim Jong Il, rationalized the decision, "The shift of generations will continue in the process of the communist movement. Under these conditions, the revolutionary task of the working class should be inherited generation after generation in order to guarantee the permanent leadership of the Party. Our succession plan has succeeded in resolving these problems ...." As of October 2003, Kim Jong Il has not formally designated his heir apparent.

Token Parties

North Korea also has two other tiny political parties:

♦ The Social Democratic Party was formed by small businessmen, craftsmen, and Christians in 1945; the membership subsequently recognized the KWP's dominate political role. This small group affords unofficial channels of communication with foreign counterparts in Europe.

♦ Chondoist Chongu Party was founded by a group of Chondo (Tonghak, see Chapter 6) followers in 1946. The party subscribes fully to the KWP's ideology and platform. This splinter party's primary role, as a member of the Democratic Front for the Reunification of the Fatherland, is to provide unofficial and informal channels of communication to counterpart groups in South Korea.

The Government

The KWP dominates all organs of government. Its main components are the National Defense Commission, the State Administrative Council or Cabinet, the Supreme People's Assembly, and the Judiciary.

National Defense Commission

In the wake of the September 1998 constitutional reforms, Kim Jong Il proclaimed his father "eternal president" of the DPRK. He then assumed the chairmanship of the National Defense Commission (NDC). Kim then filled the NDC's 10 remaining positions with 7 top generals and 3 ranking civilians.

Kim's reform of government in 1998 concentrated political, administrative, and military power in a single entity. The NDC became the preeminent policy-making body. The Constitution, however, continues to state that the NDC "is the highest military leading organ of State power and an organ for general control over national defense." In his new position as chairman of the NDC, Kim declared in September 1998, his "Military First Policy," which has continued unaltered ever since.

The Supreme People's Assembly

The Supreme People's Assembly (SPA) is the government's legislative organ. According to the constitution, it is the "highest organ of state power." In terms of political reality, the SPA serves as Kim Jong Il's rubber stamp for the annual national budget.

The tenth and most recent SPA election was held in July 1998. Its 687 representatives were elected to a five-year term of office; 11 percent, or 75 members, are lieutenant generals or higher ranks in the armed forces. This is a significant increase over the number of high-ranking officers in previous SPAs.

SPA elections are a formality. Voters can indicate either "yes" or "no" for KWP-nominated candidates. There is no option to write in another candidate. Each electoral district has about 50,000 residents. Voter turn out is usually 100 percent, and each candidate usually receives 100-percent approval.

The SPA's primary responsibility is to review the annual national budget proposal. To expedite this process, the 1998 constitution sanctions the convening of executive meetings of the SPA Presidium (an executive council of SPA members). The nation's number-two civilian official, Premiere Kim Yong-nam, chairs the Presidium, but reports to Kim Jong Il. Other members include 2 vice chairmen, a secretary, 4 honorary vice chairmen, and 11 additional representatives from the nominal political parties and other mass political organizations.

The Cabinet

The 1998 reforms designated the Cabinet responsible for oversight of national policy implementation. The Cabinet is staffed with loyal KWP officials having some administrative and technical expertise. There are 1 premier, 2 deputy premiers, 27 ministers, and 4 directors of key state institutions. The eight provincial governors and mayors of special administrative districts also are members of the cabinet. The Cabinet and provincial administrators are responsible for the implementation of policy. They do not appear to have much say, if any, in its formulation.

The Judiciary

The judicial system consists of two elements: courts and prosecutors. A hierarchy of the courts extends down from the Central Court in the capital to provincial and special municipal courts outside Pyongyang. There are separate Military and Traffic and Transportation courts.

The Central Court appoints all subordinate justices. The courts, per the constitution, are to protect the "State power and the socialist system." Individual political and other rights are not a concern.

The Supreme People's Assembly elects the prosecutor-general. He or she serves in the Central Prosecutors' Office in Pyongyang and appoints all subordinate prosecutors. Prosecutors are assigned to each court. Prosecutors, according to the constitution, are to "expose and institute legal proceedings against criminals and offenders … to protect the State power …, the socialist system, the property of the State and social, cooperative organizations and personal rights …."

The following table presents an overview of the North Korean government and its representatives.

North Korea's Government at a Glance

Government	Representatives
Korean Workers' Party (KWP)	Kim Jong Il (1)* (General Secretary)
Politburo Presidium	Kim Jong Il (1) Li Jong-ok (3) Pak Song-chol (4) Kim Yong-ju (5) Kim Yong-nam (2) Kye Ung-dae (15) Chon Pyong-ho (12) Han Song-ryong (16)
Supreme People's Assembly (SPA)	Kim Yong-nam (2) (Chairman, SPA Presidium)
The Cabinet National Defense Judiciary Commission (NDC)	Kim Jong Il (1)
People's Army	Kim Jong Il (1) (Chairman) Supreme Commander Cho Myong-rok (7) (Vice Chairman) Kim Yong-jun (8) (Vice Marshal)

*Protocol rank

The Least You Need to Know

♦ The name for communism as practiced in North Korea is juche, Kim Il Sung's interpretation of Marxism that emphasizes nationalism and man as the prime mover of nature.

♦ The Korean Workers' Party (KWP), North Korea's communist party, has three million members and dominates all aspects of the government and society.

♦ Kim Jong Il rules North Korea by holding the positions of secretary general of the Korean Workers' Party and chairman of the National Defense Commission, which controls the armed forces.

♦ The judicial system's primary role is to protect the "State and socialist system."

Chapter 11

North Korean Society

In This Chapter

- ◆ The haves and have-nots
- ◆ Clans, kinsmen, and communists
- ◆ Cultural remnants
- ◆ Internal control—secret police and informers

In this chapter, we look behind the veil of secrecy that has long prevented us from better understanding North Korea. We will look beyond the illusions and seek out the realities of life in North Korea. As we shall see, the gap between reality and illusion is profound.

For decades, Kim Il Sung painted the veil of secrecy with glossy photographs of smiling, well-fed and well-dressed North Koreans. This was the illusion he wanted us to see and to believe accurately depicted his version of a "socialist paradise." Similarly, our description of North Korea's political ideology and institutions in the previous chapter, while hopefully objective, is rather academic. It, too, tends to depict the fiction that North Korea is an orderly and efficiently governed society. Although the depiction of juche thought and political institutions is generally accurate, the overall impression of North Korean society remains similar to that of a retouched photograph, an illusion.

Keeping Order

To understand North Korea, you must enter it, encounter the government's frigid aloofness toward human beings, and experience the people's quiet agony. Here we will try to help you achieve this mentally. On this virtual journey into North Korea, you will quickly discover it is anything but a "workers' paradise." Communism promised a utopia without bureaucracy where all were treated equally and shared everything equally. North Korea's Kim dynasty created the exact opposite: a highly stratified society dominated by the twin bureaucracies of the government and communist party in which equality and egalitarianism do not exist. As for human rights, they are considered subversive to North Korea's primary political priorities: subordination to the leader's will and conformity to his thought. We will have more to say about human rights in Chapter 23.

Kim Il Sung's "Ten Commandments"

Kim Il Sung spelled out 10 rules that govern the conduct of those who wish to become and remain members of his political party, Korean Workers' Party. These rules appear in the party's charter under the title: Ten Point Principle for Solidifying the Party's Monolithic Ideological System:

1. All society must be dyed with Kim Il Sung's revolutionary ideology (that is, juche).

2. Kim Il Sung must be upheld with unswerving loyalty.

3. Kim Il Sung's authority must be made absolute.

4. Kim Il Sung's revolutionary thought must be regarded as the people's belief, and his instructions as their creed.

5. The principle of unconditional loyalty must be observed in carrying out Kim Il Sung's instructions.

6. The Party's ideological unity and revolutionary solidarity, with Kim Il Sung at the center, must be strengthened.

7. Party members must emulate Kim Il Sung and equip themselves with his Communist personality and revolutionary working methods.

8. Party members must retain the political life given to them by Kim Il Sung and return his political confidence in them with loyalty.

9. The entire Party, nation, and armed forces must establish strict discipline to behave uniformly under the monolithic leadership of Kim Il Sung.

10. The revolutionary task initiated by Kim Il Sung must be inherited and perfected generation after generation. This principle, which in fact reigns over the constitution, is regarded as the most important norm contributing to the monolithic leadership of the Suryong (that is, Kim Il Sung and Kim Jang Il).

Rank's Privileges

Hierarchy and privilege encompass all. Rank and status are everything in North Korea. Males take precedence over females, Pyongyang's residents enjoy the best of everything available, while those in other cities take what they can and share the remainder with rural residents. Party and military officials lord over all others. Each of these categories is further stratified according to occupation.

This stratification becomes apparent as soon as we board an Air Koryo flight in Beijing bound for Pyongyang. The Soviet-period TU164 has three curtain-divided sections that separate classes of service: first, business, and "the masses." Ranking North Korean Party and military officials enjoy first class. Lesser ranking officials and delegations from "friendly" countries travel in business class. U.S. citizens always enjoy being among the "masses." Actually, the "masses" are rank-and-file members of the Korean Workers' Party. Average North Korean citizens are not allowed to travel abroad.

At Pyongyang International Airport, one of the world's quietest since there is only a single daily arrival and departure to and from Beijing, we are surrounded by status symbols. The high and mighty quickly disappear into the VIP side of the terminal, step into their black Mercedes, and speed off toward Pyongyang. The rest of us patiently join the masses as we pass through immigration and wait for our luggage.

Sex as Status

Sex is the first great divider. Males always take precedent over females. Men in the cities and on the farms operate important equipment and all the vehicles. Women operate small machines, like those used in textile plants. Men handle trucks, tanks, trains, airplanes, and so on. Never does one see a woman driving any vehicle, not even a lowly farm tractor. The only exception was in soap operas. Occasionally a heroic woman drove a truck on television. But this was more fantasy than reality.

Urban and rural women carry or drag everything. Their heavy loads are balanced on their heads, carried in backpacks, or pulled in small carts. Men rarely carry anything heavy. Usually they have access to a truck or tractor.

City Versus Farm

Pyongyang has the best of everything. Access to living and working in Pyongyang is a carefully managed privilege. The capital's inhabitants have the best working and living conditions, salary, and access to food, education, and medical care. Residents of large cities outside Pyongyang enjoy similar but inferior privileges.

Among urban residents, one's position in the Party, army, and bureaucracy determine the quality, location, and size of one's living quarters. Salaries are pegged to the leadership's perceived value of an official's contribution to achieving his objectives. Children's eligibility to enroll in elite schools is determined by the status of one's parents, not on the child's demonstrated academic ability.

In Pyongyang, office workers may carry a briefcase to and from the office. Most commute via bus, trolley, or the metro. A few have bicycles, and only the privileged have access to cars.

City dwellers rank above people in rural areas. Blue collar factory workers are better off than their colleagues on the farm. Their pay, clothing, living quarters, food, and access to education and medical treatment are far superior to rural residents.

People on the farm literally struggle to survive. They work long, hard hours trying to fulfill government quotas for grain production. Over the past three decades, scarce government funds have been poured into the development of weapons of mass destruction, monuments to Kim Il Sung, and expressways to the leadership's favorite resorts. Meanwhile, the production of fertilizer lagged, and farm equipment and the irrigation system fell into disrepair.

From Black to Blue: Uniform Attire

Everywhere, there are visible indications of a preoccupation with privilege. The clothing one wears, its style and color, reveals status and authority. Ranking Party and government officials wear dark business suits decorated with a Kim Il Sung badge. Their black hair is always combed straight back. Often they wear dark or tinted eyeglasses. Their aides open doors for them and carry everything they might need.

Rank-and-file Party and civil officials prefer gray attire. In the summer, this means wearing a gray short sleeve shirt and slacks. In fall and spring, a gray "Eisenhower" jacket is added. Winter attire is usually a gray topcoat. These rank-and-file officials always live in cities, never in rural areas.

Next come uniformed personnel: the army, air force, navy, police, and drivers. Each group has its own hierarchy as displayed by its symbols of rank. Korean People Army uniforms are olive drab with red collar insignia. Air Force uniforms are black and sailors wear dark blue. Police uniforms are identified by yellow collar insignia and epaulets. Somewhat surprisingly, these military uniforms are replicas of those worn by the Imperial Japanese armed forces.

Increase Your North Korea IQ

Members of the KWP usually wear a "Kim Il Sung" badge. This is either a small colored portrait or a photograph of Kim Il Sung surrounded either by a gold wreath or a red background. It came into vogue during his life to display publicly one's loyalty to him. After his death in 1994, Party members continue to wear the badges in recognition of his heir Kim Jong Il's designation of his father as the nation's "eternal president." Similar badges of Mao Zedong were worn for the same political reason in China.

Kim Il Sung bestowed a special elite status on all men who operate vehicles—airplanes, trains, cars, trucks, and so on. The practice began during the Korean War when U.S. bombing made the driving of supply trucks a very dangerous occupation. To encourage men to volunteer as drivers, Kim awarded them special status, pay, and privileges. This practice continues. The drivers wear distinctive attire. Railroad workers dress in light gray uniforms; pilots, in black. Chauffeurs wear olive drab or light gray Eisenhower jackets and slacks.

Outside Pyongyang, the dress code changes dramatically. Persons who work with their hands in factories to operate or to maintain machines rank beneath office workers and drivers, but above farm workers. In this occupational area, males and females appear to share generally equal status. Accordingly, they both literally wear blue-collar shirts and trousers.

Personal Recollections

Riding a car in North Korea can be a frightening experience. There are no speed limits outside Pyongyang. Drivers speed everywhere, regardless of road conditions. Cars assigned to foreigners are often aging Japanese models with worn-out tires. I finally figured out the preference for excessive speed. All drivers smoke cigarettes, but smoking is not allowed while driving. To induce safety, I offered a pack of American cigarettes if we safely reached our destination. This usually kept the speed tolerable, even though still excessive.

A few women are permitted to wear uniforms. Those who do generally are in Pyongyang and young and attractive. They are police who project gentleness in their impeccably tailored, pastel blue uniforms. They direct traffic in Pyongyang's busiest intersections and maintain order at subway stations and in the airport. Macho males tremble before their glare. They know that these policewomen can send them to jail for disobedience and disrespect.

Students have status, and all wear uniforms. For males, the uniforms are dark navy blue with high collars and brass buttons. They are identical to those South Korean students wore until late in the twentieth century. All male Korean student uniforms are patterned after those worn by the Imperial Japanese Navy. Hair is always cut short. Female students wear dark navy blue shirts with white blouses. The skirts reach below the knee and the hair touches the bottom of the ear.

— Personal Recollections —

Occasionally North Korean drivers get confused while chauffeuring foreign visitors. They might think they can get away with an illegal U-turn. Not true. Three times an attractive but stern-faced young policewoman stopped my car. Each time the "guide" allowed her to complete her blistering lecture to the driver. Then she whispered to the driver that some money for makeup might resolve the matter. It did, and we promptly sped from the scene.

At the Bottom

Farm workers are clearly at the bottom. But even they have their own pyramid. The further removed from Pyongyang, the harsher the living conditions.

The most fertile farmland and the best farm equipment and housing are reserved for the rural population living south and southwest of Pyongyang. Before 1945, wealthy Koreans owned large tracts of rice paddies in this region. They were expelled and their land turned over to their former tenants during the land reform carried out between 1945 and 1955.

Farmers residing in the vicinity surrounding Pyongyang to the east, west, and north share similar advantages with their colleagues in the southwest.

After the Korean War, individuals having kinsmen in South Korea were expelled from the cities and assigned to work in the numerous mines in the far northeast or cultivate corn in the rocky soil of the northwest. Their living conditions are the worst of all.

Big Wheels, Little Wheels

Air and train travel are reserved for government officials and the military. None but a tiny minority rides in cars. Beneath them come a small number who can afford bicycles. In Pyongyang, the masses pack onto buses, trolleys, and the subway. Beyond Pyongyang, people either catch rides in dump trucks or tractor-pulled carts, or they walk.

Cars are a key indicator of power and status. The color, darkness of the rear windows, make and year of the car, and its license plate broadcast one's status. Black is reserved for the highest ranks, who prefer Mercedes Benz. In recent years, however, large Japanese Lexus and BMW sedans have become popular. Official visitors ride in rusty red and aging Mercedes or gray-colored, older model Japanese cars.

License plates indicate to check-point guards and traffic police the status of a car's occupants. A red star on a white background indicates an official State visitor. These cars roar past everything. Military and civilian officials have different color license plates. Generals never get stopped, but all others are treated equally.

Traditional Despotism

Proximity to political power determines status and wealth. Kinship ties to the powerful elevate one to the pinnacle of power. Those lacking kinship and political ties to the top fall into society's lower social and economic strata. This pyramid of power and prestige became rigid after the Korean War.

This has more in common with traditional Yi Choson society (see Chapters 5 and 6) than Marx's communist utopia. The hereditary monarchy of Kim Il Sung and his son Kim Jong Il today rule North Korea. Just as Kim Il Sung designated his son heir in 1980 and groomed him to lead the nation, Kim Jong Il is expected to designate one of his sons heir.

Nepotism in the Kim Dynasty

Nepotism is practiced with little restraint in Korea, both past and present, North and South. Kim Il Sung continued this established practice. All the members of his immediate family enjoyed prestige and received official titles and positions:

◆ Kim Il Sung (1912–1994) and his wife, Kim Chong-suk (1919–1949), had two sons and one daughter. Their first born, and only surviving son Jong Il, now rules North Korea. His younger brother Tong-il (Russian name Shura, 1944–1947) was born in Khabarovsk in the Soviet Union but drowned at the age of four. A second brother died at birth in 1949. Kim Jong Il's younger sister Kyong-hui, born in 1946, married Chang Song-t'aek. She became a prominent official in the Korean Workers' Party and served as the Minister of Light Industry. Her husband was elected to the KWP Central Committee and often handled large business transactions for the family. Their son Chang Kim-song studied in Sweden in the late 1990s.

♦ Kim Il Sung's second wife, Kim Song Ae (born 1924), had three children: daughter Kyong-jin (or Kyong-il, born 1951), son Pyong-il (born 1953), and son Yong-il (born 1955). Daughter Kyong-jin's husband Kim Kwang-sop (born 1949) served as ambassador to Austria. Son Pyong-il was ambassador to Finland. The youngest son, Yong-il, reportedly had a serious drinking problem and did not receive an official appointment.

♦ Kim Il Sung had two younger brothers: Chol-chu, who died in 1935, and Yong-chu, born in 1922. Kim Yong-chu participated in Kim Il Sung's anti-Japanese activities in Manchuria and then went to the Soviet Union in 1941. After 1945, he graduated from Moscow University with a degree in politics and economy. Kim Yong-chu helped his older brother purge the Korean Workers' Party of members from South Korea. He was elected to the Party's Central Committee in 1961, and in 1972 signed the first ever North-South Joint Statement, which has become the cornerstone for dialogue between the two Koreas. But in 1974, when Kim Il Song designated his son Jong Il heir apparent, younger brother Yong-chu left the Party and his prominence declined. Kim Yong-chu eventually made a partial political comeback in 1993, but never recovered his former stature. Rumor has it that his relationship with nephew Kim Jong Il remains contentious.

♦ Kim Il Sung's youngest sister Kim Hyong-sil had three daughters: Chong-suk, Sin-suk, and a third, who died an unnamed infant. Kim Chong-suk (same name as Kim Jong-Il's mother) married Ho Tam, a prominent official who rose to foreign minister but is now deceased. The second daughter, Kim Sin-suk (died 1986), married Yang Hyong-sop (1925–). He studied in the Soviet Union with Kim Yong-chu, Kim Il Sung's younger brother. Returning home, Yang became successful in education and in 1961 was appointed head of the KWP Central Party School, and then in 1967 minister of education. Yang's career peaked with his election as chairman of the Supreme People's Assembly. Little is known about Kim Hyong-sil's youngest daughter.

Kim Jong Il's Family

Kim Jong Il reportedly married twice and experts agree that he has had more than one mistress. His first wife, Song Hye-nim (1937–2002), was an actress when she met Kim Jong Il. At the time she starred in the North Korean film *Village at the Demarcation Line*, a reference to the DMZ. Married at the time, she sent her husband to France. Then she married Kim Jong Il. She gave birth to their first son, Kim Chong-nam (spelled Jong Nam in North Korea), in 1971.

Song Hye-nim (spelled Song Hye Rim in North Korea) later moved to Moscow, for reasons still unclear, where she died. Her niece and nephew defected to France after her death. They quickly became the source of numerous tales about Kim Jong Il. But the nephew was soon found murdered in South Korea, allegedly at the hands of North Korean agents.

According to South Korean press reports, Kim Jong Il married his mistresses Kim Yong-suk (also spelled Young-sook) who was born about 1947. She gave birth to a daughter, Kim Sol-song (also spelled Seol Song), who was born in 1974.

Kim Jong Il's current wife is the former dancer Ko Yong-hui. She gave birth to their son, Chong Chol, who was born in 1981.

The female president of Kim Hyong-jik College of Education, Hong Il-chon, also was Kim Jong Il's mistress. They reportedly had a daughter named Kim Hye-kyong who was born in 1968.

The Former Heir Apparent

Little is known about Kim Jong Il's first born son Chong-nam (Jong Nam). He briefly garnered international attention in 2001 when he was seized at Tokyo's Narita Airport for trying to enter the country under a false name and using a counterfeit Dominican Republic passport. The 30-year-old Jong Nam was accompanied by two women and a 4-year-old boy. He identified one of the women as his wife and the other as the "nanny" for his son, the young boy. At the time he was wearing a Rolex watch, a favorite gift Kim Jong Il gives those close to him, and had a pocket full of U.S. currency. He lamely explained that he wanted to visit Tokyo's Disneyland. The Japanese government promptly put them on an airplane back to Beijing.

North Korea's New Aristocracy

Kim Il Sung also formed a new aristocracy after Korea's liberation from Japanese rule in 1945. Their descendants now enjoy preferential treatment and access to power and prestige in North Korea. Many hold top positions in Kim's party, army, and bureaucracy. Their primary credentials are kinship ties to Kim Jong Il or his immediate family, and to the families of those that Kim Il Sung anointed "martyrs" and "heroes" of the "anti-imperialist struggles" against Japan and the United States.

Yi Choson's founder, a general, had established such a similar aristocracy after seizing power in 1392. He awarded his most trusted supporters the title of "Merit Subject" and bestowed upon them hereditary access to land and its produce. This reinforced their loyalty to him and ensured their future economic well being. It also enabled

Merit Subjects' sons to compete in the dynasty's civil and military service examinations, thus perpetuating their fathers' access to power and prestige.

Traces of Imperial Japan

Kim Il Sung's priority was consolidating his power, not just resurrecting Korean traditions. In his new dynasty we also find some parallels with Imperial Japan. Some of the more obvious similarities are the accent on a nationalistic ideology (North Korea's juche and Imperial Japan's *kokutai* or national essence), and reverence for a single, almighty, godlike leader (that is to say, Kim Il Sung the "Great Leader" versus Japan's emperor). Both North Korea and Imperial Japan relied on intrusive police and political associations to control society and monitor political attitudes.

Kim Il Sung's personality cult can be traced back to Imperial Japan. The similarities between the homage Japanese paid their emperor prior to World War II certainly approach what North Koreans showered upon Kim Il Sung. Both Japan's Imperial Army and Kim's followers endowed their leaders with superhuman attributes. Photographs of Japanese Emperor Hirohito appeared in official buildings and schools throughout the land. Students, civil servants, and soldiers began their day by bowing low to their emperor's picture.

Personal Recollections

Hundreds of thousands of North Koreans flocked to the foot of Kim Il Sung's huge statue in front of Pyongyang's massive Museum of the Revolution after his death on July 8, 1994. They wailed as they bowed and placed flowers at his feet. This continued for months. Even now, North Koreans returning from trips abroad carry flowers from Beijing so they can go directly from the airport to his statue to demonstrate their loyalty to him before going home.

Once my North Korean escort chastised me and threatened to seize my camera because I had taken a photograph from behind Kim Il Sung's statue. Unknown to me, it is inappropriate to photograph the "Great Leader's" backside.

In North Korea since after the Korean War, Kim Il Sung's picture was hung on the wall of every room in every official building throughout the land. Today his son Kim Jong Il's picture is similarly displayed next to his father's. North Koreans, like the Japanese of Imperial Japan, begin their day bowing to the pictures of the two Kims.

In Imperial Japan there were no statues of the emperor. In North Korea, there is a towering statue of Kim Il Sung in the center of every town. The tallest of them stands on the highest hill in central Pyongyang. It is an enormous bronze likeness. Positioned in front of the entrance to the Museum of the Revolution, Kim faces east. His right hand and arm are raised high in salute to the rising sun.

Where's Stalin?

Despite these prominent similarities to Yi Choson Korea and Imperial Japan, North Korea continues to be labeled "Stalinist." Nowhere is a picture or statue of Stalin visible. The only pictures of Marx and Engels hang from the facade of the Korean Workers' Party headquarters in Kim Il Sung Square.

Undoubtedly there are similarities, particularly the structure and role of the Korean Workers' Party. The army's tactics and equipment owe much to the Soviet Union. Still, the uniforms are replicas of those worn by the Imperial Japanese Army. For decades, economic planning owed much to Soviet economic advisers. But they have long since fallen into the dustbin of history because of North Korea's economic impotency.

Visually, Pyongyang's owes much to its Soviet-period sister city of Moscow. Pyong-yang's architecture is a mirror image of gray concrete and aesthetically lifeless Soviet architecture. Pyongyang's subway also owes much to Moscow's metro. The stations are decorated with crystal chandeliers and huge mosaics that depict the accomplish-ments of Kim Il Sung, soldiers, and workers.

Personal Recollections

I rode Pyongyang's subway and lived to tell the tale. At the station, a police-woman greeted me, "Where are you going?" Instantly, I forgot my Korean, handed her the fare, and responded in English, "I do not understand." Wearing a perplexed grimace, she waved me past. The deep station smelled of mildew and unwashed bodies. Everyone stared at the "big nose," Korean slang for Caucasian.

After a while, I realized I was lost. I asked a young woman in Korean how to get back to my hotel, and she answered, "Are you Russian?" "No," I said, "I'm an American." Wow! Mothers grabbed their children and moved to the far end of the car. But the young woman looked me in the eye, and in perfect English said, "The sol-dier following you will lead you back to your hotel."

At my hotel room there was a loud banging on my door. It was my usually calm but now agitated "guide." He said I was lucky to be alive because, he claimed, the North Korean people might have torn me apart had they known I was an "American imperialist." Grinning, he told me many people had reported a white haired, polite, and Korean-speaking "spy" loose on the subway.

Keeping the Masses Faithful

Obviously, only the minority of North Koreans in the KWP (3 million plus family members) benefit from the regime's "carrots" far more than the majority of about 18 million non-KWP citizens. Even if we add the one million soldiers to the KWP's three million, the "have-nots" far out number the "haves." Keeping this majority faithful to the regime is the work of the KWP-managed "mass" political organizations backed by internal security agencies. The foremost mass organizations are …

◆ The Democratic Front for the Reunification of the Fatherland. Formed in July 1946, this is an umbrella organization whose goal is to forge a "worker-peasant" alliance for the promotion of "peaceful" national reunification. Occasionally it serves as a government "front," issuing highly critical and stridently worded messages designed to encourage South Koreans to criticize their government's leaders and policies. North Korea's government can conveniently blame these caustic outburst on the "Front."

◆ Kim Il Sung Socialist Youth League. Its predecessor, the Democratic Youth League, was established on January 17, 1946, as a "militant" youth organization "to carry forward the Korean revolution." After a purge of the organization's leadership in 1995, Kim Jong Il gave it its current name. The organization's five million members serve as the KWP's reserve and recruiting ground.

◆ Korean General Federation of Trade Unions. The Federation is a mass political organization of urban workers. Founded in November 1945, it educates workers in the juche ideology. The Union of Agricultural Workers does the same for the rural population. Both unions also promote the three revolutions of ideology, technology, and culture. The Democratic Women's Union specializes in the education of working women in the juche ideology.

The KWP's penetration of society and professional organizations is all encompassing. The KWP's message and ideology is promoted through these additional mass organizations:

◆ Committee for the Peaceful Reunification of the Fatherland

◆ Journalists Union

◆ General Federation of the Unions of Literature and Art of Korea

◆ National Peace Committee

◆ Democratic Lawyers Association

- Students Committee

- Committee for Solidarity with the World's People

- Committee for Afro-Asian Solidarity

- The separate federations for Buddhists, Christians, Catholics, and followers of the indigenous Chondoist Church

Cracking the Whip

If inducements, education, and social pressure fall short of their intended purpose, the State Security Agency and the Public Security Ministry go to work. These are the regime's enforcers.

State Security Agency

This is North Korea's so-called "secret police" agency. It is subordinate to the National Defense Commission (NDC, see Chapter 10). The State Security Agency (SSA) has primary responsibility for monitoring citizens' political behavior as outlined in the Ten Point Principle for Solidifying the Party's Monolithic Ideological System. (see the beginning of this chapter). Kim Jong Il's personal security is in its hands.

The SSA monitors everyone, including the activities and comments of ranking Party, military, and government officials. Its Communications Interception Bureau was created to intercept, monitor, and decrypt domestic and foreign electronic communications.

The Agency oversees the nation's political prison system which houses an estimated 200,000 people imprisoned in 12 "special districts."

The SSA also conducts covert overseas operations. These included North Korea's previous acts of terrorism against South Korea and the kidnapping of at least 20 or more Japanese citizens. Through "front" trading companies, the SSA also deals in narcotics smuggling and counterfeiting.

Ministry of Public Security

The Ministry of Public Security (MPS) supervises the national police and civil defense. While it shares with the SSA responsibility for political surveillance, anyone its officers investigate or seize for political reasons is turned over to the SSA. The Ministry's staff size is estimated at about 130,000 persons, including administration and law enforcement.

The Least You Need to Know

- ◆ North Korean society is a rigid pyramid that has more in common with traditional Korean society than an egalitarian communist utopia.

- ◆ Order is maintained through a "carrot and stick" strategy. Faithful followers and their descendants receive rank and privilege. Persons of dubious political background struggle to survive at the bottom of society.

- ◆ The State Security Agency and officers of the Ministry of Public Security monitor everyone's words and deeds to enforce compliance with the dictates of the regime's leadership.

Chapter 12

Education: Managing the Minds of the People

In This Chapter

- ◆ Revising reality
- ◆ Institutions of learning
- ◆ Models and museums
- ◆ Media for the masses

Describing North Korea as a "Stalinist" state has distorted our image of North Korea. "Stalinist" brings to mind images of Stalin: a stern-faced, ruthless dictator whose power was based on the population's fear of him. He enforced his rule through brutal torture, massive purges, and banishment to frigid Siberian gulags.

Kim Il Sung likewise relied on ruthlessness to consolidate and to perpetuate his despotic power. But once in power, he developed more sophisticated techniques to manage the North Korean people. Some of these techniques are discussed in Chapter 10, specifically his "carrot and stick" strategy. In this chapter, we examine the Kim dynasty's use of education to manage the masses.

Manipulating Reality

North Korea is also often described as a "police state," but one of its more surprising aspects is the scarcity of armed men in urban areas. Few are to be seen at the airport. Armed soldiers once manned checkpoints on the main roads that lead into the capital. This practice continues except that the check point on the road between the Pyong-yang International Airport and the capital has been closed. Inside Pyongyang there is an abundance of uniformed personnel. Most of them are soldiers on leave. None carry weapons.

The Fiction of Armed Personnel

Armed men are a rarer sight in Pyongyang than in Seoul. A few sentries with rifles guard the entrance to the massive walled compound in central Pyongyang where the elite reside. A half dozen sentries are posted near the Supreme People's Assembly building and the Koryo Hotel, the aging main tourist hotel. A single policeman with a pistol can be spotted at crowded bus stops and subway stations. Then there are the traffic control police, who are attractive young women. They, too, are not armed.

Personal Recollections

While living and working at North Korea's Yongbyon Nuclear Research Center, I kept a diary of my daily observations. To avoid suspicion, I left it open on the desk in my guesthouse room just in case one of my "guides" was curious. One day I recorded seeing "young women carrying rifles." The next morning, after breakfast, my guide approached me and asked why I had written such an "inappropriate" statement. He said my journal would be seized and destroyed if I did not cross out the offensive passage. I explained I wanted an accurate record so other Americans would know what to expect in North Korea. He relented. I continued my writing but kept a small notebook of "sensitive" thoughts and observations tucked under my shirt to avoid future harassment. A few years later, the U.S. Federal Bureau of Investigation (FBI) seized my notebooks and examined every page for classified information. They found none, but left their evidence number on every page.

In the countryside, armed personnel are an even rarer sight. Headed south toward the DMZ, you are certain to spot armed soldiers training in the hills or walking beside country lanes. But the massive fortifications and huge army manning the northern side of the DMZ are all but invisible in the vicinity of Kaesong and Panmunjom.

North of Pyongyang, armed soldiers and police are as scarce. Virtually all the uniformed men you see are either on leave or working with labor battalions. Not until you reach the boundary of the Yongbyon Nuclear Research Center are armed soldiers visible.

The invisibility of armed men in North Korea is a carefully crafted illusion. North Korea is in fact a "police state." Yet having 100,000 police officers is not excessive for a population of 23 million people. Instead, North Koreans are trained to subordinate themselves to authority. Otherwise, punishment for not doing so will be swift and severe.

Confucius in a Juche Jacket

Education is central to the Kim dynasty's rule of North Korea. The North Korean people are educated from cradle to grave to follow their "great" leaders, Kim Il Sung and Kim Jong Il. As in all societies, education begins at home. North Korean parents raise their children to recognize the difference between good and bad.

North Korean parents combine traditional Confucian values with political realism when distinguishing between "good" and "bad." This renders definitions that are radically different from those of most other modern societies.

Confucius taught that all men of virtue must contribute to social harmony: humanity's foremost goal. Social harmony requires adhering to five basic relationships: ruler and subject, husband and wife, father and son, older brother and younger brother, and friend to friend.

Kim Jong Il's reverence for his father is rooted in the third of these relationships: father and son. Of course, respecting his father also has a bountiful political benefit for Kim Jong Il. It legitimizes his rule.

North Korean parents emphasize Confucius's first relationship, ruler and subject, to their children because this also has multiple benefits for the family unit. "Good" means revering "the Great Leader" because this will merit the family basic human needs (food and shelter) plus income, education, and medical treatment. "Bad" means not following the leader, which brings misfortune and possibly even imprisonment to the family.

Imbued with this basic moral frame of mind, children march off to school for formal education.

"Brainwashing" and "Reeducation"

Since the Korean War, the North Korean government has been associated with so-called "brainwashing." This colorful phrase suggests the use of techniques to cleanse one's mind of past images so that they can be replaced with politically preferred ones.

Increase Your North Korea IQ

The experiences of U.S. POWs from the Korean War, and the popular movie *The Manchurian Candidate*, imprinted vivid images of "brainwashing" upon the American public's mind. North Korean and Chinese interrogators did employ brutal torture to induce POWs to sign confessions that claimed the United States employed germ warfare and other internationally outlawed methods. Torture, however, is not a Korean invention. The methods used on U.S. POWs closely resembled those that the Imperial Japanese police and military used while the Imperial Japanese Empire ruled much of East Asia from 1904 to 1945. China, like North Korea and Vietnam, still uses torture. The authoritarian regimes that once ruled Indonesia, the Philippines, Taiwan, and South Korea between 1948 and 1990 employed similar "brainwashing" torture.

Soon after Korea's liberation in 1945, and even before North Korea's establishment in 1948, Kim Il Sung's regime launched mass movements to purge society and people's minds of "capitalistic" tendencies. The process included so-called land reform. Land was seized from its owners and redistributed to former tenants. Private businesses were seized and "nationalized," that is, taken over by the government.

Property owners who resisted either fled to South Korea or were sent to "reeducation" camps. There they endured mentally and physically abusive treatment intended to "wash" out old, politically incorrect attitudes and convert them to views more consistent with socialism. Reeducation camps still exist, but their inhabitants are temporary residents and relatively few in number, who usually return to society within a few months.

Mind-Molding Mission

Education has long been held in high esteem in Korean society. For almost a millennium, the demonstration of literacy in the civil and military examinations was mandatory for appointment to government office.

Kim Il Sung perpetuated this concept but changed the role and definition of education. He gradually forged North Korea's educational system into a tool for the Korean Workers' Party (KWP) to train young minds to defend and revere the State and its leaders, Kim Il Sung and now Kim Jong Il.

The process paralleled Kim Il Sung's consolidation of power. After liberation from Japan in 1945, the emerging North Korean government made patriotism, anti-Japanese sentiment, and respect for Marxism-Leninism core elements of education. Immediately after the Korean War, when Kim Il Sung emerged as the clear victor in the factional disputes, juche emerged for the first time to counter Soviet and Chinese communism's "dogmatism and formalism." Anti-Americanism was added to patriotism and anti-Japanese sentiment. The supremacy of socialism and communism over capitalism continued as core themes, but with increasing emphasis on Kim Il Sung's still maturing ideas about juche.

By the 1970s, Juche had ripened into the state ideology. Kim Il Sung in his 1977 essay, "Thesis on Socialist Education," set forth four principles of education:

♦ KWP control of education

♦ Juche as education's center piece

♦ Revolutionary practice

♦ State support for education

The Party as Teacher

Henceforth, the KWP would have the first and last word on all educational matters. It would determine the national curricula and content of all textbooks, accredit schools, and train, hire, and fire all educators.

The educated man in North Korea is one who knows the nation's history, respects its culture, agrees fully with juche ideology, and pays unrestrained allegiance to Kim Il Sung and Kim Jong Il. The acquisition of specialized knowledge in all areas is of secondary importance.

Education is an all-encompassing, lifelong pursuit. Study in the classroom is only the beginning of the process. The KWP has a full tool chest for molding minds beyond school.

Compulsory and Special Education

North Korea's constitution mandates that everyone attend school for at least eleven years. This includes 1 year of preschool, 4 years of elementary, and 6 years of secondary education. North Korea claims a literacy rate of 99 percent.

North Korea has special schools for handicapped children, according to UN relief workers. This is contrary to widely circulated rumors. Altogether, according to DPRK government data dated 1998, there are 52 such schools with a resident population of 10,557 children ages 1 to 16 years old.

Basic Curriculum

The school year in North Korea is the same as in South Korea and Japan. There are two semesters. The first runs from April 1 to July 31 and is followed by a one month vacation. The second semester runs from September 1 to March 31, but with a 20-day winter vacation in December.

In kindergarten, children learn the Korean language, basic counting, arts and crafts, music, and "moral science." Students in primary school continue the kindergarten curriculum, but add mathematics, history, natural science, and physical education.

Secondary schools teach Korean literature, foreign language, history, geography, mathematics, science, basic electronics, arts, crafts, and "moral science" (juche). Specialized courses in reading the biographies of Kim Il Sung and Kim Jong Il are also required. In addition, male students learn to operate machine tools and females take home economics.

Beginning in 1994, the mandatory study of English replaced Russian, reflecting the demise of the Soviet Union and the diminished role for Russia in the North Korean economy. School officials said the change was made to enable students to expand their access to knowledge, particularly modern technology, more widely available in English-language publications. Russian and Chinese are still taught, but as electives.

Personal Recollections

In July 1996, a U.S. Army officer and I visited the Pyongyang high school that Kim Jong Il had attended. My friend asked if he could try out his English-teaching skills. Once he was at the blackboard, I announced in Korean that a U.S. Army officer would begin a lesson in the English language. To the amazement and disbelief of the North Korean teachers and officials watching, the students rushed forward to welcome him and to ask questions in English.

U.S. Army LTC Marty Wisda and author Quinones at Panmunjom to arrange return of a U.S. soldier's remains to the United States.

Textbooks

North Korea no longer makes its textbooks readily available to foreigners, not even South Koreans. Access was restricted after a full set of textbooks was given to South Korean officials in the early 1990s. The reason for this restriction is the negative depiction of South Korea, the United States, and Japan in the texts. For half a century, North Korea considered South Korea a "puppet" regime of the "American imperialists" and this is dutifully recounted in North Korean textbooks.

A South Korean analysis of key terms in textbooks used in grades one through six is revealing. Kim Il Sung is mentioned 744 times and anti-Japanese Korean patriotic fighters 44 times. The "socialist fatherland" appears 270 times, "revolution" 53 times. "American imperialists" are mentioned 139 times, "Japanese imperialists" 52 times, and the "enemy" 85 times.

Higher Education

In the early 1990s, the government operated 273 universities and colleges, and 576 advanced technical and specialized institutions. An estimated 314,000 students attend these schools. Pyongyang is the apex of this higher education pyramid. It hosts 30 universities and another 40 colleges.

Some universities specialized in preparing young people for careers in the party and government. Pyongyang University of Foreign Studies prepares diplomats, the staff of trading companies, and persons who will serve in intelligence agencies. Four out of the six U.S. soldiers who defected to North Korea between 1960 and 1980 teach English at this institution. One of these soldiers is married to a Japanese-language teacher, one of several Japanese citizens that North Korean agents kidnapped to North Korea prior to 1990.

The Mangyongdae Revolutionary School, which trains children of "revolutionary martyrs" for careers as political and military party officials, is also located in Pyongyang. The Kim Il Sung Higher Party School and Pyongyang Communist University prepare young people for careers in the KWP.

Increase Your North Korea IQ

Kim Il Sung University is the peak of the education pyramid. Located in east Pyongyang, it has 12,000 students in 15 departments staffed by 5,500 teachers and researchers. The library reportedly has two million books, more than Harvard University! Kim Chaek University of Technology is North Korea's equivalent of MIT. Located in central Pyongyang, it has 13,000 students, including foreign students.

Personal Recollections

I used to take long strolls by myself during my several visits to Pyongyang. In November 1994, I was in Pyongyang with the first U.S. delegation to visit North Korea's Nuclear Research Center. One morning I happened to spot the main gate of Kimchaek University. A couple of students in their college uniforms were chatting in the guard house so I asked if I could take a couple of pictures of the students as they lined up before classes. The students proved to be very friendly, and quite curious about me, and the United States. But then a fellow who had been following me yelled at the students to shut up and to send me away. I nicknamed this fellow my "guardian angel" because later he claimed he was only protecting me from the students!

University Curriculum

Kim Il Sung University's curriculum is followed by most North Korean institutions of higher learning. Graduation requires between 5,400 and 6,600 hours of formal study. On average, this means graduation requires 30 hours per week of study for four years. Half this time is spent studying one's area of specialization.

General education requirements include the study of KWP history (280 hours), history of the international communist movement (140 hours), Marxism-Leninism (200 hours), political economy (110 hours), and foreign language (320 hours). Rounding out the curriculum are 1,200 hours of military training.

Military Training

All students enrolled in elementary schools and higher in North Korea receive military training. This begins with two to four weeks a year of training in the Juvenile Corps for students in the third year of elementary school to middle school. Training "cultivates their fighting spirit" and prepares them for farm labor. This increases to six to eight weeks per year in the League of Socialist Student Corps for final year middle school to college. Their training focuses on educating the masses about the KWP's policies and prepares them to serve as armed reserve soldiers. An estimated 400,000 boys and 380,000 girls are enrolled in these programs.

College and university students are required to put in between 12 and 14 weeks of military training each year. KWP military officials conduct the training that prepares students to serve as junior reserve military officers in the event of a national emergency. More than 170,000 male and female students receive this training.

Labor Education

All students are also required to perform mandatory farm labor. They spend between three and five months a year planting rice, weeding fields, and harvesting crops. One day each week, all urban office workers, housewives, and students are required to perform manual labor either in the fields or repairing roads and other public works facilities such as irrigation ditches.

Graduation

Graduation does not end the educational process. If anything, it certifies that an individual has been taught to suppress his or her individuality and blend into the "masses." One's mind has been filled with the words, deeds, and images ordained by Kim Il Sung and his heir as acceptable in their domain. Habits have been forged which equip the individual to submit to authority and to render selfless service to the State and "Great Leader" without pausing to consider one's own interests.

After graduation, the State and Party reinforce classroom study and military and labor training with numerous field trips to monuments and museums. Additionally, individuals enroll in politically oriented professional organizations (see Chapter 10), and nationwide mass campaigns. At the same time, access to information on a daily basis via the mass media is restricted and manipulated.

Models to Emulate

The following list provides a glance at some of the more important so-called "historical" and "revolutionary" sites on every student and soldiers' field-trip itinerary.

- ◆ **Tomb of Tangun.** Kim Il Sung directed in 1993 that, "we must build the Tomb of Tangun, … our nation's father, splendidly to hand it down to posterity." (See Chapter 4 for more details on Tangun.) The tomb's location in North Korea southeast of Pyongyang suggests continuity, thus political legitimacy, from Tangun's legendary Choson kingdom, through the Koguryo kingdom to Kim Il Sung's dynasty. It contains 1,994 white stones arranged in a pyramid 22 meters high and 50 meters wide on each side, and construction was completed two days before Kim's death.

- ◆ **Tomb of King Tongmyong.** King Tongmyong was the founder of the Koguryo kingdom which ruled the northern half of the Korean Peninsula from 277 B.C.E. to 668 C.E. Kim Il Sung directed that the tomb be reconstructed in 1993, one year before his death. The site's displays suggest linkage between Kim Il Sung's rule of North Korea and the reign of his ancient predecessor. The tomb is about 25 miles (30 kilometers) east of Pyongyang.

♦ **Korean Revolution Museum.** This enormous, 54,000 square meter building containing 90 exhibition halls, depicts Kim Il Sung's version of his struggle against Japanese colonialism and rise to power. The exhibits are convincingly displayed in life size, colorfully and with numerous photographs and documents. A huge mural (70 meters long by 12.85 meters high) across the museum's facade depicts Mount Paektu (see Chapter 3).

♦ **Mangyongdae.** This village was Kim Il Sung's birthplace. All tours of Pyongyang start here. (See Chapter 8 for more details on this village.)

♦ **Grand Monument on Mansu Hill.** Directly in front of the Museum of the Revolution is a towering bronze statue of Kim Il Sung. He faces east toward the rising sun, his right arm raised in greeting. The figure is centered in a large square. Flanking the statue to the north and south are red stone flags, each 22.5 meters high and 50 meters long (the length of half a football field). Sculptured into each are the 119 figures of soldiers, workers, farmers, and students engaged in the "anti-Japanese" and "socialist revolution and construction" struggle.

Mansu Hill is the highest spot in central Pyongyang. Hundreds of years earlier, it was surrounded by a fortress and the Koguryo kings' palace first built in the sixth century C.E. (see Chapter 5). Portions of the fortress have been restored on Moran Hill, a park just east of the hill across a board boulevard.

Personal Recollections

One beautiful clear, cool morning in October 1993, I woke before sunrise. With camera in hand, I headed out of the official guesthouse. It was located on the south cliff of Moran Hill and overlooked the Taedong River. I positioned myself to take a picture of the distant fog-shrouded rice paddies as the sun peaked over the horizon. A dark figure leaped from behind the hedge in front of me. It pointed a rifle at me and demanded in Korean, "What are you doing?" I calmly replied in Korean, "I am an American visitor and want to take a picture." Oops! In Pyongyang it is not smart, especially in the dark with a rifle pointed at you, to identify yourself as an American who wants to take a picture. The commotion attracted more sentries. Surrounded, I announced I would not take the picture, but instead go for a walk. I turned around and strolled out of the guesthouse compound, up Moran Hill and toured the ancient Koguryo fortress, shooting a full roll of film as I went. No one bothered me.

♦ **Arch of Triumph.** Modeled after the Arc de Triomphe in Paris, this much larger structure (60 meters high and 52.5 meters wide) commemorates "victory in the anti-Japanese struggle." Naturally, it pays homage to Kim Il Sung for his "immortal revolutionary exploits."

◆ **Revolutionary Martyrs Cemetery on Mt. Taesong.** Located southeast of downtown Pyongyang, 100 "revolutionary martyrs" are buried here. They are the equivalent of "merit subjects," persons the founder of a dynasty designated members of his new aristocracy. Kim Il Sung's words, inscribed in stone, read, "The noble revolutionary spirit displayed by the anti-Japanese revolutionary martyrs will dwell forever in the hearts of our Party and our People." One must climb 300 steps to reach the cemetery. The steps symbolize Kim Il Sung's "arduous march" as a youth from his home to China.

◆ **Victorious Fatherland Liberation War Museum.** No sooner had the ink dried on the Korean War Armistice than Kim Il Sung celebrated victory by opening this museum. In 1974, the museum moved to its new quarters in central Pyongyang, a massive cube of ugly gray concrete. The museum is devoted to depicting "Defeating the aggression of the imperialist Allied forces."

Its 80 large exhibition halls are filled with colorful displays that trace "U.S. imperialism" from the arrival of the USS *General Sherman* in 1866 (see Chapter 6) to the shooting down of a U.S. Army helicopter on December 17, 1994. The basement is filled with captured U.S. tanks, trucks, rifles, and aircraft.

Personal Recollections

During my third visit to the Victorious Fatherland Liberation War Museum in October 1995, I was allowed to photograph U.S. military personnel's identification cards and dog tags. The Department of Defense was able to identify three U.S. airmen who had been listed among the 8,100 Americans "missing in action" (MIA) during the Korean War. Subsequent negotiations between the United States and North Korean armies paved the way for joint operations to recover the remains of American soldiers left behind in North Korea during the Korean War. More than 160 sets of remains have since been located and returned to the United States. Fortunately, in spite of the deterioration of bilateral relations since 2002, the joint recovery operations continue, at least for the time being.

◆ **Kumsusan Mausoleum.** This is Kim Il Sung's final resting place. Like the Soviets and Lenin, Kim's body lies in perpetual display for all North Koreans and foreign visitors to see. People line up in underground tunnels and proceed slowly through X-ray machines (no cameras allowed) and then vacuum machines that cleanse one's clothing of impurities (dust and so on) before the line winds past stern faced guards into a dimly lighted room where Kim's body lies in state. As people file past, North Koreans bow at the waist and weep.

The Media—Mind-Numbing News

Only Party- and State-approved news is available in North Korea. Listening to any foreign radio and television broadcasts is outlawed. Radios and television sets sold in North Korea are equipped to receive only officially approved broadcasts. Possession of a shortwave radio is against the law.

The same is true of all foreign publications. None is sold anywhere in North Korea. Only publications sanctioned by the North Korean government are available. This includes newspapers, magazines, and books.

Access to foreign radio, television, and printed materials is restricted to selected persons in the KWP and government. The People's Grand Study Hall, North Korea's equivalent of the Library of Congress, and libraries at major universities contain foreign publications and audiovisual materials. A permit, however, is required to gain access to these materials.

Officials who work with foreigners, particularly diplomats and trading company representatives, are allowed to obtain and read foreign publications. They are also permitted to view videotapes of foreign news broadcasts, documentaries, and movies. (See Appendix C for a listing of important North Korean publications in English.)

The Least You Need to Know

- ◆ Kim Il Sung's philosophy of education evolved slowly over several decades and his son Kim Jong Il has continued it without change.

- ◆ Traditional Confucian values, as taught by parents to their children, reinforce an individual's subordination of self to the family group and, ultimately, to central authority.

- ◆ The Korean Workers' Party dominates North Korea's education system and mass media.

- ◆ Education and the mass media are designed to mold young minds into loyal, subservient followers of Kim Il Sung and Kim Jong Il and their juche philosophy.

The Economy: Supporting the Military

In This Chapter

- ◆ The changing reality
- ◆ Political goals, economic realities
- ◆ Military before all else
- ◆ Agriculture's demise
- ◆ Foreign trade

Virtually every description published outside of North Korea describes its economy using many or most of the following terms: closed, state-planned, centrally managed, Stalinist-type, communist or socialist or both, and failing. These characteristics are used to account for North Korea's dismal economic performance and the suffering of its people. This perspective tends to overemphasize Marxism's fallacies. Consequently, other key reasons are overlooked. Pyongyang, on the other hand, responds with distorted claims about its economic accomplishments and dubious allegations that nature and the "imperialists," that is the United States and Japan, are responsible for North Korea's economic shortcomings.

In this chapter we attempt to look beyond these politically shaped polarities to sort out fact from fantasy regarding the state of North Korea's economy.

The View From Pyongyang

North Korea's economy, like its political and educational institutions, is designed to serve the regime's priorities of survival and reunification. Kim Il Sung constructed the economy to supply the armed forces with what they needed to achieve these goals. Kim Jong Il repeated this set of priorities in September 1998 when he launched his campaign to build a "strong and great nation" (*kangsong taeguk)*. Central to the campaign is a "defense first" policy.

For the North Korean people, the "defense first" policy was not news. They have been trained to believe that they live in a state of perpetual war. Technically, this is true since the Korean War Armistice has yet to yield a peace treaty with the United States. The mass media daily dishes out a feast of political slogans designed to convince everyone that they stand on the front line in the war with "imperialists."

A recurring, parallel theme points to the continuing U.S. economic sanctions as evidence of the U.S. "imperialist's" attempt to "strangle" North Korea. These sanctions, and not the shortcomings of the regime's economic policies, are blamed for the persistent and widespread shortages of food and fuel that the North Korean people must endure.

Nature's Whim

In 1995, the North Korean government added nature to the list of reasons for the nation's economic woes. Torrential rains in August 1995 wrecked havoc in the nation's four western provinces. Fields, crops, homes, dikes, and roads were washed away. Electric power lines, bridges, and railroad beds were destroyed.

The effected area accounted for an estimated 70 percent of the annual rice harvest and 53 percent of its maize. High water in the flooded rice paddies prevented pollination, which must occur in August if there is to be rice by the September harvest. Blight afflicted the ears of corn, turning them hard as stone. Staple vegetables needed for *kimchi*, Koreans' favorite dish, rotted, as did the potato crop. Hunger, starvation, and disease followed the massive crop failure.

The International Federation of the Red Cross reported in December 1995 that 100,000 families had been rendered homeless and 400,000 hectares of arable land had been destroyed. At that time, damage in the nation's capital and its northeastern and eastern provinces was marginal. These areas, however, sustained significant rain-related damage the following August.

Torrential rains in summer, however, are the norm for the Korean Peninsula. Annual *monsoon rains* sweep the entire peninsula from south to north beginning in late June and continue through the latter half of July. *Typhoons* follow in August and September. Drought can be a frequent visitor to the peninsula, too, as was the case in the summer of 1997 and spring and summer of 2000. Nature intensified, but did not set the stage for North Korea's economic calamity after 1995.

Korean Concepts

The **monsoon** is a wind system that brings weather to the region, rather than a specific storm. The monsoon is an important component of the agricultural year in East Asia. It brings rain in one season, and drier weather in the other. A **typhoon** (from the Chinese "tai fung" or "great wind") is a specific, hurricane-type storm event in Asia.

The Good Old Days

North Korea actually achieved impressive economic gains between 1953 and 1985, during the height of the Cold War. Aid poured into the war-wasted Korean Peninsula from the world's superpowers, helping both Koreas rebuild. Aid from the Soviet Union and People's Republic of China quickly erased the war's damage in North Korea.

According to North Korean official data, industrial production from 1971 to 1979 climbed an average 15.9 percent annually. Meanwhile, grain production exploded from 7 million metric tons (M/T) in 1974 to a peak of 10 million M/T in 1984, or an increase of 40 percent over the decade.

Increase Your North Korea IQ

Kim Il Sung claimed that his agricultural experts had developed new and unique farming methods. These he labeled juche farm methods. He claimed they were a result of his political teaching that new ideas should conform to conditions in North Korea. The juche method of rice cultivation supposedly increased the crop yield per parcel of land. It involved the circulation of warm water through rice paddies at night. How this was accomplished was never explained. Also ignored was the steady decline of agricultural productivity after 1985. Obviously, the claims about juche farming are dubious.

North Korea in the 1970s set out to impress the so-called "developing" nations with its juche agricultural methods. The soaring grain production accompanied amazing gains in other areas of the agricultural sector. According to official North Korean data published in 1988, the nation had 40,000 kilometers of irrigation canals and 1,990 kilometers of irrigation pipe serviced by 32,200 electric pumps.

Chemical fertilizer and tractor production peaked in 1984. That year, some 4,700,000 M/T of chemical fertilizer were produced and more than 70,000 tractors worked the nation's rice paddies and corn fields.

Human Folly

Behind the well-fed smiles that appeared in North Korea's publications before 1995, a quiet disaster was in the making. Gross imbalances and excesses in economic planning and resource allocation were taking their toll on the land, people, and resources. By 1985, a downward economic trend was becoming evident.

The annual rate of increase for industrial production slowed from 15.9 percent during the period between 1970 and 1978 to 12.2 percent between 1978 and 1984.

The goals of the 2nd Seven Year Economic Plan were to have been achieved between 1978 and 1984. When results fell short of goals, the plan was extended by one year.

Still there were significant shortfalls that extra time could not make up. After 1990, as industrial production declined, agriculture also declined. At the same time, agriculture's share of GDP (gross domestic product) rose from 37.4 percent in 1992 to 45.1 percent in 1996. The country's prosperity was increasingly dependent on the agricultural sector, given the declining performance of industry.

Kim Il Sung's political goals compelled unrealistic economic goals. Building the world's fifth largest military necessarily put the armed forces' needs before the civilian sector. Soviet and Chinese foreign and military aid were poured into developing the heavy industry vital to the production of war-making equipment and munitions. Agriculture only benefited briefly between 1974 and 1985, and then only because Kim Il Sung wanted to demonstrate the "superiority" of his juche farming methods to the developing nations.

However, the North Korean economy faltered in the 1980s and then collapsed in the 1990s. The trend began at least five years before the Soviet Union's collapse in 1990. Pyongyang's economic woes paralleled those of Moscow, but pending future research, available data suggests a more complex scenario for Pyongyang's economic decline.

One phenomenon that contributed to the economic decline was the nature of the economic growth that preceded it. The North Korean and Soviet economies specialized in "extensive" growth. That is, they increased output by simply adding more inputs. They did not try to increase productivity (producing more with less). Rather, they just added more and more. In the case of North Korean agriculture, that meant more fertilizer, more tractors, more land under the plow.

Increase Your North Korea IQ

North Korea emulated the Soviet Union's approach to economic development. This emphasized centrally managed economic planning. As a guide to progress, the Soviet Union, China, North Korea, and other communist nations periodically issued such plans. Each plan had a designated period of time during which goals were to be achieved. Moscow preferred five-year plans while North Korea usually issued seven-year plans. Pyongyang, naturally, added its own unique feature. If a plan's goals were not achieved during the designated period, the time span was simply extended until the goals were fulfilled. But in the 1980s and 1990s, when goals repeatedly fell short of the allocated time period, North Korea discontinued issuing economic plans.

However, the underlying infrastructure needed improvements that were not made, in order that all available resources could be applied to increasing output. So, perversely, as each year went by, it got harder and harder to increase output, and the strain and damage to the existing infrastructure became worse and worse. Finally, the quality and quantity began to decline. What was worse, as we shall see below, industrial stock and agricultural land was being irreversibly damaged.

Old Friend's Passing

The Soviet Union's failure to follow through on some of its promises contributed to, but was not solely responsible for, North Korea's economic woes. It left a huge petrochemical plant, called the Sunchon Vinalon Complex, incomplete. The plant was to have produced fabric, carbide, and nitrogenous fertilizer. Since 1989, it has only produced a small fraction of synthetic fabric. Another Soviet-backed project, the Sariwon Fertilizer Plant, was left as a hollow concrete shell.

Two modern nuclear power plants were promised by the Soviets in 1985, but neither got started until 1997. The Korea Peninsula Energy Development Organization (KEDO) began the project as part of the inducements

North Korea Fact

The United Nations Development Program (UNDP) is a UN agency that provides technical advice and limited financial resources to promote economic development in underdeveloped nations like North Korea. The UNDP has operated in North Korea since 1992 when North and South Korea entered the United Nations.

the United States offered North Korea under their 1994 "Agreed Framework" in exchange for Pyongyang's halting of its nuclear weapons development program (see Chapters 18 and 21).

1990 Oil Shock

North Korea until 1990 relied on a steady supply of crude oil at favorable prices and credit terms from China and the USSR. The supply from the USSR ended with that nation's collapse. Without the crude oil, the production of chemical fertilizers, the generation of electricity at the Soviet-built 200-megawatt thermal power plant in northeast North Korea, and transport were severely disrupted.

China continued to supply crude oil, but in 1992 shifted from charging North Korea its discounted "friendship" price with long-term, favorable credit to requiring cash or barter payment prior to delivery. Iran and Libya became other important suppliers of crude oil.

The best available estimates of petroleum fuel consumption suggest the leading users are the military, transportation, agricultural, and industrial sectors. Experts agree that the military received preference. After 1990, the shortage of fuel for civilian use impeded the use of farm machines and fishing boats and the production of chemical fertilizer and electricity.

The aging Soviet-designed boilers and generators at North Korea's thermal power plants are prone to frequent mechanical failure and there is a shortage of repair parts. This further reduces the nation's electric generation capacity, regardless of oil supply.

Fertilizer—A Double-Edged Sword

North Korea needs more fertilizers than South Korea to sustain agricultural production. North Korea, despite its larger land area, has less arable land (2,100,000 hectares compared to 2,210,000 hectares in South Korea). Only 30 percent of this land is suitable for rice paddies compared to 60 percent in the South (630,000 hectares in the North and 1,311,000 hectares in the South). In the North, 60 percent of the soil is an infertile, brown, sandy soil that requires careful fertilization and irrigation to be productive. The different fertility levels are evident in the fact that in 1946, just after liberation, grain production in South Korea was 2.5 times that of North Korea.

Nevertheless, North Korea's misguided agricultural policies undermined grain production beginning in the 1980s. The government did little to compensate for the nation's declining chemical fertilizer production. Instead of improving domestic production, surplus grain was bartered for foreign fertilizer.

However, declining fertilizer production may have been more a blessing than a handicap. In 1991, the UNDP warned the North Korean government that intense use of chemical fertilizers had led to "land degradation." The warning appears to have gone unheeded, at least until 1996. Already by 1989, excessive use of chemical fertilizers had severely depleted the soil's fertility. But by 1994, the supply of fertilizer had dropped below need. Grain production declined accordingly.

The Environmental Disaster

Hills and mountainsides were stripped of trees and brush to make room to plant more maize. Erosion followed, filling irrigation systems with silt and washing away dikes and revetments. The increasing run off of rain water polluted with large amounts of chemicals increased soil acidification, further depleting the farmland's fertility. Wells for drinking water became unsafe for human and animal consumption. Pollution of lakes and rivers reduced fish populations. The nation's ability to produce food was severely impeded by the early 1990s.

Irrigation

By 1993, North Korea's irrigation system was in disrepair. After completion in the late 1970s, little was invested in its maintenance, that capital instead going to the military. The UNDP estimated that in 1998 North Korea had 1.9 million hectares of farm, of which 980,000 were irrigated. This is nearly a 30 percent drop from the 1,400,000 hectares claimed a decade earlier. Most of the irrigation system's 32,000 pumps were installed in the late 1960s and early 1970s. All are of Soviet design, making spare parts virtually impossible to obtain.

Where pumps and pipes still work, the shortage of electricity disrupts irrigation. This is particularly true when irrigation water is needed the most, as was the case during droughts in the spring and summers of 1996, 1997, and 2000. When drought conditions lower water levels at reservoirs, the government preserves the stored water to flood rice paddies during the spring planting of seedlings. This, however, reduces the generation of electricity, which is essential to run the pumps needed to distribute irrigation water to the rice paddies. The entire planting cycle becomes disrupted.

Where Have All the Tractors Gone?

North Korea officially claimed in 1979 that it had 70,000 tractors, but in 1998 told UNDP officials the nation only had sufficient fuel for 20,000 tractors. It also asked the UN to supply 7,500 agricultural vehicles and 30,000 tires. That same year the

UNDP estimated "motorized" farming had declined by as much as 60 percent in recent years. About 800,000 oxen are available nationwide to assist with the plowing.

One can only conjecture about the decline of farm machines. The problem extends beyond tractors to rice planting and harvesting machines and trucks. UN agricultural experts, after considerable effort, visited North Korea's largest tractor plant. Production, however, had been shifted to tracked vehicles for the military, including armored personnel carriers, and four-wheel drive military vehicles such as off-road scout cars and trucks. The production of tires for tractors had also been shifted to military use tires.

Beginning in the mid-1970s, North Korea intensified its efforts to become self sufficient in the production of many of its weapons and military support materials. Between 1984 and 1992, the army added about 1,000 tanks; more than 2,500 armored personnel carriers; and 6,000 mobile artillery pieces and rocket launchers. Production of self-propelled guns and multiple rocket launchers continued well into the 1990s. Each of these weapons requires several vehicles to transport men, fuel, parts, and ammunition.

Many of these vehicles were produced for export, primarily to nations in Africa and the Middle East to pay for oil and raw material imports. The export of arms apparently peaked in 1988 at an estimated U.S. $700 million. It has subsided ever since, falling to under US $100 million in 1994.

Monuments to Dad

In the 1980s, Kim Jong Il stepped forward to assume his father's domestic responsibilities. Resources allocated to agriculture declined as those devoted to construction and armaments increased. There was an unprecedented surge in construction, particularly in Pyongyang. Kim Jong Il appears to have been the prime mover behind these shifts.

Kim did invest some building resources to improve the crumbling industrial and agricultural infrastructure. Eight new power plants (five thermal, coal-fired plants with a generating capacity of 3,350 megawatts [MW] of electricity; two hydroelectric plants to generate 946 MW; and one 5 MW nuclear plant at Yongbyon) were built.

The huge West Sea Barrage project was completed. It dammed the Taedong River estuary. Locks allowed the passage of cargo ships to and from the port of Nampo. More than 100,000 hectares of farm land were reclaimed, the irrigation network expanded, and three electricity generating dams added on the Taedong River northeast of Pyongyang.

Five new factories were built: two to forge and press steel, one to process ore, one to make cement, and one to produce synthetic textiles. The transportation and light industry sectors, however, were virtually ignored. No new roads were built, nor were any paved. Only 252 kilometers of new railroad track were constructed. Port facilities were neither modernized nor expanded.

Sports Facilities

More impressive, however, was the surge in construction in Pyongyang. Its building boom may have been sparked by North Korea's hope to co-host the 1988 Seoul Olympiad. Pyongyang's terrorism against South Korea wiped out this possibility. Instead, Pyongyang decided to host its own so-called International Youth Festival of 1989.

Seven huge new buildings and a massive stadium were built for the festival, and another 14 major sports facilities were erected. They contained an enormous 282,000 square meters of floor space. The new May Day stadium, with 150,000 seats, was the largest ever to be built in Asia. Five huge theaters can seat 10,000 persons. An amusement park, bowling alley, golf course, and four hotels were completed, including the 45-story, twin-tower Koryo Hotel.

But the most massive project was the 105-story, 7,665-room Ryugyong Hotel that dominates the Pyongyang skyline. This towering pile of cold, grey concrete almost matches the Empire State Building in height, but the structure is useless. Elevators cannot run in its crooked shafts, so it stands empty.

Increase Your North Korea IQ

Piercing Pyongyang's sky line is the needle nosed, rocket shaped Ryugyong Hotel. This frigid, unlighted gray mass is the world's tallest and most useless pile of concrete. Its empty shell has stood 105 stories high in central Pyongyang since Kim Jong Il ordered its erection in the late 1980s. Only after the concrete had hardened was it discovered that elevators could not operate in its crooked shafts. Ever since, North Korean guides who accompany foreign visitors pretend that the structure does not exist!

Projects for the Masses

The masses were given several massive projects, as well. The Grand People's Study Hall and Mangyongdae Children's Palace (690 rooms plus a swimming pool and huge fountain) were completed in 1982 and 1989, respectively. The Changgwang Health Complex and the 13-story Pyongyang Maternity Hospital (2,000 rooms and 1,000 hospital beds) both opened in 1980. The Pyongyang Central Youth Hall (760 rooms), Pyongyang Circus (70,000 square meters of floor space in five buildings), and the Chongryu Restaurant (with room for 1,000 customers) followed.

At least 40 high-rise apartment buildings, ranging in height from 12 to 15 stories, changed the skyline. They contained more than 25,000 apartment units, all reserved for Party and government officials. New department stores were added and a new trolley line linked these residential areas to the downtown.

Pyongyang's building boom was topped off with five massive monuments and the 45,000-square-meter Mansudae Assembly Hall to house the Supreme People's Assembly. The monuments included the Juche Tower and Arch of Triumph, both completed in 1982 to celebrate Kim Il Sung's birthday.

Bullets and Bunkers

Virtually unnoticed at the time was the quiet surge of construction along the northern edge of the Demilitarized Zone (DMZ). By the mid-1980s, North Korea had deployed much of its million-man army and mechanized equipment within a 30 kilometer–wide strip of land north of the DMZ. A maze of underground, steel-reinforced concrete bunkers, roads, and support facilities were built for this purpose.

One can only guess at the enormity of resources poured into the Pyongyang and DMZ bunker building booms, plus the surge in military hardware and munitions production. Something had to give. The nation's Seven Year Economic Plan was never achieved. In fact, the practice was discontinued. The industrial and agricultural infrastructure continued to fall into disrepair.

Industrial and agricultural production plummeted. According to the International Monetary Fund (IMF), North Korea's GDP shrank from $20.9 billion in 1992 to $10.6 billion in 1996. During the same period, industrial production declined 66 percent and agricultural production by 40 percent. The flawed expansion practices of the 1970s and 1980s finally came home to roost.

Food Production

Grain harvests followed a similar pattern. The UNDP estimates that North Korea's 23 million people need a minimum of 4.1 million M/T of grain per year to supply half their food needs. Grain production between 1974 and 1991 exceeded 5 million M/T annually. By 1990, production began to decline. The production of rice, maize, and potatoes was halved from 6.9 million M/T in 1990 to a low of 3.5 million M/T in 1998.

Imports of grain, mostly international humanitarian aid, made up the deficit. By 2001, domestic production had recovered to 5.4 million M/T of rice, maize, and potatoes, but remained 1.5 million M/T below the 1990 level.

Decline in Trade

Trade underwent a similar steep slide. North Korea's international trade peaked in the late 1980s at about $5 billion. It stood at $4.7 billion in 1990, but plunged to $2.7 billion the following year. By 1999, it was a meager $1.5 billion, according to South Korea's KOTRA, Korean Traders Association. Official North Korea data suggest a similar pattern. Declining income accompanied the decline in trade, reducing the fiscal resources available for internal investments or food imports.

Ultimate responsibility must rest on the shoulders of North Korea's rulers, Kim Il Sung and Kim Jong Il. They naturally pointed the finger elsewhere. The Soviet Union's demise undoubtedly had a negative impact on the country's economy, but it did not initiate the downward spiral. U.S. sanctions, the inherent shortcomings of Marxism, and nature share some responsibility, but are not necessarily the most important factors. Perhaps the most significant cause is the extensive growth policies the leaders followed, while ignoring the need to invest in the capital stock and infrastructure of the country.

The Missing Link

North Korea's economy is changing. Beginning in 1999, according to data from the Bank of Korea (South Korea's central government bank), the North Korean economy has stabilized and a gradual, positive trend has been detected. Industrial and food production has increased. Important strides are being made to upgrade the nation's telecommunications and information technology.

More important has been the shifts away from traditional economic patterns. In 1990, North Korea's chief trading partners were the Soviet Union, China, and Japan. A decade later they are China, South Korea, and Japan. Trade has not yet returned to pre-1990 levels, but it is more diverse.

Imports from noncommunist countries comprised less than 40 percent of imports in 1990 (mostly from Japan and Germany). By 2000, more than 50 percent of imports comes from noncommunist nations. North Korea's trade with Russia has declined from 50 percent of the total, where it stood in 1990, to 5 percent 10 years later.

At the same time, South-North Korea trade has increased from 5 percent of North Korea's total trade to 15 percent. From 1998 to 1999, North Korea's exports to South Korea increased from $92 million to $121 million, and imports from $130 to $212 million.

North Korea continues its efforts to attract foreign investment. Its track record remains uneven because several formidable impediments have yet to be removed. But by 1999, considerable progress had been made in the promulgation of foreign investment laws. Implementation, however, remains wanting.

The same is true for the special trade zones established (or at least promised) by the government. The oldest of these, the Rajin-Sonbong Trade Zone on the northeast coast near the China border, even after a decade, has failed to attract significant investment. China provides a fairly steady, but relatively small flow of foreign investment. South Korean firms continue to show interest, but lingering uncertainty about the future of North-South relations remains an obstacle.

Meanwhile, investment from Japan fell significantly after North Korea launched a ballistic missile through Japanese airspace in 1998. Continuing troubled bilateral relations remain a formidable barrier to future investment.

North Korea has also diversified its diplomatic relations to include all members of the Association of South East Asian Nations (ASEAN) and most members of the European Union (EU). But North Korea's poor track record of paying its debts and political uncertainty are retarding the expansion of commercial ties.

Even with the small openings to regional economic partnerships, North Korea's economic overseers have yet to recognize the need for more fundamental shifts. Possibly the most pressing one is to shift scarce fiscal, material, and human resources from the military to the civil sectors of the society and economy.

Economic Remodeling

A program was launched in the summer of 2002 to reform selected aspects of the domestic economy. Compensation for civil and military service was shifted from payment in kind (food, housing, and so on) to cash payment. Salaries were abruptly increased, but so, too, were the costs of housing, utilities, and so on. The use of foreign currencies was legalized for the purchase of daily commodities and payment of basic services. The sale of daily necessities by profit making vendors in markets was also legalized.

The reforms' longer term impact on the overall economy remains unclear. Foreign economic observers believe these reforms are unlikely to revitalize North Korea's economy. Their failure could discredit capitalism in the eyes of North Korea's economists, impeding the apparent trend away from socialism and toward capitalism.

It is doubtful that these ill-conceived reforms will improve the quality of life for most North Koreans. Most likely they will benefit the politically influential and well-paid elite. Politically, if the nation's rulers decide that the reforms do not serve their economic purposes or erode their ability to manage and manipulate the population, the reforms could quickly be discarded. At the same time, however, these faltering reforms could set in motion a process of economic and social changes that the ruling elite would find difficult to halt and reverse.

The Ultimate Dilemma

Despite recent economic changes, North Korea's hopes of economic recovery hinge on whether it will ultimately fulfill the international community's expectation that it forgo all weapons of mass destruction and conform to internationally sanctioned norms. So long as North Korea does not, it will be ostracized from international financial institutions, live under U.S. economic sanctions, and face the risk of a second Korean War.

The Least You Need to Know

- North Korea's economy is a centrally managed, socialist system, which gives preference to the military's needs.

- After 1990, industrial and agricultural production plummeted, but the economy's downward spiral appears to have bottomed out and a tenuous recovery has begun.

- Commercial relations and exports are being diversified, but formidable impediments, particularly the risk of war, remain to foreign investment.

- North Korea's future economic development remains tied to whether the regime will conform to international norms and win admission to international financial institutions.

Part 4

North Korea's Relationship with the World

North Korea's worldview is essentially self-centered and insecure. To perpetuate the regime, Kim Jong Il is cautiously and hesitantly adjusting his nation's relations with both its former friends, Russia and China, and foes, the United States, South Korea, and Japan.

In this part, we will assess the impact that the collapse of the Soviet Union and discrediting of communism have had on North Korea and its relations with other nations.

We will explore why so many powerful nations are so concerned about North Korea.

Chapter 14

North Korea and Russia: A Marriage of Convenience

In This Chapter

- ◆ What does huge Russia gain from its friendship with tiny North Korea?

- ◆ Is Russia helping Kim Jong Il perpetuate his regime?

- ◆ Would Moscow rush to Pyongyang's aid in the event of another Korean War?

- ◆ Where does Russia stand regarding North Korea's nuclear ambitions?

The Moscow-Pyongyang alliance always has been, and continues to be, a marriage of convenience. As we discussed in Chapter 8, this relationship predates the Russian Revolution of 1917. It started long before the rise of Kim Il Sung and other anti-Japanese Korean guerilla leaders.

Marxism-Leninism eventually became the bonding force between Moscow and Korea's communist-oriented, anti-Japanese movement. But ideology was not the common ground that brought the two together in the first place, and it was not ideology that enabled the two countries to revive and repair their relationship after the Soviet Union's collapse in 1991. Understanding this mutual need helps explain how the Russia-North Korea relationship survived the discrediting of Marxism-Leninism in the late 1980s.

Moscow's present interest in the Korean Peninsula originated in Imperial Russia. The goal remains essentially the same, only the methods for attaining the goal have changed. Russia today, like its predecessors, Imperial Russia and the Soviet Union, wants to be a player in Northeast Asia. The motivations are strategic and economic, not ideological.

Ambitions in Northeast Asia

In the nineteenth century, Imperial Russia saw the Korean Peninsula as a stepping-stone to the Pacific Ocean and to trade with China and Japan. In 1896, the Korean monarch sought to enlist Russia to help expel Japan from the Korean Peninsula. After he had fled to the Russian legation in Seoul in search of safe haven (see Chapter 6), the king gave his Russian guardians exclusive commercial rights in Korea. These included the use of ports on Korea's east coast. Japanese influence on the peninsula subsided as Russian influence increased.

Japan responded by first allying with Great Britain in 1902, and then launching a surprise attack on the Imperial Russian naval base at Port Arthur on the tip of China's Liaotung Peninsula. The Russo-Japanese War of 1904–1905 ensued. Japan's victory sparked an uprising against the tsar, helping to set the stage for the Russian Revolution in 1917.

The Russo-Japanese rivalry persisted. Once Russia's new communist rulers had consolidated their rule over the new Soviet Union, their communist party's international arm, the Comintern (or Communist International), sought out potential political allies in Northeast Asia. After a decade of faltering friendship, Japan's invasion and conquest of Manchuria in 1931 gave these early probes new impetus.

Keeping Imperial Japan Preoccupied

The new Soviet Union soon moved to blunt the Japanese Empire's northward expansion. In 1937, the two nations engaged in a bloody war along the Sino-Soviet border in Manchuria. But both enemies had other pressing priorities. Stalin, the Soviet Union's ruler at the time, was increasingly concerned about Hitler's rise in Germany. Tokyo's priority was the conquest of China. An uneasy armistice ended the potentially costly armed dueling along the Manchurian-Siberian border.

Instead, Moscow began supporting anti-Japanese Korean guerillas as a way to draw the Imperial Japanese Army forces away from Siberia (see Chapter 8). Stalin's strategy paid off. During World War II, Japan was preoccupied with conquering China, Southeast Asia, and the central Pacific. Japan's large army in Manchuria was too busy dealing with anti-Japanese China and Korean guerillas to threaten the Soviet Union's Siberian and Maritime regions.

Stiff-Arming the United States

Moscow's entry into World War II against Japan a few days before the Japanese surrender paid huge dividends (see Chapter 7). Moving rapidly behind the Chinese and Korean guerilla bands it had armed and trained, the Soviet Union quickly asserted its influence in China and North Korea.

The cost to Moscow was minimal relative to its global gains. The Soviet Union became a key player in East Asia and was able to influence the rise of communist China, the northern half of the Korean Peninsula and Vietnam. It saw these new allies as ideologically compatible and economically dependent buffer states that could protect the Soviet Union's Far East flank from encroachment by the United States and its allies. Stalin apparently hoped the arrangement would enable him to concentrate on asserting control over Eastern Europe and Central Asia.

Increase Your North Korea IQ

From the end of World War II to 1990, the nations of the world divided themselves into three groups: the Communist bloc, the Western nations, and the non-aligned nations (NAN). The Communist bloc consisted of the Union of Soviet Socialist Republics (USSR or Soviet Union for short) and its allies. The Russian Republic dominated the USSR. Other members of the USSR subordinated themselves politically, economically, and militarily to Moscow, Russia's capital. Nations allied to the Soviet Union retained their national independence, but linked themselves to Moscow ideologically, economically, and militarily. They came to be called "satellites," and included the nations of Eastern Europe, North Korea, and Vietnam. China asserted its independence from the Soviet Union in 1958.

Squeezing Stalin and His Successors

But Kim Il Sung, like Mao Zedong, had a mind of his own (see Chapter 8). Kim Il Sung squeezed Stalin for all he could get. No sooner had Stalin's army installed Kim Il Sung and his anti-Japanese comrades in power in North Korea than Kim Il Sung convinced Stalin to equip and train his army to invade South Korea. Once the Korean

War had become another chapter in the Cold War, Kim got Stalin to help cover the cost of North Korea's reconstruction.

Ideology alone certainly cannot explain why Stalin's successors put up with Kim Il Sung's exploitation. By the mid-1950s, Moscow and Pyongyang were at odds, ideologically and politically. Pyongyang was already leaning toward Beijing, Moscow's rival for leadership of the world's nonaligned developing nations like India, Pakistan, and the nations of sub-Saharan Africa. Kim Il Sung had begun his purge of Soviet-educated rivals from the North Korean government and the Korean Workers' Party. Kim also was formulating his own version of Marxism-Leninism.

Moscow nevertheless persisted in cultivating Pyongyang's loyalty. Moscow did not want Beijing to dominate North Korea. The United States's influence in Japan and South Korea excluded the Soviet Union from the region's commerce, but Moscow now had new priorities. It saw North Korea as a showcase for socialism's benefits.

North Korea also served as a defensive buffer state. Access there enabled Moscow to counter Beijing's influence. It also kept distance between U.S. forces in the Pacific and the Soviet Union. Equally important was North Korea's role as an intelligence-collection base. From North Korea, the Soviet Union could monitor all US military activities in South Korea, Japan, the China Sea, and the north Pacific.

Increase Your North Korea IQ

Here is a chronology of USSR–North Korean Relations, 1948-1990:

October 12, 1948—Diplomatic relations established.

March 17, 1949—Kim Il Sung visits Moscow, first economic agreement signed.

December 1949—USSR military forces withdraw from North Korea.

August 4, 1956—The first USSR-DPRK aid agreement signed.

July 6, 1961—The first mutual defense pack signed.

December 26, 1985—Moscow promises to build two nuclear reactors for North Korea if it joins the Treaty on the Non-proliferation of Nuclear Weapons (NPT) and allows International Atomic Energy Agency (IAEA) inspections.

June 1, 1990—USSR leader Mikhail Gorbachev meets South Korea's president.

September 11, 1990—Moscow and Seoul establish diplomatic relations.

November 17, 1990—Moscow calls for both Koreas' admission into the UN.

December 25, 1990—South Korea's president visits Moscow.

The pro-Pyongyang Korean Residence Association in Japan, the *Chosen soren*, was an important link in this intelligence collection effort. Members of the Chosen soren, who traveled frequently between Japan and North Korea, provided comprehensive insight into U.S. forces, Japan's capabilities and activities, and information about the electronics revolution Japan's industry had fostered after 1960.

Pyongyang's Clinging Act

Kim Il Sung from 1953 to 1990 clung to the Soviet Union out of sheer need. Moscow's military aid had rebuilt Kim's decimated army and equipped it with state-of-the-art weaponry. When the two countries finally got around to formalizing their alliance, the July 1961 Treaty of Friendship, Cooperation, and Mutual Assistance promised:

> Should either of the Contracting Parties suffer armed attack by any State or coalition of States and thus find itself in a state of war, the other Contracting Party shall immediately extend military and other assistance with all the means at its disposal.

This treaty became the cornerstone of the alliance until December 1991 when the USSR formally ceased to exist.

Economic aid helped North Korea rebuild its industrial and agricultural infrastructure. The Soviet Union and its satellites ensured Pyongyang a market for its inferior quality exports. The Moscow-Beijing rivalry gave Pyongyang access to Soviet interest-free loans and crude oil priced below world market levels. Thousands of North Koreans traveled to the Soviet Union for low-cost training in advanced technology.

In December 1985 Moscow promised to build modern nuclear reactors for North Korea in exchange for Pyongyang's promises to join the Treaty on the Non-proliferation of Nuclear Weapons (NPT) and to allow International Atomic Energy Agency (IAEA) inspections of its nuclear facilities. Neither side fulfilled its promises. The North Korean nuclear crisis traces its origins to this accord.

Radical Makeover

The Moscow-Pyongyang relationship sustained several potentially debilitating shocks at the end of the 1980s. Soviet leader Mikhail Gorbachev initiated economic reforms and political reforms, exposing the USSR's bankruptcy. No longer could Moscow fulfill its many promises to Pyongyang and other satellites of continuing economic aid.

But the most devastating blow came in the form of warming relations between Moscow and Seoul, Pyongyang's archrival. The process had begun hesitantly in

October 1983. Seoul had won the prize of hosting the Olympiad in 1988. Having boycotted the 1984 Los Angeles Olympics (as a response to the U.S. boycott of the 1980 Moscow Olympics over the Soviet invasion of Afghanistan) the Soviet Union promptly demonstrated keen interest in participating in the Seoul event.

Personal Recollections

The first Soviet official to visit Seoul arrived in October 1983 for consultations about the safe passage for the Soviet officials who would attend the international events Seoul was scheduled to host. He arrived only one month after a Soviet fighter had blown Korean Airlines (KAL) flight 007 out of the air over the USSR's Sakhalin Island, killing everyone aboard, including a U.S. congressman. The Soviet official was to meet the influential South Korean legislator and retired army general Kwon Chong-dal.

At the time, I was the U.S. Embassy's political officer who tracked National Assembly and political party affairs. The ambassador sent me to convince Kwon, whom I knew well, to meet the Soviet official and to avoid doing anything that might complicate the improvement of relations between Moscow and Seoul. After considerable discussion, Kwon agreed. During his subsequent meeting with the Soviet official, Kwon conducted himself as a professional and put his nation's interests before his personal feelings. Kwon's daughter had died in the KAL 007 incident.

South Korea moved quickly to capitalize on its developing athletic ties with the Communist bloc. By 1985, South Korea had ties to athletic associations in the Soviet Union and most other communist nations. In 1987, many of these informal ties were expanded into commerce and trade. Shortly after the Seoul Olympiad, South Korea converted these relations into formal diplomatic ties.

Pyongyang was caught off-guard. Seoul's superior and favorably priced export goods quickly undercut Pyongyang's share of the Communist bloc market. Soviet leader and economic reformer Gorbachev recognized the benefits of doing business with Seoul. He also sanctioned commercial relations with South Korea and held the first-ever summit meeting between a leader of the USSR and South Korea. By September 1990, the Soviet Union, Pyongyang's foremost champion and defender, established diplomatic relations with South Korea.

But then the entire Communist bloc collapsed. Even the Soviet Union crumbled at the end of 1991. The negative consequences for North Korea were prompt and profound. North Korea's economic vitality suffered severe and lingering damage (see Chapter 13).

Hard Times in Paradise

Probably of greatest concern to the Pyongyang regime was the altered security situation in Northeast Asia. Without the Soviet Union, the 1961 Treaty of Friendship, Cooperation, and Mutual Assistance lost its validity. This meant North Korea no longer could benefit from the Soviet Union's nuclear umbrella.

Pyongyang remained confident, albeit briefly, in the ability of its conventional arms and massive army to deter a possible South Korea invasion. But no longer could it count on the Soviet Union to deter a possible nuclear attack by the United States.

Three more developments intensified Pyongyang's sense of insecurity. First came the United States's quick and decisive victory against Iraq in the Gulf War of 1991. In a matter of days, U.S. "smart bomb" and "stealth aircraft" technology destroyed Iraq's massive Soviet-equipped army. Suddenly, all of North Korea's arsenal of Soviet-designed armored vehicles was rendered obsolete.

Pyongyang, naturally, turned to Moscow for help. It got the cold shoulder. Gone were the days of easy "concessional" credit, which translated into free arms. Moscow insisted on its new policy of "no cash, no arms." Besides, even if more-advanced Russian equipment had been supplied, it was doubtful it could stand up to the state-of-the-art equipment that the United States had begun supplying to South Korea.

Nor could Pyongyang count on its other ally, Beijing. Relations between China and South Korea had also warmed considerably since the mid-1980s. Trade and investment between the two former enemies were expanding rapidly. Formal diplomatic ties between the two countries were established in August 1992.

As if matters were not bad enough, the new Russian government quietly informed its little ally that the former Treaty of Friendship, Cooperation, and Mutual Assistance was destined for major alteration. Moscow renewed the treaty in 1992 only because neither side had given prior notice of intent to renounce or renegotiate it.

The view from Pyongyang was dismal. Gone was the once-mighty Soviet Union. The credibility of its ideology, technology, and economy had been destroyed. Even Beijing, once Pyongyang's great defender during the Korean War, had embraced its archrival, South Korea.

Feeling lonely and vulnerable, Pyongyang seems to have settled on a dual-track policy. On the one hand, outwardly it would shift from confronting its adversaries to engaging them. But at the same time, it became determined to develop nuclear weapons. Precisely when it settled on this strategy is uncertain. But it must have been after 1985, when it put into operation its first full-scale nuclear reactor at the Yongbyon Nuclear Research Center.

Moscow Gives Pyongyang the Cold Shoulder

Pyongyang tried to keep pace with the improving relations between its former foes and Moscow. As we will discuss in Chapters 16 and 17, Pyongyang beginning in 1990 initiated high-level talks with Tokyo and Seoul. The talks with Tokyo quickly sputtered to a halt, but the Seoul-Pyongyang talks achieved impressive results. By December 1991, the two Koreas had reached a number of unprecedented agreements on reconciliation, economic cooperation, and keeping the Korean Peninsula free of nuclear weapons.

The Bush Administration was impressed. It moved to reward Pyongyang. In January 1992, U.S. and North Korean diplomats met in New York to exchange on a roadmap for the normalization of bilateral relations.

> **Increase Your North Korea IQ** _____
>
> Here is a chronology of Russian–DPRK Relations, 1991-2003:
>
> December 27, 1991—DPRK recognizes Russian-led Commonwealth of Independent States (CIS) as the USSR's successor.
>
> January 1, 1993—Russia informs North Korea it intends to revise their military alliance.
>
> March 24, 1994—Russia proposes an eight-party multilateral conference to address the nuclear crisis on the Korean Peninsula.
>
> July 1997—Bilateral talks fail to reach agreement on revisions to their military alliance.
>
> February 9, 2000—Revised treaty governing military their military alliance is signed.
>
> July 19–20, 2000—Russian president Vladimir Putin visits Pyongyang.
>
> April 27, 2001—New military cooperation accord signed.
>
> July 24, 2001—Kim Jong Il visits Moscow.
>
> August 20–26, 2002—Kim Jong Il visits Russian Far Eastern region.
>
> November 16, 2002—Russia and DPRK sign memorandum to link and expand their railway systems.

Pyongyang, seven years after promising the USSR it would do so, finally agreed to allow the International Atomic Energy Agency (IAEA) to inspect its nuclear facilities. Again, Washington reacted more positively than Moscow. Russia's President Boris Yeltsin advised his North Korean counterpart that Moscow would extend their 1961 alliance. But then it would negotiate substantive revision when it came up for renewal in 1997.

While Russia-North Korea relations remained generally cool, those with Seoul contin-ued to warm. In 1992 the Russian and South Korean presidents exchanged visits. While their two-way trade exploded, Pyongyang's total trade with Moscow dropped 70 percent between 1990 and 1991, and by 1996 had declined to a meager $50 million annually. Any purchases Pyongyang made, moreover, were on a strictly cash basis. This policy effectively prevented North Korea from buying advanced military equipment from Moscow.

But Seoul, to help Russia pay for its imports from South Korea, began purchasing mil-itary armaments from Moscow. The purchases included state-of-the-art fighter aircraft, T-80 tanks, BMP-3 armored fighting vehicles, and antiaircraft missiles. But the United States twisted South Korea's arm when in 1997 it sought to purchase Russian S-300 surface-to-air missiles instead of U.S.-made Patriot missiles.

Still, Seoul-Moscow military ties continued to warm. In November 1997, the two nations signed an agreement to increase bilateral cooperation between their defense ministries. It called for mutual assistance in technology transfer and information on design, testing, and production of weapons systems.

Washington reacted negatively to Seoul's eagerness to purchase military equipment from Moscow. Granted, Moscow was hard-pressed to pay its growing debt to Seoul. But Seoul had other priorities. It wanted to break Washington's virtual monopoly on equipping South Korean forces. Pride was a greater concern than price. Despite Washington's protests, Seoul persisted. But when Seoul said it would purchase Russian air-to-surface missiles, Washington drew the line, compelling Seoul to buy "America."

Moscow's relations with Pyongyang hit rock bottom in 1997–1998. Bilateral efforts to renegotiate their old alliance ended inconclusively in the summer of 1997. Moscow insisted on dropping its former promise of "automatic response" in the event North Korea was attacked. Russia also wanted wording that called on Pyongyang and Seoul to work out their differences according to the UN Charter and international law. Pyongyang refused.

Putin to the Rescue

Russian President Vladimir Putin moved decisively after his election to improve rela-tions with North Korea. He dispatched a diplomatic delegation to Pyongyang in the summer of 1999 to resolve longstanding differences over the wording of the treaty of alliance. Moscow replaced the Soviet Union's former assurances that it would come to Pyongyang's aid in the event of external attack, but promised to consult with North Korea on how to address the situation prior to taking action. This time, Pyongyang conceded to the new wording.

Friendship Redefined

Portions of the new treaty, signed on February 9, 2000, remain secret. But when President Putin visited Pyongyang in July 2000, he and Kim Jong Il signed the "Russia-DPRK Joint Declaration." Article 2, paragraph 2 reads:

> Russia and the DPRK express the willingness to get in touch with each other without delay if the danger of aggression to the DPRK or to Russia is created or when there is the need to have consultations and cooperate with each other under the circumstances where peace and security are threatened.

This wording is certainly much more ambiguous than the previous treaty in defining Russia's commitment to defend North Korea.

The joint declaration contains numerous other bilateral pledges, but no promises of Russian economic or technological assistance to North Korea. Instead, Russia promised "cooperation in trade, economy, science, and technology …" Also, the two leaders agreed to the "drawing up (of) gigantic plans for cooperation in various fields such as metal, power, transport, forestry, oil, gas, and light industries."

Three new accords followed the 2000 joint declaration. In April 2001, the two nations signed a new military pact. It promises both sides will work to oppose the United State's national Missile Defense initiative. It also promises "cooperation between the armed forces" of the two nations, but no specifics have been revealed.

When Kim Jong Il traveled to Moscow in August 2001, a second declaration, the Russia-DPRK Moscow Declaration, was issued. In it the two countries promised to strengthen the role of the United Nations, work to settle disputes peacefully and through negotiations, and to oppose the spread of international terrorism. They also declared progress toward the linking of their rail systems.

In the August 2001 declaration, North Korea called the "pullout of the U.S. forces from south Korea" a "pressing issue." Moscow cautiously "expressed understanding" and "stressed the need to ensure peace and stability in this part of Asia by non-military means."

When North Korea's foreign minister visited Moscow in May 2002, he and his Russian counterpart signed a "Plan of Exchanges for 2002–04." In it, the two nations affirmed that they would cooperate on the linking of their rail systems. Also, the two nations agreed to resume the exchange of students and cultural groups and exhibitions.

Nuclear Fallout

Moscow helped North Korea get started in the nuclear business. It trained North Korean scientists and technicians in nuclear sciences and power plant operation during the 1970s and 1980s. Moscow provided the technology in the first place as part of its ongoing effort to assert its influence in North Korea. But the Soviet Union also sought to minimize the chances that North Korea might develop its own nuclear weapons capability. It insisted that Pyongyang join the NPT and cooperate with IAEA inspections.

When Pyongyang announced in March 1994 its intention to withdraw from the NPT, Moscow joined other nuclear powers in condemning North Korea and insisting that it remain in the treaty. Russia watched with keen interest as the United States engaged North Korea in negotiations aimed at halting and eventually dismantling North Korea's nuclear weapons program.

Moscow's Multilateral Solution

In March 1994, Moscow sought to break the impasse between the United States and North Korea by calling for a multilateral conference that would bring together North and South Korea, the United States, Russia, China, Japan, the IAEA, and the UN secretary general. Not wishing to promote Moscow's efforts to reassert its influence on the Korean Peninsula, the United States rejected the proposal. Other nations subsequently distanced themselves from it. Three months later, the impasse between the United States and North Korea was broken and their bilateral talks eventually yielded the October 1994 Agreed Framework that "froze" North Korea's nuclear activities until sometime after the year 2000.

Moscow tried repeatedly to become a party to the accord, but Washington consistently opposed this.

The New Korean Nuclear Crisis

Once again Moscow has teamed up with the international community to block Pyongyang's efforts to build its own nuclear arsenal. While Moscow shares Washington's goal of keeping the Korean Peninsula free of nuclear weapons, it disagrees on how to achieve this goal. Like President George W. Bush, the Russian leadership, too, wants a peaceful, diplomatic solution. Russia favors bilateral US-North Korea negotiations to induce Pyongyang to return to the NPT and to rid itself of nuclear weapons.

Russia eagerly accepted China's invitation to the August 2003 Six Party Talks in Beijing that were also attended by the United States, Japan, and the two Koreas. Nevertheless, Moscow, like Beijing, believes only bilateral U.S.–North Korea negotiations can ultimately break the nuclear impasse between Washington and Pyongyang.

The Least You Need to Know

◆ Russia's interests in the Korean Peninsula are rooted in strategic and commercial interests that predate the rise of the Soviet Union and communist North Korea.

◆ USSR-North Korea ties faltered during the 1980s when Moscow found it commercially advantageous to do business with North Korea's archrival, South Korea.

◆ After the fall of the Soviet Union in 1990, Russia-North Korea relations remained frigid for a decade as Moscow courted Seoul for economic benefits.

◆ Since 2000, Russia-North Korea relations have warmed, but Pyongyang's renewed nuclear ambitions, and Moscow's opposition to them, are a serious irritant in their relationship.

Chapter 15

North Korea and China: A Love-Hate Relationship

In This Chapter

- ◆ Beijing and Pyongyang's mutual need
- ◆ Beijing's balancing act on the Korean Peninsula
- ◆ Pyongyang's economic dependency on Beijing
- ◆ China and the North Korean nuclear issue

China's relationship with the Korean Peninsula has undergone profound change over the past century. For two millennia, China had reigned supreme in East Asia. China compared its traditional relations with Korea to that between older and younger brothers. China assumed responsibility for Korea's protection. In exchange, Korea's king recognized China's political and cultural superiority, emulated China's governmental institutions, and regularly dispatched tribute-bearing diplomatic missions to China.

But then China's world order crumbled at the end of the nineteenth century (see Chapters 5 and 6).

The "Lips and Teeth" Alliance

Since China's entry into the Korean War in 1950, leaders in Beijing and Pyongyang have considered their two nations' relations as close as "lips and teeth." In other words, one could not function without the other. Actually, however, the phrase is quite misleading. Relations between the two allies have swung back and forth between friendship and animosity, collaboration and competition.

This first became evident when the Sino-Soviet dispute erupted between China and the Soviet Union in 1960 and placed a heavy strain on the China–North Korea alliance. For the next 30 years, Kim Il Sung maneuvered to play Beijing against Moscow so he could maximize economic and military aid from both capitals. Moscow put up with Kim's antics to prevent him from becoming a hostile neighbor on the Soviet Union's distant border in East Asia. Beijing put up with Kim to preserve his domain as a buffer against the United States's military in South Korea.

The developments of 1990-1992 changed all this. The Soviet Union's collapse ended Kim's double dipping game with Moscow and Beijing. This freed China to turn its attention for the first time toward South Korea. For 40 years, the PRC had dealt only with the government of North Korea on Korean issues. Then Beijing established full diplomatic and commercial relations with Kim's rival, South Korea.

Beijing and Pyongyang continued to toast their "lips and teeth" alliance, but the relations quickly became chilly. North Korea's push for nuclear weapons further estranged the relationship. China, adamantly opposed to nuclear weapons on the Korean Peninsula, welcomed North Korea's signing of the Agreed Framework with the United States in 1994 (see Chapters 1, 18, and 21). Thereafter, Beijing–Pyongyang relations began to warm.

In 1995, with North Korea on the brink of famine and bankruptcy, China rushed food, oil, coal, and other aid to prop up Kim Jong Il's wavering regime. The "lips and teeth" alliance seemed to be making a full recovery.

North Korea's persistent nuclear ambitions, however, have once again put the alliance under severe strain. China initially reacted with calculated calm when, in October 2002, North Korea confirmed to the United States that it had initiated a second nuclear weapons development program (see Chapters 1 and 21).

The escalation of tensions between Pyongyang and Washington eventually convinced Beijing that it had to intervene. In April 2003, it brought together representatives from the two quarreling capitals in the hope of setting the stage for a diplomatic end to North Korea's nuclear ambitions. When this failed, it pressured Pyongyang into attending a second diplomatic gathering, the Six Party Talks which convened between

China, Japan, North Korea, South Korea, Russia, and the United States in Beijing in August 2003.

China's worst fears about the Korean Peninsula, either a second Korean War or a nuclear armed North Korea, could materialize unless Beijing can convince Pyongyang to give up its quest for a nuclear arsenal. Beijing hopes it can achieve this by persuading Kim Jong Il that he has more to gain from giving up his nuclear weapons than from possessing them.

Washington shares China's goal, but differs with its strategy. President Bush is pursuing a two track strategy of diplomacy and economic pressure backed by an option to use military force, if deemed necessary. China instead prefers that the international community, particularly the United States, would rely on security and economic inducements to persuade North Korea. Meanwhile, Beijing publicly opposes pressuring Pyongyang, but has quietly used brief disruptions of its economic aid to restrain Pyongyang's conduct and to convince it to attend diplomatic gatherings in Beijing.

North Korea's future course regarding its nuclear weapons will make or break the "lips and teeth" alliance. Beijing seems determined to confront Pyongyang with a choice between nuclear weapons or the continued diplomatic and economic support of China. This choice, more than anything else, could eventually compel Pyongyang to give up its nuclear ambitions.

Personal Recollections

During one of my many tours of Pyongyang's Memorial Hall to Victory in the War to Liberate the Fatherland (in other words, the Korean War), I asked why no display explained the Soviet Union's contribution to North Korea during the war. The guide took me to the "Hall of Heroes" and pointed to a young man's picture and said, "This is Mao Zedong's son. He died in our war, killed by a U.S. airplane." The guide added that Stalin had promised air cover for the Chinese troops helping North Korea, but Soviet pilots only fought against U.S. pilots along the China-North Korea border; they did not provide air support further down the peninsula. There was no need, the guide concluded, to devote an entire room to the Soviet Union.

The "Blood-Bonded" Partnership

Annually, Chinese and North Korea officials, when toasting the shared trauma of the Korean War, refer to their "blood-bonded" alliance. No one will ever know how many tens of thousands of Chinese soldiers died in the Korean War. Had China not rushed to Kim Il Sung's aid in that war, his regime would have been overwhelmed and Korea reunited under U.S. auspices. Kim Il Sung has died, but the generals who surround his son Kim Jong Il remember well the debt they owe China.

During the first decade of the DPRK-PRC alliance, Pyongyang sought to maintain balance in its dealings with Beijing and Moscow. North Korea benefited in two ways from this approach. While Moscow provided significant amounts of economic aid and technical assistance, Beijing maintained a sizable army in North Korea through 1958. But after a decade of close collaboration and coordination, cracks in the triangular alliance widened into deep crevices.

Increase Your North Korea IQ

Here is a chronology of (PRC)–North Korea Relations, 1949–1961

May 1949—Mao Zedong transfers ethnic Korean troops to Kim Il Sung's army.

October 6, 1949— Diplomatic relations established.

May 13, 1950—Kim Il Sung and Mao Zedong meet to discuss Korea's forceful reunification of Korea.

June 25, 1950—North Korea invades South Korea.

July 2, 1950—Beijing tells Moscow it will intervene in the Korean War if U.S. troops enter North Korea.

July 5, 1950—Stalin promises air support for Chinese in North Korea.

October 2, 1950— "Chinese People's Volunteers" enter North Korea.

November 23, 1953—China and North Korea sign first economic agreement.

October 1958— Chinese troops withdraw from North Korea.

July 11, 1961—China and North Korea sign Treaty of Friendship, Cooperation, and Mutual Assistance that is identical to North Korea's treaty with the Moscow.

Yo-Yo Diplomacy (1960–1991)

The Sino-Soviet dispute undermined the camaraderie of the Moscow-Beijing-Pyongyang alliance. Kim Il Sung successfully exploited the situation for 30 years until the Soviet Union's demise in 1990 (see Chapter 14).

During the 1960s, North Korea's economy made impressive gains in large part due to the bountiful economic aid it received from its two allies (see Chapter 13). Low-cost Chinese oil and coal fueled the boom in North Korea's steel and mining industries. The steady supply of diesel oil fueled Soviet-designed tractors and irrigation pumps, produced chemical fertilizers and pesticides, and powered fishing boats. North Korea was able to achieve impressive gains in food production.

Cheap Chinese and Soviet oil also produced explosives and fueled North Korea's rapidly expanding arsenal of Soviet-designed tanks, armored vehicles, mobile artillery, and modern fighter aircraft. By the end of 1959, North Korea was again confident in its ability to defend itself. China's army was advised the time had come for it to withdraw from the Korean Peninsula. Beijing was quite willing to accommodate the request. China at the time needed all its young men to help end its famine and to revitalize its own economy.

North Korea contributed to China's effort to preserve North Vietnam as a buffer against the United States. During the Vietnam War, North Korean pilots flew Soviet- and Chinese-supplied fighter aircraft against U.S. pilots over North Vietnam. North Korea supplied Soviet-designed weapons to the North Vietnamese army.

But then Beijing stunned Pyongyang. Beginning in 1971, China began a fundamental makeover of its foreign and domestic policies. The Nixon Administration initiated diplomatic contact with Beijing in 1971. The PRC's normalization of diplomatic relations with the United States and numerous other former Chinese enemies followed. After Mao Zedong's death, China's new leaders initiated domestic economic reforms to attract foreign investment. From Pyongyang's perspective, China seemed to be shifting from communism to capitalism.

Increase Your North Korea IQ

Here is a chronology of PRC–North Korean Relations, 1980–1992

May 1983—PRC civilian airliner hijacked to South Korea, first diplomatic talks held.

June 1983—North Korea's future leader Kim Jong Il visits Beijing.

August 1983—First visit to the PRC by a South Korean official.

March and April 1984—South Korea and China exchange hosting athletic events.

May–July 1984—Kim Il Sung visits the Soviet Union.

November 1984—Kim Il Sung visits China.

October 1986—Beijing competes in the Asian Games in South Korea.

October 1988—Beijing participates in the Seoul Olympiad.

January 1992—China changes trade with North Korea from barter to cash-payment basis.

August 24, 1992—Beijing and Seoul initiate diplomatic relations.

North Korea's confidence in its closest ally was shaken. The China-North Korea alliance seemed to be spinning up and down like a yo-yo. The 1980s brought new surprises as Beijing hesitantly opened channels of communication with Seoul, Pyongyang's archrival.

These developments severely undermined North Korea's sense of security. Pyongyang watched Beijing first turn toward the capitalist world. As Beijing opened commercial ties with South Korea, the Soviet Union stumbled toward bankruptcy, economic reform, and political chaos. The strategy of playing the Soviets off of the Chinese was now obsolete. No sooner had the Soviet Union collapsed in 1991 than China established diplomatic relations with South Korea in 1992. Amid these developments, North Korea decided to develop a nuclear weapons capability.

Seesaw Diplomacy Since 1992

China, since its 1992 opening of diplomatic relations with South Korea, has maintained clear and consistent goals regarding the Korean Peninsula. Beijing strives to sustain a balance in its dealings with the two Koreas. Its effort resembles standing on the middle of a seesaw and trying to prevent either end from tilting toward the ground.

Fundamental to its balancing act are the so-called "three principles." These are ...

◆ Keep the peninsula free of nuclear weapons.

◆ Maintain peace and stability on the peninsula.

◆ Settle issues through dialogue.

Beijing's early efforts to normalize diplomatic and commercial relations with Seoul promptly tipped the seesaw in South Korea's favor. Actually, the first blow to the China-North Korea relationship predated Beijing's opening of relations with Seoul.

No More Free Ride

Early in 1992, before China and South Korea opened diplomatic relations, Beijing decided to stop supplying North Korea crude oil, coal, fertilizer, and other basic commodities on terms highly favorable to North Korea. Traditionally, the Chinese central government had subsidized the trade with interest-free loans and the artificially low, subsidized "friendship" prices. Instead, Pyongyang henceforth would have to pay up front for what it sought to purchase from Beijing.

At the same time, however, regulation of so-called border trade was relaxed. China's central government allowed provincial authorities to conduct trade on a barter basis. For North Korea, this was a double-edged sword. North Korea could acquire through barter essentials like grain, fertilizer, and light industrial goods (small machines, processed foods, and so on). But the range of goods available via barter did not include what North Korea needed most—fuel for its struggling economy.

Bilateral Beijing-Pyongyang trade continued to tail off. China's food exports to North Korea fell by more than half in just one year, between 1993 and 1994. China's exports of crude oil and coal to North Korea slipped more than one third in value. At the same time, North Korea's exports to China covered only half the value of its imports from China, even at the reduced levels.

Trading Places

For almost half a century, China had been North Korea's second largest trading partner after the Soviet Union. But then China's economic reforms allowed its new breed of capitalist-leaning leaders to put profit before politics. One glance at North Korea convinced these new Chinese leaders to embrace South Korea. North Korea's rusting Soviet-designed industrial infrastructure was incapable of competing with South Korea's shiny new, modern, efficient, and high-technology infrastructure.

China's trade with its long-time enemy South Korea lunged past that of trade with its long-time friend North Korea. In 2001, Beijing-Seoul trade reached US $35.9 billion. China's exports to South Korea amounted to US $12.5 billion, and imports totaled twice as much, US $23.4 billion.

In 2001, by comparison, China-North Korea trade came to about US $325 million. China's exports to North Korea declined about 20 percent and its imports from North Korea increased more than 300 percent. Nevertheless, their total bilateral trade was a fraction of trade between China and South Korea.

Personal Recollections

North Korea's "oil shock" of 1992 was evident when I first visited Pyongyang in December 1992. A chauffeur-driven Mercedes Benz rushed me through the city's dark streets. Not a single streetlight brightened the way. In countless apartment buildings, only dim lights shined in stairways. The apartments were dark. After being told there would be no supper, I was taken to a modern Western-style house—one of several in the official guest compound. Having flown from Tokyo to Beijing, and then Beijing to Pyongyang, I was eager to take a hot shower. It never happened. The water temperature remained just above freezing as I showered. This proved to be the first of many cold showers I was destined to take in North Korea.

Investment

Similarly, cash-starved North Korea could not compete with the bulging pockets full of investment cash that South Korea's savvy businessmen carried to China. Between 1992 and 2001, South Korea's entrepreneurs have poured US $13.5 billion into more than 20,000 investment projects in mainland China, worth US $25.1 billion. At the same time, China's investment in North Korea added up to a paltry US $5.1 million in just 13 North Korean enterprises.

Border Crossings

Long-term relations rely on a growing exchange of people and ideas, not just the exchange of money and goods. Recent developments in this regard suggest China's ties with South Korea have and will continue to strengthen relative to its ties with North Korea. At the end of 2000, 15,000 South Koreans were studying in China, and 1,615 young Chinese were doing likewise in South Korea.

At the same time, North Korea was reluctant to allow its youth to spend long periods of time in China. Pyongyang feared these young people's commitment to socialism would be eroded by China's turn toward capitalism. Coinciding with North Korea's official reluctance to enable exchanges with China, the PRC is struggling to keep out the hundreds of so-called "illegal" North Korean immigrants who slip into northeast China in search of food and employment (see Chapter 2).

The Warming Trend

Beijing-Pyongyang ties turned frigid by the fall of 1992, and continued that way until the end of 1994. The flow of oil from China diminished to a trickle. The supply of high-quality Chinese coal to North Korea's steel industry plummeted. Just as the Soviet Union's declining ability to defend North Korea may have contributed to Kim's decision to develop nuclear weapons, China's shift from barter trade to cash basis could have inadvertently increased North Korea's dependence on missile exports to obtain crude oil.

Playing Hard to Get

Pyongyang faced a bleak future by the winter of 1992. The Soviet Union had disappeared (see Chapter 14) and China seemed to have betrayed it for Seoul. Faced with these developments, Kim Il Sung decided upon drastic action.

In March 1993, North Korea announced that it would withdraw from the Treaty on the Non-proliferation of Nuclear Weapons (NPT) and resume its nuclear development program. Pyongyang claimed it had to develop nuclear energy to replace its lost supply of crude oil.

The First Korean Nuclear Crisis

Most experts believed North Korea's primary goal was to develop a nuclear weapons capability. These experts believed nuclear power stations were a secondary consideration.

China shared with the United States, Russia, South Korea, Japan, and most European nations, a distinct concern for North Korea's nuclear ambitions. The United States rather reluctantly agreed to engage North Korea in negotiations aimed at "freezing" its nuclear program. But Washington was hesitant about extending economic inducements to Pyongyang to keep it in the NPT.

While the Clinton Administration in Washington, D.C., haggled with itself and the South Korean leadership about what, if any, inducements to provide, China quietly initiated its own program of economic inducements aimed at getting Pyongyang to drop its nuclear program.

Fueling Relations

China began by reversing its trade guidelines with North Korea at the end of 1994. It resumed supplying crude oil on favorable terms. Since then, China has provided North Korea with 90–100 percent of its annual oil imports. Between 1996 and 2001, China each year provided North Korea 1.2 million M/T of crude oil and 1.5 million M/T of coal.

This tactic had several positive effects. Beijing's relations with China have warmed steadily ever since. This has increased its leverage in dealing with its sometimes exasperating ally. With access to energy imports on favorable terms, North Korea's dependence on ballistic missile exports to generate revenues has subsequently subsided. Also, North Korea's industrial and agricultural production has made gradual but steady gains.

Nurturing Relations

China's food aid to North Korea has been equally generous. Its food aid dates from 1994, one year before torrential rains and floods devastated North Korea's grain crops and compelled it to seek international humanitarian aid. According to official Chinese data, Beijing each year between 1996 and 2001 supplied North Korea at least 10 percent of its annual food grain requirements. This amounts to 500,000 M/T of grain each year. Additionally, food aid from China's provincial governments came to an additional 50,000 M/T of grain per year.

Courting Pyongyang

China also swallowed its pride and began courting North Korea's new leader, Kim Jong Il. The Chinese government had reacted negatively to Kim's choice as heir apparent in 1981. But now that Kim Il Sung was dead and the Soviet Union was gone, China sought to reassert its influence over North Korea. To do so, the PRC had to officially recognize Kim Jong Il as North Korea's new leader and stroke his ego.

Initially the courtship required that Beijing dispatch high-ranking, official delegations to Pyongyang. Kim Jong Il was unresponsive. Between 1993 and 2000, Beijing sent four of its highest ranking officials to Pyongyang to meet with Kim Jong Il. Between November 1991 and June 1999, no ranking North Korean official made an official visit to China. All the while, China continued shipping, at no cost, crude oil, grain, fertilizer, and other basic necessities to North Korea.

Making Up

The impasse was finally broken in May 1999. North Korea's Foreign Ministry issued a statement that condemned the United States bombing of the Chinese embassy in Yugoslavia. China welcomed Pyongyang's support and invited Pyongyang to send a ranking official to Beijing. The visit produced a joint statement that reaffirmed the two nation's "traditional friendship."

Beijing expressed full support for the Korean people's "struggle to achieve peace and stability"—and "its endeavors for peaceful reunification." Beijing also urged Pyongyang to improve its relations with the United States, Japan, and the European Union countries.

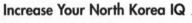

Increase Your North Korea IQ

Here is a chronology of PRC–North Korean Relations, 1992–2003

June 3–7, 1999—Kim Yong Nam, President of the Supreme People's Assembly, visits Beijing, the highest level visit since Kim Il Sung's 1991 visit.

June 23, 1999—Kim Jong Il makes his second visit to China; the first was in 1983 with his father.

May 29, 2000—Kim Jong Il makes a third visit to China, his second since becoming North Korea's ruler.

July 25, 2001—North Korea and China commemorate the fortieth anniversary of their Treaty of Friendship, Cooperation, and Mutual Assistance.

September 3–5, 2001—Chinese President Jiang Zemin visits North Korea, the first Chinese leader's visit in 11 years.

April 17, 2003—Beijing hosts nuclear talks between Washington and Pyongyang.

As icing on the cake, China pledged to send North Korea 150,000 M/T of grain and 40,000 tons of coal. Within days, the North Korean government announced that Kim Jong Il would make his first visit to China since 1983, when he accompanied his father on an official visit.

Finding Common Ground

Beijing welcomed Kim Jong Il at the end of May 2000, two weeks before his history-making summit with South Korean President Kim Dae-jung. There was no joint statement in Beijing, only numerous toasts. But Pyongyang's official media cleared away yet another hurdle to the normalization of relations. Kim Jong Il had long viewed China's rush toward capitalism as a betrayal of socialism and of its socialist partnership with North Korea. But on his visit to China, Kim Jong Il saw first hand the benefits of "modernizing" socialism. He apparently liked what he had seen. After returning home, he commended China for its "great successes … in the socialist modernization drive …."

A senior Chinese military delegation visited Pyongyang in October 2000. Although there was no official announcement about the discussions that took place, the rank of the visitors and the length of the stay indicated that their military alliance remained very strong.

"Illegal Immigrants" or "Refugees"?

The two allies discovered more common ground in December 2000. China reaffirmed its three decade–old agreement with North Korea that governed the movement of both nations' citizens between their two countries. China officially designated as illegal immigrants any North Koreans who had entered China without travel permits. China assured North Korea it would not extend refugee status to these people and would return them to North Korea (see Chapter 2).

By 2001, Beijing and Pyongyang relations were back on track. The two nations' leaders exchanged visits. First Kim Jong Il made his second visit to China as North Korea's leader in January 2001. China's President Jiang Zemin visited Pyongyang in September 2001, the first visit by a Chinese leader in 11 years.

The two nations also reaffirmed their 40-year-old Treaty of Friendship, Cooperation, and Mutual Assistance. Unlike Russia, Beijing maintained without change its commitment to defend North Korea in the event of invasion.

The Chinese leader commended Kim for his progress toward reconciliation with South Korea and improvements in North Korea's economy. The North Korean leader congratulated China on its impressive economic gains. They assured one another of continued efforts to improve relations.

Without naming names, the two communist leaders voiced opposition to selected U.S. policy goals in East Asia. Pyongyang pledged unwavering support for a "one China" policy and for Beijing's desire for reunification with Taiwan. Both leaders expressed opposition to the United States's development and intended deployment of antiballistic missile systems.

Again, China topped off each visit with pledges of additional fuel and food aid. Jiang on his September 2001 promised "grant-in-aid" of 200,000 M/T of food and 30,000 M/T of diesel fuel. No longer was Pyongyang delivering tribute to Beijing—in some ways, the roles were reversed. Instead, by 2001, China's aid to Pyongyang had resumed in earnest.

Nukes and Yankees Keep Out

China's strategy of inducing North Korea to abandon nuclear weapons appears to have yielded very disappointing results. No sooner had China and North Korea repaired their alliance, and Chinese aid resumed, than North Korea stunned the world by claiming to a visiting U.S. official delegation in October 2002 that it had initiated a second, clandestine nuclear weapons development program.

The particulars of this new program and the crisis it sparked will be discussed in Chapters 18, 21, and 24. Here we will concentrate on Beijing's reaction to Pyongyang's revelation in October 2002 and its preferred solution for resolving the crisis.

Direct Talks—Yes

China prefers to deal with North Korea through diplomatic channels, not publicly via the mass media. But Pyongyang's persistent escalation of the second nuclear crisis on the Korean Peninsula since 1992 finally compelled the Chinese government to speak out publicly in February 2003, after years of private diplomacy.

The Foreign Ministry's statement of policy came after North Korea had expelled the International Atomic Energy Agency (IAEA), restarted its old five megawatt nuclear reactor at the Yongbyon Nuclear Research Center, and then withdrew completely from the Treaty on the Non-proliferation of Nuclear Weapons.

For the sake of accuracy, we repeat what the Chinese Foreign Ministry spokeswoman said on February 13, 2003, regarding her nation's policy about nuclear weapons on the Korean Peninsula. She said:

> China believes that a nuclear-free Korean Peninsula should be safeguarded, and … the security concerns of the DPRK should also be taken into consideration. The key … is the dialogue between the parties concerned at an early date, the only effective way to settle their disputes. *The relevant parties should make positive efforts to promote the dialogue between the US and the DPRK. China has done a lot in this regard.* [Emphasis added.]

She repeatedly emphasized direct dialogue between the United States and North Korea as the only effective way to resolve the situation. She also pointed to the 1994 U.S.–North Korea Agreed Framework as the "the important basis" and starting point for any future resolution.

When asked about a European proposal that the United States and North Korea convene their direct talks within a "multilateral framework," the spokeswoman responded:

> China believes that direct dialogue … constitutes the only effective way to settle this issue … We adopt a flexible attitude towards the method and framework of the dialogue. But the key is that the relevant parties must agree to dialogue.

Multilateral Talks—Yes; Sanctions—No

China opposes the use of multilateral pressure to compel North Korea's unilateral submission to United States's demands, a point made in the Foreign Ministry's February 13, 2003, press conference, "China is *not* in favor of the willful use of sanctions or pressure to address some issues in the world." (Emphasis added.)

In light of the above remarks, China's reluctance to pass the Korean nuclear issue to the UN Security Council is understandable. Instead, China supports efforts of the IAEA to resume its monitoring and inspections of North Korea's nuclear facilities. At the same time, Beijing urges the international community to demonstrate continuing patience. Also, it calls on the community to nurture an atmosphere conducive to direct dialogue between Washington and Pyongyang.

China clearly shares with Moscow, Seoul, and Tokyo a preference for direct negotiations between the United States and North Korea to resolve the Korean Peninsula nuclear issue. But it officially expressed flexibility regarding the format of diplomatic dialogue. In other words, while Beijing rejects multilateral pressure on North Korea, it can accommodate multilateral diplomatic dialogue.

China in March 2003 took the lead in promoting a compromise between North Korea's insistence on direct, bilateral talks with the United States, and the United States' adamant rejection of this. At the end of April, after intense diplomatic effort,

China convened the so-called Three Party Talks between representatives from Pyongyang and Washington in Beijing. While the talks failed to achieve any progress toward breaking the impasse, they did intensify China's determination to promote a peaceful resolution through dialogue.

Four months of persistent diplomacy finally produced the Six Party Talks that convened in Beijing on August 27–29, 2003. The participants included China, Japan, North Korea, South Korea, Russia, and the United States. Again, there was no progress toward a resolution. Nevertheless, the talks created a calm atmosphere conducive to diplomatic dialogue. All the participants, particularly North Korea and the United States, were able to clarify their positions.

Also, the meeting concluded with Chinese Vice Minister of Foreign Affairs Wang Yi issuing a statement of consensus. In it, the participants concurred that the Korean Peninsula must remain free of nuclear weapons and urged that the United States and North Korea work to achieve a peaceful resolution of their differences through diplomacy. See Chapter 24 for an assessment of prospects for achieving the goals established at the first round of the Six Party Talks.

The Least You Need to Know

- ◆ North Korea appears to have successfully resumed its position in the triangle of cooperation between itself, Beijing, and Moscow.

- ◆ Without support from its triangle relations with China and Russia, North Korea would be hard pressed to sustain itself, as became evident in the 1990s.

- ◆ Russia, preoccupied since 1985 with its internal problems, has relinquished its dominant role in the triangle to China.

- ◆ China has steadily increased North Korea's dependence on it for economic aid, which gives Beijing considerable leverage in Pyongyang.

- ◆ Beijing has taken the lead in pressing for a diplomatic resolution to the nuclear impasse between North Korea and the United States.

North Korea and South Korea: The North-South Courtship

In This Chapter

- ◆ Estrangement between the Koreas (1949–1972)

- ◆ Sputtering dialogue (1972–1989)

- ◆ Lunge toward reconciliation (1990–1992)

- ◆ Estrangement persists (1993–1997)

- ◆ Engagement begins (1998–Present)

The North Korean regime has been in a struggle to survive since 1990. The Soviet Union's collapse and China's turn toward capitalism ended Kim Il Sung's economic and political free ride. Gone is the security of the Soviet nuclear umbrella, its military alliance, and aid. The Communist bloc's market for North Korea's exports has evaporated. South Korea, at the same time, has excelled politically and economically.

In 1990, Kim Il Sung initiated a two-track policy to save his regime. His son is continuing the same dual-track strategy, with just minor tactical adjustments. Survival remains the primary goal of the regime. Since 2000, reconciliation with South Korea has become an important means to that goal.

Both Kims faced the same problem: how to convince the international community to give them what they need to maintain their regime. Kim Il Sung traditionally used a double-edged sword. One edge was crafty diplomacy that pitted Beijing against Moscow and yielded a continuous supply of the basic needs for national defense and economic growth. The other edge was armed deterrence. Insulting rhetoric juxtaposed with pictures of a multitude of goose-stepping soldiers became the audible and visible images of North Korean deterrence. The aim was to compel enemies like the United States and South Korea to keep their distance.

The developments of 1990 called for drastic measures. Kim Il Sung stuck to his double-edged strategy, but refined it. He turned to his worst enemies for his needs. In succession, North Korea engaged in diplomatic dialogue with Seoul, Tokyo, and Washington. In this and the next two chapters, we examine North Korea's efforts at reconciliation. We begin with South Korea.

Halfway There?

An old Korean adage proclaims, "The beginning is half the journey." The epic meeting of South Korean President Kim Dae Jung and North Korea's Supreme Commander Kim Jong Il on June 15, 2000, in Pyongyang took 50 years to occur. If the Korean adage is accurate, reconciliation between the two Koreas would require another half century.

The Korean Peninsula's role as a flashpoint during the Cold War has experienced a profound alteration since the Soviet Union's demise. This once highly unstable intersection of superpower rivalry has benefited from the growing détente between the superpowers. Easing tensions have fostered dialogue and economic cooperation between North and South Korea.

In 2002, more than 12,000 South Koreans visited North Korea. They went as tourists to the famous Kumgang Mountains. Many others visited Pyongyang bearing humanitarian aid, to meet long-lost relatives, or to negotiate future economic cooperation.

However, today's tranquility may prove to be just a temporary illusion. Looking at the past will bring this illusion into focus.

Distrust One's Kinsman

North and South Koreans harbor deep mutual distrust. It is rooted in the memories of a ghastly half century of national division, war, and economic destitution that parents, teachers, friends, and colleagues retell to one another and their children.

National division in 1945 (see Chapter 7) initiated the process that shredded the fabric of Korean society. Tens of thousands of Korean Christians and land owners fled the north to escape the North Korean regime's persecution of Christians, seizure of land, and nationalization of privately owned enterprises.

War followed in 1950 (see Chapter 9). Like the U.S. Civil War, death and physical separation tore apart families, but in Korea the division continues. The DMZ remains a deep physical and figurative scar across the Korean Peninsula's waist.

Containment

The Korean War and its aftermath intensified and prolonged North-South animosity. Despite his near defeat by United Nations forces, Kim Il Sung proclaimed victory after the Korean Armistice had been signed. For the next 40 years, he pursued policies aimed at destroying the South Korean government.

Kim's invasion of South Korea demonized him in the eyes of all South Koreans and the multitude of nations aligned against the Communist bloc. Washington and Seoul teamed up for the next 40 years to diplomatically isolate, economically undermine, and militarily deter North Korea.

From 1948 to 1972, North and South Korea struggled to destroy one another. Intense competition for diplomatic recognition ensued for 40 years. Each Korean government equated the establishment of diplomatic ties to other nations to be recognition of its legitimacy as the sole government of Korea. The superpowers encouraged and assisted this rivalry until 1991, when both Koreas were admitted into the United Nations, conferring legitimacy on both governments.

Deterrence's Double-Edged Sword

Each Korea sought to deter the other's anticipated aggression. Effective deterrence requires a balance of terror projected through massed armies and weapons. The idea is to convince the other side that attack would be too costly and inevitably futile. The desired result is the perpetuation of the status quo—a military stalemate.

Prior to the collapse of the Soviet Union, neither Korea had, or believed it needed, a nuclear arsenal. Each relied instead on their superpower allies' nuclear umbrellas to add nuclear punch to their deterrence. This strategy meant, however, that the failure of deterrence could escalate rapidly into a nuclear holocaust that would extend far beyond the Korean Peninsula.

Deterrence is a two-way street. While it has prevented the resumption of war, it also has made the Korean Peninsula a potentially volatile place. Deterrence cannot promote reconciliation and durable peace, since it sustains an arms race. No sooner had North Korea lost its Soviet nuclear umbrella than it began building its own nuclear weapons capacity. The United States, South Korea, and Japan responded by improving their military capabilities on the Korean Peninsula.

Confrontation

The Korean rivalry often was deadly and sometimes projected far beyond the Korean Peninsula. In the 1960s, the two Koreas competed militarily along the DMZ in Korea and in Vietnam. Exchanges of rifle and artillery fire erupted almost weekly along the DMZ from 1963 to 1972. North Korean infiltrators trying to sneak through no-man's land into South Korea triggered many of these incidents. In Vietnam, North Korean pilots flew Soviet-supplied fighters against U.S. pilots over North Vietnam while South Korean troops fought the Viet Cong, or Vietnamese communists, in South Vietnam.

Pyongyang occasionally turned to terrorism between 1968 and 1988. North Korean soldiers and covert agents repeatedly tried to assassinate South Korea's president. In a failed 1968 effort, a platoon of North Korean soldiers almost reached the Blue House, the residence of South Korea's president. In 1974, a pro–North Korea resident of Japan killed the wife of South Korea's president when trying to shoot the president. In Rangoon, Burma, in October 1983, North Korea agents detonated a bomb that was intended to kill the visiting South Korean president but instead murdered several members of his cabinet. The last act of North Korean terrorism occurred in 1987 when a North Korean–planted bomb on a South Korean civilian airliner exploded, killing everyone aboard.

Mirror Imaging One Another

Containment, confrontation, and deterrence have not been conducive to reconciliation. The North-South rivalry has infected all aspects of post-war reconstruction, politics, and communication between the two societies.

North Korea's covert assault on the South Korean government has backfired. South Koreans have rejected communism and despotism and instead embraced capitalism and steadily pushed for democracy. But U.S. economic sanctions did not weaken

Pyongyang. Instead, North Korea gained strength from its membership in the Communist bloc.

Both regimes used each other's threat to rationalize their authoritarian rule. They claimed moral superiority and mouthed the slogans of democracy, but authoritarian regimes ruled in Pyongyang and Seoul for much of the Cold War. Opposition to established authority and officially sanctioned ideology was severely punished on both sides of the DMZ. Both Korean rulers claimed to be "defending the fatherland" from either the "imperialist" or "communist" aggression, and "capitalist" or "communist" infiltration.

Spies and Subversives

On either side of the DMZ, anyone who advocated engagement and dialogue with the other side was promptly labeled either a traitor to socialism or a communist sympathizer and imprisoned. Even in South Korea, anyone seeking to contact a person in North Korea, regardless of reason, first had to apply for permission to do so.

Under South Korea's notorious *National Security Law*, citizens of South Korea are still not permitted to contact any North Koreans, including kinsmen, without explicit written permission. Possession of any materials, especially printed literature from or even about North Korea and communism, was outlawed until the early 1990s. Even the exchange of mail with relatives in North Korea was once considered a subversive act. North Korean television and radio broadcasts were jammed. Disobeying the law was punishable by execution. Conditions in the North were and still are much harsher.

> **Korean Concepts**
>
> South Korea's **National Security Law** prohibits all contact between a South Korean citizen and a person from North Korea, unless prior written permission has been granted. There is no such law in North Korea, but every North Korean knows contact with anyone other than a fellow North Korean requires either prior permission or a detailed written report to the Internal Security Bureau.

In both Koreas, the language of reconciliation became equated with disloyalty and even treason. Compromise—the essence of diplomacy and democracy—was associated with appeasement.

The only institutionalized and politically acceptable channel of communication between the two Koreas from 1953 to 1971 was the Military Armistice Commission (MAC; see Chapter 9). There, dialogue occurred between representatives of hostile armies. Their purpose was to maintain the Korean War Armistice and its military stalemate, not to resolve the conflict's causes or to promote reconciliation.

Can We Talk?

Since 1971, despite these formidable obstacles, South and North Korea have built a dialogue that has become increasingly substantive and productive. In so doing, they have focused on reconciliation rather than reunification.

Round One

The first tentative effort at reconciliation began in 1971. The United States's disengagement from Vietnam and pursuit of détente with Beijing appear to have motivated South Korean president Park Chung Hee (the preferred spelling for Pak Chong-hui) to initiate secret contact with Kim Il Sung in the aftermath of President Nixon's February 1971 visit to Beijing.

Increase Your North Korea IQ

President Park Chung Hee ruled South Korea from 1963 to 1979. A graduate of the Imperial Japanese Army's Military Academy, he joined South Korea's new army after World War II and fought in the Korean War. In 1963, he seized power in a military coup. After normalizing relations with Japan in 1965, Park used central management of the economy and five-year economic plans to engineer South Korea's rapid economic revitalization. But he earned the scorn of young South Koreans in 1972 when he proclaimed a new constitution that made him president for life and outlawed dissent. The director of the Korean Central Intelligence Agency assassinated Park in 1979.

Progress initially appeared promising. On July 4, 1972, the first *South-North Joint Communiqué* was signed. The rigid mold set in place by the Korean War had at last been cracked. The legitimacy of dialogue between the two Korean governments had been established. So, too, had been the principle that the two sides should pursue reconciliation without regard for foreign concerns.

The first North-South dialogue also set the agenda for future talks. President Park in August 1972 urged North Korea to "… exhibit their fraternal love by beginning the humanitarian task of reducing the pains of the separated families." A year later, he advocated South Korea's "… admittance into the United Nations together with North Korea …" These were forward-looking proposals that Kim Il Sung initially rejected, but eventually embraced.

> **Korean Concepts** _____
>
> The first **South-North Joint Communiqué** has become the cornerstone of the two Koreas' dialogue. It states, "First unification shall be achieved through independent efforts without being subject to external imposition or interference." These were oblique references to superpower intervention in the relationship between the two Koreas. The two Korean leaders reaffirmed this statement at their June 2000 Pyongyang summit.

Return to Rivalry

Just as quickly as it had begun, this early dialogue sputtered to an end. Mutual hostility promptly resumed. Neither side tried to foster an atmosphere conducive to reconciliation. Both sides persisted in insulting each other. Neither Korean leader had anything to gain politically from compromise. Besides, South Korea after 1972 became preoccupied with internal political unrest as President Park's oppressive rule sparked public outrage. One of Park's closest advisers shot him to death while they dined in 1979.

Soul Searching in Seoul

In the turmoil that followed Park's assassination, General Chun Doo-hwan seized power in December 1979 and set about putting Seoul's house in order. Law and order topped his agenda, not dialogue with North Korea. This was particularly true after North Korean agents tried to assassinate him in Burma in 1983.

> **Increase Your North Korea IQ** _____
>
> Chun Doo-hwan, South Korea's president from 1980 to 1987, was an army general who seized power in December 1979, shortly after President Park Chung Hee's assassination. Chun ruthlessly suppressed dissent in the name of countering communism. He achieved infamy for the Kwangju Incident of 1980 during which troops under Chun's command killed hundreds of antigovernment demonstrators in the southwest city of Kwangju. Chun blamed his critic Kim Dae Jung and sentenced him to death. A political deal between Chun and U.S. president Ronald Reagan allowed Kim to go to the United States.
>
> Korea's economic development surged during the Chun administration. But massive demonstrations in 1987 forced him out of power. He was later imprisoned for his political and financial excesses. Chun's nemesis Kim Dae Jung was elected president in 1998.

Olympic Strategy

The awarding of the 1988 Olympiad to Seoul convinced Chun to form ties with the Communist bloc to ensure its broad participation. Chun's so-called "Nord politick" also called for dialogue with Pyongyang to disarm its hostility. Chun reluctantly agreed to open talks with Pyongyang in September 1984 after it sent rice, cement, and cloth to flood-stricken South Korea. The talks yielded the first-ever reunion of long-separated family members and athletic and cultural exchanges. But then the progress stalled.

In the 1980s, Seoul enjoyed tremendous success establishing athletic and cultural ties to all of Pyongyang's allies. Pyongyang found itself isolated and outflanked when everyone from the Communist bloc showed up at the 1988 Seoul Olympiad (see Chapters 14 and 15).

Trading Places

The balance of power and prosperity on the Korean Peninsula was reversed in the 1980s from the picture we have of the two countries today. Pyongyang began the decade out in front. Its grain production had record highs while Seoul still needed U.S. food aid. North Korea's army was modernizing its huge army with Soviet-designed tanks, armored vehicles, and ballistic missiles. Pyongyang was a picture-perfect city of two million well-fed and clothed people.

Seoul then was a chaotic city of narrow streets. The poor and unemployed rioted in government-built slums. Tear gas filled the streets around campuses where students spent most of their time demonstrating against the government. Labor disputes were harshly suppressed, journalists jailed, and politicians corrupted. South Korea's export- and light industry–oriented economy was depressed by mounting competition from Taiwan, Hong Kong, and other newly awakening economies in East Asia.

By decade's end, however, the situation was reversed. Seoul had won the world's acclaim for its hosting of the Seoul Olympiad and its impressive progress toward democracy. It had become a power in the world market. Seoul had diplomatic or commercial ties with virtually every nation in the world except North Korea. Seoul had become a city of parks, colorful nightlife, cultural diversity, and a rapidly expanding middle class. A modernized, apolitical South Korean army focused on national defense instead of domestic politics. Problems persisted, but increasingly South Koreans were acquiring the material means and political practices to deal with their society's shortcomings.

Pyongyang on the other hand was on the brink of decline by 1990. Aid from Moscow and Beijing had stopped (see Chapters 14 and 15). Agricultural and industrial production were in steep decline (see Chapter 13). Pyongyang had lost its markets in Eastern Europe and Central Asia. Its lower-quality goods simply could not compete with the much better, more favorably priced and financed South Korean goods.

After the Cold War

In 1988 and 1989, South Korea's newly elected president, Roh Tae Woo, repeatedly invited North Korea to reopen a dialogue. Absent from Roh's proposals was the harsh Cold War rhetoric. In August 1989, he urged Kim Il Sung, "It is … imperative that we establish an interim stage toward unification in which the South and North should … seek co-existence and co-prosperity on the basis of mutual recognition."

Increase Your North Korea IQ

President Roh Tae Woo ruled South Korea from 1987 to 1993. Like his close friend and predecessor President Chun, Roh was a retired army general. South Korea's first popularly elected president, he oversaw the hosting of the Seoul Olympiad, restored political freedom and rights to thousands of imprisoned and blacklisted professionals, and achieved the first substantial reconciliation between the two Koreas. Once out of office, however, Roh was imprisoned for having accepted upward of $500 million in bribes from South Korea's business community.

An envious and insecure Kim Il Sung listened cautiously to Roh's proposals. The Cold War's end had freed the two Koreas of their ideological straitjackets, and Kim Il Sung was aging. These factors plus Pyongyang's growing uncertainty about its future could have convinced Kim to accept Roh's invitations.

Once the dialogue started in 1990, it lunged forward. The Koreas signed two unprecedented agreements in February 1992: the *Agreement on Reconciliation, Non-aggression, and Exchanges and Cooperation*, plus the *Joint Declaration on the Denuclearization* (sic) *of the Korean Peninsula*.

> **Korean Concepts**
>
> The **South-North Korea Agreement on Reconciliation, Non-aggression, and Exchanges and Cooperation** was signed in February 1992. Both parties promised to work toward "national reconciliation," "to avoid armed aggression and hostilities," and "to realize … exchanges and cooperation to advance common national interests and prosperity …."
>
> The **Joint Declaration on the Denuclearization (sic) of the Korean Peninsula,** signed the same day, promised, "The South and the North shall not test, manufacture, produce, receive, possess, store, deploy or use nuclear weapons." Nor will either side "possess nuclear reprocessing and uranium enrichment facilities." North Korea has subsequently broken all these promises.

The First Nuclear Crisis (1992–1997)

The dialogue abruptly ended, however, at the end of 1992 before Pyongyang could reap any economic benefits from the new opening. International Atomic Energy Agency (IAEA) inspections sparked suspicions in August 1992 that North Korea had not accurately reported its inventory of plutonium. Pyongyang's adamant refusal to cooperate with the IAEA seemed to confirm these suspicions. The first Korean nuclear crisis ensued (see Chapter 18 for specifics).

Mutual distrust between the North and South quickly replaced the reconciliation. South Korea's new president, Kim Yong-sam, put dialogue with Pyongyang near the bottom of his agenda. After the U.S.–North Korea nuclear negotiations began in June 1993, President Kim sought to manage the U.S. initiative. Although South Korea did not participate in the talks, he compelled Washington to link the negotiation's continuation to the resumption of North-South dialogue.

The Agreed Framework

Washington came to regret the linkage. The harder it pressed Pyongyang to reengage Seoul, and the closer the U.S. and North Korea came to an agreement, the more President Kim demanded of his ally. Finally in June 1994, North Korea agreed to resume IAEA inspections and invited Kim Yong-sam to a summit. South Korea's president agreed to the arrangement, but then Kim Il Sung died two weeks later.

Kim Yong-sam reacted by labeling Kim Il Sung a "war criminal" yet still said that he was ready to meet North Korea's new leader, Kim Jong Il. The South Korean leader's disparaging comments about his father had angered Kim Jong Il and he rejected the offer.

The Clinton Administration concentrated on ending North Korea's nuclear program. In September 1994, the United States reluctantly shelved South Korea's last lingering concerns and closed a deal with North Korea. The so-called Agreed Framework, signed in October 1994, was the first-ever accord between the United States and North Korea (see Chapter 18 for the accord's specifics).

The deal pleased Pyongyang and angered Seoul. North Korea was promised two modern nuclear reactors, and Seoul and Tokyo got the bill. Seoul felt the accord gave North Korea too much in the way of economic benefits in exchange for the promise to "freeze" its nuclear program. The Republican-dominated and budget-minded U.S. Congress echoed Seoul's concerns.

The Clinton Administration was caught in the middle. Pyongyang grumbled about Seoul's oversight of the nuclear reactor construction project while Seoul complained about having to cover the cost. North-South dialogue languished. In 1995, as Pyongyang's food shortage approached famine proportions and its economy dived toward bankruptcy, President Kim, among others, concluded North Korea would soon collapse.

Four Party Talks

To buy time while waiting for North Korea's collapse, President Kim proposed, and the Clinton Administration agreed to pursue, so-called four party talks (Seoul, Washington, Beijing, and Pyongyang) to negotiate unresolved issues. Six months after their joint proposal of April 1996, a North Korean submarine ran aground on South Korea's East Coast. According to a crew member, the sub had landed a platoon of North Korean commandoes. All were later found inside South Korea, shot to death by their commander.

Only after the United States had convinced North Korea to make its first-ever public apology to the Seoul government did the public outcry subside in South Korea and the four party talks began. Pyongyang finally agreed to participate, but only after Washington had promised it large amounts of food aid. Just as the talks commenced, Kim Yong-sam's term expired. His successor, Kim Dae Jung, discontinued the four-party talks.

Sunshine Diplomacy

In December 1997, South Koreans elected Kim Dae Jung president. The aging champion of Korea's democratization, Kim was determined during his seven-year term to achieve an unprecedented level of reconciliation with North Korea.

President Kim Dae Jung successfully orchestrated the first-ever North-South Korea summit in June 2000 by doing exactly the opposite of what his predecessors had done for half a century. First he rallied the support of the superpowers. Never before had Moscow, Beijing, Tokyo, and Washington together backed Seoul's approach to Pyongyang. Simultaneously, Kim Dae Jung shifted from trying to overpower Pyongyang diplomatically to engaging it while maintaining South Korea's deterrence posture. The South Korean press nicknamed Kim's strategy toward North Korea *sunshine diplomacy*.

Korean Concepts

South Koreans nicknamed President Kim Dae Jung's strategy of engaging North Korea diplomatically and economically **sunshine diplomacy.** His effort was viewed as projecting warmth (i.e., sunshine) toward the frigid North in the hope of getting the North to warm its attitude toward the South. South Korean businessmen were urged to invest in the North and humanitarian organizations to send food and medical aid. The strategy set the stage for the unprecedented June 2000 summit in Pyongyang between the two Korean leaders. Most South Koreans, despite sunshine diplomacy's subsequent uneven record, still prefer it over previous strategies. Kim Dae Jung's successor, President Noh Moo-hyun, in compliance with the public's preference, is continuing the strategy.

The June 2000 North-South summit was an epic event, but there was no breakthrough in terms of relations between the two Koreas. The two leaders essentially reaffirmed past agreements and pledged to renew efforts to implement them.

Perhaps the summit's most important aspect was that the key participants represented a new generation of Korean leadership. Their focus is oriented more toward achieving reconciliation in the future than seeking revenge for past transgressions.

There has been a fundamental shift of goals and the balance of power on the Korean Peninsula since 1980. Both Koreas, for different reasons, appear intent on pursuing coexistence rather than mutual destruction. South Korea, now a prosperous economic power in Northeast Asia, prefers peace to the risk of war that would only disrupt its prosperity. North Korea is equally intent upon survival. Peace with South Korea thus better serves Pyongyang's priorities.

But political realities in both societies remain formidable obstacles to reconciliation. Mutual mistrust is pervasive in the two Koreas, particularly the North. While South Korea continues to make impressive progress toward democracy, North Korea clings to despotic political institutions and practices. Economically, South Korea continues to rush toward prosperity while North Korea languishes on the edge of bankruptcy and many of its people live in poverty and linger near famine.

South Korea's government since 1990 has allowed its people greater freedom to decide for themselves about North Korea. South Koreans can now watch and listen to North Korean television and radio broadcasts, read its literature, and engage its professionals in conferences and joint projects. But North Korea persists in trying to manipulate people's thinking by blinding them to the reality beyond their homeland and regulating access to the outsiders.

If there is to be further, durable reconciliation, North Korea's government must cease trying to isolate its people from reality and extensively revise what it teaches young North Koreans about South Korea and the rest of the world. North-South dialogue and sunshine diplomacy alone cannot bring the two societies closer together.

The Least You Need to Know

- ◆ Memories of national division and the Korean War perpetuate mutual distrust and complicate reconciliation between South and North Korea.

- ◆ From 1950 to 1983, the two Koreas dueled to destroy each other. North Korea preferred military might and terrorism while South Korea favored diplomatic and commercial isolation of the North.

- ◆ The two Koreas eventually shifted to dialogue that has gradually gained momentum toward reconciliation.

- ◆ The possibility of war, however, still haunts the Korean Peninsula, largely because of North Korea's nuclear ambitions.

Chapter 17

North Korea and Japan: Old Animosities Die Hard

In This Chapter

- Why does North Korea want to reconcile with Japan?
- What issues are perpetuating their mutual animosity?
- What are the prospects for reconciliation?

Japan's relationship with North Korea is haunted by the legacy of Imperial Japan's colonial rule of Korea. Kim Il Sung pointed to this legacy as evidence that Lenin's theory of imperialism fit the Korean experience. He placed anti-Japanese sentiment at the core of modern Korean nationalism, as viewed in North Korea, and made it a recurring theme of the history taught to all North Koreans. Anti-Japanese sentiment in North Korea will remain a formidable obstacle to the two nations' reconciliation until the North Korean government ceases the propagation of distrust and hatred of the Japanese people.

Japan is to be commended for its efforts since 1989 to achieve reconciliation with North Korea. North Korea, however, has been generally unresponsive. Every time progress appears to be underway, Pyongyang's leaders take steps that revive old animosities. For the Japanese people, the most objectionable aspects of North Korea's policies are its pursuit of weapons of mass destruction, particularly nuclear weapons and ballistic missiles, and its refusal to resolve the cases of the Japanese adducted citizens (see Chapters 2 and later in this chapter). Not until North Korea resolves these issues will prospects improve for normal relations between the two nations.

Pyongyang to Tokyo—You Owe Me!

Since 1989, Japan and North Korea have alternately enticed and rejected each other. Numerous Japanese delegations have gone to Pyongyang hoping to defuse its hostility and to promote normal diplomatic relations. Yet their relations remain estranged.

Pyongyang's official attitude toward Tokyo is, "You owe me!" North Korean officials and mass media repeatedly rattle off a litany of claims against Japan. These are intended to pressure Japan into giving North Korea monetary compensation for Japan's past misdeeds and to sustain the North Korean people's distrust and disdain for Japan.

Pyongyang's goal since 1989 has been to cash in on Japan's sense of guilt for its colonization of Korea in 1910 (see Chapters 6 and 7). North Korea's leaders once believed political forces within Japan could compel Japan's government to give North Korea a huge sum of money plus aid just as Japan gave to South Korea in 1965.

When Japan and South Korea normalized their relationship in 1965, the Japanese government extended full diplomatic recognition to Seoul and pledged to provide US $800 million, then a substantial sum, in grants and loans over a 10-year period. Many believe, including North Koreans, that the settlement's financial benefits sparked South Korea's rapid economic development.

Talking the Talk

Beginning in 1990, Pyongyang eagerly accepted several overtures from Japan to engage in diplomatic negotiations. It hoped to emulate South Korea's successes both with Japan and its economic development. Since 1998, however, the Japanese government has made it adamantly clear that before any settlement of old scores, Pyongyang must begin to resolve a list of outstanding issues.

The most recent effort came in September 2002, when Japan's Prime Minister Junichiro Koizumi went to Pyongyang to meet North Korean leader Kim Jong Il. The unprecedented summit raised hopes of speedy reconciliation. But no sooner had the prime minister returned to Japan than such expectations collapsed. Like all the previous efforts, progress proved temporary.

Looking back will allow us to better project the probable future of Japan–North Korea relations.

Tokyo Tries It Alone

Members of Japan's parliament, the Diet, pioneered efforts to normalize Japan's relations with North Korea. Shin Kanemaru, one of Japan's most powerful politicians in the 1980s, led a bipartisan parliamentary delegation to North Korea in September 1990. The Communist bloc had just collapsed and the Soviet Union would soon disappear. North Korea's economy was in a steep decline (see Chapter 13), and North Korea's primary benefactor, China, was turning toward capitalism and curtailing the favorable aid to its small neighbor.

Select elements of Japan's business community and North Korean leader Kim Il Sung were eager for reconciliation. Kim was feeling increasingly insecure without his protectors' backing. Also, his economy needed a quick injection of cash and a new market. Rumors rumbled around political circles in Japan that the government might give North Korea upward of $10 billion, a formal apology, and diplomatic relations in exchange for settling old scores.

Beating the "Four Dragons"

Japan's politicians, pressed by the business community, pushed the Foreign Ministry to find new markets for Japan's export-driven economy. Japan's exports were encountering stiffening competition from the so-called Four Dragons: South Korea, Hong Kong, Singapore, and Thailand. The opening of the China market had given Japan's economy a boost since the mid-1970s. But competition there, too, was heating up.

Trade with North Korea had started years earlier, but failed to expand because of North Korea's impotent economy. Some Koreans living in Japan had profited from this trade since the 1960s because of their political connections to Pyongyang. In 1986, the Japanese government stopped insuring Japanese investment in North Korea. At the time, North Korea owed Japanese investors US $600 million. An expansion of trade, some Japanese hoped, would enable North Korea to pay off this debt.

Japan's broader business community wanted in on this trade. It believed that once Japan–North Korea relations were normalized, North Korea could replicate South Korea's economic "miracle." The North then could become a sponge for Japanese exports and investment.

Japan's North Korea "Lobby"

Japan, then and now, has a North Korea lobby, the pro-Pyongyang Association of Korean Residents in Japan. Its name in Japanese is the *Chosen soron*. This group has been, and remains the prime moving force behind efforts to establish diplomatic relations with North Korea.

Korean Concepts

The **Chosen soron** (or *Choson chongnyon* in the Korean language) is the Japanese name of the Association of Korean Residents in Japan. Established in 1955 to protect members from pervasive Japanese prejudice against Koreans, the organization received money from North Korea. Kim Il Sung hoped through it to form ties to Japan's Communist and Socialist Parties.

Some association members channeled profits from illegal activities through the association to North Korea where their money garnered them preferential treatment and investment in some of North Korea's more profitable enterprises.

Improving Japanese treatment of Koreans, acculturation, and the discrediting of communism sapped the association of its previous political and economic prowess. By 1994, the Japanese government put the association's membership at 56,000, less than 10 percent of the Korean population in Japan.

Japan's Korean minority numbered about 700,000 Koreans in 1990. Most are descended from Koreans enticed or forced to go to Japan during the colonial period (1910–1945). Of the 1.5 to 2 million Koreans in Japan at the end of World War II, the majority went home. About 600,000, despite ill treatment in Japan, opted to remain for various reasons. Some chose to stay once they learned they would be blacklisted as being pro-Japanese traitors if they went home.

Korean Concepts

Yakuza is the Japanese word for "mobster" or "gangster." They excel at the same illegal activities of their counterparts in United States and Italy. A small number of Japan's Yakuza are Korean residents of Japan.

The Japanese once despised their Korean minority. The Korean minority since 1960, however, has shared in Japan's prosperity. Most Korean residents now are respected members of Japan's business and professional communities. Prejudice persists today, but attitudes have moderated greatly.

Given the harsh conditions in post–World War II Japan, combined with Japanese prejudice against Koreans, some Koreans had to earn their living from petty theft, extortion, and black marketing. Those who excelled in these vocations then invested in more sophisticated criminal activity. These Koreans retain ties to Japan's gangster element, the so-called *Yakuza*. Working together, Korean and Japanese mobsters deal in prostitution, smuggle and distribute drugs, and finance gambling. Some of their profits eventually were invested in North Korea.

More than half of Japan's Korean population initially flocked to the pro–North Korean association when it was founded in 1955 to protect themselves from prejudice. They were also enticed with promises of employment and the Korean-language schools that the association established. Kim Il Sung's Korean Workers' Party pumped money into the organization.

Cashing In

By the 1980s, the pro–North Korean association was a potent, cash-rich organization with close ties to several influential Japanese politicians. This group bankrolled Kanemaru's 1990 trip.

Kanemaru probably made the trip for two reasons. First, he sought to magnify his political influence by drawing Japan's Socialist Party closer to the conservative political mainstream, a move that would further isolate the Japanese Communist Party.

At the same time, the businessmen who funded the trip gave Kanemaru a large sum of money for his services. This fact did not become public knowledge until years later and after his death.

Japan and North Korea—Round One (1990)

Accompanying Kanemaru to Pyongyang were leaders of the Japan Socialist Party. They carried with them a letter from Japan's prime minister addressed to Kim Il Sung. Kim Il Sung personally greeted the delegation at his residence, a rare event for a visiting delegation from a nation that did not have diplomatic ties to North Korea.

Roadmap to the "Yellow Brick Road"

The two sides proudly and confidently signed a "Joint Declaration." Ever since, it has served as a roadmap to bilateral normalization. The Japanese government was urged to "fully and officially apologize and compensate" North Korea for Japan's colonization of the Korean Peninsula.

North Korea's desire for apologies had been anticipated. The delegation brought along letters of apology from several powerful Japanese politicians, including the current and former prime ministers. Kim Il Sung, however, wanted an apology from the Japanese emperor, but that was not then forthcoming, and is still pending North Korea addressing Japan's wish list of outstanding issues between the two countries.

The two countries also agreed to develop two-way exchanges between politicians, businessmen, and cultural groups. To facilitate these exchanges, direct air service and satellite communications were urged.

Direct telephone service was soon established. While chartered Japanese flights between Japan and North Korea are possible for Japanese citizens, North Koreans cannot fly directly to Japan. Instead, they can either fly from Pyongyang to Japan via Beijing or make the trip aboard a small North Korean ocean liner that travels weekly between the two countries.

Japan's political leaders promised an end to discrimination against Koreans living in Japan and the enforcement of laws designed to guarantee their human rights.

Then came the hard part. The two sides' political party leaders agreed to the need to end the "abnormal state" of relations "as soon as possible." The Japanese side agreed to consider "that Korea is one," but stopped short of referring to "one nation" in order to avoid suggesting agreement with North Korea's claim that it was the sole legitimate government of Korea. Doing so would have outraged Seoul and Washington.

To assuage such concerns, Japan won inclusion of two significant points. North Korea agreed to include the phrase, "… peaceful reunification through north-south dialogue …" Also, the joint statement calls for the "building of a peaceful and free Asia and elimination of nuclear threats from all regions of the globe."

Toward these ends, Japan's politicians promised to "strongly recommend" to their government the start of bilateral diplomatic negotiations "within (the month of) November 1990" to resolve outstanding issues and to clear the way to normalized diplomatic relations.

The Never-Ending Talks

The Japan–North Korea "normalization" talks began in November 1990, five weeks after Kanemaru and his delegation had returned to Tokyo. Eight rounds of formal talks followed until 1992. As the talks dragged on, North Korea tried to make itself as attractive as possible to potential Japanese investors.

Pipe Dreaming on the Tumen River

North Korea sought to entice Japanese investment. In October 1991, it hosted a UN Development Program (UNDP) conference that aspired to establish the Tumen River

Development Project. The Tumen River, which flows from west to east (see Chapter 3), forms the northeast border between China and North Korea. The conference brought together representatives from China, Russia, Mongolia, North and South Korea, and Japan. The goal was to attract foreign investment to the construction of transportation and industrial infrastructure in the area where the Russian, Chinese, and North Korean borders intersect. Japan's representatives listened politely, and then went home to consult with their colleagues in government, business, and political circles.

Increase Your North Korea IQ

Here is a chronology of Japanese–Korean relations, 1945–1992

1945—Korea liberated from Japanese colonial rule.

1955—Pro-Pyongyang Association of Korean Residents in Japan (Chosen soron) formed in Tokyo.

1957—North Korea sends first "education aid funds" to the Chosen soron in Tokyo.

1959—Repatriation to North Korea of 100,000 Korean residents in Japan begins.

1965—Japan–South Korea relations normalized.

September 1990—Kanemaru Parliamentary Delegation visit to Pyongyang.

November 1990—First round of Japan–North Korea normalization talks held.

October 1992—Normalization talks suspended because of the Korean Peninsula nuclear crisis.

Pyongyang's Radical Makeover

As its contribution to the Tumen River Project, North Korea proposed in December 1991 to establish the Rajin/Sonbong Free Economic and Trade Zone (FETZ). The zone was named after the small twin ports of Rajin (or Najin as it is spelled in South Korea) and Sonbong. Rajin at the time was actually a fishing village with one small pier. Sonbong was the site of a Soviet-designed thermal power plant that burned heavy fuel oil.

The concept had shortcomings. The area lacked infrastructure. There were no piers (save the small one at Rajin), warehouses, paved roads, or industry. Next, North Korea lacked the funds and credit to finance the construction of such facilities. Finally, North Korean attempts to entice foreign investment always fell far short of expectations.

The High Cost of Friendship

The talks dragged on. North Korea demanded that Japan's emperor apologize for Japan's colonization of Korea, plus provide compensation worth $10 billion in cash, aid, and investment.

Japan countered that it had already paid compensation to South Korea. Instead, Tokyo offered loans, investment, and technology valued at about half of what Pyongyang demanded. Japan also insisted that North Korea first address allegations that its agents had kidnapped Japanese citizens to teach North Korean covert agents the Japanese language and culture. North Korea, however, continued to deny any responsibility for the abductions until September 2002 (see this chapter's conclusion).

Some Japanese businessmen nevertheless continued to press the government for rapid normalization of relations with North Korea. In July 1992, a 60-member private Japanese trade mission arrived in Pyongyang seeking joint venture opportunities in North Korea's light industries and mining sectors. Their dreams of profit soon evaporated.

Let's Not Make a Deal

The first nuclear crisis on the Korean Peninsula heated up at the end of 1992. Japan closed ranks with Washington and Seoul. Tokyo told Pyongyang that it first had to give up any thoughts of building a nuclear weapons arsenal before normal diplomatic ties could be formed. Japan–North Korea normalization talks sputtered to a halt.

Increase Your North Korea IQ

Here is a chronology of Japanese–North Korean relations, 1997-1998

September 1997—Japan and the United States agree on expanded defense guidelines.

November 1997—Japanese parliamentary delegation to Pyongyang issues a second joint communiqué.

November 1997—First home visit of Japanese spouses of Koreans repatriated from Japan to North Korea.

January 1998—Second home visit of Japanese spouses of Koreans previously resident in Japan.

March 1998—Third Japanese Parliamentary Delegation visit to Pyongyang.

June 1998—North Korean Red Cross denies North Korea responsible for the disappearance of any Japanese citizens.

Japan and North Korea–Round Two (1997)

Once the U.S.–North Korea Agreed Framework had resolved the nuclear crisis in October 1994, the Japanese government quickened efforts to restart the normalization talks. A trickle of humanitarian aid flowed to North Korea beginning in the summer of 1995 and continuing until 1998.

Two Japanese parliamentary delegations visited North Korea in 1997. The first in March accomplished nothing. The visit by the heads of three major Japanese political parties in November 1997 resulted in a joint statement. It urged resumption of the bilateral normalization talks. Both sides agreed to the need to resolve "humanitarian and cooperation issues … before the normalization of bilateral diplomatic ties."

North Korea Blinks

North Korea offered to allow the Japanese spouses of some North Koreans to visit Japan. Beginning in 1958, Japan allowed Korean residents of Japan and their Japanese spouses to move to North Korea. Once in North Korea, however, and despite earlier assurances, the Pyongyang government had never allowed these Japanese citizen spouses to visit their homeland. In 1997, Pyongyang finally offered to do so.

Increase Your North Korea IQ

The welfare of 6,637 Japanese spouses of North Koreans remains a divisive issue between Japan and North Korea. These Japanese women accompanied their spouses, when they voluntarily repatriated to North Korea after 1959. About half of these women retained Japanese citizenship, but with the exception of two small groups who visited Japan in 1997–98, the North Korean government did not allow them to visit Japan.

At the same time, however, North Korea labeled as "false" Japan's claims that North Korea was responsible for the disappearance of some Japanese citizens. Nevertheless, North Korea offered to investigate the allegations.

These were promising first steps by North Korea. At the beginning of 1998, Pyongyang allowed 14 Japanese spouses of former Korean residents of Japan to make short visits to their homeland.

Behind the Blink

Pyongyang rarely gives something for nothing. A deciphering of the motives for North Korea's conciliatory attitude must await further research.

One possibility is that Pyongyang hoped to stiffen opposition in the Japanese Diet to the U.S.–Japan Defense Guidelines. The 40-year-old U.S.–Japan alliance's foremost purpose remains Japan's defense. But shared concerns about the Korean Peninsula caused the allies to develop a contingency outline of Japan's role if a second Korean War erupted. Japan's politicians would have to sanction the plan before it took effect, which was expected to happen in 1998.

Increase Your North Korea IQ

Japan's constitution, written when General Douglas MacArthur ruled Japan after World War II, bars Japan from having armed forces. After the U.S.-Japan Mutual Defense Treaty was signed in 1954, the constitution was revised, at Washington's urging, so that Japan could have "self-defense forces." According to the revised constitution, these forces could not to be deployed beyond Japan and its territorial waters. In the 1980s, again at Washington's urging, Tokyo agreed to expand the operational range of these forces so they could defend Japan's sea lanes extending 200 miles from Japan. Beginning in 1993, the United States encouraged Japan to further expand its defense role in the event of another Korean War. The specifics of their September 1997 agreement are spelled out in the expanded U.S.–Japan Defense Guidelines. Japan's Diet approved the new guidelines in 1998.

Pyongyang alleged that the guidelines were a "plot to strangle" it. Finalization of the draft outline coincided with the 1997 Japanese parliamentary visit to North Korea. By demonstrating a conciliatory attitude toward the visiting Japanese politicians, Pyongyang may have hoped to entice their opposition to the U.S.–Japan Defense Guidelines.

A possibly related motive may have been Pyongyang's hope to deter further defense cooperation between Seoul and Tokyo. The United States since the early 1980s had been urging the two neighbors to begin such cooperation, but military talks between them did not begin until much later.

Kim Jong Il Pops Off

The warming trend in Japan–North Korea relations was abruptly reversed on August 31, 1998, when North Korea launched a three-stage, long-range *Taepodong* ballistic missile through Japanese airspace into the northern Pacific Ocean.

North Korea's intention probably was to draw the world's attention to Kim Jong Il's formal succession as heir to Kim Il Sung. Its missile launching backfired. The claim of having put a satellite in orbit was nothing but hot air. Actually, the launch was a failure. The missile flew only about 300 kilometers before falling into the ocean.

Increase Your North Korea IQ

Here is a chronology of Japanese–North Korean relations, 1998–2003

August 1998—North Korea launches a long-range ballistic missile through Japanese airspace.

March 1999—North Korea "spy" ship spotted near Japanese coast.

December 1999—Japanese parliamentary delegation visits North Korea. Bilateral Red Cross talks follow.

April 2000—Normalization talks resume.

October 2001—Normalization talks end again without results.

September 2002—Japanese prime minister holds summit meeting with Kim Jong Il in Pyongyang, but relations soon sour.

May 2003—North Korea condemns Japan's launching of a "spy" satellite to monitor military activities in North Korea.

Outrage in Japan

The missile launching had a profound and enduring negative impact on the Japanese public's view of North Korea. For years, the Japanese people had approached North Korea with a sense of humility and guilt because of Imperial Japan's colonization of Korea. The missile launching, however, convinced the Japanese people that North Korea presented a serious threat to their national security.

The Japanese government also reacted with uncharacteristic outrage. Food aid and nine cargo flights per week between the two countries were immediately halted. Japan's Diet condemned the launch. South Korea's defense minister happened to be in Tokyo at the time. He and his Japanese counterpart the day after the launch announced an expansion of Japan–South Korean defense cooperation. Opposition to the expanded U.S.–Japan Defense Guidelines evaporated. Also, the Japanese government announced it would co-develop with the United States the Theater Missile Defense System (TMD).

For the Association of Korean Residents in Japan, the *Taepodong* launching was a public relations disaster. The Association had chartered 16 flights to transport members to the festivities to

Increase Your North Korea IQ

Since North Korea's August 1998 missile launch, the Japanese public has insisted that the abducted Japanese citizens' issue be resolved before relations could be normalized. For the Japanese public, this issue ranks higher than their government's priorities of nuclear weapons and ballistic missiles.

commemorate Kim Jong Il's succession. Fourteen of the flights were cancelled after members decided not to make the trip. This deprived Kim Jong Il's regime of the large amount of hard currency that these people would have spent to pay their expenses while in Pyongyang and as gifts to the new leader.

Jump Start Summit

Japanese Prime Minister Junichiro Koizumi stunned the world on September 17, 2002, when he landed in Pyongyang for the first-ever summit between a Japanese ruler and his North Korean counterpart Kim Jong Il. Secret diplomacy over the previous year had set the stage for the surprise summit.

Kim Jong Il then stunned the world by admitting that North Korean agents had in fact kidnapped approximately 12 Japanese citizens, one more than the Japanese government had long claimed. Kim claimed that a thirteenth alleged Japanese victim never entered North Korea. Amazingly, Kim apologized to the Japanese prime minister and people for these misdeeds. He claimed that those responsible for the abductions had been punished, but declined to provide any further details about the punishment. Kim also confirmed the deaths of eight of the abducted persons and identified the four survivors. According to Kim, all these persons had died from illness or natural disasters.

Abruptly, Japan–North Korea relations seemed on the verge of surging toward normalization after 12 years of inconclusive diplomatic negotiations. Once again, expectations proved premature (see Chapter 2 for additional details).

> **Increase Your North Korea IQ**
>
> The Department of Defense lists six U.S. soldiers as defectors to North Korea. Four defected between 1961 and 1965 while assigned to units in South Korea. One, Private Roy Chung, defected in June 1979 from his post in Berlin, and another one, PFC Joseph Timothy White, defected in 1981 while assigned to South Korea. Chung reportedly died in a North Korean prison and White while swimming in a river. The four survivors, including Private Charles R. Jenkins, live in Pyongyang and teach English. All are married—two to North Korean women, Jenkins to a former Japanese abductee, and one to a Lebanese abductee, who was allowed to leave North Korea, but returned to Pyongyang to live with her husband. No American prisoners of war from the Korean War are known to survive in North Korea.

As soon as the prime minister returned to Tokyo, the Japanese public was outraged to learn that the North Korea government refused to allow the four kidnapped persons to return to Japan. Even more shocking was the news that several of the kidnapped

Japanese had died in their youth and possibly from unnatural causes. The Japanese government promptly demanded, but received, no further details from Pyongyang.

After a month of haggling, Pyongyang allowed four of the previously abducted Japanese to visit Japan. Their spouses and children, however, were kept in North Korea. One of the Japanese women revealed that she had two children by her marriage to a former U.S. Army soldier, Private Charles R. Jenkins, who had defected to North Korea on January 5, 1965, from his unit in South Korea and now teaches English in Pyongyang. (Jenkins also has acted as an American officer in North Korean movies.)

At the end of their visit, the four former abductees refused to return to North Korea. Their spouses and children, however, remain in North Korea. Jenkins, in an interview with a Japanese newspaper, said he would not seek to leave North Korea until the statute of limitations runs out in 2005 on his alleged crime of desertion from the U.S. Army. The Department of Defense has stated that it would prosecute Jenkins if he were to leave North Korea prior to 2005. Jenkins's Japanese wife in June 2003 asked the U.S. Ambassador to Japan, Howard Baker, to seek a presidential pardon for Jenkins. Apparently, President Bush is not inclined to issue one.

Personal Recollections

In July 1996, U.S. Army Lt. Col. Martin Wisda and I were in Pyongyang in connection with the recovery of U.S. soldiers' remains left behind during the Korean War. We asked the foreign ministry if we could meet Private Jenkins and three other U.S. Army defectors known to be living in Pyongyang. We were told they did not wish to meet us. But we were assured that all four men were in good health and enjoying their life in North Korea. Actually, Private Jenkins had played the role of U.S. Army generals in North Korean movies about the Korean War and was teaching English at the Pyongyang University of Foreign Languages.

Japan and North Korea, on the margins of the August 2003 Six Party Talks in Beijing, briefly discussed the abducted Japanese issue. A second informal meeting was held at the end of September in New York. Neither effort yielded any progress toward a resolution. Prospects for a prompt resolution of this issue appear bleak. Kim Jong Il might be awaiting the calming of Japanese outrage before attempting again to resolve the abduction issue.

Bleak Prospects

Japanese–North Korean relations remain at an impasse because of the unresolved issues related to North Korea's abduction of Japanese citizens. Further reinforcing the impasse are North Korea's ballistic and nuclear threats to Japan's security.

Japan since 1992 has supported the efforts of the United States and South Korea to convince North Korea not to pursue a nuclear arsenal and to dismantle its ballistic missile capability.

Japanese Prime Minister Koizumi continues to consistently support U.S. President Bush's policies toward North Korea and Iraq. Japan's alliance with the United States remains the cornerstone of Japan's defense posture. In keeping with this, the Japanese government, for the first time since the end of World War II, will dispatch a small contingent of Self Defense combat troops to Iraq to demonstrate unity with the United States. Koizumi's administration also has won legislative approval for the co-development, with the United States, of a Theater Missile Defense (TMD) system designed to protect Japan from North Korea's ballistic missiles.

Japan's government supports the peaceful diplomatic resolution of the continuing impasse between the United States and North Korea regarding the nuclear issue on the Korean Peninsula. Tokyo, however, would prefer that Washington demonstrate greater flexibility in its posture toward North Korea by agreeing to engage it in diplomatic negotiations.

For North Korea, Japan's alliance with the United States remains the foremost obstacle to the normalization of relations. In Pyongyang's eyes, the U.S.–Japan alliance is the embodiment of the "imperialist threat" to its survival.

So long as North Korea refuses to satisfy Japan's demands regarding the abduction issue and continues to develop weapons of mass destruction, further progress toward the normalization of Japanese–North Korean relations will not be possible.

The Least You Need to Know

- Japan–North Korea relations remain estranged even after more than a decade of intense diplomatic effort to resolve outstanding issues.

- For the Japanese public, the priority issue awaiting resolution involves North Korea's abduction of Japanese citizens.

- The Japanese government's priority concerns are North Korea's nuclear and ballistic missile development programs.

- Japan continues to closely coordinate with the United States and South Korea all aspects of its policy and strategy for dealing with North Korea.

Chapter 18

North Korea and the United States: A Dangerous Tango

In This Chapter

- The U.S. shift from containment to engagement

- The former Bush Administration's approach

- The Clinton Administration's handling of the first Korean nuclear crisis

- The Agreed Framework's demise

Pyongyang's leaders must have felt isolated and frustrated by early 1991. Moscow and Beijing had turned away from their long-time ally. The Soviet Union had simply disappeared. Its successor, the Commonwealth of Independent States (better known as Russia), was too preoccupied with its own problems to assist North Korea. Even worse, China had opened relations with Seoul, Pyongyang's foremost rival.

Pyongyang's negotiations with Seoul and Tokyo held out the promise of better times. Both extended enticements of economic aid and monetary compensation, but at a cost and at some future time. North Korea's economy was in crisis now. It urgently needed a large infusion of hard currency to reverse its downward slide. But before it could cash in, Seoul and Tokyo insisted that Pyongyang address their lists of grievances.

Pyongyang balked at this requirement. Its leadership seemed convinced that the more it conceded, the more Seoul, Tokyo, and Washington demanded. Pyongyang drew the line in the fall of 1992. Its aging leader Kim Il Sung insisted that either his foes give his regime what it needed to survive, or he would restart his nuclear program.

In this chapter, we concentrate on how the United States has dealt with North Korea's intensified sense of insecurity and persistent efforts to develop a nuclear arsenal. We will review the numerous hurdles to the normalization of U.S.–North Korean relations, and assess U.S. policy toward North Korea from 1988 and 2000. The discussion of U.S.–North Korean relations since is presented in Chapters 19, 21, and 24.

Gathering Storm

During the summer of 1992, the International Atomic Energy Agency (IAEA) conducted its first inspections of North Korea's nuclear facilities. The UN's nuclear watchdog agency found evidence that suggested North Korea might not have accurately reported its inventory of plutonium, the core material of a nuclear weapon.

In August 1992, satellite photographs seemed to confirm these suspicions. Workers at North Korea's Yongbyon Nuclear Research Center (spelled Nyongbyon in North Korea) were spotted creating a rice paddy to camouflage the nuclear waste dump where the IAEA had obtained its suspicious samples. Trees also were being planted to conceal the road that once led to the site.

Patiently and repeatedly for five months, the IAEA and the international community, led by the United States, pressed North Korea to allow the IAEA to collect additional samples of nuclear waste from the concealed site so it could either confirm or discard its earlier findings. North Korea adamantly refused to cooperate, declaring that the inspections would undermine its sovereignty.

Pyongyang's Coercive Diplomacy

On March 12, 1993, Pyongyang declared that it would pull out of the Treaty on the Non-proliferation of Nuclear Weapons (NPT). The first Korean Peninsula crisis was born.

The move was a classic example of Pyongyang's coercive diplomacy. Pyongyang had grown accustomed to getting its way by threatening to do what others did not want it to do. Time and again, Moscow or Beijing had given Pyongyang something to deter it from taking steps detrimental to their interests. But when Kim Il Sung tried out his favorite diplomatic ploy on the international community, it backfired.

Rogue Nation

The international community in the spring of 1993 unanimously censured North Korea for threatening to undermine the system that had been designed to prevent the proliferation of nuclear weapons. While a debate raged inside the young Clinton Administration over what to do, the international community acted. The IAEA Board of Governors urged Pyongyang to comply with its international responsibilities. Pyongyang dismissed the resolution.

Russia called together the NPT's depository nations: Russia, the United Kingdom, France, and the United States. These are the world's foremost nuclear powers. They had negotiated the NPT and designated themselves responsible for its implementation. They jointly chastised North Korea.

Then the European Union (EU), the political and economic association of European nations, passed a resolution that supported the IAEA and censured North Korea.

On April 1, the IAEA Board of Governors directed that North Korea's "noncompliance" be reported to the UN Security Council (UNSC). Indicative of North Korea's isolation, 28 nations approved the resolution; 4 nations (India, Pakistan, Syria, and Vietnam) abstained; and 2 nations (China and Libya) voted no.

In the UNSC, China held the trump card. As one of five permanent members of the Council, its single veto could block the Council's passage of any resolution. The UNSC president sidestepped this possibility by issuing a statement. In it, he called for a peaceful diplomatic solution, avowed support for the NPT and the IAEA, and urged North Korea to comply with its earlier pledges to cooperate with international nuclear safeguards. China voiced its support for the statement.

North Korea continued to escalate the crisis. On May 2, a North Korean machine-gunner fired southward across the DMZ. No one was hurt, and fortunately the South Korean army did not respond. Four days later, Pyongyang told the IAEA that it would refuel its nuclear reactor at Yongbyon. Doing so would give it 8,000 spent nuclear fuel rods from which to extract enough plutonium to make five or six nuclear weapons.

Tensions peaked on May 11 when the UNSC passed a resolution that urged, "… all member states to encourage the DPRK to respond positively to this resolution, and encourage them to facilitate a solution." Two of North Korea's supporters, China and Pakistan, indicated their growing displeasure with Pyongyang by abstaining, which allowed the resolution to pass. The UN General Assembly then unanimously voted to censure North Korea. Pyongyang was completely isolated.

Squabbling in Washington

Pyongyang's timing had been impeccable. It caught the two new presidential administrations in Washington and Seoul completely unprepared. In Washington, the Clinton Administration was only a few weeks old. Many senior positions remained vacant. President Clinton, moreover, was preoccupied with justifying to the Defense Department his new policy regarding homosexuals in the U.S. Armed Forces.

The debate over how to deal with North Korea intensified. Opponents of negotiations, promptly labeled hawks, argued that talking to North Korea would "reward" its misconduct and coercive tactics. They warned that other small, would-be nuclear powers might try to emulate North Korea's coercive diplomacy. The hawks advocated a show of force to enforce North Korea's compliance with the NPT. A few pushed for "taking out" Yongbyon with an aerial attack.

The Ticking Clock

The doves, as those who advocated negotiations were called, urged decisive diplomatic action. They pointed to the clock. Ninety days after North Korea's announcement, per the NPT's provisions, Pyongyang would automatically cease to be a party to the treaty. A solution had to be found by June 11. Otherwise, they cautioned, the international nuclear nonproliferation regime would collapse. Saving the NPT and preserving peace, they contended, justified negotiating with Pyongyang. These "moderates" called for inducing North Korea to give up its nuclear ambitions by drawing it into the international community.

Containment

Part of the problem was that the United States had never engaged North Korea in diplomatic negotiations. For 40 years, U.S. policy toward East Asia's communist regimes was designed to contain communism. Diplomatic and commercial isolation reinforced by armed deterrence were designed to estrange these nations from the international community and eventually bring about the collapse of the People's Republic of China, North Korea, and North Vietnam.

U.S. policy toward two of these regimes had undergone dramatic alteration in the 1970s. The Nixon Administration had broken with the policy of containment, initiated by President Harry S. Truman in Europe in 1947, and established diplomatic relations with Beijing. At the same time, North Vietnam crushed the U.S.–backed South Vietnamese government and unified Vietnam.

On the Korean Peninsula in 1993, the United States and South Korea persisted in their Cold War containment policy despite both the Soviet Union's collapse and their opening of diplomatic relations with the People's Republic of China.

Reagan's Modest Initiative

Paradoxically, it was the hard-line administration of President Ronald Reagan that set in motion a process that eroded the containment policy on the Korean Peninsula. Aiming to defuse Pyongyang's frustration over being excluded from the 1988 Seoul Olympiad, Seoul and Washington teamed up to declare their "modest initiative" on July 7, 1988.

The initiative was linked to South Korea's *nordpolitik* strategy of engaging communist nations (see Chapter 16). For the first time, Washington offered Pyongyang inducements, if its diplomacy complied with internationally acceptable norms. As a goodwill gesture, the United States offered the modest inducement of opening the first diplomatic channel to North Korea through the U.S. Embassy in Beijing. This became known as the Beijing Channel.

Personal Recollections

The first U.S. export license involving North Korea was given to retired Admiral Dan Murphy in 1991. He was then-President Bush's long-time friend, foreign policy adviser when Bush was vice president, former deputy director of the Central Intelligence Agency, and a retired naval officer. The license authorized Murphy's firm, Nikko of New Jersey, to export up to $1 billion worth of grain to North Korea. Murphy and his partner, David Chang, were also prominent fundraisers for the Republican National Committee and the Republican Party in New Jersey. Murphy's firm eventually exported more than $100 million worth of grain to North Korea, but North Korea stopped payment in 1993. My duties as the North Korea desk officer from 1992 to 1994 required that I work with both men.

The Beijing Channel was opened in 1989. Whenever the United States sought to send a message to Pyongyang, it directed the U.S. Embassy in Beijing to telephone the North Korean mission to set a time and place for a meeting. The State Department's North Korea desk officer drafted the message and circulated it to concerned parties in the Departments of State and Defense, then to the National Security Council. Once approved, the classified message was cabled to Beijing for the embassy's political minister to pass to his North Korean counterpart at Beijing's International Club. At these brief encounters, no talking was permitted unless one side sought clarification of the message's content. This cumbersome process was not conducive to resolving crises.

The U.S. government also promised to issue export permits to U.S. businessmen to sell and export to North Korea basic human needs such as food grain, educational materials, and so on.

Bush's "Carrot and Stick" Strategy

In 1991, the former President Bush, at the behest of South Korea, continued the "carrot and stick" strategy. The "carrots" included the admission of both Koreas into the United Nations in September 1991. President Bush announced later that same month the withdrawal of all U.S. tactical nuclear weapons from around the world. Early in January 1992, he agreed to discontinue the huge annual U.S.–South Korea military training exercise called "Team Spirit."

Two weeks later, the first-ever high-level meeting between U.S. and North Korean officials convened for one day in New York. U.S. State Department political affairs undersecretary Arnold Kantor met with North Korean Workers' Party secretary Kim Yong-sun. There were no negotiations. Instead, they tabled lists of what each side wanted before relations could be normalized.

At the January 1992 meeting, the United States called on North Korea to …

- ◆ Forgo the development of nuclear weapons.

- ◆ Halt the export of ballistic missiles and join the Missile Technology Control Regime (MTCR).

- ◆ Renounce the use of terrorism.

- ◆ Engage in dialogue with South Korea to resolve outstanding issues.

- ◆ Cooperate with the United States. in the recovery and repatriation of the remains of 8,000 U.S. military personnel who died in North Korea during the Korean War.

- ◆ Show respect for the North Korean people's human rights.

U.S. policy since has emphasized that North Korea must satisfy these requirements before relations can be normalized.

Pyongyang seemed to respond positively. Dialogue between South and North was achieving unprecedented progress (see Chapter 16). North Korean officials initiated dialogue with the chairman of the Senate's Committee on Prisoners of War and Missing in Action (POW/MIA) regarding the recovery of U.S. Korean War dead from North Korea. Pyongyang even began to cooperate with the IAEA and allowed it to begin inspections in June 1992.

The IAEA's suspicions about North Korea's previous plutonium production, however, abruptly shifted the Bush Administration's strategy from proffering "carrots" to threatening to use "sticks." Meanwhile, the hawk and dove debate raged on through the transition from the Bush to Clinton Administrations.

U.S.–North Korea nuclear negotiations, June 1993: U.S. and North Korean chief negotiators size up each other as author Quinones takes notes.

The Agreed Framework

Finally in May 1993, international pressure and President Clinton's preference for diplomacy over war ended the debate in Washington in favor of the first-ever diplomatic negotiations between the United States and North Korea. The talks commenced in New York in June 1993 and then moved to Geneva the following month.

Uncertain Beginning

In the negotiations, State Department assistant secretary for political-military affairs, Robert Gallucci, was pitted against North Korea's first vice minister of foreign affairs Kang Sok-ju. Their first three days of talks at the U.S. Mission to the UN in New

York ended in a draw. Although just one week remained before the June 11 deadline for North Korea's withdrawal from the NPT, the U.S. delegation packed up Friday afternoon and returned to Washington, D.C. Before leaving, Gallucci told Kang to call when he was ready to resume the talks.

Personal Recollections

I was munching my lunch in my State Department office when the secretary appeared with an expression of amazement in her face. "Some guy on the telephone says he's North Korea's ambassador and he wants to talk to you! What do I tell him?" At the time, U.S. diplomats were not authorized to speak to North Koreans without written authorization. I told her I would talk to him. It was North Korea's deputy permanent representative at the UN. He said his government wanted to start negotiations about the nuclear crisis. I answered that I had to talk to my supervisor before I could respond. A couple hours later, I called him back and we agreed to meet the next day in New York. The U.S.–North Korea nuclear talks began two weeks later. At those talks, I was designated the "New York Channel" and became the primary point of contact between the two governments.

The following Monday, the North Korean delegation called the State Department's North Korea affairs officer Kenneth Quinones and said they wanted to talk only to him. With authorization, he jumped on a shuttle flight and headed to New York carrying nothing but a notebook. The next three days were spent sipping orange juice with three North Koreans in a bagel shop on 42nd Street across from the Helmsley Hotel (the shop has undergone a complete makeover).

After one day of explaining the U.S. delegation's membership and how U.S. foreign policy is made, the North Koreans turned to substance. They said they would resume the negotiations if the United States agreed to issue a joint statement. In it, they wanted assurances that the United States would not attack North Korea during the negotiations. Washington somewhat reluctantly agreed.

Personal Recollections

A couple colleagues joined me at the U.S. Mission to write the first U.S. draft of the joint statement. Some of the wording was borrowed from the UN Charter, such as the Preamble's phrase, "armed force shall not be used ..." and Article 2's, "settle disputes by peaceful means ...." We called the National Security Council for approval. The initial response was, "Where the hell did you get that language?" We got approval shortly after we explained our source was the UN Charter.

"Suspended Withdrawal"

The negotiations resumed. On the day of the deadline, the United States and North Korea issued their first joint statement. North Korea agreed to "suspend withdrawal" from the NPT. Without this, the negotiations would not have continued, North Korea would have left the NPT, and its nuclear weapons program would have resumed. The "U.S.–DPRK Joint Statement" of June 11, 1993 (see Appendix B for the text) became a cornerstone of U.S.–North Korean relations.

Wish Lists

Eighteen long, tense months of hard negotiation followed. Actually, there were three simultaneous negotiations. Washington was the scene of constant debate over how to deal with Pyongyang. Most of the discussion focused on whether to offer Pyongyang more carrots (economic and diplomatic concessions) or wave a big stick (U.S. military might) at it.

Washington also dueled with Seoul. Nuclear nonproliferation topped the U.S. agenda. Washington wanted Pyongyang to resume IAEA inspections at North Korea's nuclear facility. Seoul wanted this, too, but first it wanted North-South Korea dialogue to resume.

The United States and North Korea stunned each other at the second round of talks in Geneva in July. Pyongyang said all could be resolved if the United States built two modern nuclear reactors for it, normalized diplomatic relations, ended economic sanctions, and stopped the annual Team Spirit military exercise.

Washington demanded that Pyongyang resume IAEA inspections and restart dialogue with South Korea before the next round of U.S.–North Korea negotiations could be held. Both sides returned to their capitals unhappy and grumbling. From August 1993 to May 1994, there were no negotiations. Instead, 31 so-called working-level meetings were held in New York.

Beyond the "Red Line"

Then in May 1994, Pyongyang crossed the "red line" Washington had drawn. It began to refuel its reactor at Yongbyon. Washington had warned that "serious" consequences, such as a call for UN economic sanctions on North Korea, would follow. Pyongyang countered that it would consider sanctions "an act of war." Kim Il Sung earlier had declared a "state of semi-war alert," which mobilized his people for war.

Washington began preparations for sanctions and war in April. The U.S. military sent antiaircraft Patriot missiles and several hundred headquarters personnel to South Korea. At the State Department, draft resolutions calling for UN sanctions were drawn up. At the United Nations, U.S. diplomats met counterparts on the UN Security Council to discuss possible sanctions against North Korea. In May, the U.S. ambassador in Seoul suggested that the spouses and children of Americans living there return to the United States to begin "an early summer vacation."

By early June, Kim Il Sung knew he had pushed the United States too far. He was under increasing pressure from Moscow and Beijing to back down and resume negotiations. He needed a face-saving way out of the corner he had painted himself into.

Saving Face

Former U.S. president Jimmy Carter's visit to Pyongyang in mid-June 1994 gave Kim what he needed. In a private chat, Kim told Carter he was ready to "freeze" his nuclear program, restart IAEA inspections, and convene a summit with his South Korean counterpart if the United States would agree to resume the negotiations.

When Carter called President Clinton about the good news, Clinton was chairing a war-planning meeting in the White House and would not take the call. Carter, to get Clinton's attention, called CNN's headquarters in Atlanta and offered to tell the world via a live interview on CNN what Kim Il Sung had promised. That got Clinton's immediate and full attention.

Kim Il Sung Is Mortal!

After South Korea's president Kim Yong-sam accepted Kim Il Sung's invitation to a summit, the United States agreed to restart its negotiations with North Korea. But the day after the talks resumed on July 7, Kim Il Sung died.

South Korea's president soon enraged North Korea's new leader Kim Jong Il by labeling his father a "war criminal." When Kim Jong Il subsequently refused to meet Kim Yong-sam, the South Korean president tried to block the resumption of the U.S.–North Korea negotiations.

Washington was forced to pick between Pyongyang or Seoul. Restarting the talks with Pyongyang would anger Seoul but improve prospects for avoiding war with North Korea and salvaging the global nuclear nonproliferation system. The risk of war was renewed when Washington backed Seoul's insistence that North Korea restart dialogue with it.

Personal Recollections

The telephone rang in my Geneva hotel room at 4 A.M. The Japanese diplomat on the line had been up all night drinking and playing cards with Japanese journalists when one of their Tokyo offices informed them that Kim Il Sung had died. He had called me for confirmation. I called a friend at CNN and asked him to call a Russian journalist I knew in Pyongyang—I was not authorized to call anyone in North Korea. My CNN friend soon called back to confirm Kim Il Sung's death. I first informed the State Department Operations Center, and then the White House situation room.

Next, I called the North Korean delegation. They adamantly denied that their leader was dead. Then I woke up Bob Gallucci and told him. He gathered some members of our delegation and walked to a nearby bakery for breakfast. I returned to my room to await further news. My embarrassed but grateful North Korean counterpart called me to officially confirm Kim Il Sung's death. Later, the North Korean delegation awarded me a "Kim Il Sung badge" in recognition of my effort.

U.S.–North Korea negotiations resumed in August. A tentative agreement was worked out by the end of the round. A final agreement, the so-called Agreed Framework, was signed on October 21, 1994, in Geneva. (See Appendix B for the accord's text.)

Yongbyon Senior Nuclear Engineer and author Quinones plan storage work for 8,000 plutonium-filled nuclear fuel rods.

Devil in the Details

The pros and cons of the Agreed Framework will long be argued. So, too, will it be argued whether the accord itself failed, or whether those responsible for making it work failed to implement it effectively. The undeniable fact is that implementing the accord proved far more difficult than negotiating it.

The Agreed Framework consisted of four major components:

♦ The freezing of all North Korean nuclear programs; this included the halting of all activities at North Korea's primary nuclear facilities, constant IAEA monitoring of these facilities, and the long-term, safe storage of 8,000 spent nuclear fuel rods.

♦ Movement toward normal diplomatic and commercial relations by opening of diplomatic liaison offices in each other's capitals, phasing out economic sanctions, and negotiating resolution of outstanding issues regarding ballistic missiles, and so on.

♦ The construction of two light-water nuclear reactors in North Korea by an international consortium, the Korean Peninsula Energy Development Organization (KEDO), to be funded primarily by South Korea, Japan, and the United States.

♦ North Korea's compensation for the electricity that would have been generated if construction of its two older model reactors had been completed, by supplying 500,000 M/T of heavy fuel oil each year until the reactors are operating. (Heavy fuel oil or HFO is the sludge remaining after all useable fuels and lubricants have been extracted from crude oil. HFO is normally used to power electric generators and ships.)

No sooner had the Agreed Framework been signed than it became the focus of bipartisan political bickering in Washington, Seoul, and Tokyo. The accord gave the United States responsibility for the implementation but saddled Seoul and Tokyo with 90 percent of the cost.

None of the participants was comfortable with this arrangement. South Korea's president resented it, and for a year after the accord's signing tried to complicate and delay implementation. Pyongyang responded in kind by squabbling over every detail ranging from selection of the nuclear reactor design to the project's prime contractor and financial arrangements. Meanwhile, Japan's foreign ministry wrestled with a hesitant legislature to get funds needed to cover Japan's portion of the costs.

In Washington, the Republican-dominated Congress challenged every aspect of the accord and quibbled about its expense. Pyongyang became increasingly concerned that the United States would not be able to follow through with the accord's implementation.

Helicopter Down!

The first crisis came in December 1994, two months after the accord's signing. On a clear winter day near the DMZ, a U.S. Army helicopter pilot invited his replacement to take a short orientation flight. No sooner had they taken off than the pilot became disoriented and flew north over the DMZ into North Korea.

On the ground, North Korean soldiers watched in dismay. In keeping with their nation's paranoia, they assumed the unarmed helicopter was on a spy mission. A shoulder mounted antiaircraft missile was fired at the helicopter, blowing it out of the sky. One of the Americans died immediately and the other was taken prisoner.

The incident was resolved through diplomatic dialogue and the captured American was returned unharmed to South Korea. Confidence in the Agreed Framework's potency to end U.S.–North Korea hostility, however, had been shaken severely.

February 1995 brought more problems. The U.S. Treasury Department balked at beginning the phasing out of U.S. economic sanctions. The State Department had to pressure it to comply. Then progress toward the opening of liaison offices stalled. Never would it resume nor have the liaison offices been opened. Again, Pyongyang's confidence in the U.S. commitment was shaken.

Nevertheless, North Korea froze its nuclear activities and allowed IAEA monitoring at its primary nuclear facilities. The U.S. was allowed to begin preparations to place the 8,000 spent nuclear fuel rods in monitored, long-term safe storage. Here Congress's hesitancy to fund the project caused a six-month delay. South-North Korean bickering delayed for several months the beginning of the nuclear reactors' construction. North Korea later demanded "compensation" for the delay, but the United States refused citing Pyongyang's partial responsibility for the delay.

Making Nice with Congress—The Perry Report

To quiet Republican criticism of the Agreed Framework, Clinton asked retired secretary of defense William Perry to thoroughly review U.S. policy toward North Korea. After several months of earnest effort and consultations with all the concerned parties, including a May 1999 visit to Pyongyang, Perry in October 1999 issued a report to Congress that essentially called for a continuation of diplomatic engagement backed by armed deterrence.

Flourishing Finish

Progress quickened in 2000. The Clinton Administration felt pressured by President Kim Dae-jung's June 2000 summit with Kim Jong Il to highlight its progress. North Korea was invited to send a high-level official to Washington, D.C. Kim Jong Il sent Vice Marshal Jo Myong Rok, first vice chairman of the National Defense Commission. Dressed in his medal-decorated uniform, the general called on President Clinton. A joint statement reaffirmed the 1993 Joint Statement and the 1994 Agreed Framework.

President Clinton then sent Secretary of State Madeleine Albright to Pyongyang later in October. Kim Jong Il suggested to her a willingness to "negotiate an immediate freeze on long-range missile testing and development and to stop all exports of missiles and missile components provided the United States offered sufficient economic aid and other inducements ...."

The secretary returned to Washington confident that a deal could be worked out. In November, the two sides met in Kuala Lumpur, Malaysia, to discuss a deal on ballistic missiles. Expectations on both sides proved excessive. Pyongyang wanted too much for too little. The Clinton Administration's efforts with Pyongyang ended on a sour note. Discussion of U.S.–North Korean relations since the end of the Clinton Administration follows in Chapters 19, 21, and 24.

The Least You Need to Know

◆ Presidents Reagan and Bush initiated a "carrot and stick" strategy to induce North Korea to give up nuclear ambitions and ballistic missile exports in exchange for normal relations.

◆ North Korea's threat to withdraw from the Treaty on the Non-proliferation of Nuclear Weapons (NPT) in March 1993 sparked an international crisis and almost led to war with the United States.

◆ U.S.–North Korea negotiations from June 1993 to October 1994 deterred a second Korean War and produced the Agreed Framework that "froze" North Korea's nuclear program and restarted international inspections of its nuclear facilities.

◆ Implementation of the accord, despite numerous obstacles, made steady progress toward the ultimate goal of dismantling North Korea's nuclear weapons development facilities.

Part 5

North Korea Tomorrow

North Korea's leaders struggle to reconcile themselves with the reality that they must cease past practices if their regime is to survive. The international community faces its own struggle over how to deter and defuse North Korea's threat.

In this part, we assess the options available to both North Korea and the international community, and prospects for success or failure. Success would mean peace, but failure could bring war.

Chapter 19

North and South Korea: An Estranged Relationship

In This Chapter

- ◆ The odds for reconciliation or reunification between the two Koreas

- ◆ Problems to overcome before reunification

- ◆ Recent progress toward reconciliation

- ◆ Prospects for Korea's future

Northeast Asia remains the world's potentially most volatile area. North Korea's possession of the knowledge and materials to make weapons of mass destruction makes the region even more dangerous than the Middle East. Compounding the danger are the mingling of superpower rivalries and the tensions of a divided Korea.

North Korea's paranoia and weapons of mass destruction threaten East Asia's peace and stability. Even without their use, North Korea's possession of them might compel Japan and South Korea to decide that they, too, must have nuclear weapons to deter a North Korean nuclear attack. If so, the global nuclear nonproliferation system would be severely damaged, and other non-nuclear nations might decide to acquire their own nuclear arsenal.

Also, Pyongyang might add plutonium to its exports. North Korea's bleak economic future, perpetuated by its estrangement from the international community, causes Pyongyang to continue exporting weapons and munitions. These include ballistic missiles. In the future, they could include deadly plutonium, given North Korea's disregard for international nuclear nonproliferation norms.

Options for dealing with North Korea are limited and have not changed since the Korean War. Essentially, they are Korean reconciliation and reunification, war, regime change, or co-existence. Co-existence poses a choice between negotiating with North Korea or so-called benign neglect—that is, ignoring it.

Collapse of the North Korean regime is not really an option. Instead, the option would be regime change of some form. In this chapter, we assess these options and prospects for Korean reconciliation and reunification.

The Possibilities for Unification

Korea's reunification is the preferred option to end North Korea's threat to peace. War or regime change could accomplish rapid reunification, but at a horrendous price. Peaceful reunification is a much slower process, and one that first requires the removal of numerous obstacles.

While prospects for Korea's future do range from war to peaceful reunification, neither extreme is likely in the foreseeable future. More realistic possibilities lie between these extremes. Peaceful co-existence could continue, but a return to hostile confrontation also remains possible.

War

War could swiftly unify Korea, but the price in lives lost and property destroyed would be enormous. The international community agrees that a war to reunify Korea is the least desirable of all the options.

War on the Korean Peninsula would devastate the Korean population and quite probably rain death and suffering on Japan as well as the region's large U.S. population. The world's economy would be severely disrupted. Three of the world's most dynamic economies are in Northeast Asia—Japan, South Korea, and China. All three are among the United States's top 10 trading partners. The ramifications of war in the region would ripple around the world.

U.S. policy regarding this option changed during the transition from the Clinton (1993–2001) to the Bush Administration. The Clinton Administration in its June 1993 Joint Statement (see Appendix B) with North Korea pledged, "assurances against the threat and use of force, including nuclear weapons …." President George W. Bush and his senior officials have rejected North Korea's repeated demands for the United States to reaffirm this promise.

Increase Your North Korea IQ

The 1993 U.S.–North Korea Joint Statement was the first diplomatic agreement between the two nations. Issued on June 11, the two nations agreed on principles that included: "assurances against the threat and use of force, including nuclear weapons …." In exchange, North Korea "decided unilaterally to suspend … its withdrawal from the Treaty on the Non-proliferation of Nuclear Weapons." These pledges opened the way for continued negotiation of the first nuclear crisis on the Korean Peninsula that concluded with the 1994 Agreed Framework. (See Appendix B for the Joint Statement's full text.)

Instead, the Bush Administration prefers a "peaceful, diplomatic solution" to disagreements with North Korea. At the same time, the administration emphasizes that it will not rule out a military option for dealing with North Korea. This reference to a "military option" is a less alarming use of words that still adds up to war.

South Korea and Japan, however, would prefer that the United States reaffirm the previous assurances made during the Clinton Administration. South Korean president Roh Moo-hyun, in his May 14, 2003, summit with President Bush in Washington, pressed the United States to publicly rule out the military option. But President Bush declined to do so.

Increase Your North Korea IQ

U.S. president George W. Bush and South Korean president Roh Moo-hyun issued a joint statement after their first summit held in Washington, D.C., on May 14, 2003. Their statement affirmed "… their strong commitment to work for the complete, verifiable and irreversible elimination of North Korea's nuclear weapons program through peaceful means based on international cooperation." The statement then asserted that, "[w]hile noting that increased threats to peace and stability on the peninsula would require consideration of further steps, they expressed confidence that a peaceful resolution can be achieved." (Emphasis added.) Experts have interpreted the highlighted phrase to refer to the so-called military option.

Regime Change

Regime change could also bring about Korea's rapid reunification, but it could also complicate the situation. This option implies forcefully ending the current Kim Jong Il regime. In the North Korean situation, regime change suggests two possibilities. Either a foreign power, like the United States, forcefully removes Kim Jong Il from power, or else North Korea's political elite remove him from power. South Korea's government has ruled out pursuing regime change. Regime change is inconsistent with several pledges South Korea made in the South-North 1992 Agreement on Reconciliation, Nonaggression, and Exchanges, and reaffirmed in the South-North Joint Declaration of June 15, 2000 (see Appendix B). Specifically, in the 1992 accord, "The two sides shall not attempt any actions of sabotage or overthrow against each other." The 2000 Joint Declaration reaffirmed this pledge.

On the other hand, there does not appear to be any group within North Korea intent upon, or powerful enough to remove Kim Jong Il from power. Kim Jong Il has dealt decisively with grumbling in the ranks since coming to power in 1994. In 1996, a group of generals was executed for allegedly plotting against him. Afterward, he promoted 147 generals out of the army's 800 and gave many of them luxury foreign cars and other gifts and exclusive privileges. In 1998, he carried out a sweeping anticorruption campaign. An unknown number of middle- and high-ranking officials in the Korean Workers' Party (KWP) and the Korean People's Army (KPA) were purged. They included the chairman of the Committee for the Promotion of External Trade, Kim Jong-u, who had worked closely with Kim Il Sung and was well known to the international business community. Both purges suggest Kim Jong Il's supporters far outnumber those critical of his leadership.

President George W. Bush and senior-ranking officials in the State Department have publicly suggested they are considering regime change as an option for dealing with North Korea.

President Bush in an August 2002 interview with Washington Post journalist Bob Woodward was quoted as having said, "I loathe Kim Jong Il. I've got a visceral reaction to this guy, because he is starving his people. ... They tell me, we don't need to move too fast, because the financial burdens on people will be so immense if we try to—if this guy were to topple."

A ranking Defense Department official has indicated that the Bush Administration was considering the option of regime change as a way to deal with North Korea. He stated in an off-the-record interview in December 2002, "I think we need to stop thinking about what we're going to give [North Korea]. Instead, we need to think about how we're going to change this [Kim Jong Il] regime. How are we going to bring this [North Korean] government down? That is the threat, the [North Korean] government … That's what President [Bush] thinks. Our diplomats are uneasy with it but that's what our president thinks."

Regime change is not the U.S. government's, nor the Bush Administration's, preferred option for dealing with North Korea. But it is one of several possible options under consideration.

Like war, regime change has distinct disadvantages. Either Kim Jong Il's death or his forceful removal from power would not necessarily solve the problem. If anything, it could complicate it further. It would not prevent the rise of a new authoritarian regime, nor automatically lead to reunification.

Instead, political chaos and armed conflict could ensue. In North Korea, the army is the only political force capable of decisively resolving a succession dispute. Squabbling over a successor could ignite a civil war, either between contending North Korean rivals or between the two Koreas.

The new North Korean regime, brought about by outside pressure to bring down Kim Jong Il by nonmilitary means, most likely would be authoritarian and dominated by the military. To legitimize its authority, the Korean People's Army might strike out against South Korea to rally the political support of North Korea's Communist Worker's Party. On the other hand, South Korea might be tempted to intervene in North Korea's dispute. This would lead to a civil war that could quickly escalate into an armed dispute that involved other nations.

Collapse

Collapse implies more than regime change. It suggests that the entire North Korean political system might become so unstable that it would disintegrate. Mention of this possibility brings to mind the dramatic demise of the Eastern bloc of communist regimes like East Germany, Poland, Romania, even the Soviet Union.

Theoretically, South Korea could rush into the political vacuum that would follow the North Korean government's demise and reshape the society into its own likeness. But prospects for collapse appear to be diminishing. On top of that, the difficult experience of West Germany (now Germany) in assimilating East Germany shows that even a dynamic, capitalist power on the border of a failing communist state will have significant problems trying to achieve unification.

North Korea still faces formidable challenges to its survival. Its economy remains on the verge of bankruptcy, the international community supplies about 20 percent of its food in the form of aid, and it is hard-pressed to increase its production and export of goods that are competitive in the world market.

But prospects for North Korea's survival have steadily improved since the darkest days of 1996 when its people were near famine and its economy was at a virtual standstill.

During the past decade, North Korea has achieved several important diplomatic breakthroughs. It has diversified its relations while repairing relations with old friends. Generally amiable relations have resumed with its former champions, Russia and China (see Chapters 14 and 15). Never before have relations between Pyongyang and Seoul been better (see Chapter 16). Since 1998, Pyongyang has normalized diplomatic and commercial relations with most members of the European Union (EU) and the Association of South East Asian Nations (ASEAN), as well as several nations in South America. Also, North Korea is a full member of the United Nations.

North Korea is gradually restoring its economic vitality. China, South Korea, and the United Nations now make up for the aid and markets that North Korea lost when the Soviet Union disappeared. Investment capital and new technology flow into North Korea from South Korea and China, plus a continuing trickle from Japan. Japan remains an important market for North Korea's exports, particularly processed seafood products. The European Union, because of diplomatic normalization, is a potential market for North Korean goods.

Economic Sanctions

One way to reverse North Korea's gradual return to economic health is to multiply and tighten the economic sanctions on it. The United States first imposed economic sanctions on North Korea during the Korean War when it applied the Trading with the Enemy Act to North Korea. The original aim was to isolate North Korea commercially in the hope of undermining its economic vitality. The effort backfired. Instead of weakening North Korea, economic sanctions increased its dependence on Moscow and Beijing.

The Reagan Administration used economic sanctions both as a stick and a carrot. It imposed additional sanctions on North Korea because of its acts of international terrorism. As we discussed in Chapter 18, the Reagan Administration also sought to use economic sanctions as an inducement. In the Modest Initiative, this administration held out the promise of phasing out economic sanctions as an inducement for North Korea to end its isolation and conform its behavior within internationally acceptable norms.

Increase Your North Korea IQ

The United States imposed economic sanctions on North Korea in 1950 after the Korean War started. These sanctions, established under the "Trading with the Enemy Act" Foreign Assets Control Regulations, imposed an embargo on U.S. trade and financial relations with North Korea. More sanctions were added under the Arms Export Control Act and the Export Administration Acts of 1979. In 1987, more sanctions were imposed and North Korea was labeled a terrorist nation. The 1988 "Modest Initiative" (see Chapter 18) allowed U.S. exporters to obtain licenses to sell "basic human needs" to North Korea. After 1994, some sanctions were phased out, but an extensive array of U.S. sanctions remains. The international community excluded North Korea from international financial institutions like the World Bank, Asian Development Bank (ADB), and International Monetary Fund (IMF).

Carrots and Sticks

Both the first Bush and former Clinton Administrations viewed economic sanctions as both a carrot and a stick. The Clinton Administration continued the Bush strategy and offered to begin phasing out economic sanctions as an inducement for Pyongyang to sign the 1994 Agreed Framework. The new Bush Administration has given some thought to tightening enforcement of economic sanctions as a way to influence North Korea's conduct and possibly to undermine its economy.

Opposition to Sanctions

South Korea and China are reluctant to tighten the economic embargo on North Korea. Japan seeks a middle position between that of the Bush Administration and those of South Korea and China. Tokyo favors tightening the implementation of existing sanctions, but not the addition of more sanctions.

China relies on North Korea as a buffer between it and the United States. Economic sanctions, Beijing believes, are partially responsible for Pyongyang's threatening behavior. Rather than more sanctions, China prefers that the United States use the phasing out of sanctions as an inducement to entice North Korea toward preferred conduct. Consequently, Beijing since 1994 has become North Korea's largest provider of humanitarian and economic assistance.

South Korea shares similar views with China, but for different reasons. Since 1998, South Korea's government has pursued a strategy nicknamed sunshine diplomacy (see Chapter 16). This involves extensive economic engagement with North Korea aimed at defusing its hostility toward South Korea, tempering the North's intense sense of insecurity and paranoia, and influencing the director of its future economic development in the hope of making the two economies more compatible.

Sanctions' Impact

The success or failure of sanctions must be determined relative to their goals. Historically, economic sanctions have never brought a nation to its knees nor caused its collapse. A half century has passed since the United States imposed its first sanctions on North Korea. Collapse due to sanction is not likely to happen in the near future in light of China, South Korea, and Japan's continuing economic engagement of North Korea.

Sanctions nevertheless play a vital role regarding North Korea. U.S. and international sanctions limit North Korea's ability to modernize its military-oriented economy. Used as inducements, the easing of sanctions has influenced North Korea's behavior. Also, sanctions work both ways. Not only can they be eased, they can also be restored in the event Pyongyang resumes objectionable behavior.

Peaceful Co-existence and Reconciliation

Most nations prefer peaceful reunification of the two Koreas, but this option also has disadvantages. Peaceful reunification would require a gradual, time-consuming process given the incompatibility of North and South Korea's political, economic, and educational systems. Even more challenging would be the erasing of a half century of mutual distrust and animosity. Most difficult might be the forming of a shared political system. One only has to look at the economic, social, and political struggles of the united Germany to get an idea of what would be in store if the two Koreas were to become one country.

Increase Your North Korea IQ

The 1992 South-North accord on Reconciliation, Non-aggression, and Exchanges and Cooperation declares in Chapter I, Article 1, that "[t]he South and North shall recognize and respect each other's system." In Chapter III, Article 15, they pledge "[t]o promote an integrated and balanced development of the national economy and the welfare of the entire people, the two sides shall engage in economic exchanges and cooperation ...."

Renewed Dreams

The most important aspect of the Pyongyang Summit of 2000 between Korea's two leaders (see Chapter 16) may have been the reaffirmation of the Korean people's dream of national reunification. The summit confirmed to a new generation of Koreans the aspirations and hopes contained in the 1992 South-North Agreement on Reconciliation (see Appendix B).

The two Koreas affirmed their long-term goal of national reunification, but since the 2000 summit have focused on the difficult task of reconciliation. Placed in the context of their troubled relationship during the past half century, Seoul and Pyongyang have made significant, albeit gradual and uncertain, progress toward reconciliation.

Ever since, the process of South-North reconciliation has experienced some significant progress, occasional armed conflict, and several substantial reverses.

The Positive Side

Never before have the two Koreas been so engaged with one another. Since the 2000 summit, inter-Korean ministerial talks have become a standard feature. First held in 1991, the first nuclear crisis disrupted them until July 2000. Several rounds have been held since to further implementation of the June 2000 summit's Joint Statement (see Appendix B for the text).

The following list presents some of the key results of these talks:

- **Open liaison office.** The South-North Liaison Office at Panmunjom, the neutral area within the Demilitarized Zone, has remained open. It facilitates direct, rapid communication between the two governments. The Office is entirely separate from channels of communication that the Korean Armistice established in 1953 between the UN Command and the North Korean army.

- **Tourism in the Diamond Mountain region.** The two Koreas also have undertaken several joint projects aimed at linking their economies. The first was the opening in the fall of 1998 of North Korea's Diamond Mountain (Kumgangsan) National Park to South Korean tourists. This large park is located at the eastern end of the DMZ inside North Korea. Despite numerous problems, the project remains active and has benefited from constant improvement.

- **Holes in the DMZ.** In February 2003, two roads opened between North and South Korea. Each is a two-lane, paved road that passes through the DMZ. The one on the east side of the Korean Peninsula carries tourists from South Korea through the DMZ to the Diamond Mountain Park in North Korea. Previously, the visit took a minimum of three days. Tourists first boarded a ship in South Korea and spent a day sailing north. After remaining overnight on the ship, they were admitted to the park. The third day was spent returning to South Korea via ship. Now, the trip can be done in a single day.

  The second road links South Korea to Kaesong, a North Korean city located about 20 miles north of the DMZ. The North Korean government hopes to establish near the city a South Korean–funded industrial park consisting of joint ventures between the two Koreas. The Kaesong project, first conceived in 1991, is a manifestation of the increasing inter-Korean trade.

◆ **Inter-Korean trade and investment.** In 2002, trade between the Koreas amounted to US $642 million, more than a 59 percent increase over the 2001 amount of US $403 million. Looking back, their trade in 1989, when it began, totaled US $89 million. Today, it accounts for almost 30 percent of North Korea's entire trade, making South Korea the North's third-largest trading partner after China and Japan.

◆ **Railroads.** Since the 1992 Reconciliation Agreement, the two Koreas have endeavored to link their railroads. Doing so was delayed by the first nuclear crisis of 1992–1994, and then complicated by the need for the UN Command and North Korean army to work out an agreement on how to breach the DMZ. Meanwhile, the growing inter-Korean trade relied on seaborne shipping. In 2001, 838,000 M/T of cargo were transported between the two Koreas via sea. Obviously, the reopening of overland shipping routes is of mutual benefit, as it will enable more efficient transport of trade goods.

After seven rounds of ministerial talks and six rounds of working-level talks between both sides' militaries, an agreement was reached on September 18, 2002. Work to relink two major railroad lines began immediately. Reopening of South-North rail traffic is scheduled for 2009 on the East Coast.

Increase Your North Korea IQ

Russia has been working with both Koreas to link the entire Korean Peninsula railroad network to Russia's Trans-Siberian Railroad. This project envisions transporting goods from the Korean Peninsula and Japan to Europe through Russia. North Korea and Russia signed agreements to this effect in July 2000 and August 2001. South Korea has yet to join the project but is giving it serious consideration. China is also considering linking its railroads to this proposed network.

◆ **Nuclear power plants.** The Korean Peninsula Energy Development Organization (KEDO) continues to build two nuclear light-water reactors (LWR) in North Korea. The project was agreed upon in 1994 as part of the Agreed Framework between the United States and North Korea to resolve the first nuclear crisis. (See Appendix B for details on the Agreed Framework's provisions.) The prime contractor, a South Korean company, employs several hundred South Koreans at the site. The South Korean and Japanese governments provide most of the project's costs. In 2002, KEDO invested US $59 million in the project.

- **Humanitarian aid.** South Korea's combined government and private humanitarian assistance to North Korea in 2002 amounted to US $131 million. This includes the value of 400,000 M/T of rice that South Korea sent to North Korea in 2002. This grain was provided on a "loan basis" subject to eventual repayment, but South Korea considers it to be humanitarian aid. South Korea's continuing humanitarian aid also includes farm equipment, pesticides, chemical fertilizer, and medicines and medical equipment.

- **Exchanges.** In 2002, 12,300 South Koreans, excluding visitors to the Diamond Mountain Park, visited North Korea. About 1,000 North Koreans visited South Korea in the same year. These are not large numbers, given the two Koreas populations of about 70 million people. But they are significant when one considered how many people are involved in facilitating the exchanges and have contact with the visitors.

The range of people-to-people exchanges continues to expanded. They include travel to the North by government officials attending one of 34 inter-Korean meetings held during the year, businessmen seeking to invest in North Korea, and representatives of humanitarian organizations monitoring the distribution of aid to North Korea. Meetings in 2002 between long-separated family members reunited 1,724 kinsmen from both Koreas. Another 1,635 persons reestablished contact with their families.

Increase Your North Korea IQ

Since 2000, North Korean athletic teams participated in the Asian Games held in South Korea. South Korean orchestras performed in Pyongyang, athletic teams competed with their North Korean counterparts, and professional groups, including academics and journalists, attended conferences in their subject areas.

Remaining Hurdles

Despite all the impressive progress toward reconciliation, formidable obstacles remain. Memories of war, and the North's impoverished socialist authoritarianism, clash with the South's more prosperous, egalitarian democracy. Memories of national division, family separation, and war haunt the older generation of Koreans while their children are exposed daily to negative images of their northern or southern kinsmen in school textbooks, daily media coverage, and popular films and books.

Actually, the more the two Koreas attempt to achieve reconciliation, the greater the gap between their political and economic systems. As South Koreans press their government for greater individual freedom, and respect for political and human rights, the government of North Korea intensifies its control of the population. While South Koreans enjoy greater prosperity, North Koreans must endure poverty, disease, and hunger.

Ideologically, the two Koreas have embraced incompatible systems of thought. Most North Koreans remain resolutely loyal to their political leader and his ideology of juche, and they have been educated to dismiss foreign religious beliefs. South Koreans, on the other hand, enjoy philosophical and religious diversity. Most South Koreans view communism and socialism as having been discredited. At least a quarter of the population subscribes to Christianity, and many others practice Buddhism.

Future Prospects

The all peaceful merger of North and South Korea into a single united country does not appear to be a realistic possibility, in either the near- or long-term future. Common ancestry, shared culture and language, nationalism, and distrust of foreign powers will continue to sustain a bridge of dialogue between the two states. Economic cooperation is strengthening and broadening their common meeting ground, enhancing prospects for continuing peaceful co-existence.

Reconciliation can continue, but only if North Korea breaks with its pattern of relying on armed might and coercive diplomacy to defend itself through intimidation. Specifically, North Korea will have to relinquish its weapons of mass destruction, particularly nuclear weapons, if it is earnest about pursuing reconciliation with South Korea.

Peaceful reunification can come only if one of the two sides' political and ideological systems is thoroughly discredited in the eyes of the Korean people. This is not likely to happen soon. Continued engagement of South and North Korea, however, will gradually make North Koreans more aware of the gap between their government's promises and deeds. This process could slowly erode support within North Korea for the current regime.

The Least You Need to Know

- ◆ Northeast Asia will remain the world's most potentially volatile region so long as Korea is divided into two rival and mutually hostile nations.

- ◆ South and North Koreans recognize that peaceful reunification is not now a realistic goal.

◆ Since 2000, the two Koreas have been pursuing and have made significant progress toward reconciliation (but not actual reunification) particularly through economic cooperation.

◆ North Korea's pursuit of a nuclear arsenal could undermine future progress toward reconciliation.

◆ The ideologies and political and economic systems of the two Korean states remain incompatible, making peaceful reunification unlikely until one of the two systems has been fully discredited in the eyes of the Korean people.

Chapter 20

Conventional Forces: How Will They Be Used?

In This Chapter

- ◆ Estimating North Korea's military capability
- ◆ National priorities and military strategy
- ◆ Conventional weapons arsenal
- ◆ The best defense is a good offense

North Korea's ambitions to become a nuclear power and its development of ballistic missiles have captured the international community's concern. Lurking behind these weapons of mass destruction is an equally awesome arsenal of conventional, non-nuclear weapons manned by North Korea's more than one million soldiers. These conventional weapons include thousands of rapid firing artillery pieces and multiple rocket launchers aimed at South Korea's capital, speedy amphibious landing craft, and submarines. This enormous army and its massive arsenal could wreck havoc on South Korea in a matter of hours.

Opposing it is an even more powerful military force armed with sophisticated conventional weapons. It includes more than 600,000 South Korean military personnel plus 100,000 U.S. military personnel in South Korea and Japan.

They are equipped with the most advanced weapons mankind has ever seen such as laser and satellite guided missiles and bombs, huge tanks with computer guided guns, rockets and artillery, and jet aircraft. Backing them from distant bases are aircraft carriers and long range, high-flying bombers.

Fortunately for the people of Northeast Asia and the tens of thousands of American civilians and military personnel living in this region, the massive might of the United States and South Korean forces have deterred North Korea from attempting to repeat the Korean War.

If, however, the impasse between the United States and North Korea over the latter's nuclear ambitions is not resolved through diplomacy, a second Korean War could abruptly explode on the Korean Peninsula. In this chapter, we review the conventional military forces concentrated in Northeast Asia and assess prospect that they might clash.

Spying on North Korea

North Korea's June 25, 1950, invasion of South Korea has similarities with Japan's surprise attack on the U.S. Pacific Fleet at Pearl Harbor, Hawaii, in 1941. The North Korean attack also was unprovoked and began on a Sunday morning. It, too, was a surprise. And in both cases, the U.S. military claimed beforehand that it could counter any attack.

Ever since the Korean War, spying on North Korea has been a huge business in South Korea and the United States. Both nations have devoted a vast treasure of mental energy, technology, and money into trying to size up and figure out North Korea's armed forces.

North Korea is one of the most watched and closely monitored nations in the world. The South Korean and U.S. intelligence communities make it one of their top priorities. There is a wall of video screens in the "tank" at the Pentagon in Washington where the Joint Chiefs of Staff meet. High on the wall there is a list of priority concerns. In early 2003, North Korea was second only to Iraq.

Super Snoopers

High above Earth, satellites watch and photograph every inch of North Korea every day, 24 hours a day. In May 2003, Japan joined the North Korea–watching business by launching its first "spy" satellite. It, too, is aimed at North Korea.

Cold War–era, slow, high-flying (but very reliable) U-2 aircraft, loaded with special cameras, radar monitoring, and voice-recording devices, fly back and forth along the southern edge of the DMZ. Low-flying electronic monitoring aircraft fly in circles near North Korea's coastline, just beyond North Korea's territorial waters. Korean-speaking linguists, posted on ships along the coast or in bunkers south of the DMZ, record and transcribe every word picked up by monitors in the aircraft.

Personal Recollections

After my first year of college, I joined the army hoping to study French and complete my college foreign language requirement. Many tests later, and after basic training, I was sent to Monterey, California, to study Korean! Then I went to the National Security Agency (NSA) at Fort Meade, Maryland, to learn how to break codes, both South and North Korean. After landing in South Korea at the end of 1963, I worked 12-hour shifts, six days a week, in a windowless building on the southern edge of Seoul. My job was to break North Korean army codes. I have been trying to figure out both Koreas ever since.

A small fleet of U.S. nuclear attack submarines cruise beneath the frigid waters of the East Sea, also known as the Sea of Japan. Undetected, they track North Korean ships, military and civilian.

In Seoul, the U.S. Foreign Broadcast Information Service (FBIS) records every North Korean television and radio broadcast. Hard-working Korean translators quickly convert reams of dialogue transcripts from Korean into English. Each morning, anyone in the U.S. government, anywhere in the world, can read in English every word aired on North Korea's radio and television the day before.

Bean Counting

Each day, a literal flood of data, classified and unclassified, streams back to Seoul and Washington, D.C. Small armies of photographic interpreters examine every photograph looking for some small hint about North Korea's military capability. So-called bean counters in Seoul and at the Defense Intelligence Agency (DIA) in Washington try to count literally every person, vehicle, rifle, and bullet available to the North Korean military.

At South Korea's National Intelligence Service (NIS) headquarters on the southern edge of Seoul, and at the U.S. National Security Agency (NSA) on the northern edge of Washington, linguists and cryptanalysts labor to decipher encrypted North Korean messages.

The Intelligence Community

Eventually, the most significant pieces of information find their way into daily intelligence summaries prepared for the presidents of South Korea and the United States, and their senior foreign policy and military officials. These highly classified summaries are prepared separately at the Central Intelligence Agency (CIA), DIA, NSA, National Reconnaissance Center (NRC), Department of Energy and the State Department's Bureau of Intelligence and Research.

Personal Recollections

I worked in the State Department's Bureau of Intelligence and Research from 1994 to 1997. My primary job was to try to figure out North Korea. I was the member of a small, highly knowledgeable team of East Asia and technical experts. We had access to incredible research resources. But we had no travel budget and our offices were cold in the winter and hot in the summer. The offices were then located on the eighth floor of the "Old State" building. During World War II, the "Manhattan Project," code word for the atomic bomb, was housed in these same offices.

National Intelligence Estimates

Nevertheless, the best we can do is guess about North Korea's military capability. On a frequent basis, the U.S. intelligence community gathers at the CIA to draft and finalize a National Intelligence Estimate (NIE). These highly classified estimates reflect the best guesses that the intelligence community can make. Those who put together these classified essays are highly intelligent, experienced, and trained professionals.

However, North Korea is very good at concealing and camouflaging its massive military establishment. Everything about its armed forces is secret. We have to guess at its military budget, numbers of uniformed personnel, and location of units.

North Korea is like a piece of Swiss cheese, with holes and tunnels everywhere. Entire factories have been built inside mountains. Key airfields, their runways and hangers, are housed inside mountain ridges. Enough food and fuel is believed to be stored underground to keep the North Korean army going for up to six months. Some military facilities are visible here and there, but these are few and far between. They give the casual visitor the image of a nation without a large military. Actually, these visible facilities may be decoys intended to mislead the visitor or a possible attacker.

_____ **Personal Recollections** _____

When the U.S. Army returned to North Korea in July 1996 to locate and retrieve the remains of U.S. Korean War dead, they brought six Jeep Cherokees with them. When the battery in one proved faulty, I was dispatched to find a new battery in Pyongyang. Only then did it dawn on me that I had never seen a single gasoline station or auto repair shop in the entire country! Of course there are many, but no foreigner can go to one without a special permit and help of the ever-present "guide." These facilities are designated "military sites" and are thoroughly camouflaged. I finally found a Toyota battery in a place that looked like a grocery store on the outside. Because of North Korea's embargo on the importation of U.S. goods, no U.S. autos, and so no U.S. auto parts, are available in North Korea!

All foreigners are banned from entering several areas of the country where there is a concentration of military facilities. Most of these areas are along the northern edge of the DMZ. Others are along the coasts where there are naval bases. Some mountainous areas are also off limits because they host ballistic missile sites.

Keeping this in mind, let's size up North Korea's armed forces. North Korea has an estimated 1.1 million people on active military duty. Another 7.45 million are believed to be in the ready reserve. These reserves are divided into 4.1 million in the Red Guard of Workers and Peasants; 1.2 million in the Red Youth Guard (high school and college students); 1.7 million in the Paramilitary Training Unit personnel; and 400,000 People's Guard (internal security and police).

This is a huge armed force for a population of about 23 million people. Actually, the North Korean army ranks as the fifth largest in the world after China (3 million), the United States (1.4 million), Russia, and India.

Military Objectives

North Korea shifted its military objectives after the collapse of the Soviet Union and democratization of South Korea. Previously, from before the Korean War until the late 1980s, North Korea's foremost military objective was reunification of Korea. The use of military force and covert subversion of South Korea were integral parts of the nation's overall military strategy. Since 1990, these have been pushed into the background.

Instead, North Korea since the early 1990s has accented peaceful co-existence with South Korea while it strives to reinforce its deterrence posture by upgrading the quality and technological sophistication of its major weapons systems.

Forcing the Issue

Peaceful reunification was preferred. This preference translated into North Korea's covert efforts in South Korea to agitate political turmoil and overthrow of the incumbent government. The expectation in Pyongyang, albeit groundless, was that South Koreans would consider shifting their support to the North Korean regime. Lacking this, North Korea was prepared to use armed force to achieve reunification, if the occasion presented itself.

The solid U.S.–South Korea alliance for 40 years deterred North Korea from attempting armed reunification. The cornerstone of U.S. security strategy in South Korea remains armed deterrence (see Chapter 2). Numerous exchanges of gunfire along the DMZ, and a multitude of covert infiltrations into South Korea, and vice versa, fortunately never escalated to war largely because of the reliability of U.S.–South Korea deterrence. Reinforcing this was both sides' recognition of the potential cost of war.

Changing Posture

Since the early 1990s, Pyongyang has shifted its military priorities from offensive to defensive intentions. Changing circumstances, more than benign intentions, brought about this shift. Ever since, regime survival has been Pyongyang's foremost priority. This priority puts the accent on deterring invasion and maintaining an in-depth defense posture.

As we discussed in Chapters 13 and 16, South and North Korea's economic fortunes were reversed in the 1980s. Seoul far outpaced Pyongyang in terms of economic development and diversification of diplomatic supporters and commercial markets.

South Korea's rapidly increasing economic prowess enabled it to upgrade the quality, technology, and mechanization of its armed forces. By 1990, South Korea's uniformed armed forces were smaller in number than North Korea's military. But South Korea by 1990 was able to achieve military parity with North Korea through technology and weaponry. This was particularly true when we include the strength of U.S. forces deployed in Northeast Asia.

As important, North Korea's primary allies had become less reliable. The Soviet Union was collapsing in 1990, and the communist East European bloc had evaporated. China at the same time was leaning toward capitalism and opened diplomatic and commercial relations with South Korea.

Playing Catch Up

North Korea in the 1980s decided the best way to catch up to South Korea, at least militarily, was to shift from its traditional reliance on a massive ground force to striving for technological superiority for its armed forces. This translated into the development of ballistic missiles and nuclear weapons. It may also have included refinement of its chemical and biological warfare capabilities. We will examine these weapons systems in the Chapter 21.

National Strategy

Subsequently, North Korea's military strategy was adjusted to reflect its revised national priorities and changing circumstances. China's establishment of diplomatic ties with South Korea compelled North Korea to reduce its reliance on China as an ally. Pyongyang can still count on Beijing to come to its rescue, but only if North Korea is attacked, not if North Korea does the attacking. Furthermore, after the Soviet Union's collapse, Pyongyang no longer can rely on Moscow for a *nuclear umbrella.*

Since the early 1990s, Pyongyang has put defending national sovereignty and pursuing reconciliation before reunification. On the one hand, it maintains a formidable ground army deployed both to deter and attack but also be ready to lunge south into South Korea. At the same time, the number of covert operations inside South Korea has been reduced. Also their purpose appears to have shifted away from fomenting political turmoil toward gathering intelligence.

> **Korean Concepts**
>
> **Nuclear umbrella** is a Cold War–period term that refers to the protective nuclear shield a nuclear-armed superpower projected over its close allies. The United States and the Soviet Union promised their loyal allies that they would retaliate if one or the other superpower launched a nuclear attack. The U.S. nuclear umbrella over South Korea and Japan remains in effect. North Korea, however, has lost its Soviet nuclear umbrella.

These changing circumstances and priorities suggest a reduced risk that small-scale armed clashes between the two Koreas might explode into a full-scale war. Despite several major clashes between 1996 and 2002, including substantial naval clashes in the West Sea, both sides quickly moved to prevent escalation.

Accidents do happen, however. Reconciliation appears to be fostering a less hostile rivalry between the two Koreans. Yet the possibility of gross miscalculations combined with unintended accidents could trigger a major conventional war.

Pyongyang's War Machine

Regardless of intent or reason, North Korea's mighty military still is poised for instant war. An estimated 70 percent of its ground force is forward deployed in the southern one third of the country. If you drew a line east from Pyongyang to the east coast port of Wonsan (see Chapter 2 for a map), about 600,000 armed men are housed in steel reinforced bunkers south of that line and north of the DMZ.

Everything they need to fight a war is there with them below ground. Food, fuel, ammunition, weapons, equipment—everything is stored in underground bunkers and inside mountains. In front of them are thousands of landmines buried inside the DMZ and along its northern edge.

Also positioned with them are an estimated 12,000 field artillery pieces. Some fire at long ranges and can hit a target 40 kilometers (about 24 miles away). They also have about 2,300 multiple rocket launchers that fire tactical artillery missiles in rapid succession. All are hidden in bunkers.

Heavy Metal

North Korea's forward-deployed ground forces are highly mechanized. The tank force is awe-inspiring. It consists of 3,800 Soviet-designed tanks. Most are of recent vintage, but a few date from the Korean War period, according to South Korean estimates. DIA puts the number of North Korean tanks at about 4,000. Estimates of the number of armored personnel carriers range from 2,300 (U.S. estimate) to 2,800 (South Korean estimate). All of this equipment is sheltered in bunkers.

As further protection from air attack, North Korea has deployed between 10,800 (U.S. estimate) to 12,500 (South Korean estimate) antiaircraft guns. Plus it has 1,100 surface-to-air antiaircraft missiles deployed at about 54 sites.

North Korea is believed to have about 15,000 shoulder-fired, surface-to-air antiaircraft missiles. At least one was used to shoot down a U.S. Army helicopter that had strayed across the DMZ into North Korea on December 17, 1994. These small missiles could prove to be a formidable counter to U.S. attack helicopters and low-flying jet aircraft.

Special Operation Forces

About 100,000 North Korean soldiers are in Special Operations Force (SOF) units. Their mission is to establish a second front in the enemy's rear area (that is, South Korea), conduct reconnaissance, carry out combat operations in coordination with main battle units, and neutralize any South Korean special operations units that might enter North Korea.

These SOF units have access to several means of stealthy deployment. They have an estimated 300 AN–2 aircraft, which is a small, slow, low-flying transport. These could virtually glide silently across the DMZ below radar detection and distribute by parachute undercover Special Operations Forces (SOF) troops in areas around Seoul.

American-Supplied Helicopters

North Korean SOF troops could also fly south aboard U.S.-made Hughes MD-500 helicopters. In 1984–1985, North Korea managed to circumvent U.S. sanctions and acquire 87 of these civilian-version helicopters. Appropriately equipped, they could be used against U.S. and South Korean forces. South Korea has a large inventory of the antitank version. But in North Korea, a special unit was formed around these U.S. helicopters and painted with South Korean air force markings. Inability to purchase spare parts probably has reduced the number of these helicopters that are still operational. But still at least a significant number remain available to SOF troops.

Several SOF units could be deployed on South Korea's coastlines using small submarines. Other units could be landed using the North Korean navy's 130 or so landing craft. Each can carry up to 60 combat equipped troops. Deployment using these craft requires the troops to get into small rubber boats to reach the shore. To overcome this handicap, North Korea has developed and built about 130 air-cushion landing craft that would ferry troops directly onto the beach.

The "Back Benchers"

Waiting in the rear area, if war comes, will be the "back benchers" ready and eager to support the frontline units. Air and navy support units, plus ballistic missiles and covert operatives pre-positioned in South Korea and Japan, would be activated. The entire nation would be mobilized. The seven million plus reservists would be armed and posted to guard strategic facilities, to man coastal and antiaircraft guns, and to provide logistical support.

Antique Air Power

North Korea's 85,000–personnel air force has impressive numbers. Technologically, however, its inventory of 1,100 combat aircraft is unsophisticated and obsolete. This number includes 80 medium-range bombers that were designed and manufactured in the Soviet Union in the 1950s. Another 650 fighter aircraft are Soviet-era antiques designed and built in the 1950s and 1960s. North Korea's most modern fighters, about 130 of various design, date from the 1980s. The remainder of its aircraft are either transports or helicopters.

Armament for fighters likewise is unimpressive. The air force does have several kinds of Soviet-era and Chinese air-to-air missiles. Most bombs are "dumb," which means they predate the laser-guided smart bombs in the United States and South Korea arsenals. But North Korea may have a few laser-guided bombs, possibly purchased from Russia.

Fast Attack Navy

The 46,000 sailors of the navy man 990 combat ships. Most ships displace 200 tons or less. The largest ship is a fast frigate. North Korea has just one of these, but no destroyers or larger combat ships. Instead of size and numbers, the navy relies on speed and stealth. There are 423 patrol craft of various types. Most are fast and can launch torpedoes. About 43 of these patrol craft can launch antiship missiles. Most other craft are minesweepers and various kinds of support ships.

The submarine is North Korea's most dangerous combat vessel. The DPRK is believed to have about 30 submarines. The attack version carries torpedoes while the reconnaissance version is designed to support covert operations. It also has about 24 midget submarines that can either attack shipping or support covert operations.

Command and Control

North Korea continues to invest in qualitatively upgrading its dual-purpose communications and computer infrastructure. With the help of Swiss technicians, an extensive system of fiber-optic communication cables are linking key industrial and military areas to Pyongyang.

Impressive strides are being made in the acquisition, installation, and networking of a nationwide, government-operated, secure intranet. North Korea is known to have trained an impressive cadre of sophisticated computer hardware and software specialists.

Modern radar and sophisticated electronic warfare equipment (both for the interception of communications and the jamming of radar and communications) have been installed in concrete and steel hardened fortifications.

Blitzkrieg!

Regardless of who started the war, once started, the rush of events would render the question futile. Again, we must keep in mind that our knowledge about North Korea's military is limited. But because of North Korea's secrecy and the forward deployment of most of its army, there would be little advance notice if North Korea decided to attack first. At most, the U.S. intelligence community estimates, there would be only 24 hours advance indication. Preparedness requires that we make our best "guesstimate" about what North Korea would do in the event of an all-out war.

If North Korea Attacks: South Across the Border

Unseen in the darkness of night, 300 AN-2 aircraft would scatter hundreds of special operations forces in the hills around Seoul. Teams of commandos would silently paddle their rubber boats to numerous spots along the shoreline. Surely many would land near South Korea's nuclear power plants. Before the crack of dawn, these forces would cut communication and power lines, and blow up bridges and power plants. Massive confusion in and around Seoul and other urban areas of South Korea would ensue.

The roar of a massive artillery barrage would follow, launched by 12,000 artillery guns and hundreds of multiple rocket launchers. Seoul and its suburbs would be leveled and millions of people sent screaming into the dim dawn light.

Beneath the multitude of screaming shells, hundreds of tanks and armored personnel carriers loaded with combat troops would emerge from their protective bunkers and rush southward. They would attempt to punch holes in South Korea's defensive line before troops and equipment could be concentrated to counter the formidable attack.

Farther south, in the Tsushima Straits between Korea and Japan, submarines would take up positions to intercept and sink any U.S. troop and supply ships coming from Japan. U.S. military bases in Japan most likely would be the target of North Korea's ballistic missiles and terrorist squads.

Within hours of the first explosions, tens of thousands of people would be dead or wounded. Northeast Asia would be consumed in intense warfare, and the world economy would be severely disrupted.

Deterrence

North Korea's surprise attack would create havoc and kill tens of thousands of civilians and soldiers. But North Korea's eventual defeat would be inevitable. This is the essence of U.S. and South Korean deterrence.

South Korea's 600,000–strong army is an even more formidable force. Its equipment is far superior to anything the North Koreans have. All of the North Korean military equipment, including its tanks and other mechanized equipment, is mostly of Soviet design, and it has already been defeated twice in U.S. wars with Iraq.

The South Korean army has much of the same cutting-edge equipment that the U.S. military used in those wars. It has the most advanced U.S. battle tanks, and antitank guns and rockets. Its long-range artillery and multiple rocket launchers are equipped with radar that can quickly locate and fire on enemy artillery.

Attack helicopters and U.S. Air Force A-10 "tank busters" would quickly devastate North Korea's armored columns, clearing paths for South Korean forces to launch counterattacks into North Korea. U.S. and South Korean fighter-bombers would destroy North Korea's lines of communication and transportation while long-range heavy bombers flew north from Guam. Once over Pyongyang, these huge bombers with their massive payloads would pulverize Pyongyang and other major North Korean cities and ports.

The cost of war to both sides would be horrendous. Neither side could claim total victory, but the North Korean regime would be destroyed and Korea subsequently unified.

North Korea's Achilles' Heel

Further deterring a North Korean attack on South Korea is the fact that North Korea depends on China for more than 80 percent of its oil and 20 percent of its food. South Korea and the UN World Food Program supply another 20 percent of North Korea's food needs. Despite large stockpiles of these essential commodities, the North Korean regime could not survive long without these supplies. Making war on South Korea would certainly cut access to China's oil, not to mention the food it now receives from China and South Korea.

Beyond the Facade

North Korea's formidable conventional military force is a facade, one designed more to deter than to make war. Thus North Korea's eagerness for the world to see a multitude of rifle-carrying troops goosestep from Kim Il Sung Square is clearly intended to intimidate. Having the same purpose are the display of ballistic missiles that follow the troops, the sea of red flags, and stiff youths saluting Kim Jong Il.

It is a potentially deadly facade because of its huge size and deadly equipment. But we must remember, its one million–man army is equipped with obsolete equipment, and its supply of food and fuel uncertain. Equally important, it faces a foe even more formidable than itself. But to this picture we must add North Korea's weapons of mass destruction, which we discuss in the following chapter.

The Least You Need to Know

- ◆ North Korea's armed forces are a formidable military force of more than one million soldiers.

- ◆ Their primary mission since the early 1990s has shifted from achieving national reunification by force to defending the regime.

- ◆ Despite its impressive numbers, North Korea's military capability has gradually declined since the 1980s relative to that of South Korea.

- ◆ North Korea could launch a deadly and devastating attack on South Korea, Japan, and U.S. forces in these two nations, but it would inevitably be defeated.

21

North Korea's Weapons of Mass Destruction

In This Chapter

- ◆ Reasons for development
- ◆ Ballistic missile inventory
- ◆ Nuclear weapons capability
- ◆ Chemical and biological weapons

We first introduced you to North Korea's arsenal of weapons of mass destruction (WMDs) in Chapter 1. These weapons include chemical and biological weapons, ballistic missiles and, quite possibly in the near future, nuclear weapons. North Korea's development of weapons of mass destruction has a long history.

Pyongyang is believed to have first acquired chemical and biological weapons (CDW) as early as the Korean War. The Japanese Imperial Army during World War II had developed such weapons and stockpiled them in the mountainous regions along the North Korea–China border. None of these weapons, however, were used during the war. Nevertheless, the United States intelligence community believes North Korea maintains a significant arsenal of modern chemical and biological weapons.

Its development of ballistic missiles dates from the 1980s. By reserve engineering Soviet period ballistic missile engines and rocket bodies, North Korea was able to rapidly develop short- and medium-range missiles, which can deliver a conventional (non-nuclear) warhead with good accuracy on any target in South Korea and Japan. Efforts to develop a longer-range, multiple-stage ballistic missile have faltered since North Korea first tested such a missile in August 1998.

The most destructive and feared weapon of mass destruction is a nuclear bomb. North Korea's experimentation with nuclear physics dates from 1985 when it put into operation its infamous reactor at the Yongbyon Nuclear Research Center (see Chapter 1). Eventually, North Korea produced enough plutonium from the spent fuel rods extracted from this reactor to make one or two nuclear weapons. But before it actually made any bombs, the U.S.–North Korean Agreed Framework halted North Korea's nuclear weapons development program.

But in October 2002, North Korea confirmed to the United States that it had initiated a second nuclear weapons program. A diplomatic stand off ensued between the two nations. Tension escalated after North Korea early in 2003 restarted the reactor at their nuclear research center, bragged that it was producing more plutonium for nuclear weapons, and declared repeatedly that it was prepared to "demonstrate" a nuclear weapon.

The international community, including China and Russia, is agreed that North Korea should not be allowed to maintain a nuclear arsenal. The United States and Japan further advocate that North Korea should not possess any weapons of mass destruction. Pyongyang counters that it must have these weapons to deter possible attack from the United States and its allies.

In this chapter, we assess the current potency of North Korea's arsenal of weapons of mass destruction and review continuing efforts to halt its maintenance and possible use of this arsenal.

Pyongyang's Paranoia

Pyongyang has reason to be paranoid. Picture yourself standing on top of the forty-fourth floor of the Koryo Hotel in downtown Pyongyang. About one quarter of a mile to the east is the residential area for North Korea's elite. Kim Jong Il and his most trusted colleagues live in this tightly guarded, fenced compound. Beneath that placid, park-like setting is a maze of steel-reinforced concrete bunkers. This is the bull's-eye for U.S. cruise missiles in the event of war on the Korean Peninsula.

The South Korean "Threat"

From the high perch in the Koryo Hotel, you can see distant danger in any direction. About 150 miles due south is the DMZ. On its southern side waits the highly trained and modernized 690,000 members of the South Korean armed forces, plus a reserve force of about 3 million. Their inventory of armored vehicles, field artillery, missiles, naval vessels, and combat aircraft are fewer in number than those of North Korea. But their quality is far superior to their northern counterparts.

The U.S. "Imperialist" Threat

Backing the South Korean soldiers are the U.S. armed forces forward-deployed in Northeast Asia. Their strength is anchored at Pearl Harbor, Hawaii. From there, the Commander-in-Chief, Pacific Area Command (CINCPAC) overseas three mighty U.S. military forces available to rush to South Korea's aid.

These commands include the U.S. Seventh Fleet, headquartered at Pearl Harbor, U.S. Forces Japan, and U.S. Forces Korea. Included in these forces are a total of 100,000 military personnel. They include about 38,000 combat troops (16,000 in South Korea and 22,000 in Japan), several aircraft carrier battle groups, nuclear attack submarines armed with cruise missiles, and hundreds of fighter aircraft equipped with "smart" bombs. On the island of Guam, a fleet of flying fortresses—B-52s and B-1s—stands ready to drop "smart" bombs and cruise missiles all over North Korea.

Personal Recollections

In the 1990s, I served as the deputy director of the U.S. Mutual Defense Office (MAO) at the U.S. Embassy in Tokyo. My job was to monitor Japan's coproduction of U.S.-designed and highly sophisticated weapons systems. But the highlight was a cruise on the USS Indianapolis, a nuclear attack submarine. In September 1992, I showed North Korean Vice Minister of Foreign Affairs Kim Kye Gwan photographs of sailors sleeping on top of this submarine's cruise missiles as proof that the United States had withdrawn its tactical nuclear weapons from around the world as former President Bush announced in his speech a year earlier.

The Threat of a "Remilitarized" Japan

Supporting this impressive force are Japan's Self-Defense Forces (JSDF). They make up in quality and technological sophistication what they lack in numbers (about 200,000 personnel). Japan for two decades has acquired some of the most advanced weapons systems that the United States produces. These include AWACs command and control aircraft, P3C antisubmarine warfare aircraft, E2C radar and electronic warfare aircraft, supersonic FX and F-15 fighters, *PAC-3* Patriot missiles, destroyers equipped with *Aegis* over-the-horizon radar, a fleet of fast-attack submarines, and minesweepers equipped with cutting-edge detection devices.

Korean Concepts

Aegis and **PAC-3** are core elements of "Lower-Tier" Theater Missile Defense (TMD). The United States is building a three-tier antiballistic missile defense system. The lower-tier is TMD, which is designed to defend against short-range missiles like those in the North Korean arsenal. Japan helped develop this system and has deployed it on its destroyers. Japan is also working with the United States to develop the second-level, upper-tier (High-Altitude) Theater Missile Defense (or THAAD). It is designed to destroy missiles at a much longer distance than PAC-3. The third tier is National Missile Defense (or NMD). This system will consist of long-range antiballistic missiles based in the United States and designed to destroy missiles beyond the atmosphere. Japan has contributed technological assistance to this system's development.

Japan's forces could not be deployed to the Korean Peninsula because of Japanese constitutional barriers that date from the U.S. occupation and rule of Japan after World War II. JSDF, however, would fill in behind U.S. Forces in Japan (usually abbreviated as USFJ) as they are transferred to Korea in the event of a crisis.

Faltering Friends

From the vantage point back on the Koryo Hotel, looking west and north only increases the sense of insecurity. In both directions are unreliable allies, China and Russia. Prior to 1990, they had promised to rush to Pyongyang's help in time of threat. Russia's predecessor, the Soviet Union, had extended its nuclear umbrella over North Korea to shield it from the might of the U.S. nuclear arsenal. But Moscow since has retracted its nuclear umbrella. China remains a helpful ally. But it, too, like Russia, has become an unreliable ally because of its expanding diplomatic and highly profitable commercial relations with South Korea.

Pyongyang's Options

After 1989, changing circumstances in Northeast Asia (see Chapters 14 through 16) have redefined North Korea's military strategy. During the 1980s, Pyongyang shifted from preparing for armed reunification to maintaining peaceful co-existence with South Korea. Deterrence capability assumed greater importance than assault ability.

Pyongyang's leadership must have realized that the balance of military might on the Korean Peninsula was tilting toward Seoul. South Korea's rapid economic development in the 1980s enabled it to greatly enhance its defense capability.

The events of 1990 seriously eroded Pyongyang's peace of mind and sense of security. First, its foremost champion and protector, the Soviet Union, collapsed. Gone in a flash was Moscow's nuclear umbrella. Pyongyang stood naked before the awesome might of the U.S. nuclear arsenal. Then Seoul's courtship of China paid big dividends in the form of expanding diplomatic and commercial ties.

On top of this, the U.S. military's quick defeat of Iraq's Soviet-equipped armed forces shook Pyongyang's confidence in the deterrence and combat capabilities of its huge conventional forces. All of its equipment was based on now obsolete Soviet designs.

No one except Pyongyang's leadership can explain why North Korea decided to pursue the development of nuclear weapons, ballistic missiles, and CB (chemical and biological) weapons. Historical developments tracing back to the 1980s suggest that decision was rooted in Pyongyang's intensifying sense of paranoia and insecurity. Survival, not a desire to forcefully achieve reunification, appears to have been the primary consideration for the North Korean pursuit of WMDs.

Deterring the United States

U.S. military capability in the region was central to North Korea's decision to pursue the development of WMDs. North Korea's official media has repeatedly made this point. In a statement, Korean Central News Agency (KCNA) alleged,

> … the nuclear issue on the Korean Peninsula is a product of the U.S. hostile policy toward the DPRK … the successive U.S. regimes have pursued this hostile policy toward the DPRK and threatened it with nukes (sic).

We need not agree with this view, but we would do well to be aware of it. It has and continues to be the essence of Pyongyang's paranoia.

Kim Il Sung and his generals appear to have decided sometime in the late 1980s to reinforce North Korea's "self reliant" (juche) defense posture with a combined ballistic missile and nuclear weapons capability.

Instead of investing heavily to upgrade its conventional forces, North Korea opted to deter perceived threats from the United States and South Korea by "fighting fire with fire." In other words, North Korea would try to create its own nuclear umbrella with nuclear weapons equipped ballistic missiles.

While pursuing this option, Kim Il Sung simultaneously pursued a diplomatic offensive aimed at engaging the United States. His aim probably was to defuse U.S. suspicions about North Korea's intentions while revitalizing North Korea's economy by linking it to the international market. It would allow North Korea to generate the income needed to upgrade its conventional forces. Peaceful co-existence with its foe, particularly the United States, may well have been a parallel objective.

Ballistic Missiles

Nuclear weapons are virtually useless unless they can be delivered at the enemy. The fastest and most reliable delivery system is a ballistic missile. North Korea by the late 1980s was making impressive progress in this area. Today, North Korea leads the Third World in the development and deployment of ballistic missiles.

Technology Genealogy

North Korea has relied on several nations to develop its ballistic missile technology. Most of it is based on Soviet technology acquired in the 1960s. Engine and guidance designs were generally refinements of German equipment seized by the Soviets at the end of World War II. When the Soviet Union hesitated about cooperating further, Pyongyang turned to China in the early 1970s.

China in the 1970s provided North Korea with a variety of missile technology. This included surface-to-air (SAM) antiaircraft missiles and antiship *cruise missiles*. North Korea still deploys these missiles. They include the short-range, antiship coastal defense cruise Silkworm and ship-launched Safeflower missile. China is also believed to have helped North Korea improve upon *ballistic missile* engine and airframe design, as well as production and metallurgy processes.

Korean Concepts

Ballistic and **cruise missiles** are fundamentally different. A ballistic missile is powered by a rocket engine that pushes the rocket upward to the edge of the atmosphere. After the engine has burnt its fuel, the missile's warhead breaks away from the main body of the rocket and falls back to Earth, unguided (this is what is called a "ballistic" trajectory). A cruise missile is propelled by an engine similar to a jet engine. The missile is first thrust upward to few thousand feet and then levels out and flies parallel to the ground. Unlike a ballistic missile, a cruise missile never leaves the atmosphere and is guided to its target. North Korea has both kinds of missiles.

North Korea, reportedly working alone, subsequently refined these Soviet and Chinese designs with missile technology acquired from Egypt, Iran, Libya, Pakistan, and Syria.

South Korea at this same initiated its own surface-to-surface missile project. Code-named Yulgok, it relied on U.S.–based missile technology. Seoul's first successful launch was accomplished in September 1978. The missile was designed with a range of 180 kilometers (about 120 miles), but U.S. pressure blocked production of the missile.

Hwasong–North Korea's Scud

North Korea's ballistic missile program has continued. Pyongyang circumvented Moscow's and Beijing's reluctance to provide further assistance by turning elsewhere. Egypt and Syria transferred some Soviet-based missile technology to North Korea in the mid-1970s. Egypt also sold North Korea a few Soviet-designed Scud missiles. This was the basic Soviet tactical missile. The Scud was essentially a replica of Germany's World War II V-2 rocket that terrorized London during the last year of World War II.

North Korea engineers slowly learned to *reverse engineer* the Scud's key components. North Korea gave its version of the Scud the name *Hwasong*. The earliest tests of this missile took place in 1984.

Iran's interest in purchasing North Korea's *Hwasong* missile added further impetus to the program. Iran sought to acquire a ballistic missile that could retaliate for Iraq's use of Soviet supplied Scud missiles during the Iran-Iraq War. North Korea's *Hwasong* filled Iran's needs.

North Korean refinements increased the missile's range from 280 to 320 kilometers (about 192 miles) with a 1,000 kilogram (one-ton) warhead. This gave the missile sufficient range to hit Seoul when launched from a site hidden in North Korea's rugged central mountains. *Hwasong* production probably began in 1985. North Korea is thought to have between 300 and 625 operational *Hwasong 5* and *6* missiles.

> **Korean Concepts**
>
> **Reverse engineering** is the process of acquiring a piece of technology and then figuring out how to make it by taking it apart and analyzing its components. It is a common technique when trying to develop complex systems quickly, without access to the research that created the technology in question.

The Medium-Range *Nodong*

North Korea's medium-range ballistic missile is called the *Nodong*. Development is believed to have begun in the late 1980s by refining the technology and design of the *Hwasong 6*. Engineering refinements, plus new technology acquired from China and Pakistan, give the *Nodong* a range of about 1,300 kilometers (about 780 miles) carrying a 1,200-kilogram (about a 1.5-ton) warhead. The range can be increased to 1,500 kilometers (900 miles) if the warhead is reduced to 1,000 kilograms (slightly more than one ton).

North Korea first tested the *Nodong* in 1993. The results were less than impressive. Iranian and Pakistani officials were present. The *Nodong* traveled 500 kilometers, compared to its estimated range of 1,300 kilometers. Of the three *Hwasong* missiles tested at the same time, one flew 100 kilometers, and the other two fell short of 100 kilometers, despite their estimated range of 320 kilometers.

An estimated 75 to 150 *Nodong* missiles had been built by 1999. Of this number, a few were used in tests, 50 to 100 are deployed in North Korea, and the remainder, an estimated 24 to 50 missiles, were exported.

*Nodong*s in Disguise

North Korea continues to work closely with Pakistan and Iran on missile development. Pakistani-North Korea collaboration dates from 1988. In 1993, Pakistani Prime Minister Benazir Bhutto visited North Korea and China. Despite her public denial of interest in North Korea's ballistic missile program, the two nations worked closely together on missile development. Pakistan still denies officially that its *Ghauri* ballistic missile, first tested in 1998, is in fact a North Korean–designed and built *Nodong*.

Similar cooperation has continued with Iran since the late 1980s. In 1994, General Cho Myong-rok (who called on President Clinton at the White House during his October 1999 visit to Washington, D.C.) visited Iran; he met its nuclear experts and toured its missile test facility. Experts agree that Iran has purchased an unknown number of *Nodong* missiles from North Korea.

Iran launched in 1998 a ballistic missile it designated a *Shehab 3*. Actually, this missile was a North Korean–built *Nodong*.

The *Taepodong* Missile

North Korea is trying to develop a three-stage, long-range *Taepodong* ballistic missile. Two versions are believed to be under development. The *Taepodong I* would have a range of 1,500 to 2,500 kilometers (600 to 900 miles) and deliver a 1,000- to 1,500-kilogram warhead. The *Taepodong II* could deliver a similar size warhead between 4,000 and 8,000 kilometers (2,400 to 4,800 miles). This would give North Korea an intercontinental ballistic missile (ICBM) capability.

On August 31, 1998, North Korea tested its first *Taepodong II*. The launch had the primary purpose of placing a satellite in orbit. Western intelligence indicates that the first two stages thrust the payload about 1,100 kilometers high but the third stage failed. Nevertheless, Pyongyang proudly proclaimed that it had successfully placed a satellite in orbit. North Korea has never admitted the launch was a failure, and it has not tested the *Taepodong* again.

Missile Exports

The export of ballistic missiles and related equipment has been a major hard currency earner for North Korea. Payment on occasion has been in the form of crude oil from Middle Eastern countries. But missile sales have slackened in recent years because of North Korea's difficulties thus far in achieving a more sophisticated technological plateau.

North Korea is believed to have made between 600 and 1,000 *Hwasong 5* and *6* missiles by 1999. Some 350 to 500 were exported. Iran purchased between 90 and 100 of the *Hwasong 5* missiles as part of a US $500-million arms sale in 1987. Iran launched 77 of these missiles at Iraq during a 52-day period in 1988. North Korea is believed to have provided Iran with chemical warheads for a few of these *Hwasong 5* missiles.

In 1989, North Korea sold the United Arab Emirates (UAE) 25 *Hwasong 5* missiles. The deal, worth US $160 million, also included self-propelled artillery, multiple rocket launchers, and munitions. The UAE reportedly was displeased with the missiles' quality and has put them in storage.

Hwasong missile exports between 1987 and 1992 are estimated to have totaled 250 missiles worth US $580 million. These missiles and related equipment were sent to Egypt, Iran, Libya, and Syria.

Target Countries

North Korea's ballistic missiles pose threats to world peace. The most immediate threat is to North Korea's neighbors South Korea and Japan. In the event of war, North Korea's *Hwasong* and *Nodong* missiles could hit any target in South Korea (indeed, North Korean conventional artillery can hit Seoul). *Nodong* missiles could hit most U.S. military facilities and population centers in Japan.

The U.S. homeland need not be concerned about North Korea's ballistic missiles, at least not until North Korea succeeds in producing and testing its *Taepodong II.* Central Intelligence Agency (CIA) Director George Tenet and Defense Intelligence Agency (DIA) Director Vice Admiral Lowell Jacoby, however, both claimed to the U.S. Senate Armed Services Committee on February 11, 2003, that North Korea has "the capability to reach the western U.S. with a long-range ballistic missile."

While it may possess the technical capability, North Korea is not known to have actually built or successfully tested a ballistic missile capable of reaching the continental United States. At this point, it is possible for a *Nodong* missile to reach one of the tiny islands in the U.S.–owned Aleutian Island chain that extends west from Alaska into the North Pacific Ocean.

U.S.–North Korea Missile Talks

Several rounds of U.S.–North Korea missile negotiations between 1995 and 2002 failed to produce an agreement. The last round of missile negotiations convened in Kuala Lumpur in November 2000. Despite expectations of a breakthrough, the talks ended inconclusively and none have been held since.

The United States, backed by South Korea and Japan, insists that North Korea halt the export of its missiles and all further development of ballistic missiles. In addition, the U.S. has demanded that North Korea halt the production and deployment of all ballistic missiles.

North Korea has indicated a willingness to phase out its export of missiles, but at a high price. In 1997, it demanded US $1 billion as payment for doing so. The United States offered to phase out selected economic sanctions, but only if North Korea also halted its ballistic missile research and development programs. North Korea responded that this was expecting too much while offering too little.

Continued North Korean development of ballistic missiles poses the possibility that one day it will have the capability to put nuclear and chemical/biological warheads on its ballistic missiles. This would undercut the effectiveness of U.S. deterrence around the world. Furthermore, North Korea could even begin to sell such weapons of mass destruction to other small nations that aspire to be regional nuclear powers, not to mention terrorist organizations.

Making Nukes

In April 2003, a North Korean official claimed to U.S. Assistant Secretary of State for East Asian and Pacific Affairs James Kelly that North Korea has nuclear weapons.

If true, this would confirm the U.S. intelligence community's long-standing estimate that North Korea possesses at least one or two nuclear weapons.

Prior to this meeting, senior North Korean Foreign Ministry officials admitted to Assistant Secretary Kelly on October 4, 2002, that North Korea had established a program to enrich uranium for the production of nuclear weapons. The admission confirmed long-held suspicions that North Korea would not fulfill the terms of the 1992 South-North Joint Declaration of the Denuclearization of the Korean Peninsula and the 1994 U.S.–North Korea Agreed Framework (see Appendix B for texts).

Yongbyon's infamous five megawatt nuclear reactor, producer of North Korea's plutonium for nuclear weapons.

In the Beginning

North Korea's nuclear program dates from the late 1970s. With Soviet help, Pyongyang trained a cadre of nuclear engineers and nuclear power plant operators in the Soviet Union and East European bloc nations during the 1970s and 1980s.

The Soviet Union opposed North Korea's acquisition of nuclear weapons, however. Moscow pressed Pyongyang to become a party to the Treaty on the Non-proliferation of Nuclear Weapons (NPT) and to submit its nuclear facilities to International Atomic Energy Agency (IAEA) inspections.

In 1985, as an inducement for doing so, Moscow signed an agreement with Pyongyang that committed Moscow to building two nuclear reactors for North Korea. The agreement was never implemented. Moscow's economic woes prevented it from following through on its promises. Meanwhile, North Korea failed to sign up for IAEA inspections.

The Plutonium Program

At some unknown point in the late 1980s, North Korea initiated a clandestine nuclear weapons program at its Yongbyon Nuclear Research Center. Beginning on a small scale, scientists at the center learned how to extract plutonium, the core element of a nuclear weapon, from nuclear-spent fuel removed for the center's five megawatt reactor. By 1992, North Korea's nuclear program was in full stride. Satellite photographs established that North Korea had built a large nuclear-spent fuel reprocessing plant at Yongbyon, a couple of kilometers from the five megawatt reactor. North Korea claimed it was a radio-chemical laboratory. IAEA inspection in 1992 confirmed it was a plutonium extraction facility. More worrisome was the discovery of evidence that North Korea was concealing plutonium.

The U.S.–North Korea Agreed Framework of 1994 (see Chapter 18 and Appendix B) froze North Korea's plutonium-based nuclear weapons program.

Highly Enriched Uranium

Intelligence reports indicated that North Korea might have developed a second nuclear weapons program based on highly enriched uranium (HEU). Just when this HEU program began has become a political hot potato in Washington, D.C. Some members of the U.S. intelligence community claim they saw indications of this HEU as early as 1998 or 1999. Others push the date into 2001 after the second Bush Administration took office.

Apparently, the intelligence community lacked sufficient information upon which to make a clear-cut assessment. The dimensions of the HEU program remained a mystery until June and July 2002.

Assistant Secretary Kelly, armed with the U.S. intelligence community's best information, asked his North Korean counterparts in Pyongyang whether their nation had an HEU program. After an initial denial, the next day the first vice minister of foreign affairs, who had been North Korea's chief negotiator during the 1993–1994 nuclear talks with the United States, confirmed that his country had an HEU nuclear program.

Ever since, tensions in Northeast Asia have escalated. Washington insists that Pyongyang dismantle its entire nuclear weapons program in front of IAEA inspectors before negotiations can commence. Once these talks begin, Washington insists all the concerned nations must be represented at the negotiating table. This would include the United States, South Korea, Japan, China, and North Korea.

North Korea has insisted that the impasse can only be broken by convening direct, bilateral U.S.–North Korea negotiations. Pyongyang, after repeatedly rejecting Washington's call for multilateral talks, participated in such talks in Beijing in August 2003 (see Chapter 15). But Pyongyang continues to reject Washington's demand that it first dismantle its HEU program and shut down its plutonium program before negotiations can begin. Also, North Korea insists it must have U.S. assurances that it will not attack North Korea nor insult it while negotiations are underway.

The Bush Administration, shortly after the first round of Six Party Talks in August, indicated a significant shift in its long-held approach. Secretary of State Colin Powell confirmed the shift on September 5. Until then, the Bush Administration had adamantly rejected any possibility of giving North Korean any "concessions." But on September 5, Powell dropped the usual insistence that North Korea first "verifiably" dismantle its entire nuclear weapons program before the United States would consider engaging North Korea in negotiations. Instead, he said, "Well, I would be pleased if North Korea would say that … they are prepared to undertake a process to verifiably dismantle their nuclear weapons program."

He also indicated that the United States was willing to provide North Korea the security assurances it had been demanding for almost two years. Until this occasion, the Bush Administration had adamantly rejected any possibility of providing the assurances along the lines North Korea sought. But on September 5, Powell said, according to a U.S. government transcript, "And we are looking at ways in which we can given them (North Koreans) the kind of (security) assurances that they say they need." President Bush reiterated this new stance on October 20, 2003.

Even if both sides do eventually decide to negotiate a settlement to the dispute over WMD, intense mistrust on both sides is certain to complicate the implementation of any accord.

Gas and Germs

Little is known about the actual capability of North Korea's chemical and biological weapons (CBW) programs because both are shrouded in tight secrecy. North Korea has never demonstrated this capability in battle.

Our best insight into this aspect of North Korea's WMDs comes from the U.S. intelligence community. In February 2002, the Department of Defense released the following unclassified CIA assessment of North Korea's biological weapons program:

> North Korea has acceded to the Biological and Toxin Weapons Convention (BWC), but nonetheless has pursued biological warfare capabilities since the 1960s. Pyongyang's resources include a rudimentary (by Western standards)

bio-technical infrastructure that could support the production of infectious bio-logical warfare agents and toxins such as anthrax, cholera, and plague. North Korea is believed to possess a munitions-production infrastructure that would allow it to weaponize (sic) biological warfare agents and may have biological weapons available for use.

Regarding chemical warfare, the CIA report continued:

Like its biological warfare effort, we believe North Korea has had a long-standing chemical warfare program. North Korea's chemical warfare capabilities include the ability to produce bulk quantities of nerve, blister, choking, and blood agents, using its sizable, although aging, chemical industry. We believe it possesses a sizeable stockpile of these agents and weapons, which it could employ should there be renewed fighting on the Korean Peninsula.

The carefully worded CIA assessments clearly indicate two things. First, U.S. knowl-edge of North Korea's biological and chemical weapons capabilities are very limited and of uncertain reliability. Secondly, however, the U.S. intelligence community is confident that North Korea has sufficient expertise, infrastructure, and capability to produce and utilize such weapons in the event of a war.

Japan's Imperial Legacy

Actually, North Korea acquired its first knowledge and infrastructure for the develop-ment of weapons of mass destruction from Imperial Japan. Secret U.S. Army docu-ments, declassified in 1996, document that the Imperial Japanese Army maintained a nuclear weapons research program in Hungnam on North Korea's northeast coast. The research, according to a declassified secret U.S. Army report, included the enrichment of uranium for use in nuclear weapons.

The Japanese army also developed chemical and biological weapons during World War II. Chinese and Korean prisoners were used as test subjects in Manchuria to determine these weapons' potency. The Japanese army stockpiled its CW and BW weapons along the China–North Korea border. What became of these stockpiles remains a mystery.

During the Korean War, U.S. and South Korean forces reached Hungnam and con-ducted an extensive survey of the area's weapons research and production facilities. A similar survey of the CBW stockpiles was not conducted before they were forced to retreat.

How Dangerous Are Pyongyang's WMDs?

North Korea's potent arsenal of weapons of mass destruction makes it one of the world's most dangerous nations. It has a growing arsenal of increasingly sophisticated ballistic missiles, two nuclear weapons development programs, possibly an unknown number of nuclear weapons, and a CBW capability. In war, North Korea would be a most formidable foe.

North Korea's primary purposes for developing this deadly arsenal appear to be more defensive than offensive. Its WMD capability accents defensive deterrence more than offense. Nevertheless, its WMD capability allows it to intimidate its neighbors, specifically South Korea and Japan, and enable it to engage in a destructive war.

This capability also gives North Korea the option to proliferate WMD to all parts of the world. This might eventually include the sale of plutonium and CBW weapons to terrorist groups.

In Chapter 24, we will assess North Korea's future intentions regarding its WMD.

The Least You Need to Know

- ◆ North Korea's potent arsenal of weapons of mass destruction makes it one of the most dangerous nations in the world.

- ◆ North Korea's ballistic missiles can reach any target in South Korea and Japan, but North Korea has not yet developed a reliable intercontinental ballistic missile (ICBM) that could reach populated U.S. territory or the U.S. mainland.

- ◆ The U.S. intelligence community remains uncertain about North Korea's self-proclaimed nuclear weapon capabilities, but is convinced North Korea has sufficient plutonium to fabricate several nuclear weapons and has the ability to test one or more of them.

- ◆ North Korea has not yet developed a nuclear warhead for its ballistic missiles.

- ◆ North Korea is believed to have both chemical and biological weapons, and it may have developed ballistic missile warheads that can deliver these agents to distant targets.

Chapter 22

Terrorism—War Without Battles

In This Chapter

- ◆ Why North Korea is on the U.S. government's list of nations that support terrorism
- ◆ Economic sanctions because of terrorism
- ◆ Changing U.S. policy toward North Korea
- ◆ North Korea's legacy of terrorism

Prior to graduating to weapons of mass destruction, North Korea repeatedly attempted to promote its national interests using terrorism against South Korea and Japan. North Korea is not known to have committed an act of terrorism since 1987, yet it remains on the U.S. list of terrorist nations. In this chapter, we review this legacy of terror and assess what North Korea must do to stop being labeled a terrorist nation.

Joining the Big Leagues

An aging Japanese father and his young daughter boarded Korean Airline (KAL) flight 858 at Baghdad Airport on November 29, 1987. Only three hours earlier, they had arrived from Pyongyang via Moscow, Budapest, Vienna, and Belgrade.

No one thought it strange that the two Japanese citizens boarded the KAL flight 858 just for the relatively short hop from Baghdad to Abu Dhabi. They stayed in Abu Dhabi after KAL 858 departed for Bangkok, Thailand. Nine hours later, KAL 858 exploded. All 115 passengers and crew died.

Shortly after receiving word of the explosion, South Korean authorities decided a bomb must have destroyed the aircraft. An intense search began for the 15 passengers who had left the flight at Abu Dhabi. Highly professional intelligence work quickly focused attention on the "Japanese" couple.

Two weeks later, South Korean authorities caught up with the couple at Bahrain's airport just as they were about to fly out of the country. The elderly man, 70 years old, quickly swallowed a tablet of poison and died. His young companion tried but failed to swallow her pill and lived.

Covert Espionage

The two "Japanese" proved to be members of North Korea's Workers' Party and highly trained terrorists. The man was Kim Sung-il, a 70-year-old father of seven from Pyongyang. His "daughter" was actually Kim Hyon-hui, the 26-year-old eldest daughter of a Foreign Ministry official who had served in Cuba from 1962 to 1967. Both had trained together as father and daughter since 1984. He had actually sneaked into South Korea in 1984, stayed in a downtown hotel for a week, and then departed undetected.

The woman had been recruited as a covert operative in 1980. After a year of secret, paramilitary training, she began the study of Japanese. For two years, she shared a house in Pyongyang with her language teacher—a Japanese woman. The purpose of the arrangement was to teach her Japanese customs and manners, and to polish her Japanese language. This Japanese teacher turned out to be one of the Japanese citizens that North Korean agents had abducted from Japan.

After a month of questioning, Kim Hyon-hui confessed her crimes. She explained that she and her deceased colleague had left a radio on KAL 858 when they left the flight at Abu Dhabi airport. Inside was a powerful bomb made of C4 plastic explosive attached to a timer.

This was not North Korea's first act of terrorism against South Korea, but North Korea has not repeated such a deadly and despicable act since.

For both Koreas, covert espionage has been routine for years. North and South Korean agents have been slipping in and out of each other's halves of the Korean Peninsula since their nations were established. But collecting intelligence is one thing, assassinating political leaders is an entire different matter.

Birds of Feather

The first Japan Airlines (JAL) flight to Pyongyang was unscheduled. Actually, the flight had been hijacked by the international terrorist group that called itself, among other things, the Japanese Red Army (JRA). This proved to be the international debuts of one of the most brutal and feared terrorist groups before the birth of Al Qaeda.

The JRA group seized the flight and ordered the pilot to fly to Pyongyang. He landed at Seoul instead, hoping to trick the hijackers.

Not so fast, the hijackers said, and they demanded to see a North Korean flag and a picture of Kim Il Sung. When the South Korean authorities could not fulfill either demand, the hijackers forced the pilot to resume the flight to Pyongyang.

Eventually, the aircraft and its passengers would be allowed to return to Japan. But the hijackers sought, and the North Korean government granted them, safe haven. Actually, one or two of these aging JRA terrorists still reside in Pyongyang where they teach the Japanese language.

Many years later, a member of this JRA group was arrested on the Thai-Cambodia border while riding in a car with North Korean diplomats. He was eventually arrested for allegedly carrying counterfeit U.S. currency, but these charges were later dropped.

Shoot-Out in Seoul

North Korea excelled in trying to murder South Korea's political leadership. The first highly publicized effort failed in 1968 when a platoon of North Korean soldiers, in full combat dress and heavily armed, managed to hike undetected through the DMZ to the fence that encloses the Blue House, the official residence of South Korea's president. But early in the morning, an alert policeman sounded the alarm and an intense battle erupted on the northern edge of Seoul. All but one North Korean was killed.

Remember the *Pueblo!*

January 23, 1968, began as just another bitterly cold winter day on the Korean Peninsula. Then the only North Korean soldier to survive the raid on the Blue House appeared on South Korean television to tell what he and his colleagues had tried to do. As he spoke, a small U.S. naval ship quietly bobbed in calm seas beyond North Korea's territorial waters on its east coast.

This was not your usual U.S. Navy ship. This was the USS *Pueblo.* It did the work of the United States's super-secret National Security Agency (NSA). The small ship bristled on the outside with antennae of all kinds. Inside, highly trained Korean language specialists, code breakers, and electronic intelligence (ELINT) operators listened, recorded, and translated every word that the North Korean military and civilian authorities were sending to one another.

The small dots on the horizon quickly grew into fast patrol and torpedo boats. From their mast fluttered in the frigid breeze was the red, white, and blue flag of North Korea. The rest is history, as they say.

The North Koreans fired on the *Pueblo* as it tried to flee, wounding several crew members and killing one. The *Pueblo's* radio man sent repeated pleas for help. Many promises were received in response, but none was fulfilled.

The North Korean navy had caught a U.S. naval vessel full of top-secret equipment and intelligence, completely unprotected and defenseless. The *Pueblo* was towed into Wonsan port. There its crew was rushed to Pyongyang, interrogated, and tortured for one year. The crew did not regain its freedom until a high-ranking U.S. officer signed an apology for the incident and passed it to his North Korean counterpart.

For the Americans that were aware of this incident, it was an extremely frustrating and humiliating experience. For the crew of the USS *Pueblo* and their families, first it was an ordeal in North Korea's capacity to inflict suffering on others. Then the U.S. Navy insisted on using the USS *Pueblo's* captain as the scapegoat for the entire ordeal. U.S.–North Korean relations had reached a new low.

Assassination of a Lady

North Korea remained focused on killing South Korea's increasingly unpopular and authoritarian ruler, Park Chung-hee. Apparently, North Korea's leaders believed that killing Park would cause his regime to collapse and in the turmoil that would have followed the South Koreans might use the opportunity to unite with North Korea. This might have made sense to a few isolated officials in Pyongyang, but to South Koreans, this thinking was sheer folly.

On August 15, 1974, South Korea's president and his popular and sophisticated wife were together on the National Theater's stage at a celebration of Korea's independence from Japan. A young man in the audience leaped to his feet and quickly emptied his pistol at the people on stage. President Park ducked behind his bulletproof podium and was saved. His wife, seated behind him, was hit and killed. The assassin proved to be a Korean resident of Japan with pro-Pyongyang sympathies.

Increase Your North Korea IQ

North Korea's chronology of terror:

1968—North Korean soldiers attacked South Korea's presidential residence.

1968—North Korea seized the U.S. intelligence ship USS *Pueblo* in international waters off its east coast and tortured the crew for one year prior to releasing them.

1970—Japanese Red Army (JRA) hijacked a Japan Airlines (JAL) flight to Pyongyang, and North Korea granted them safe haven.

1972—A North Korean bomb exploded prematurely at South Korea's National Cemetery hours before the president's arrival.

1974—South Korea's first lady murdered at the National Theater by a pro-Pyongyang Korean resident of Japan.

1976—Two U.S. Army officers killed with an axe handle in the DMZ by North Korean soldiers.

1983—Rangoon bombing killed several members of South Korea's presidential cabinet.

1987—KAL flight 858 exploded over the Gulf of Thailand, killing 115 people on board.

Death by Hatchet

It was just another hot, humid summer day in the DMZ north of Seoul. A work party of U.S. and South Korean soldiers set out to chop down a tree inside the no-man's land that separates North and South Korea. They wanted to remove it because blocked their ability to observe that corner of the so-called Joint Security Area (JSA).

No sooner had the cutting begun than a North Korean army officer approached. He insisted that the work stop. The U.S. officer in charge explained that the project had the Military Armistice Commission's approval. Enraged, the North Korean officer and his fellow soldiers attacked the work party. Two U.S. officers were beaten to death in the ensuing melee, by an axe handle wielded by North Korean soldiers.

The incident brought the United States and North Korea to the edge of war. Tempers calmed only after North Korean leader Kim Il Sung signed an apology for the incident.

Personal Recollections

Lt. Col. Marty Wisda was the first U.S. soldier to travel from Pyongyang to Panmunjom since the hasty withdrawal of the U.S. Eighth Army from North Korea in the winter of 1950. Marty and I were the liaison officers between the first U.S. Army Joint Recovery Team to search for the remains of U.S. Korean War Missing in Action (MIA). We traveled from Pyongyang to Panmunjom in July 1996 to negotiate the return of a U.S. soldier's remains to South Korea. The contingent of North Korean officers at Panmunjom treated Marty with unexpected respect. They invited us to visit their museum about the Korean War Armistice. Toward the end of our highly educational tour, we approached a large axe prominently displayed in a glass case. Marty's face turned ashen as I translated the Korean explanation, "This axe was used to defend our fatherland …" Marty bolted from the museum, enraged. I followed. After a few minutes, he had regained his composure. Our North Korean guides apologized for their insensitivity. The so-called axe murders, like many of North Korea's acts of terror, are not yet history. For many, they remain painful, living memories and retard reconciliation on all sides.

Murder in Rangoon

The worst was yet to come. President Park was finally assassinated, but not by a North Korean. The director of the Korean Central Intelligence Agency shot his president while they dined at the presidential residence. Another general, Chun Doo-hwan, promptly seized power and proclaimed himself ruler of South Korea.

President Chun traveled to Rangoon in October 1983. There he was scheduled to deliver a wreath at a national monument. The night before, two North Korean agents hid a powerful bomb in the monument's ceiling. The next morning, they hid in the nearby jungle, waiting to explode the bomb by remote control as South Korea's president entered to place his wreath.

They literally blew it! Chun's motorcade was behind schedule, but members of his cabinet had arrived earlier and lined up inside the monument. As a television camera recorded the scene, there was a terrible explosion. Dust and debris filled the air. As it settled, blood pouring from the dead and dying became visible. The living struggled to their feet and wandered in shock, moaning from the pain their wounds caused.

Quick-thinking security forces caught the two North Korean agents as they attempted to flee through the jungle to a waiting North Korean ship. They and the ship were seized, and yet another treacherous North Korean plot was exposed.

Personal Recollections

In October 1983, I was a political officer at the U.S. Embassy in Seoul, Korea. At the time of the Rangoon bombing, I was with a U.S. congressman as he shopped on a Sunday afternoon. Security was extremely tight because for days North Korean radio had warned that the congressman's hotel would be blown up.

The day after the explosion in Rangoon, the U.S. ambassador dispatched me to the National Assembly to deliver his message to the chairmen of the Foreign and Defense Affairs Committees. Many powerful national assemblymen were retired generals. They demanded armed retaliation against North Korea. My job was to tell them that United States would defend South Korea, but not if it attacked North Korea first. They and other South Koreans, in a most admirable demonstration of self-restraint, peacefully mourned their dead and then resumed their normal lives.

North Korea Makes the List

U.S. legislation finally empowered the U.S. secretary of state to designate nations a "terrorist country" and impose selected economic sanctions on them. On January 20, 1988, North Korea was finally labeled a terrorist nation because of the KAL 858 incident. North Korea remains on the U.S. government's list of terrorist nations along with Cuba, Iran, Iraq, Libya, Sudan, and Syria.

The 1988 designation increased the economic sanctions on North Korea. Originally, the U.S. government in 1950, after North Korea invaded South Korea, imposed an embargo on North Korea as provided for in the Trading with the Enemy Act of 1918.

The sanctions added in 1988 bar North Korea from receiving food aid under Public Law 480 on a loan or subsidized-purchase basis. This same law, however, allows the U.S. government to send food aid to nations with "high levels of malnutrition and emergency food requirements." North Korea thus remained qualified for food aid because of this provision. But North Korea was barred from obtaining credit from the Export-Import Bank to finance its international trade.

In 1989, a year after North Korea was placed on the "terrorist list," the U.S. Export Administration Act of 1979 was amended by the Anti-Terrorism and Arms Export Amendments. This imposed economic sanctions on nations that the U.S. government had designated terrorist states. The sanctions added in 1989 outlaw the export of any munitions by the U.S. government or a U.S. citizen to North Korea. Also, the export of selected nonmunitions items must be licensed.

Congress gave the president limited discretion in waiving the prohibition for a particular transaction. But first he had to decide that it is "essential to the national security interest of the United States," and then both consult with and submit a report to Congress 15 days prior to the transaction.

There are two ways for a country to get off the "terrorist list." First, the president must certify to the Congress that "there has been a fundamental change in the leadership or policies of the terrorist country, that the government … is not supporting acts of international terrorism, and that the government has provided assurances that it will not support actions of international terrorism in the future."

The second path requires the president send Congress for its review, 45 days prior to the effective date of the nation being dropped from the list, an explanation that the nominated government has not supported international terrorism during the previous six months and has provided assurances that it will not support acts of international terrorism in the future.

On top of all of this, the fiscal year (FY) 1995 Foreign Operations Appropriations (funding for the conducting of foreign relations) required that the secretary of the treasury oppose any loan to a country that the secretary of state has designated a terrorist state. In other words, North Korea cannot borrow any money from the World Bank, International Monetary Fund (IMF), or the Asian Development Bank (ADB) until it gets off the terrorist list.

Japan's Abducted Citizens

Nobody knows how many Japanese citizens North Korean agents have kidnapped and taken to Pyongyang. The estimates reach as high as 50 people. But beginning in the late 1970s, rumors spread across Japan that young men and women were disappearing as they strolled along Japan's scenic coastline and beaches.

After a quarter of a century of denial by North Korea, agony by the loved ones of the missing, and intense effort by the Japanese government, North Korean leader Kim Jong Il admitted the truth.

North Korea had kidnapped several Japanese citizens to teach the Japanese language, customs, and manners to North Korea's covert agents.

The agony and mystery began in 1977. In September 1977, a 52-year-old woman disappeared off the beach of Japan's northwest coast. Japanese police arrested a North Korean resident living in Japan who confessed that he had handed the woman over to North Korean agents. Thirteen-year-old Megumi Yokota, a middle school student, disappeared two months later.

Language Teachers

A year later in Lebanon, two Asian men recruited 20 women to apply for language instruction positions. Four of the women were promised flights to Japan. Instead they were flown to Pyongyang. Two of the four managed to escape to tell their tale. But then one of the escapees voluntarily returned to Pyongyang. She was pregnant by her husband, an American soldier named Jerry Parish (Koran name Kim Il Woo), who had defected to North Korea in 1963.

Then came the bizarre story told by the North Korean terrorist Kim Hyon-hui. Her Japanese-language teacher was identified as another Japanese woman who had disappeared. The stories continued along with North Korea's official and adamant denials.

Normalization Talks Stalled

In 1992, Japan raised the issue of the abducted Japanese at the October round of normalization talks with North Korea. When Pyongyang repeated its denial and refused to discuss the matter any further, Japan broke off the talks (see Chapter 17). Ever since, the issue has remained at the top of Japan's agenda of outstanding issues to resolve with North Korea.

"Comfort Women"

Pyongyang for a decade sought to deflect international attention away from the abducted Japanese citizens to the so-called comfort women issue. Beginning in approximately 1937, and continuing until the end of World War II in 1945, the Japanese Imperial Army recruited young women to provide sexual comfort to its soldiers. The practice was adopted from the French army's tradition of having groups of prostitutes attached to military units.

But Japan's Imperial Army turned to trickery and coercion to force many of the estimated 200,000 women from Korea, Taiwan, China, Japan, and other Asian nations to serve as so-called comfort women. Out of shame, these women remained silent for decades until historians brought their humiliation and agony to the public's attention.

Human rights and women's advocates brought the issue to the attention of the UN Human Rights Commission in 1992. The subsequent public furor compelled a reluctant Japanese government to recognize that a serious problem existed and that it had to take compassionate and concrete steps to address the former comfort women's demands.

Japan Responds

In August 1996, Japan's prime minister issued a personal letter of apology and expression of remorse regarding the comfort women. He also contributed a large sum of atonement money to establish the Asian Women's Fund to provide compensation to the victims.

North Korea in August 1997 rejected Japan's efforts as being insufficient, and officially informed the UN subcommission on the Prevention of Discrimination and Protection of Minorities of its displeasure. Pyongyang demanded that the government of Japan accept responsibility, officially apologize, contribute government money to the Asian Women's Fund, supplement this with atonement money, and fund medical welfare and education programs for the victims and their family members.

South Korea teamed up with North Korea at the 54th Session of the UN Commission on Human Rights held in Geneva, Switzerland, in the spring of 1998. The South Korean delegation expressed disappointment with the Japanese government's response to the comfort women's plight. South Korea, unlike North Korea, did not press for the Japanese government to respond with money. Instead, the South Koreans pressed for "an honest admission on the part of the Japanese government."

Japan Judged

A ranking member of the UN Commission on Human Rights and Violence Against Women convened a "Women's International War Crimes Tribunal." The tribunal "indicted" several ranking World War II–period Japanese generals (all deceased) for their promotion of the comfort women program. The common indictment also found the Japanese government responsible for rape and sexual slavery, and other crimes against humanity. The tribunal recommended that the Japanese government fulfill all of North Korea's demands regarding settlement of the matter.

Thus far, the Japanese government has not taken steps to address the tribunal's recommendations. Instead, Tokyo continues to insist the current government of Japan should not be held responsible for the misdeeds of the Imperial Japanese government during World War II. However, the Japanese government continues to quietly and unofficially provide funds for the Asian Women's Fund.

North Korea continues its clamor about the case, but much of the international community, including concerned South Koreans, consider the matter settled.

Kim Jong Il Confesses

The Japanese people's concerns about their abducted citizens were ignited into outrage by North Korean leader Kim Jong Il's inept effort to resolve this matter in September 2002.

Japan's energetic prime minister Junichiro Koizumi stunned Japan's allies and friends around the world in August 2002 when he announced his plan to travel to Pyongyang for a summit with North Korean leader Kim Jong Il. After 12 years of on-again, off-again tedious negotiations, the prime minister was pushing for a dramatic breakthrough in Japan–North Korea relations.

Initially, his efforts seemed to pay huge dividends. When he met Kim Jong Il on September 17, Kim admitted to North Korea's kidnapping of several Japanese citizens, apologized for this, and assured the prime minister that those responsible were punished.

Koizumi returned to a triumphant welcome in Tokyo that same day. But by the next day, the public outcry had begun. The Japanese people demanded to know why so many of the missing Japanese had died apparently untimely deaths. Koizumi sought to repair the damage by demanding a follow-up meeting with North Korea. A meeting was promptly held, but North Korea refused to provide any details about the circumstances of death, or particulars about which North Korean officials had been punished and how.

In a rather lame effort to restore good will, Kim Jong Il allowed a small number of the Japanese victims to visit Japan. The North Korean government, however, insisted on their return to North Korea. As insurance for this, the victims' children and spouses were not allowed to leave North Korea. Once in Japan, however, the victims decided not to return to North Korea.

Since September 2002, Kim Jong Il's fumbling attempt to resolve this highly emotional issue has only worsened the situation. The unresolved issue of the abducted Japanese citizens will remain well into the future as a major impediment to the normalization of Japan-North Korea relations.

More Sanctions

Japan and the United States are agreed that North Korea will not be removed from the terrorist list until this issue is resolved. The two allies also agree that North Korea will be denied admission to the World and Asian Development Banks until North Korea satisfies Japan's demands regarding its abducted citizens. Without membership in the World Bank, North Korea is not able to obtain low-interest loans to fund its economic development.

Trying to Make Nice

Meanwhile, North Korea was trying to improve ties with the United States. In 2000, at the end of a series of diplomatic discussions between the U.S. and North Korea, the two nations issued a "Joint U.S.–DPRK Statement on International Terrorism." In it, North Korea "affirmed that ... it opposes all forms of terrorism ...." The statement, released on October 6, two and one half months prior to the end of the Clinton Administration, has generally been ignored by the Bush Administration.

The former Bush Administration in 1992 had told North Korea that its public renunciation of international terrorism and release to Japan of the Japanese Red Army members would qualify it for removal from the terrorist list. The Clinton Administration added the requirement that North Korea must satisfy Japan's requirements regarding the abducted Japanese citizens.

The new Bush Administration further adjusted the preconditions North Korea must fulfill before it can get off the terrorist list. First, it has reaffirmed the requirements of previous administrations. Then, through its annual reports on international terrorism, the Bush Administration has added the requirements that North Korea do more to combat international terrorism and that it halt the export of ballistic missiles. In July 2003, the Bush Administration reaffirmed its support for Japan's efforts to compel North Korea to satisfactorily address Japan's requirements regarding the abducted Japanese issue (see Chapter 17).

In light of Kim Jong Il's poor handling of the situation with Japan, and continuing effort to develop nuclear weapons, North Korea seems destined to remain on the terrorist list well into the foreseeable future.

The Least You Need to Know

- ◆ North Korea practiced terrorism against South Korea beginning in the 1960s and against Japan since the 1970s.

- ◆ North Korea is not known to have carried out an act of international terrorism since 1987.

- ◆ North Korea was named to the U.S. Department of State's List of Terrorist Nations in 1988, and is highly likely to remain on the list into the foreseeable future.

- ◆ Being on the list imposes severe economic sanctions on North Korea.

Chapter 23

Human Rights and Refugees

In This Chapter

- ◆ Obligations versus individual rights
- ◆ Prospects for political change
- ◆ Strategies for change
- ◆ Flood of foreigners in, flow of refugees out

North Korea's huge army and weapons of mass destruction impose enormous burdens on at least 20 million of the nation's 23 million people. This majority must work longer and harder, eat less, shiver more in the winter, and sweat more in the summer than the privileged minority of 3 million.

The situation excites some very logical questions. Why do the North Korean people put up with this situation? Why don't they just rise up and overthrow their government, or at least pack up and walk out? Actually, these questions pose a more fundamental one: What will it take to change North Korea?

In this chapter, we address this issue, not to rehash the U.S. Department of State's annual human rights report. In Part 3, we looked at how the North Korean government asserts its control over the population through education, mass political organizations, and coercive monitoring. Here we shift our view from Pyongyang to the rice paddies, cornfields, factories, and offices. At the end of a long, hard day of working for marginal self gain, what prevents an individual North Korean from turning on the system?

Far-Out Ideas

The North Korean people have an outlook on life that is alien to the Western reader. But the Western ideas of human and individual political rights are just as alien to them, and to East Asian culture in general. North Korea's human rights record is bad, but at various times the same can be said of the other East Asian nations.

Japan's democratization dates from the 1920s, but did not pick up momentum until after World War II. Iron-fisted despots ruled the Philippines, South Korea, and Taiwan until the 1980s. Only then did democracy take hold, and governmental respect for human rights (consistent with the Western concept) improve. China, Vietnam, and North Korea still lag behind.

Judging a nation's human rights record is easily done. Saying that North Korea's human rights record is appalling does not require much mental energy. Pyongyang's record obviously is very bad. But knowing and saying this does not change the situation.

Before outside governments and peoples can start telling the North Korean people what they should do to help themselves, we need to understand how difficult it will be to replace the deeply rooted authoritarian practices with ones more conducive to respect for human rights. Then we can begin to look at ways to bring about the changes needed before respect for human rights can take root.

Obligations Versus Rights

Let's leap back to Korea's Confucian heritage and traditional social pyramid. Modern North Korean society retains many of the traditional traits outlined in Chapters 10, 11, and 12.

North Korea's authoritarian legacy left no room for democracy or individual and human rights. According to Confucius, the monarch's foremost responsibility is to maintain social harmony. Five key relationships were to be respected, particularly the one that required subjects to respect their king. Collectivism was revered while individualism was equated with evil. Why? The assertion of one's desires could arouse others to do likewise. Anarchy could quickly ensue, destroying social harmony. The Western concept of individualism runs contrary to this philosophy.

None of this has anything to do with Stalinism or communism, but it is the bedrock upon which Kim Il Sung built his dynasty. He named himself the monarch and grafted selected elements of Confucianism onto his juche ideology. To further justify the individual's submission to the "Great Leader," Kim took the Confucian value of loyalty and remolded it into nationalism.

The sum result is a blending of Confucianism's accent on submission to authority and modern nationalism. Combined with this was an emphasis on collectivism over individualism. No room remained for the individual or the Western concept of "rights." Instead, we end up with the individual subordinated to a group and heavily burdened with obligations to his group (the party, army, or both), the nation, and its leader.

Individualism thus acquires an evil, subversive meaning. Individuals who assert their personal desires and claim "rights" vis-à-vis the state and ruler are perceived as disloyal and subversive. They are easily categorized as the "enemy of the state" and purged, either through execution or banishment to a labor camp.

Personal Recollections

I accidentally discovered that a strong sense of individuality survives in North Korea. After several stays at Pyongyang's Koryo Hotel, I got to know the hotel staff as individuals. One evening, I took my camera to the dining room and asked if I could take a picture of each individual waiter and waitress. They said yes, and I photographed each. A month later I returned and presented each with copies of their picture. They were thrilled. At long last they had pictures of themselves to send to their parents for display to other family members and friends. The photograph of an individual is a most highly prized possession in North Korea.

Legalized Tyranny

The North Korean constitution legalizes all of this. Thus, anyone who breaks stride makes him- or herself an outlaw. In the Constitution, juche is singled out as the sole acceptable ideology in Article 3, "The DPRK is guided in its activities by the Juche idea ..." Then in Article 4, "democracy" is squeezed out of the political system, "All State organs in the DPRK are formed and function on the principle of democratic centralism."

Finally, in Article 10, we get to "social harmony" expressed in modern political jargon, "The DPRK rests on the politico-ideological unity of all the people ... The State shall revolutionize all the members of the society, and assimilate them into the working class by intensifying the ideological revolution, and shall turn the whole of society into a collective, united in a comradely way."

The constitution's Chapter V has the promising title, "Fundamental Rights and Duties of Citizens." But right away, duties jump ahead of rights. In Article 63 it is explained that, "In the DPRK the rights and duties of citizens are based on the collectivist principle, 'One for all and all for one.'" Subsequent articles "guarantee" freedom of speech, and so on. Article 78 goes so far as to guarantee "the inviolability of the person and the home and privacy of correspondence."

Thereafter, however, we get into the list of duties. It begins with, "Citizens shall firmly safeguard the political and ideological unity and solidarity of the people." Farther down the list we find, "collectivism is the basis of life of a socialist society." The bottom line, simply put, is that the nail that sticks up gets banged down. In other words, the individual that steps out of the mold is labeled an outlaw.

Give Me a Break

What value are the Western concepts of human and political rights to the majority of North Koreans? Most North Koreans simply do not know what they mean. No one has ever taught them about human rights in school. There is no mention of them in textbooks, popular literature, or the daily mass media.

We must keep in mind that, in North Korea, there is no window to the outside world. The majority of people have never seen a foreign book, magazine, or newspaper, nor have they heard or seen a foreign broadcast. Only a tiny, select elite has been allowed to travel abroad. When they return home, they say little to others about the outside world. The less said, the better to safeguard oneself from possible allegations of wavering loyalty.

Personal Recollections

One of the first North Korean interpreters I got to know well asked me to bring him some English-language novels so on my next visit he could catch up on current American slang. At the time, I happened to be reading The Hunt for Red October, *a Cold War–thriller about a Soviet submarine captain's effort to defect to the United States. Not thinking about the book's political theme, I gave him my copy. Back in the United States, a member of the North Korean diplomatic delegation to the UN called me at the State Department and cautioned that I was not to give anyone in North Korea a book of any kind. When I returned a month later to North Korea, I asked to see the interpreter. His replacement explained that he had been sent to reeducation camp because he had accepted the book from me without permission from the Korean Workers' Party. I later saw him, but he said it was better for him not to be seen with me.*

In fact, it is against the law to ask foreigners about the outside world. Regular access to foreigners requires the permission of one's superiors. Every time a North Korean has an accidental encounter with a foreigner, he or she is required to submit a written report to the authorities. This requirement is enough to deter a busy worker or farmer from speaking to a foreigner.

Nor can a North Korean (or foreign visitor for that matter) turn on the radio or television set and tune into a foreign broadcast. All radios and television sets in North Korea are designed so that they can receive only domestic broadcasts. Owning a shortwave radio is outlawed.

Survival First

For a half century, the majority of the people in North Korea have been preoccupied with the struggle to survive. Life is an endless cycle of hard labor in the factories, fields, offices, and army. Spare time is spent reflecting on family, friends, and one's natural surroundings. Certainly you do not sit around Sunday afternoon over a couple of beers grumbling about how the "Great Leader" combs his hair or that his generals strut about showing off their medals. This will get you nowhere fast.

Personal Recollections

An ashen-faced U.S. Army officer stood in my hotel room door. Flanking him were three stern-faced North Koreans. They accused him of a most grievous crime—showing disrespect to their "Great Leader." That morning, he had crumpled up a copy of the weekly English-language newspaper Pyongyang Weekly *and tossed it in the wastebasket in his room. The room maid found it and immediately reported him to the police. On the front cover was a picture of Kim Jong Il. The North Koreans insisted upon a signed apology. I dismissed the demand as excessive. At that point, my American companion suggested that he be expelled from the country. He said he would promise to tell everyone in foreign countries about his "crime." Then he apologized to me for having created such a horrendous situation.*

I turned to the irate North Koreans and in my best Korean explained that the U.S. Army officer had apologized for this incident. (The that fact that he had apologized to me, and not to them, was irrelevant.) Also, he promised to humiliate himself by telling every American he met about his misdeed. This wiped the stern look from their faces and they quickly headed off to report their victorious struggle with the American army.

The incident at the time was rather traumatic, but since then it brings a smile to my face and fond memories of my colleague.

North Koreans, however, share all the same human traits we know so well. They do complain, have quarrels and rivalries with one another, criticize their colleagues or boss, and commit all the same crimes that people around the world commit each day.

The difference between their reality and ours, however, is enormous. Complaining, criticizing, rivalry, and other forms of expressing individual frustration are crimes in North Korea. In many cases, punishment is unbelievably harsh. Criticizing a local official for unfair food allocations can get you executed in public by a firing squad. Officials who hoard food suffer the same punishment. Complaining about the size of one's ration could get you set off to a reeducation or labor camp.

Survival in North Korea means you do not complain, and you most certainly do not dissent. Instead, the individual seeks shelter from government authority by clinging to a group and conforming to sanctioned norms.

Those who do not conform are "crossed out." In North and South Korean society, the government maintains "family registers." These are similar to birth certificates in the United States and elsewhere. The difference is that in both Koreas, the individual is registered with their family group.

Traditionally, individual misdeeds brought punishment to the entire family group. This practice continues in North Korea. When a person dies, a red "X" is slashed across their name. Getting "crossed out" in North Korea means receiving the worst possible punishment—either execution or disappearance into a labor camp.

The Bottom Line

Tallying all these factors leads to the inescapable conclusion that North Koreans face the ultimate choice everyday. Either they can endure what their government demands of them, and survive, or they can criticize the situation, and in all likelihood, end up dead or in prison. The basic human urge is to survive. Therefore, we should not expect to see much dissent in North Korean society.

The Push for Change

Who can start the process of political change in North Korea? Obviously, Kim Jong Il and his colleagues are out to keep their despotic system intact. Democracy and human rights are not on their agenda.

North Koreans are hardly in a position to do much about their situation. To begin with, most do not have any basis for comparison. Those who have acquired knowledge of the outside world have a vested interest in preserving the current authoritarian system. Any who might venture to advocate political change from within the system would most likely be labeled "traitors" and banished.

This tosses the task to people living outside the North Korean system. South Koreans and others in the international community are the best candidates for the job. As democracy matures in South Korea, its people will be prone to press harder for their government to promote change in North Korea. High on their list of reforms is pushing for increased North Korean government concern for North Koreans' welfare and respect of their human rights.

Frequent social and educational exchanges, economic cooperation, and family visits are only the beginning. Progress toward North-South Korea reconciliation will require narrowing the gap between the two Koreas' political philosophies and systems. This will require extensive overhauling of North Korea's entire political system. Otherwise, any official North Korean demonstration of respect for human rights would be superficial and temporary.

Nor is this simply a matter of replacing Kim Jong Il as North Korea's ruler. The lack of human rights is not merely a consequence of his one-man rule. Kim Jong Il's disappearance tomorrow would not automatically give birth to human rights. The causes of the problem permeate the political and social systems, the state ideology, and both the educational and legal systems.

Soft Versus Hard Landings

How to achieve these changes is the subject of an intense and continuing debate between advocates of a "soft landing" or a "hard landing." South Korea's official approach to North Korea favors the "soft landers." They urge engagement of North Korea. Using economic and other inducements, their immediate goal is to gain access to North Korea's population and expose it to the concepts and practices of democracy and benefits of capitalism. Their hope is to initiate a gradual, peaceful process inside North Korea that will lead to the regime's "soft landing" (read: transformation).

"Hard landers" counter that such an approach cannot succeed. Instead, they favor direct, assertive action. Their techniques range from toppling the regime through covert action or an economic embargo, inducing North Koreans to rise up and overthrow their government, or shaming the regime into changing.

The debate focuses more on tactics than goals. Both groups want to see North Korea's political and economic systems transformed, the sooner the better. But there is also a debate over the extent of change needed.

Repair or Revamp?

Some advocates of North Korea's political transformation believe the current system can be "reformed." But this suggests that the system is worth salvaging and that it only needs repair, not a complete revamping. Soft landers would seem to prefer this limited, repair approach.

Soft landers tend to favor engagement of North Korea. This means entering into the society and exposing its population to outside influences, knowledge, and images that conflict with those their government has long fostered. They point to the East-West German experience as an example of when such a strategy succeeded.

They favor contact at all levels—government, private, commercial, social, and educational, as we discuss in Chapter 16.

Advocates of the hard landing generally agree that the entire system must be replaced. But they disagree over how to accomplish this. Some want to topple the regime, covertly or otherwise. Others want to foster dissent from within North Korean society in the hope that the North Korean people will topple their government. And yet others contend that benign neglect, the isolation of the regime from international commerce and similar measures would inevitably lead to its demise.

Big Brother Is Listening

Each approach has its pros and cons, benefits and price, yet there is a common denominator. Kim Jong Il is listening to the debate in South Korea, the United States, and elsewhere. Surely, he does not like what either side is saying because both are working to change, even end, his regime. We should anticipate that he will work to obstruct to the maximum extent possible the influence of outsiders, especially South Koreans and Americans, on his subjects. Once outsiders recognize this fact, they can better pace and refine their efforts to promote change in North Korea.

The Ancestors Have Spoken

After his father's death, Kim Jong Il appears to have struggled with the question of how best to deal with his crumbling regime and dilapidated economic infrastructure. He fears that change and reform would undermine the political cohesiveness of his regime. On the other hand, without some change, he could not revive the North Korean economy and maintain the military might needed to defend his regime.

The immediate cause for Kim Jong Il's recent willingness to allow change was the August 1995 floods and subsequent food crisis. Kim Jong Il in 1995 seemed on the verge of losing the Mandate of Heaven. This ancient Confucian concept (see Chapter 5) cautioned rulers that if they failed to care for the welfare of their people, the long-deceased ancestors might unleash the forces of nature. Flood and famine would follow, setting in motion a political cycle that would thrust up a new claimant to the throne and the Mandate of Heaven.

It would appear the ancestors yelled in Kim Jong Il's ear in the late summer and fall of 1995. Torrential rains that year wreaked havoc in North Korea's four western provinces. Flooding washed away fields, crops, homes, dikes, and roads. Electric power and telephone lines were knocked down, bridges and railroad beds washed away.

An estimated 70 percent of the nation's annual rice harvest and 53 percent of its maize production were destroyed. The International Red Cross estimated that 100,000 families lost their homes and 400,000 hectares of arable land (25 percent of the nation's total) were destroyed or flooded.

A Flood of Foreigners

That fall, North Korea's 23 million people became the focus of a sustained global humanitarian effort. More than 30 governments, over 130 nongovernmental private voluntary humanitarian relief organizations, and virtually every major international relief organization has contributed to this effort.

Their combined food aid between September 1, 1995, and October 31, 2001, amounts to nearly 6 million M/T worth close to US $1 billion. Additional assistance in the areas of public health, agricultural recovery and development, sanitation, and education increased gradually from approximately US $8 million in the winter of 1995–1996 to US $60 million in 2001, largely because of assistance from South Korea.

Accompanying the aid was a relative multitude of foreigners. Never before had North Korea allowed so many foreigners to reside in Pyongyang and to visit and survey most areas of the nation.

UN relief organizations that responded had opened an office in Pyongyang staffed by foreign citizens. UNICEF representatives from Hong Kong took up residence in the Koryo Hotel, Pyongyang's premiere hotel for foreign visitors.

The flood of foreigners into North Korea continues. Most important is the increasing number of South Koreans going to North Korea (see Chapter 19). Adding to their growing number are businessmen from all the nations of East Asia and many from the European Union, relief workers from around the world, and technical advisers on everything from agriculture to computers and communications.

Foreigners now can visit every province of North Korea and all but a relatively small number of districts. Access and visibility to the North Korean population continues to expand. At the same time, North Koreans can see for themselves that not all foreigners are a threat to their security and nation's survival.

The Flow of Refugees

Along with the increase of foreigners streaming in to North Korea, the floods and pervasive food shortages that followed expanded the outward flow of refugees. Most headed northeast to China's Korean Autonomous Region. A few survived the trek or a ride atop railroad cars through central North Korea's rugged mountains into China. Others crossed the west end of the China-North Korea border and disappeared into the Chinese city of Dandong.

Beginning as a trickle in the winter of 1995, the number of North Koreans seeking food, work, and escape from North Korea's oppressive conditions steadily increased until 1998. The number appears to have peaked in 1999, and has slowly and steadily declined since.

No one can say for certain how many North Koreans have fled to China. Estimates range from 30,000 to 10 times this number. One organization that has closely monitored the situation since 1998 estimates that between 50,000 and 150,000 North Koreans reside in the Yanbian region.

China's *Yanbian* (*Yonbyon* in Korean) Korean Self Autonomous Region is the most hospitable place for North Korea's refugees. The region is a special administrative district within China's northeast Jilin Province in the area previously known as Manchuria. Korean-Chinese dominate the region's government, commerce, and professions. The Korean language has legal equal status with Chinese.

Of the some 2 million Chinese of Korean ancestry residing in China, about 850,000 people live in the Yanbian region. The remaining 1.2 million Chinese of Korean ancestry are scattered elsewhere in China. Most of these people fled to China from the Korean Peninsula during Japan's colonial occupation of Korea. It is believed that the number of Koreans living in China at the end of the war reached 750,000. The larger part of the Korean population in Yanbian traces its ancestry to the southern part of the Korean Peninsula. Korea's division in 1945, however, blocked their return home.

It may come as a surprise to some people, but a significant number of Chinese of Korean ancestry moved back to North Korea during China's great famine in the late 1950s. At the time, conditions in North Korea were superior to those in China, particularly regarding the food supply. North Korea's food shortages in the 1990s reversed this flow.

Monitoring the Flow

The North Koreans who have sought refuge in China have become a political football. Advocates of North Korea's hard landing interpret the flow of North Korean refugees into China as proof that Kim Jong Il's regime is on the verge of collapse. Others in this school hope to undermine the regime by enticing more North Koreans to flee their homeland. Several organizations have monitored the flow of refugees hoping to assign political significance to their data. All agree that these people's plight is a humanitarian tragedy.

One organization's efforts have put the compilation of accurate data before political motives. It has conducted this work quietly on the China-North Korean border since the spring of 1998. The data it has accumulated from several thousand interviews suggests some relatively reliable characteristics and trends about this population flow.

No less than 80 percent of the North Koreans crossing into China come from North Korea's northern two provinces. Only a very small number of North Koreans risk imprisonment, and even their lives, to leave from the southern areas of North Korea. Most are young, between the ages of 10 to 39. The number of persons older than 39 years of age appears to have dropped off since 1998. The same can be said for young children, nine or younger. The split between males and females is almost equal.

Refugees or Migrants?

In recent years, refugee and human rights activists from South Korea and Japan have tried hard to focus attention on the North Korean population in China. Since 2001, some American activists, with encouragement and funding from the Republican Heritage Foundation and the congressionally funded National Endowment for Democracy, also have become advocates for legislation that would enable North Korean refugees to immigrate from China to the United States.

These activists prefer to label all of the North Koreans residing in China as "refugees," that is, people who have fled their homeland in search of safe haven from political repression. The Chinese government rejects this claim, and instead calls all these North Koreans "migrants," a politically neutral label that implies economic motivation as the primary reason for leaving their homeland.

Usually ignored is the fact that it is not illegal for North Koreans to visit China. For decades, it has been fairly common for Chinese to cross over into North Korea and vice versa. North Koreans can obtain a—travel permit to visit relatives in Yanbian or to conduct business there. Beginning in 1995, however, the flow of North Koreans to China underwent a significant change.

Carefully collected data suggests there is truth in both views. The majority of these North Koreans identify themselves as migrants, but there is also a significant number of apparently bona fide refugees. About half of the North Koreans interviewed claimed that they would return to North Korea in a few days. Their primary motive for entering China was to acquire food or medicine. Many of these people were in contact with kinsmen who resided in the Yanbian region. Also, many had made the trip more than once.

Another significant group said they had come to China in search of employment. Many of these people had kinsmen or friends in the Yanbian region to whom they would turn for assistance. The men in this group tended to find employment on farms or in cities some distance from the border. Most of the young women sought work in restaurants and factories. Eventually, a fair number would marry long-time Korean residents of China. Some would return to their families in North Korea. Claims that some of these women were being sold into prostitution or virtual slavery proved grossly exaggerated.

Those North Koreans claiming political motivation were consistently the smallest group. These people claimed they would never return to North Korea. Their numbers, however, do not substantiate claims that the Kim Jong Il regime is crumbling, at least not yet. On the other hand, there is no doubting that there is a continuing flow of politically motivated North Koreans out of North Korea.

Continuity or Change?

Kim Jong Il faces a politically complex dilemma. Either he pursues change or his regime collapses. His primary goal we already know is regime survival. Toward this end, he has initiated a program of carefully managed change. To rationalize this program, he has turned to juche for political justification. This also has assured his inner circle of advisers that his goal is to perpetuate his father's legacy, not to strike out on his own or to compromise with the "capitalists" and the "imperialists."

Lest we be confused, we need to keep in mind that Kim's goal is regime preservation, not its transformation. Democracy and human rights are not on his agenda. Yet the urgency of his needs, the near bankruptcy of his economy, and the erosion of his army's fighting capability compels him to turn to the outside world for assistance.

For him, the primary challenge is how to manage the change so that it serves his political purposes, does not undermine his authority, yet allows his regime to absorb sufficient foreign influence to revitalize the economy.

But the more Kim Jong Il needs the international community, the greater should be the international community's ability to influence North Korea's conduct, and the pace and direction of change inside North Korea. This would suggest the possibility of eventually achieving a gradual transformation of North Korea, possibly even a soft landing.

Whether this is a realistic expectation, however, will be determined by whether Kim Jong Il's preference is for continuity of his regime based on a nuclear capability, or for change and a shift from military might to diplomacy and commerce as the primary propagators of his regime.

The Least You Need to Know

- North Koreans have no idea what is meant by the Western concept of human or political rights.

- Only the radical political transformation of North Korea's political, social, and educational systems will make it possible for North Koreans to enjoy individual political rights.

- Some changes are underway inside North Korea, but we should not expect them to inevitably lead to greater democracy and respect for human rights in North Korea.

- There is a steady, small flow of North Korean refugees into China, but this phenomenon is not necessarily an indication that the Kim Jong Il's regime is crumbling from within.

- North Korea's fate and that of its people now hinges on whether Kim Jong Il continues to link his regime future to the building of a nuclear arsenal, or whether he foregoes that ambition and instead ties his regime's future to commercial and diplomatic engagement with the international community.

Chapter 24

Where Is North Korea Heading—War or Peace?

In This Chapter

◆ North Korea's dilemma

◆ What does North Korea want?

◆ The United States's dilemma regarding North Korea

◆ What does the United States want from North Korea?

Throughout this book, we have looked at the past and present in an effort to make North Korea more understandable. Now we come to the final questions—where do we go from here? What is the future for North Korea and its relationship with the West, particularly the United States?

Ending the Cold War

July 27, 2003 marks the fiftieth anniversary of the signing of the Korean War Armistice. Unfortunately, there is little to celebrate. The Korean War left the Korean Peninsula divided into two hostile camps. Despite the two

Koreas' promising progress toward reconciliation, peace and stability remain tenuous on the Korean Peninsula. Relations between Washington and Pyongyang are still intensely hostile.

Before the Cold War can end in Northeast Asia, and a durable peace prevail on the Korean Peninsula, a peace treaty will have to replace the Korean Armistice. Both sides at least agreed to the need for a peace treaty. The devil, however, remains in the details. Washington wants Seoul included in any peace talks. Pyongyang first wants to work out a "peace mechanism" directly (and unilaterally) with Washington to replace the armistice, after which it wants a peace treaty. Seoul, from Pyongyang's point of view, can get involved later. The potentially dangerous squabbling most likely will continue well into the foreseeable future.

The 1994 U.S.–North Korea Agreed Framework held out hope that a deal could eventually be worked out. It provided a roadmap for a nuclear-free Korean Peninsula, the normalization of U.S. relations with North Korea, and eventually even a peace treaty. Between 1994 and 2001, the agreed process seemed to be making promising progress.

One tactic the United States deployed during the nuclear negotiations of 1993–1994 was to confront North Korea with a stark dilemma. Repeatedly the U.S. negotiators contrasted North Korea's increasingly humiliating reality of isolation, international disdain, and economic decline with the potential for spectacular diplomatic and economic gains if Pyongyang would only shut down its nuclear program.

This enticement strategy seemed to have accomplished its goal. North Korea's leadership appeared to realize that regime survival was best accomplished through engagement with the international community. Clinging to its traditional coercive diplomacy and pursuit of a nuclear arsenal only seemed destined eventually to doom the regime. So, in response to the pressures, Kim Jong Il ordered his nuclear program frozen and opened his country to international humanitarian workers and their aid.

Then he allowed the other shoe to drop. Hesitantly, he permitted his once-quarantined bureaucracy to participate in international educational and technical exchanges, to travel abroad and to have access to a widening range of information from outside the country. Next came a resumption of reconciliation with South Korea, economic cooperation, and an increasing number of academic, cultural, and social exchanges. The international community reacted by increasing its diplomatic and commercial interaction with North Korea.

DPRK officials watch as nuclear fuel rods are stored. Extraction of their plutonium for nuclear weapons began early in 2003.

About Face!

Just as abruptly, Kim Jong Il turned everything around. The reasons remain unclear and are certain to be debated for years. The facts are that in October 2002, Kim Jong Il's diplomats let it be known to their American counterparts that North Korea considered the Agreed Framework "nullified." In rapid succession, North Korea broke all its promises to the international community and to South Korea not to pursue a nuclear weapons program. (See Appendix A for a timeline on related North Korean activities in 2002–2003.)

By April 2003, North Koreas declared it was producing plutonium and that it possessed nuclear weapons. North Korea proudly proclaimed that it merely was exercising its national "sovereignty." To many, its brashness seemed almost suicidal.

Kim Jong Il's Dilemma

Kim Jong Il wants more than regime survival. He wants to perpetuate his father Kim Il Sung's legacy, his juche ideology, and most of all, his own power. At the same time, however, he must preserve and modernize his nation's military might, revitalize the economy, and yet continue to control and manipulate the population.

There are some serious contradictions on his wish list. The more he cooperates with the international community regarding his nuclear program, humanitarian aid, and so on, the more he must surrender national sovereignty. "Sovereignty" in North Korea really means Kim Jong Il's absolute power to do as he wishes.

Paralleling Kim Jong Il's shrinking sovereignty has been his people's exposure to the outside world. European and American visitors are easily managed. They have limited knowledge of the Korean language and culture and stand out in a crowd in downtown Pyongyang.

But the growing number of South Korean visitors are much harder to handle. They can penetrate all sectors of North Korean society, almost without being noticed. Even more threatening is their ability to explain, in the Korean language and as fellow kinsmen, the benefits of breaking with the past. Otherwise innocent conversations could become blatantly subversive.

In some respects, all of this tension between what Kim Jong Il wanted—power and control—and what he had to do—cooperate with the international community—suggests the Agreed Framework and South-North reconciliation efforts were profoundly affecting North Korea's internal situation. Kim, in other words, may have sensed that he was losing control of his domestic situation.

At the same time, the new Bush Administration began to shift from a conciliatory to a confrontational posture. Kim Jong Il's sense of insecurity swiftly increased. The sum result has been an abrupt turnaround in North Korea, from Agreed Framework to unilateral declarations of nuclear capability.

Clinging to the Past

Kim Jong Il now clings to the past. He has declared that he needs nuclear weapons to deter a U.S. attack. Now he wants to preserve his ballistic missiles and huge arsenal of conventional weapons. At the same time, tight controls on his population will not only remain in place, but will be refurbished to ensure their thorough effectiveness.

The sum result is that North Korea has opted to resume a coercive and threatening posture. However, unlike the past, North Korea is, or is poised to quickly become, a nuclear power. Chances are that Kim's new nuclear muscle will prompt him to become even more threatening and brash as he asserts his goals.

The United States's Dilemma

Just like Kim Jong Il, the United States and its close allies in Northeast Asia face a potentially dangerous dilemma. Does the U.S. administration want to risk encouraging Kim Jong Il to continue his coercive diplomacy, which some would term "nuclear blackmail," by engaging him in negotiations? Or would the United States prefer to risk the possibility of war and destroy his military might now?

Kim Jong Il might make the choice himself by provoking an armed clash on the Korean Peninsula. Short of this very real possibility, the current administration would do well to size up its options now.

Soft Landing

Convincing North Korea once again to trade in its nuclear weapons for a promising economic future remains a hope in some quarters, particularly South Korea. The tools to accomplish this have been reviewed in the previous chapters: engagement, reconciliation, negotiation, economic cooperation, inducements, and so on.

This course of action has several benefits. First of all, it would greatly reduce the risk of war on the Korean Peninsula and between North Korea and Japan. It would allow North-South reconciliation and economic cooperation to continue without destroying the progress achieved thus far. Ultimately, North Korea might be induced to engage the international community so extensively, diplomatically and commercially, that the price of resuming its old ways would simply become too costly.

On the negative side, pursuing a soft landing would require the reopening of negotiations with North Korea and provision of bountiful inducements that undoubtedly would strengthen the regime economically and, indirectly, militarily. Plus, there would be no guarantee that North Korea would eventually forgo its nuclear program, hostile posture, and authoritarian system.

Hard Landing

Advocates of a hard landing envision the collapse of Kim Jong Il's regime, not its transformation as assumed in the previous scenario. A hard landing could be brought about by diplomatic and commercial isolation (what some call benign neglect), armed confrontation, or regime change.

All of these techniques have been tried before. Armed confrontation failed in the Korean War to end the regime. The United States and many in the international community imposed an extensive economic and diplomatic embargo on North Korea over the previous half century. North Korea survived by turning to China and the Soviet Union. Today, such measures would require enlisting the very unlikely support of China and South Korea.

Most of all, the pursuit of a hard landing—regardless of means—would unavoidably mean the resumption of the Korean War with all the hostilities and risks.

Another Agreed Framework?

Proponents of a hard landing also argue that negotiations would be futile because North Korea cannot be trusted. Even if a revised Agreed Framework were negotiated, they asked, how could North Korea be trusted to adhere to it? They have a point. North Korea's actions in 2002 and early 2003 have destroyed the limited amount of trust built after 1994. Even worse, the potential for rebuilding that trust has been severely undermined.

At the same time, however, hard landers advocate a verifiable dismantling of North Korea's two nuclear weapons programs, its plutonium and highly enriched uranium (HEU) programs. But "verifiable" is a false hope. Technically, 100 percent verification is impossible to achieve. A more realistic figure would be 80 to 90 percent.

A verifiable end to North Korea's nuclear weapons program would have to await, therefore, the building of mutual trust between the two antagonists. This suggests the potential for a vicious cycle even if a new negotiated settlement is put together.

Living with Danger

A third option not involving a soft or hard landing is possible. The U.S. and its allies in Northeast Asia could decide to live with a nuclear-armed North Korea. This idea makes advocates of nuclear nonproliferation nervous. Their concern is that allowing North Korea to retain a nuclear arsenal could encourage other small nations to acquire nuclear weapons. A further concern is that North Korea might begin exporting its surplus plutonium and nuclear weapons–related technology to such nations.

Others contend that U.S. allies would move to build their own nuclear arsenals. Of particular concern in this case are Japan and South Korea.

Stalemate

U.S.–North Korean relations have been stalled since 2001. President George W. Bush put the talks with North Korea on hold during his first five months in office so that his administration could review U.S. policy toward Pyongyang. In June 2001, the president announced he was ready to talk. The North Koreans, however, responded with "thanks but no thanks."

Not until the summer of 2002 did both sides finally agree to meet for substantive discussions of outstanding issues. But no sooner had they met in Pyongyang in October 2002 than the North Koreans confirmed that they had broken their promises. They claimed to the United States to have started clandestinely a new nuclear weapons program. Promptly, however, North Korea offered to talk. Faced with this new information, Washington just as quickly said "no thank you."

The Dragon Puffs

China let it be known to both sides (see Chapter 15) that it wanted both sides to come together and negotiate a peaceful resolution of their differences. After intense effort, China managed to bring U.S. and North Korean diplomats together in Beijing in April 2003. The talks were inconclusive, but at least they were a new beginning in an already seriously estranged relationship.

North Korea's Wish List

Mysteries about North Korea are plentiful, but not its wish list of what it wants in exchange for dismantling its nuclear program. To begin with, North Korea wants what the Clinton Administration promised to provide in the Joint Statement of June 1993, the Agreed Framework of 1994, and the October 2000 Joint Statement.

Specifically, North Korea wants the United States to …

- Provide assurances that it will not use force, either nuclear or conventional, against it.

- Respect its sovereignty.

- Engage in direct, bilateral negotiations.

- Move toward the normalization of diplomatic and commercial relations, which includes North Korea's removal from the list of terrorist nations and the phasing out of all economic sanctions.

- Promise to replace the Korean War Armistice with a peace treaty.

Washington's Wish List

Washington's wish list has not changed significantly since 1992, when George H. W. Bush's administration initiated talks with North Korea. The U.S. wish list includes …

- The full verifiable dismantlement of North Korea's plutonium and highly enriched uranium programs.

- International Atomic Energy Agency (IAEA) inspections of North Korea's nuclear facilities.

- North Korea's compliance with its previous pledges regarding keeping the Korean Peninsula nuclear-free as stated in the North-South Joint Declaration on the Denuclearization of the Korean Peninsula, the Treaty on the Non-proliferation of Nuclear Weapons, and the Agreed Framework.

- An end to North Korea's development, deployment, and export of ballistic missiles.

- Negotiations regarding the reduction of conventional forces.

- An end of all support for terrorists and related activities, including the release of all abducted Japanese citizens and their family members for return to Japan.

- Continuing cooperation in the location and return of the remains of several thousand U.S. soldiers in North Korea.

- Continued dialogue with South Korea and progress toward reconciliation.

- The demonstration of increased respect for the North Korean people's welfare and human rights.

Shall We Talk or What ...?

Washington and Pyongyang would prefer to talk rather than to fight. But, the longer they do not negotiate away their differences, the greater the chances that they will end up fighting.

North Korea continues to assemble a nuclear arsenal. It now has the choice between making plutonium-based bombs or highly enriched uranium (HEU) bombs. The best intelligence estimates that the North Koreans are making plutonium-based bombs. North Korea most likely has reprocessed most, if not all, of its 8,000 nuclear spent-fuel rods. Depending on a nuclear weapon's explosive power, this gives North Korea enough material to make several more nuclear bombs.

"Ball" or "Gun" Bomb

Fabrication of a plutonium "ball"-type nuclear bomb, however, could still be beyond North Korea's technical sophistication. This type of weapon requires sophisticated techniques for the shaping of a bomb's inner core, complex timing devices, and other demanding technologies that North Korea may not yet have accomplished.

North Korea's new HEU program most likely is still in its infancy. The tools essential for putting together this program probably have been acquired. A facility may already have been built. But producing sufficient HEU would place a heavy burden on an already energy-hungry nation. It would also require an extended period of time to produce a large enough amount of HEU for a "gun"-type nuclear weapon.

The gun type of nuclear weapons is relatively simple to make. Two lumps of HEU are mounted inside a chamber. A conventional "trigger" or explosive smashes the two halves together and the ensuing nuclear reaction causes the ball to explode.

In either case, North Korea very likely has not "weaponized" its nuclear arsenal. The U.S. intelligence community appears confident that North Korea cannot yet "wed" a nuclear warhead to a ballistic missile. The most likely delivery system for a North Korean nuclear weapon would be a cargo ship. Once inside a port, quite likely a Japanese port, North Korean agents using a remote-control device, could explode the nuclear weapon. This doomsday scenario, however, does not appear to be imminent.

Future Escalation

Long, drawn-out U.S.–North Korea negotiations would allow North Korea to refine its nuclear weapons related technologies. Once equipped with nuclear weapons, we should expect North Korea to attempt to test them, first secretly to make sure they work, and then publicly to give credibility to its nuclear capability.

Once North Korea has established that it can make working nuclear weapons, prospects for a peaceful resolution of the U.S.–North Korea impasse will quickly wane. North Korea can be expected to jack up the price for dismantling its nuclear program to a level higher than what the United States and its allies are willing to pay.

Even more worrisome is the possibility that a negotiated settlement might not settle anything. Few, if any, people outside the North Korean government believe that North Korea would fulfill all of its promises and discard all of its plutonium and nuclear weapons. The post-agreement atmosphere would be poisoned by deep, mutual distrust.

Six Party Talks

Fortunately for all the concerned nations, the Six Party Talks have achieved modest success. When representatives of China, Japan, the two Koreas, Russia, and the United States gathered in Beijing, an atmosphere conducive to diplomatic dialogue was established. Thoughts shifted from confrontation to resolution of the nuclear issue through peaceful diplomatic discussions.

The August meeting established common ground among the participants, as stated by China's Vice Foreign Minister Wang Yi at the end of the meeting. Reading from a prepared statement that reflected the participants' consensus, he announced that "each country had agreed, including North Korea, to the following six points (unofficial translation) …"

1. Each country agreed through dialogue to solve the nuclear issue on the Korean Peninsula peacefully, and to maintain peace and stability on the peninsula and construct permanent peace.

2. Each country asserted that the de-nuclearization of the Korean Peninsula should be achieved and at the same time consideration should be given to addressing North Korea's security concerns.

3. Each country agreed that either parallel or simultaneous steps should be taken to find a fair and rational solution.

4. Each country agreed not to take any measures to escalate or accelerate the situation during the Six Party process.

5. Each country asserted that it would continue dialogue, build mutual confidence and reduce differences in their views while expanding commonly held views.

6. Each party agreed to continue the process of six party meetings and through diplomatic channels to decide the next meeting date and venue as soon as possible.

These points did not solve any of the many complex problems that plague the Korean Peninsula, but they established a common meeting ground for the pursuit of peaceful resolutions.

Hopeful sight—North Korea's Liaison Office Negotiating Team toured Washington with author Quinones, December 1994.

It's in the Hands of the United States

In the previous pages we have laid out for you a bounty of factors and possible scenarios that affect U.S. relations with North Korea. Obviously, this is a very complicated situation. Equally apparent is the danger to all of us if the two governments ultimately prove unable to work out their differences over a negotiating table.

No one can say for certain that another war on the Korean Peninsula is inevitable. But the longer the two sides squabble, the greater the chances that North Korea will make a working nuclear weapon. Ultimately, this could mean the next Korean War might involve nuclear weapons.

You are looking right at the fundamental difference between you and the North Korean people. You have the freedom to read and judge this book. They do not. The chance for open dialogue between North Korea and the United States, or other democracies such as South Korea and Japan, is diminished by the fact that only one side has a multifaceted view of the situation. But even in democratic societies like ours, inaccuracies and confusion cloud our perceptions and hinder our ability to engage North Korea in constructive dialogue.

We hope that this book has helped remove some of the barriers that surround this ancient and troubled land.

The Least You Need to Know

- ◆ Kim Jong Il, for reasons still unclear, abruptly shifted his strategy for regime survival from engagement of the international community to a resumption of coercive diplomacy and the building of a nuclear arsenal.

- ◆ The more time Kim Jong Il has to develop nuclear weapons, the greater the likelihood that he will have both nuclear weapons and the means to deliver them.

- ◆ Kim Jong Il can be expected to test one or more nuclear weapons to give credibility to his nuclear arsenal and to intimidate his adversaries into giving him what he needs

- ◆ So long as the six nations most concerned about achieving a durable peace in Northeast Asia continue their diplomatic dialogue, prospects for achieving a durable peace will improve while the risk of war will subside.

Appendix A

A North Korean Timeline

Korea Colonized

1866—U.S. merchant ship *General Sherman* is destroyed near Pyongyang. Kim Il Sung later claims his grandfather participated in the destruction.

1871—U.S. naval expedition destroys Korean forts near Seoul in retaliation for the *General Sherman* incident.

1882—The United States and Korea sign a "Treaty of Peace, Amity, Commerce, and Navigation."

1894–1995—Sino-Japanese War; Japan defeats China in a war over Korea.

1904–1905—Russo-Japanese War; Japan defeats Russia in a war over Korea. President Theodore Roosevelt wins the Nobel Peace Prize for having helped negotiate the peace agreement in Portsmouth, New Hampshire.

1905—Signing of the Taft-Katsura Accord, a so-called gentlemen's agreement in which the United States recognized Japan's sphere of influence on the Korean Peninsula and Japan did likewise regarding U.S. interest in the Philippine Islands.

1910—Japan formally annexes Korea into its empire.

1912—Kim Il Sung is born near Pyongyang.

Korea's Early Communist Movement

1919 (March 1)—Modern Korean nationalism is born during nationwide anti-Japanese demonstrations and armed clashes with Japanese colonial authorities.

1919 (April)—Lee Tong-hwi organizes the first Korean communist party, the Koryo Communists Party.

1929—Kim Il Sung joins the communist movement in Manchuria and is promptly arrested and imprisoned.

1932—Released from jail, Kim Il Sung joins the anti-Japanese guerilla movement.

1942—Kim Il Sung's first son and eventual heir, Kim Jong Il, is born.

Liberation and Division

1943—Cairo Declaration promises Korean independence "in due course."

1945

February 8—Yalta Conference; Allies propose that an international trusteeship will temporarily rule Korea.

June—San Francisco Conference; the Allied Powers and supporting nations establish the United Nations. The U.S. secretary of state denies representatives of the provincial government of Korea access to the conference.

July 22—Berlin Conference; Allies agree to establish a trusteeship to temporarily rule liberated Korea.

July 26—Potsdam Conference; U.S. and Soviet commanders agree to divide the Korean Peninsula along the 41st parallel into a Soviet zone of operation to the north and a U.S. zone to the south of the 41st parallel.

July 26—Potsdam Proclamation; the four Allied powers call for Japan's unconditional surrender and affirm that the terms of the Cairo Declaration "shall be carried out."

August 15—Japan surrenders, Korea is liberated. The United States occupies southern Korea, and the Soviet Union occupies northern Korea.

1948

May 10—UN Temporary Commission on Korea conducts a plebiscite in South Korea to elect representatives to a national assembly.

July 20—National assembly elects Syngman Rhee president of the Republic of Korea (ROK).

September 9—North Korea's Supreme People's Council proclaims the establishment of the Democratic People's Republic of Korea (DPRK).

October 12—The Soviet Union establishes diplomatic relations with the DPRK.

1949—All USSR military forces are withdrawn from the DPRK.

The Korean War

1950

June 25—North Korea invades Republic of Korea (ROK).

June 27—UN Security Council urges UN members to help ROK.

July 8—General MacArthur named UN commander in chief.

September 15—U.S. marines land at Inchon, ROK.

October 1—ROK troops cross 38th parallel into North Korea.

October 14—Chinese Communist forces enter North Korea.

October 26—Chinese forces defeat ROK units northwest of Yongbyon.

November 5—UN Command confirms Chinese forces in North Korea.

November 24—MacArthur orders start of "end of war" offensive.

November 26—Chinese troops start an offensive against UN forces.

December 4—UN forces retreat from Pyongyang.

1951

January 4—Communists capture Seoul.

March 15—UN retakes Seoul.

April 10—President Truman dismisses General MacArthur.

May—Stalemate.

1953

July 27—Korean War Armistice is signed.

August—Immediately after the armistice is signed, the UN Command unilaterally establishes the so-called Northern Limit Line (NLL), which declares that South Korea has the right to enter fishing grounds within 12 miles of North Korean–occupied islands in the West (Yellow) Sea. North Korea disputes the NLL, claiming the waters are within its 12-mile territorial waters.

October 1—The United States and the Republic of Korea sign their Mutual Defense Treaty.

Post War Reconstruction

1956—The USSR and DPRK sign their first aid agreement.

1958—All Chinese troops withdraw from North Korea by year's end.

1960 (April)—The student uprising in South Korea forces President Rhee to flee to the United States.

1961 (July)—North Korea signs treaties of friendship with the Soviet Union and China that contain identical mutual defense clauses.

1961 (May 16)—South Korean army general Park Chung Hee overthrows the civilian government and seizes power.

1968

January 20—A platoon of North Korea soldiers reaches the grounds of the South Korean president's official residence before being discovered and killed in a vicious battle.

January 23—Soon afterward, North Korea seizes the U.S. Navy "spy" ship, USS *Pueblo* in international waters east of North Korea's Wonsan harbor. The crew is released one year later, after very harsh treatment and a U.S. military officer signs an apology for the incident.

1972 (July 4)—North and South Korea issue their first joint statement after holding several rounds of secret talks. The talks prove inconclusive.

1976 (August)—In the infamous "axe murder incident," North Korean soldiers brutally kill two U.S. Army officers with axes inside the Joint Security Area of the DMZ.

1978—U.S. president Jimmy Carter convinces South Korea's president to cease his clandestine nuclear weapons development program.

North Korea Begins Its Nuclear Program

1979—South Korea's president is assassinated.

1982—DPRK begins construction of five megawatt (electric) graphite-moderated nuclear reactor at Yongbyon.

1983 (October)—North Korean agents attempt to assassinate South Korea's president in Rangoon, Myanmar, but fail and instead kill several presidential cabinet members.

1985

December 26—USSR-DPRK signs agreement on light-water reactors (LWR); the USSR promises to construct an LWR for the DPRK if it joins the Treaty on the Non-proliferation of Nuclear Weapons (NPT).

December—DPRK joins the NPT.

1986 (January)—Yongbyon five megawatt (electric) reactor begins operation.

1988

October—The United States announces "Modest Initiative" directed toward the DPRK.

October—Seoul Olympiad is held. Both China and the Soviet Union participate, as well as most other communist nations.

December—"Beijing Channel" between the United States and the DPRK opens.

1989

Spring—Yongbyon reactor is shut down and spent nuclear fuel is withdrawn for later reprocessing.

September—Japanese parliamentary leader Shin Kanemaru leads a delegation to North Korea.

October—Japan–North Korea normalization talks begin.

1990

June 1—USSR leader Gorbachev visits South Korea.

September 11—South Korea and the USSR establish diplomatic relations.

December 25—South Korea's president visits Moscow.

The First Bush Administration Engages North Korea

1991

September 4–7—North-South Prime Ministerial talks began in Pyongyang.

September 17—South and North Korea (ROK) entered the United Nations.

September 27—President Bush announces the withdrawal back to the United States of all U.S. tactical nuclear weapons.

December 27—North Korea establishes diplomatic relations with the Commonwealth of Independent States (CIS), Russia.

December—The two Koreas announce their Joint Declaration on the Denucleariza-tion of the Korean Peninsula.

1992

January—The two Koreas sign their Agreement on Reconciliation, Non-aggression, and Exchanges and Cooperation.

January—South Korea announces suspension of the annual U.S.–South Korea mili-tary exercise Team Spirit '92.

January 21—The first U.S.–North Korea high-level diplomatic talks convene in New York. The U.S. Department of State undersecretary for political affairs exchanges views on bilateral issues with his North Korean counterpart, Korean Workers' Party (KWP) secretary Kim Young-sun.

January 30—North Korea signs a full scope nuclear safeguards agreement with the International Atomic Energy Agency (IAEA).

March—North-South Korea Joint Nuclear Control Committee is established to implement their denuclearization accord.

April—North Korea's Supreme People's Assembly (SPA) ratifies the IAEA nuclear safeguard agreement.

May—DPRK submits its inventory of nuclear materials to the IAEA, and the IAEA conducts its first ad hoc inspection of DPRK's nuclear facilities.

May—The seventh round of Japan-North Korea normalization talks is held in Beijing, China.

July—IAEA director general Hans Blix visits the DPRK. The second IAEA inspec-tion suggests possible inaccurate inventory, or concealment of plutonium.

August—North Korea's vice premier visits Seoul.

August—Satellite imagery indicates North Korea camouflages a nuclear waste site at Yongbyon, intensifying suspicions that it has more plutonium than it claims to have.

August 24—China and South Korea establish diplomatic relations.

September—North-South prime ministerial talks are held in Pyongyang.

October—The United States and South Korea warn North Korea that Team Spirit '93 military exercise will be held unless North Korea cooperates with the IAEA regarding verification of North Korea's declared inventory of plutonium nuclear inspections.

November—The fourth IAEA ad hoc inspection is conducted.

November—William Clinton elected U.S. president.

November—The eight round of Japan–North Korea normalization talks rupture when Japan raises issue of North Korea's alleged kidnapping of a Japanese woman.

December—Senator Bob Smith heads the first congressional delegation to North Korea and holds talks with First Vice Minister of Foreign Affairs Kang Sok Ju.

The Clinton Administration and the First Nuclear Crisis

1993

January—IAEA passes resolution finding North Korea in noncompliance with its nuclear safeguards obligations.

January—South Korea and the United States announce Team Spirit '93 will be held, and Russia informs North Korea of its intention to revise their mutual defense treaty.

February—IAEA calls for the first ever "special inspection" of a member of the NPT to compel North Korea to allow IAEA inspectors access to the concealed North Korean nuclear waste site.

February—Kim Young Sam inaugurated South Korea's president.

March 11—North Korea announces intention to withdraw from the NPT.

March—The United States, ROK, and Japan convene trilateral consultations about North Korea.

April—UN Security Council (UNSC) president issues a statement that calls on members to help resolve the crisis through negotiations.

May—The United States and North Korea decide to meet in New York to negotiate a resolution to the nuclear crisis.

June—The U.S.–North Korean nuclear talks begin.

June—The first U.S.–North Korea Joint Statement is issued.

July—Round two of the U.S.–North Korean nuclear talks convene in Geneva, Switzerland.

September—The U.S.–North Korea nuclear talks reach an impasse. Working-level meetings begin in New York.

October—Chairman of the House Foreign Affairs Subcommittee on East Asia and the Pacific, Congressman Ackerman of New York, visits Pyongyang and meets President Kim Il Sung.

1994

February—U.S.–North Korea Agreed Conclusions are finalized in New York. They are designed to restart the U.S.–North Korean nuclear talks; implementation falters in March.

March—North-South Korea efforts to restart their long suspended dialogue end when the North Korean delegate threatens to turn Seoul into a "sea of flames." Tensions rapidly intensify.

March 24—Russia proposes convening an eight-party multilateral conference to address the nuclear crisis on the Korean Peninsula.

April—North Korea notifies IAEA it will refuel its nuclear reactor.

April—North Korea declares 1953 armistice invalid.

May—The United States and North Korea begin preparations for war.

June—Former President Carter announces he will visit North and South Korea.

June—North Korea withdraws from the IAEA.

June—The Clinton Administration accepts Kim Il Sung's proposal to resume nuclear negotiations.

July—U.S.–North Korea nuclear talks resume, but Kim Il Sung's death interrupts them.

August—U.S.–North Korea nuclear talks resume, Agreed Conclusions is reached.

September—U.S.–North Korea technical talks are held in Berlin, Germany.

October 21— Washington and Pyongyang sign the Agreed Framework.

November 12—U.S. nuclear spent fuel delegation arrives in Pyongyang and makes its first visit to Yongbyon Nuclear Research Center.

November 14—U.S.–North Korea light-water reactor (LWR) talks begin.

December 6–10—U.S.–North Korea Liaison Office talks are held in Washington, D.C.

December 17—North Korean People's Army shoots down an unarmed U.S. Army helicopter north of the DMZ.

December 31—U.S. Deputy Assistant Secretary of State for East Asian and Pacific Affairs Thomas Hubbard signs an apology to obtain the release from North Korea of the U.S. Army helicopter pilot and the body of his deceased companion.

1995

February 20—The U.S. administration begins to ease economic sanctions on North Korea.

March 9 —The Korean Peninsula Energy Development Organization is established in New York.

June 13—North Korea agrees to cooperate with Korean Peninsula Energy Development Organization (KEDO).

June—South Korea agrees to send food aid to North Korea.

August—Torrential rains devastate northwestern North Korea.

September—International humanitarian aid to North Korea begins.

December 15—KEDO and North Korea sign the LWR Supply Contract in New York.

1996

January—U.S.–North Korea armies' representatives meet in Honolulu to discuss joint operations to recover the remains of U.S. missing in action (MIA) from the Korean War.

April—South Korea and the United States jointly propose four-party peace talks to resolve outstanding issues on the Korean Peninsula.

July—U.S.–North Korean army MIA joint recovery operations begin.

September—A North Korean submarine is found on South Korea's East Coast after it offloads commandos, triggering a crisis.

December—North Korea makes its first public apology to South Korea concerning the submarine incident.

1997

January—North Korea signs two agreements with KEDO.

February—North Korean Workers' Party Secretary for International Affairs Hwang Chang-yop defects.

April—Representatives from North and South Korea and the United States meet in New York to discuss North Korea's possible participation in the proposed four-party peace talks.

August—KEDO conducts a groundbreaking ceremony at Sinpo, North Korea, construction site for the two LWRs promised North Korea in the Agreed Framework.

August—North Korea joins the first preliminary round of the four-party talks.

November—The so-called Asian Financial Crisis thrusts South Korea and other East Asian nations to the brink of bankruptcy.

December—Kim Dae-jung is elected president of South Korea.

1998

February—Kim Dae-jung inaugurated president of South Korea, and initiates so-called sunshine diplomacy toward North Korea.

June—Hyundai Corporation founder starts private food aid to North Korea and wins approval to arrange South Korean tourist visits to the Diamond (Kumgang) Mountains in North Korea.

June—Generals representing the UN Command and North Korean army hold inconclusive talks at Panmunjom.

June—A second North Korean submarine is discovered on South Korea's coast.

August—Press leaks arouse suspicion that North Korea has built a secret nuclear facility at Kumjangni. The U.S. administration demands access to the site.

August—North Korea launches a long-range ballistic missile, *Taepo-dong*, over Japan.

September—Kim Jong Il formally assumes the chairmanship of the North Korean National Defense Commission.

September—South Korea and Japan agree to increase their defense cooperation.

October—The United States and Japan initial their agreement to expand the U.S.-Japan Defense Guidelines regarding Japan's role in the event of war on the Korean Peninsula.

December—The South Korean navy sinks a North Korean spy ship.

December—North Korea accepts Russia's proposal to revise and reduce their mutual defense commitment in their basic bilateral treaty of friendship.

1999

January—The fourth and final round of the four-party peace talks ends inconclusively.

March—The United States and North Korea agree to terms for the U.S. inspection of the suspected nuclear site at Kumjangni.

March—North Korea denies it has sent two spy ships into Japanese territorial waters.

June—The South Korean Navy sinks a North Korea torpedo boat after the two ships collided in contested waters south of the Northern Limit Line (NLL), the UN-established maritime border between the two Koreas in the West (Yellow) Sea. About 30 North Korean sailors reportedly are killed.

September—North Korea declares the Northern Limit Line (NLL) invalid and threatens to use military force to defend what it claims are contested waters in the area.

September—The United States eases additional economic sanctions on North Korea, per former defense secretary William Perry's recommendation, allowing trade and investment as well as U.S. aircraft and merchant ships to enter North Korea.

2000

February 9—Russia and North Korea sign a revised Treaty of Friendship, Good-neighborliness, and Cooperation, which ends Russia's commitment to defend North Korea.

May 27—The second U.S. inspection of North Korea's suspected nuclear site at Kumjangni is completed without finding anything suspicious.

June 12–14—The first North-South Korea Summit is held in Pyongyang.

June 19—The U.S. government further eases economic sanctions in view of North Korea's assurances that it will continue its moratorium on testing long-range ballistic missiles.

July 10–12—Another inconclusive round of U.S.–North Korea missile negotiations held in Kuala Lumpur, Malaysia.

July 19–20—Russian president Vladimir Putin visits Pyongyang.

September 27—U.S.–North Korea negotiations about the Agreed Framework's implementation, missiles, and terrorism convene in New York.

October 9–12—North Korea's Vice Chairman of the National Defense Committee Jo Myong Rok visits Washington, D.C., and calls on the president.

October 23–24—U.S. Secretary of State Madeleine Albright visits Pyongyang and meets with North Korean Leader Kim Jong Il.

November 1–3—Another round of U.S.–North Korea missile talks ends inconclusively.

The Bush Administration

2001

January 21—President George W. Bush takes his oath of office.

March 7—South Korea's president meets President Bush in Washington, D.C.

March 27—The United States, South Korea, and Japan reaffirm commitment to continue the 1994 Agreed Framework.

April 27—Russia and North Korea sign a new military cooperation agreement.

June 6—President Bush announces the end of the review of U.S. policy toward North Korea. He promises a "comprehensive approach" that "will expand our efforts to help the North Korean people, ease sanctions, and take other political steps" if North Korea responds appropriately. He urges North Korea to improve implementation of the Agreed Framework, end its missile programs, and reduce the threat of its conventional forces.

July 24—North Korea's leader Kim Jong Il visits Moscow.

September 11—Al Qaeda terrorists crash civilian airliners into the World Trade Center and the Pentagon.

2002

January—President Bush identifies North Korea as a member of the "Axis of Evil" in his State of the Union speech. North Korea claims his remarks threaten North Korea and are contrary to the Agreed Framework.

January 29—President Bush announces a new global partnership to stop the spread of the weapons of mass destruction.

February 19–21—President Bush meets South Korea's president in Seoul. President Bush affirms his administration's willingness to engage North Korea in dialogue. He also says, "I will not change my opinion on the man, on Kim Jong Il until he frees his people and accepts genuine proposals from countries such as South Korea or the United States to dialogue; until he proves to the world that he's got a good heart, that he cares about the people that live in his country." North Korean official media allege President Bush has insulted their leader.

April 1—President Bush warns Congress he will not recommend further funding in 2003 for the (KEDO), responsible for building two nuclear reactors in North Korea, unless North Korea promptly complies with all the terms of the Agreed Framework.

April 20—North Korea informs the U.S. administration that it is ready to engage in dialogue. The U.S. State Department defers its response pending discussions between U.S. government agencies in Washington.

July 1—A North Korean warship sinks a South Korean naval vessel in the West (Yellow) Sea, killing at least 4 South Korean sailors and wounding another 19.

July 2—The U.S. State Department announces that it has postponed its July 10 visit to Pyongyang to begin U.S.–North Korea talks.

August 20–26—Russian president Putin and North Korean leader Kim Jong Il hold their third summit.

September 20—The U.S. government releases its National Security Strategy of the USA. Regarding weapons of mass destruction, the policy calls for "proactive counter-proliferation efforts. We must deter and defend against the threat before it is unleashed."

September 17—Japanese prime minister Junichiro Koizumi and North Korean leader Kim Jong Il convene the first summit between their two nations in Pyongyang.

October 3–5—U.S. Assistant Secretary of State James Kelly visits Pyongyang to begin talks with North Korea. His North Korean counterparts first deny, and then confirm, that their nation "has been pursuing a highly enriched uranium (HEU) program."

October 16—The State Department confirms that North Korea told Kelly that they have a clandestine nuclear program. The National Security Council says North Korea is in "material violation" of the Agreed Framework.

October 25—North Korea issues a statement outlining demands for a settlement of the nuclear issue with the United States.

October 26—The United States, South Korea, and Japan jointly call upon North Korea to dismantle its HEU program "in a prompt and verifiable manner and to come into full compliance with all its international commitments …."

November 14—KEDO suspends the shipment of heavy fuel oil to North Korea as provided for in the U.S.–North Korea Agreed Framework.

November 15—President Bush states that, "the United States has no intention of invading North Korea." Also, "the only option for addressing this situation is for North Korea to completely and visibly eliminate its nuclear weapons program."

November 16—Russia and North Korea sign a agreement to link their railroads.

November 29—The International Atomic Energy Agency (IAEA) board of governors adopts a resolution that deplores North Korea's repeated violation of its obligations under the Treaty for the Non-proliferation of Nuclear Weapons (NPT), and urges North Korea to promptly cooperate with the IAEA and allow inspection of all relevant nuclear facilities.

December 2—Leaders of Russia and China at their summit in Beijing urge North Korea to end its nuclear weapons program and call on the United States to engage in diplomatic negotiations with North Korea.

December 10—The U.S. government releases its National Strategy to Combat Weapons of Mass Destruction, which calls for "country-specific strategies that best enable us and our friends and allies to prevent, deter and defend against weapons of mass destruction and missile threats from each of them."

December 10—A Spanish naval vessel, at the behest of U.S. military authorities, seizes a Cambodian-registered cargo ship en route to Yemen to deliver North Korea manufactured ballistic missiles.

December 11—The White House spokesman explains that "there is no provision under international law prohibiting Yemen from accepting delivery of missiles from North Korea." Consequently, the Cambodian ship is allowed to complete its delivery of North Korean ballistic missiles to Yemen.

December 19—Roh Moo Hyun is elected South Korea's president.

December 22—North Korea announces it will restart its nuclear program at the Yongbyon Nuclear Research Center and reopen its plutonium reprocessing plant.

December 27—North Korea announces it will expel IAEA inspectors, ending eight years of IAEA monitoring of North Korea's nuclear facilities.

December 30—President Bush, after telephone conversations with South Korea's president-elect and China's leader, describes the situation involving North Korea, "not a military showdown; this is a diplomatic showdown," and says he "intends to resolve this peacefully."

2003

January 10—North Korea announces that it has "effectuated its withdrawal from the Treaty on the Nonproliferation of Nuclear Weapons."

January 14—President Bush reaffirms his commitment to a peaceful resolution and reminds North Korea about his June 6, 2001, offer of a "bold initiative, an initiative which would talk about energy and food …."

April 23–25—Diplomats from China, North Korea, and the United States meet in Beijing to discuss North Korea's nuclear program. North Korea's representative claims North Korea has nuclear weapons and has produced more plutonium. The talks end inconclusively.

May 12—North Korea announces that it considers the Agreed Framework nullified.

May 14—President Bush hosts South Korean president's visit to Washington. They "reaffirm that they will not tolerate nuclear weapons in North Korea." They also express the hope of a "peaceful resolution," but note that, "increased threats to peace and stability on the (Korean) Peninsula would require consideration of further steps …."

August 27–29—Six Party talks convene in Beijing, China between China, Japan, the two Koreas, Russia, and the United States in an effort to achieve a peaceful diplomatic resolution to the impasse North Korea created by its persistent efforts to acquire a nuclear capability.

Treaties, Declarations, and Joint Statements

The nations most concerned about peace and stability on the Korean Peninsula repeatedly refer to a set of agreements and understandings that outline their relationships with one another. These documents also contain several commitments that these nations have made to one another regarding the Korean Peninsula. This appendix presents the texts or key passages from these documents.

All of these documents remain current, and none is historical in nature, although the first document was signed in 1953. They include ...

- ◆ The Korean War Armistice signed June 8, 1953, and effective on July 27, 1953.

- ◆ South-North Joint Communiqué of July 4, 1972.

- ◆ The U.S. Department of State Modest Initiative of October 31, 1988.

- ◆ President George H.W. Bush, New Initiatives to Reduce U.S. Nuclear Forces, Address to the Nation, September 27, 1991.

- ◆ The South-North Korea Agreement on Reconciliation, Non-aggression, and Exchanges and Cooperation. Signed December 13, 1991, and effective on February 19, 1992.

♦ Joint Declaration of the Denuclearization of the Korean Peninsula, February 19, 1992.

♦ Joint Statement of the Democratic People's Republic of Korea (DPRK) and the United States of America (USA), June 11, 1993.

♦ Agreed Framework Between the United States of America and the Democratic People's Republic of Korea, October 21, 1994.

♦ U.S. president Bill Clinton's Letter of Assurances in connection with the Agreed Framework to "His Excellency Kim Jong Il, Supreme Leader of the DPRK" dated October 20, 1994.

♦ South-North Joint Declaration of June 15, 2000.

♦ U.S.-DPRK Joint Communiqué of October 12, 2000.

The Korean War Armistice

The Korean War Armistice was signed June 8, 1953, and became effective on July 27, 1953. It ended combat, but not the Korean War. The commander in chief of the United Nations Command, a U.S. Army general, the supreme commander of the Korean People's Army, and the commander of the Chinese People's Volunteers signed the armistice which remains in effect.

North Korea, however, declared the armistice ineffective in 1994, and continues to demand that it be replaced with a "new peace mechanism."

South Korea and the United States maintain that the armistice must remain in effect pending a peace treaty between Seoul and Pyongyang as called for in the two Koreas' 1992 Agreement on Reconciliation, Nonaggression, and Exchanges and Cooperation between the South and the North. Here are some excerpts from the Armistice:

> Preamble: ... The undersigned, ... with the objective of establishing an armistice which will insure a complete cessation of hostilities and of all acts of armed force in Korea until a final peaceful settlement is achieved, ... mutually agree to accept and to be bound and governed by the conditions and terms of armistice ...
>
> Article I.
>
> 1. A military demarcation line shall be fixed and both sides shall withdraw two kilometers from his line so as to establish a demilitarized zone ...
>
> 7. No person, military or civilian, shall be permitted to cross the military demarcation line unless specifically authorized to do so by the Military Armistice Commission.

Article II.

12. C. Cease the introduction into Korea of reinforcing military personnel … No military personnel of either side shall be introduced into Korea if the introduction … will cause the aggregate of the military personnel of that side admitted into Korea since the effective date of this armistice agreement to exceed the cumulative total of military personnel of that side who have departed from Korea since that date.

South-North Joint Communiqué of July 4, 1972

Both Seoul and Pyongyang consider this communiqué the cornerstone of their relationship, and progress toward normalization dates from it. The communiqué was the result of several months of secret communication between the two Koreas that began after the United States initiated its secret contacts with the People's Republic of China. The two sides intentionally selected July 4 so that the issuance of their joint statement coincided with the anniversary of the U.S. Declaration of Independence. Article one below asserted the two Koreas' desire for self-determination regarding their reunification.

> With the common desire to achieve peaceful unification of the fatherland as early as possible, the two sides had a frank and open hearted exchange of views … In the course of the talks, the two sides … reached full agreement on the following points:

> First, unification shall be achieved through independent efforts without being subject to external imposition or interference.

> Second, unification shall be achieved through peaceful means, and not through use of force against one another.

> Third, a great national unity, as a homogeneous people, shall be sought first, transcending differences in ideas, ideologies and systems.

The U.S. Department of State Modest Initiative of October 31, 1988

The first steps toward the normalization of diplomatic relations between the U.S. and North Korean governments dates from 1988. President of the Republic of Korea, Roh Tae Woo, in his speech to the UN General Assembly on October 18, 1988, and in his declaration of July 7, 1988, called for joint efforts to draw the Democratic People's Republic of Korea (DPRK) out of isolation and encourage it to abandon its longstanding policies of confrontation and violence.

Selected passages from the U.S. Department of State's October 31, 1988 Review of Relations with the DPRK follow:

> The U.S. Government will encourage unofficial, non-governmental visits from the DPRK in academics, sports, culture and other areas so long as prospective DPRK visitors are eligible under our visa laws.

> To facilitate the travel of U.S. citizens to the DPRK, the U.S. government will be reviewing financial regulations affecting travel to the DPRK with a view toward permitting travel services for exchanges and group travel on a case-by-case basis.

> The United States is reviewing Commerce regulations with a view toward permitting certain limited commercial exports of humanitarian goods to the DPRK on a case-by-case basis. U.S. law already permits the donation of certain humanitarian goods such as foodstuffs, clothing and medicine.

> General commercial trade remains unlawful; it remains regulated strictly under provisions of the Trading with the Enemy Act and the Export Administration Act. Furthermore, the DPRK remains on the list of states, which support or are engaged in international terrorism.

> The Department of State is instructing U.S. diplomats that they may once again hold substantive discussions with officials of the DPRK in neutral settings. We issued such guidance in September 1983 and March 1987 in the hope that such contacts could lead to increased mutual understanding and perhaps eventually, to improved relations these hopes were not realized and the guidance was withdrawn. We are again authorizing substantive diplomatic exchanges.

> We have taken these steps in close consultation with our ROK ally and with other interested parties.

President George H. W. Bush, New Initiatives to Reduce U.S. Nuclear Forces, Address to the Nation, September 27, 1991

This speech by President George H. W. Bush followed the collapse of the Communist bloc and the Soviet Union. Although not aimed specifically at North Korea, its ruler Kim Il Sung responded promptly to it and engaged in discussions with South Korea's president that opened the way for the South-North Declaration on the Denuclearization of the Korean Peninsula.

> I am announcing today a series of sweeping initiatives affecting every aspect of our nuclear forces—on land, on ships and on aircraft.

I am, therefore, directing that the United States eliminate its entire worldwide inventory of ground-launched short-range—that is, theater—nuclear weapons. We will bring home and destroy all of our nuclear artillery shells and short-range ballistic missile warheads.

…, the United States will withdraw all tactical nuclear weapons from its surface ships (and) attack submarines, as well as those nuclear weapons associated with our land based naval aircraft. This means removing all nuclear tomahawk cruise missiles from U.S. ships and submarines, as well as nuclear bombs aboard air-craft carriers. The bottom line is that under normal circumstances, our ships will not carry tactical nuclear weapons.

The South-North Korea Agreement on Reconciliation, Non-aggression, and Exchanges and Cooperation.

This agreement was signed December 13, 1991, and took effect on February 19, 1992. It remains the basic accord between Seoul and Pyongyang regarding their rela-tionship. Implementation has been hesitant and uneven, making it more a statement of mutual aspirations than actual reality. There continues to be, however, a continuing increase in the number of exchanges and areas of cooperation.

The South and the North, in keeping with the yearning of the entire Korean people for the peaceful unification of the divided land;

Reaffirming the three principles of unification set forth in the July 4, 1972, South-North Joint Communiqué;

Determined to remove the state of political and military confrontation and achieve national reconciliation;

Also determined to avoid armed aggression and hostilities, reduce tension and ensure peace;

Expressing the desire to realize multi-faceted exchanges and cooperation to advance common national interests and prosperity;

Recognizing that their relations, not being a relationship between states, consti-tute a special interim relationship stemming from the process towards unifica-tion, … hereby have agreed as follows;

Chapter I. South-North Reconciliation

Article 1. The South and North shall recognize and respect each other's system.

Article 2. The two sides shall not interfere in each other's internal affairs.

Article 3. The two sides shall not slander or vilify each other.

Article 4. The two sides shall not attempt any actions of sabotage or overthrow against each other.

Article 5. The two sides shall endeavor together to transform the present state of armistice into a solid state of peace between the south and the North and shall abide by the present Military Armistice Agreement (of July 27, 1953) until such a state of peace has been realized.

Chapter II. South-North Non-Aggression

Article 9. The two sides shall not use force against each other and shall not undertake armed aggression against each other.

Chapter III. South-North Exchanges and Cooperation

Article. 15 To promote an integrated and balanced development of the national economy and the welfare of the entire people, the two sides shall engage in economic exchanges and cooperation, including the joint development of resources, the trade of goods as domestic commerce and joint ventures.

Joint Declaration of the Denuclearization of the Korean Peninsula, February 19, 1992

South and North Korea agreed in December 1991, and confirmed in writing on January 20, 1922, that on February 19, 1992, this declaration would take effect. Selected passages are quoted below. North Korea, however, 11 years later in October 2002, told U.S. State Department Assistant Secretary of State James Kelly in Pyongyang that it had broken the terms of this agreement. Then in April 2003, North Korea declared this agreement nullified.

The South and the North, desiring to eliminate the danger of nuclear war through denuclearization of the Korean Peninsula, and thus to create an environment and conditions favorable for peace and peaceful unification of our country and contribute to peace and security in Asia and the world,

Declare as follows;

1. The South and the North shall not test, manufacture, produce, receive, possess, store, deploy or use nuclear weapons.

2. The South and the North shall use nuclear energy solely for peaceful purposes.

3. The South and the North shall not possess nuclear reprocessing and uranium enrichment facilities.

4. The South and the North, in order to verify the denuclearization of the Korean Peninsula, shall conduct inspection of the objects selected by the other side and agreed upon between the two sides, in accordance with procedures and methods to be determined ...

Joint Statement of the Democratic People's Republic of Korea (DPRK) and the United States of America (USA), June 11, 1993

This statement "suspended" North Korea's withdrawal from the Treaty on the Non-proliferation of Nuclear Weapons (NPT) and allowed continuation of U.S.–North Korea negotiations that eventually yielded the U.S.–North Korea Agreed Framework of October 21, 1994 (see the following).

North Korea maintains that the U.S. Bush Administration failed to maintain key elements of the agreement, specifically the "assurances against the threat and use of force, including nuclear weapons."

The United States asserts that North Korea has broken promises made in the statement, specifically support for the North-South Joint Declaration on the Denuclearization of the Korean Peninsula in the interest of nuclear non-proliferation goals. Yet both sides set in the agreement elements that remain essential to the normalization of their relationship.

> The DPRK and the USA held government-level talks in New York from the 2nd through the 11th of June, 1993. Present at the talks were the delegation of the DPRK headed by First Vice Minister of Foreign Affairs Kang Sok Ju and the delegation of the USA headed by Assistant Secretary of State Robert L. Gallucci, both representing their respective Governments. At the talks, both sides have discussed policy matters with a view to a fundamental solution of the nuclear issue on the Korean Peninsula. Both sides expressed support for the North-South Joint Declaration on the Denuclearization of the Korean Peninsula in the interest of nuclear non-proliferation goals.

The DPRK and the USA have agreed to principles of:

— assurances against the threat and use of force, including nuclear weapons;

— peace and security in a nuclear-free Korean Peninsula, including impartial application of full-scope safeguards, mutual respect for each other's sovereignty, and non-interference in each other's internal affairs; and

— support for the peaceful reunification of Korea.

In this context, the two Governments have agreed to continue dialogue on an equal and unprejudiced basis. In this respect, the Government of the DPRK has decided unilaterally to suspend as long as it considers necessary the effectuation of its withdrawal from the Treaty on the Non-proliferation of Nuclear Weapons.

Agreed Framework Between the United States of America (USA) and the Democratic People's Republic of Korea (DPRK), October 21, 1994

The Agreed Framework is the first, formal agreement signed by diplomatic representatives of the USA and DPRK. (Although a U.S. general signed the Korean War Armistice, he did so in his capacity as the Commander of United Nations Command, not as a representative of the U.S. Army.) The accord is not a treaty, only an understanding. It has no binding force under international law and it was not submitted to the U.S. Senate for its review and formal consent.

However, the accord defused the escalating nuclear crisis on the Korean Peninsula by "freezing" North Korea's nuclear activities and facilitating the resumption of International Atomic Energy Agency (IAEA) inspections of North Korea's primary nuclear facilities. In exchange for these promises, the United States promised to build two nuclear reactors in North Korea, to end its annual joint military exercise Team Spirit with South Korea, among other promises.

Attached to the agreement was a "confidential" minute that specified definitions for key terms and phrases used in the agreement. The content of this minute is included below.

The Bush Administration in 2001 first declined to affirm or renegotiate the accord with North Korea. North Korea subsequently claimed in October 2002 that U.S. government actions had "nullified" the agreement. North Korea's withdrawal from the Treaty on the Non-proliferation of Nuclear Weapons in January 2003 did in fact nullify the agreement.

South Korea, Japan, China, and Russia agree among themselves that the accord will have to be revived if the second U.S.–North Korea nuclear crisis is to be resolved.

Delegations of the governments of the USA and the DPRK held talks in Geneva from September 23 to October 21, 1994, to negotiate an overall resolution of the nuclear issue on the Korean Peninsula.

Both sides reaffirmed the importance of attaining the objectives contained in the August 12, 1994, Agreed Statement between the United States and the DPRK and upholding the principles of the June 11, 1993, Joint Statement of the

United States and the DPRK to achieve peace and security on a nuclear-free Korean Peninsula. The U.S. and the DPRK decided to take the following actions for the resolution of the nuclear issue:

1. In accordance with the October 20, 1994, letter of assurance from the U.S. President (see Item 9), the U.S. will undertake to make arrangements for the provision to the DPRK of a Light Water Reactor (LWR) PROJECT WITH A TOTAL GENERATING CAPACITY OF APPROXIMATELY 2,000mw(e)BY A TARGET DATE OF 2003.

— The U.S. will organize under its leadership an international consortium to finance and supply the LWR project to be provided to the DPRK. The U.S., representing the international consortium, will serve as the principal point of contact with the DPRK for the LWR project.

— The U.S., representing the consortium, will make best efforts to secure the conclusion of a supply contract with the DPRK within six months of the date of this Document for the provision of the LWR project. Contract talks will begin as soon as possible after the date of this Document.

— As necessary, the U.S. and the DPRK will conclude a bilateral agreement for cooperation in the field of peaceful uses of nuclear energy.

2. In accordance with the October 20, 1994, letter of assurances from the U.S. President, the United States, representing the consortium, will make arrangements to offset the energy foregone due to the freeze of the DPRK's graphite-moderated reactors and related facilities, pending completion of the first LWR unit.

— Alternative energy will be provided in the form of heavy oil for heating and electricity production.

— Deliveries of heavy oil will begin within three months of the date of this Document and will reach a rate of 500,000 tons annually, in accordance with an agreed schedule of deliveries.

3. Upon receipt of U.S. assurances for the provision of LWRs and for arrangements for interim energy alternatives, the DPRK will freeze its graphite-moderated reactors and related facilities and will eventually dismantle these reactors and related facilities.

— The freeze on the DPRK's graphite-moderated reactors and related facilities will be fully implemented within one month of the date of this Document. During this one-month period, and throughout the freeze, the International

Atomic Energy Agency (IAEA) will be allowed to monitor this freeze, and the DPRK will provide full cooperation to the IAEA for this purpose.

— Dismantlement of the DPRK's graphite-moderated reactors and related facilities will be completed when the LWR project is completed.

— The U.S. and the DPRK will cooperate in finding a method to store safely the spent fuel from the 5 MW(e)experimental reactor during the construction of the LWR project, and to dispose of the fuel in a safe manner that does not involve reprocessing in the DPRK.

4. As soon as possible after the date of this Document, U.S. and DPRK experts will hold two sets of experts talks.

— At one set of talks, experts will discuss issues related to alternative energy and the replacement of the graphite-moderated reactor program with the LWR project.

— At the other set of talks, experts will discuss specific arrangements for spent fuel storage and ultimate disposition.

II. The two sides will move toward full normalization of political and economic relations.

1. Within three months of the date of this Document, both sides will reduce barriers to trade and investment, including restrictions on telecommunications services and financial transactions.

2. Each side will open a liaison office in the other's capital following resolution of consular and other technical issues through expert level discussions.

3. As progress is made on issues of concern to each side, the U.S. and the DPRK will upgrade bilateral relations to the Ambassadorial level.

III. Both sides will work together for peace and security on a nuclear-free Korean Peninsula.

1. The U.S. will provide formal assurances to the DPRK against the threat or use of nuclear weapons by the U.S.

2. The DPRK will consistently take steps to implement the North-South Joint Declaration on the Denuclearization of the Korean Peninsula.

3. The DPRK will engage in North-South dialogue, as this Agreed Framework will help create an atmosphere that promotes such dialogue.

IV. Both sides will work together to strengthen the international nuclear non-proliferation regime.

1. The DPRK will remain a party to the Treaty on the Non-proliferation of Nuclear Weapons (NPT) and will allow implementation of its safeguards agreement under the Treaty.

2. Upon conclusion of the supply contract for the provision of the LWR project, ad hoc and routine inspections will resume under the DPRK's safeguards agreement with the IAEA with respect to the facilities not subject to the freeze. Pending conclusion of the supply contract, inspections required by the IAEA for the continuity of safeguards will continue at the facilities not subject to the freeze.

3. When a significant portion of the LWR project is completed, but before delivery of key nuclear components, the DPRK will come into full compliance with its safeguards agreement with the IAEA (INFCIRC/403), including taking all steps that may be deemed necessary by the IAEA, following consultations with the Agency with regard to verifying the accuracy and completeness of the DPRK's initial report on all nuclear material in the DPRK.

"Confidential" Minute

The two sides decided upon the following understandings and definitions applicable to the actions described in the Agreed Framework:

1. The LWR project will consist of two reactors with a generating capacity of approximately 1,000 MW(e)each. It is anticipated that completion of the second reactor unit will occur approximately one to two years after completion of the first LWR unit.

2. In the event that U.S. firms will be providing any key nuclear components, the U.S. and the DPRK will conclude a bilateral agreement for peaceful nuclear cooperation prior to the delivery of such components. Such agreement will not be implemented until a significant portion of the LWR project is completed.

3. The freeze on the DPRK's graphite-moderated reactors and related facilities will consist of: no refueling or operation of the 5 MW(e)experimental reactor; freezing construction of the 50 MW (e)and 200 MW (e)reactors; foregoing reprocessing; sealing and ceasing activities at the Radio-chemical (Reprocessing) Laboratory; and ceasing operation of the fuel fabrication plant.

4. The DPRK will not construct any new graphite-moderated reactors or related facilities.

5. The schedule of delivery of heavy oil to the DPRK in the first year after the date of the Agreed Framework will proceed as follows: within the first three months, 50,000 tons of heavy oil will be delivered, and an additional 100,000

tons of heavy oil will be delivered before the end of the one-year period. Thereafter, annual deliveries of 500,000 tons of heavy oil will be made for heating and electricity production.

6. When a significant portion of the LWR project is completed, as described in the Agreed Framework, the DPRK will come into full compliance with its safeguards agreement (INFCIRC/403), including permitting the IAEA access to additional sites and information the IAEA may deem necessary to verify the accuracy and completeness of the DPRK's initial report on all nuclear material in the DPRK.

7. For purposes of this minute and the Agreed Framework, "a significant portion of the LWR project" means the following:

a. Conclusion of the contract for the LWR project;

b. Completion of site preparation, excavation, and completion of facilities necessary to support construction of the project;

c. Completion of initial plant design for the selected site;

d. Specification and fabrication of major reactor components for the first reactor unit as provided for in project plans and schedules;

e. Delivery of essential non-nuclear components for the first LWR unit, including turbines and generators, according to the project plans and schedules;

f. Construction of the turbine buildings and other auxiliary buildings for the first reactor unit, to the stage provided for in project plans and schedules;

g. Construction of the reactor building and containment structure for the first reactor unit to the point suitable for the introduction of components of the nuclear steam supply system, and

h. Civil construction and fabrication and delivery of components for the second reactor unit according to project plans and schedules.

8. When the first reactor unit is completed, the DPRK will begin dismantling its frozen graphite-moderated reactors and related facilities, and such dismantlement will be completed when the second reactor unit is completed. Dismantlement of the DPRK's frozen graphite-moderated reactors and related facilities will mean their disassembly or destruction so that their components and equipment are no longer useful.

9. When delivery of the key nuclear components for the first reactor unit begins, the transfer of spent fuel from the DPRK for ultimate disposition will

begin and will be completed when the first reactor unit is completed. Within the period required by technical and safety consideration, following discussions with the U.S., the DPRK will select and begin to implement a method of spent fuel storage that permits ultimate transfer.

10. For purposes of this minute and the Agreed Framework, the term "key nuclear components" means components controlled under the Export Trigger List of Nuclear Suppliers Group.

U.S. President Bill Clinton's Letter of Assurances in Connection with the Agreed Framework to "His Excellency Kim Jong II, Supreme Leader of the DPRK," October 20, 1994

At the request of North Korea's negotiating team, President Clinton sent his North Korean counterpart Kim Jong Il the following letter of assurances that the U.S. would fulfill its commitments under the Agreed Framework.

Excellency:

I wish to confirm to you that I will use the full powers of my office to facilitate arrangements for the financing and construction of a light-water nuclear power reactor project within the DPRK, and the funding and implementation of interim energy alternatives for the DPRK pending completion of the first reactor unit of the LWR project. In addition, in the event that this reactor project is not completed for reasons beyond the control of the DPRK, I will use the full powers of my office to provide, to the extent necessary, such a project from the United States, subject to approval of the U.S. Congress. Similarly, in the event that the interim energy alternatives are not provided for reasons beyond the control of the DPRK, I will use the full powers of my office to provide, to the extent necessary, such interim energy alternatives from the United States, subject to the approval of the U.S. Congress.

I will follow this course of action so long as the DPRK continues to implement the policies described in the Agreed Framework between the USA and the DPRK.

Sincerely

South-North Joint Declaration of June 15, 2000

The leaders of South and North Korea convened their first ever summit in Pyongyang on June 13, 2000. The unprecedented meeting raised expectations on the Korean Peninsula, and around the world, that the two Koreas might soon achieve reconciliation and quicken the nation's reunification. These expectations and aspirations are reflected in the joint declaration issued after the summit.

The June 13–15, 2000, summit did not achieve a breakthrough in South-North relations, a fact reflected in the Joint Declaration. Both sides essentially reaffirmed earlier South-North agreements beginning with the July 4, 1972, joint communiqué. Subsequently, progress toward reconciliation continues, albeit at a hesitant and uncertain pace.

> In accordance with the noble will of the entire people who yearn for the peaceful reunification of the nation, President Kim Dae-jung of the Republic of Korea and National Defense Commission Chairman Kim Jong Il of the Democratic People's Republic of Korea held a historic meeting and summit talks in Pyongyang from June 13 to June 15, 2000.
>
> The leaders of the South and the North, recognizing that the meeting and summit talks, the first since the division of the country, were of great significance in promoting mutual understanding, developing South-North relations and realizing peaceful reunification, declared as follows:
>
> 1. The South and the North have agreed to resolve the question of reunification independently and through the joint efforts of the Korean people, who are the masters of the country.
>
> 2. Acknowledging that there is a common element in the South's proposal for a confederation and the North's proposal for a loose form of federation as the formulae for achieving reunification, the South and the North agreed to promote reunification in that direction.
>
> 3. The South and the North have agreed to promptly resolve humanitarian issues such as exchange visits by separated family members and relatives on the occasion of the August 15 National Liberation Day and the question of unswerving communists who have been given long prison sentences in the South.
>
> 4. The South and the North have agreed to consolidate mutual trust by promoting balanced development of the national economy through economic cooperation and by stimulating cooperation and exchanges in civic, cultural, sports, public health, environmental and all other fields.
>
> 5. The South and the North have agreed to hold dialogue between relevant authorities in the near future to implement the above agreement expeditiously.
>
> President Kim Dae Jung cordially invited National Defense Commission Chairman Kim Jong Il to visit Seoul, and Chairman Kim Jong Il decided to visit Seoul at an appropriate time.

U.S.-DPRK Joint Communiqué of October 12, 2000

The United States and DPRK appeared to achieve a breakthrough in their relationship in the fall of 2000 as suggested by the exchange of high level visits. First, North Korean leader Kim Jong Il sent his special envoy, Vice Marshal and First Deputy Chairman of the National Defense Commission Jo Myong Rok to Washington, D.C., where he called on President Clinton and other ranking U.S. officials. Secretary of State Madeleine Albright then visited Pyongyang.

Subsequent to these visits, U.S.-DPRK relations gradually declined into another diplomatic impasse because of North Korea's nuclear ambitions.

At the conclusion of Vice Marshal Jo's October 9–12, 2000, visit, the U.S. and DPRK issued a joint communiqué, the full text of which is reproduced here.

> As the special envoy of Chairman Kim Jong Il of the DPRK National Defense commission, the First Vice Chairman, Vice Marshal Jo Myong Rok, visited the USA from October 9–12, 2000.
>
> During his visit, Special Envoy Jo Myong Rok delivered a letter from the National Defense commission Chairman Kim Jong Il, as well as his views on US-DPRK relations, directly to U.S. President William Clinton. Special Envoy Jo Myong Rok and his party also met with senior officials of the U.S. Administration, including his host secretary of State Madeleine Albright and secretary of Defense William Cohen, for an extensive exchange of views on issues of common concern. They reviewed in depth the new opportunities that have opened up for improving the full range of relations between the United States and the DPRK. The meetings proceeded in a serious, constructive and businesslike atmosphere, allowing each side to gain a better understanding of the other's concerns.
>
> Recognizing the changed circumstances of the Korean Peninsula created by the historic inter-Korean summit, the U.S. and the DPRK have decided to take steps to fundamentally improve their bilateral relations in the interests of enhancing peace and security in the Asia-Pacific region. In this regard, the two sides agreed there are a variety of available means, including Four Party talks, to reduce tension on the Korean Peninsula and formally end the Korean War by replacing the 1953 Armistice Agreement with permanent peace arrangements.
>
> Recognizing that improving ties is a natural goal in relations among states and that better relations would benefit both nations in the 21st century while helping ensure peace and security on the Korean Peninsula and in the Asia-Pacific region, the U.S. and the DPRK sides stated that they are prepared to undertake a new direction in their relations. As a crucial first step, the two sides stated that

neither government would have hostile intent toward the other and confirmed the commitment of both governments to make every effort in the future to build a new relationship free from past enmity.

Building on the principles laid out in the June 11, 1993 U.S.-DPRK Joint Statement and reaffirmed in the October 21, 1994 Agreed Framework, the two sides agreed to work to remove mistrust, build mutual confidence, and maintain an atmosphere in which they can deal constructively with issues of central concern. In this regard, the two sides reaffirmed that their relations should be based on the principles of respect for each other's sovereignty and non-interference in each other's internal affairs, and noted the value of regular diplomatic contacts, bilaterally and in broader fora.

The two sides agreed to work together to develop mutually beneficial economic cooperation and exchanges. To explore the possibilities for trade and commerce that will benefit the peoples of both countries and contribute to an environment conducive to greater economic cooperation throughout Northeast Asia, the two sides discussed an exchange of visits by economic and trade experts at an early date.

For More Information

Magazines, Newspapers, and Speeches

In general, these publications are good sources of information on developments in North Korea:

Associated Press

Foreign Affairs

The New York Times

USA Today

U.S. Department of State Dispatch

The Washington Post

Here are some recent articles and speeches that were used in writing this Guide:

Bolton, John, State Undersecretary for Arms Control and International Security. "Beyond the Axis of Evil: Additional Threats from Weapons of Mass Destruction, Remarks to the Heritage Foundation, May 6, 2002." www.state.gov/t/us.

———. "North Korea: A Shared Challenge to the U.S. and the ROK, Remarks to the Korean-American Association, August 29, 2002, Seoul, Korea." www.state/gov/t.

———. "Remarks to the Second Global Conference on Nuclear, Bio/Chem Terrorism: Mitigation and Response, November 1, 2002." www.state.gov/t/us.

Boucher, Richard. State Department Spokesman, "Status of Political Dialogue with North Korea." www.state.gov, 2 July 2002.

———. "North Korean Nuclear Program, October 16, 2002." www.state.gov.r/pa/prs.

Bush, George, President. "New Initiatives to Reduce U.S. Nuclear Forces—Address to the Nation, September 27, 1991." *US Department of State Dispatch*, 30 September 1991, p. 715.

———. "The U.S. and Korea: Entering a New World—Address Before the Korean National Assembly, Seoul, January 6, 1992." *US Department of State Dispatch*, 13 January 1992, p. 23.

Bush, George W., President. "Statement by the President on North Korea Policy." White House Press Release, www.whitehouse.gov, 6 June 2001.

———. "Remarks by President Bush and Prime Minister Koizumi in Joint Press Conference, Tokyo, Japan, February 18, 2002." www.state.gov/p/eap.

———. "Remarks by President Bush and President Kim Dae-jung in Press Availability, Seoul, Republic of Korea, February 20, 2002." www.state.gov/p/eap.

———. "Memorandum to the Secretary of State, Presidential Determination No. 2002-12, April 1, 2002." www.whitehouse.gov/news/releases.

———. "Statement Regarding KEDO, November 15, 2002." www.whitehouse.gov/news/releases.

———. "Remarks by President Bush and Polish President Kwasniewski, Washington, D.C., January 14, 2003." www.state.gov/p/eap.

China, People's Republic of. "China, Russia Issue Joint Statement, December 3, 2002." www.china.org.cn/english/international.

CNN. "U.S. Envoy Gets North Korean Invite," www.cnn.worldnews.com, 29 April 2002.

Craner, Lorne, Assistant Secretary of State for Democracy, Human Rights and Labor. "Remarks to the Congressional Human Rights Caucus." Washington, D.C., www.state.gov, 17 April 2002. www.state.gov.

Department of State. "U.S. Review of Relations with the DPRK." *US Department of State Dispatch*, January 1989, p. 17.

Department of State. "Joint Press Statements—Trilateral Coordination and oversight Group (TCOG) Meetings." www.state.gov/p/eap, 27 March, 26 May, and 27 November 2001; 25 January, 9 September, 26 October, and 9 November 2002; etc.

"DPRK Foreign Minister Attends ARF, Talks with Powell, Japanese Prime Minister." www.korea-np.co.jp/pk, 31 July 2002.

Fleischer, Ari, Presidential Spokesman. "Press Briefing, December 12, 2002." www.whitehouse.gov/news/releases.

———. "Statement by the Press Secretary." www.whitehouse.gov/news/releases, 30 April 2002.

Gordon, Michael. "U.S. Toughens Terms for North Korea Talks." *New York Times*, 2 July 2001.

Kelly, James, Assistant Secretary of State for East Asian and Pacific Affairs. "Remarks at the Woodrow Wilson Center, Washington, D.C., December 11, 2002." www.state.gov/p/eap.

Kessler, Glenn. "North Korea Says it Has Nuclear Arms." *Washington Post*, 25 April 2003, p. A1.

Mufson, Steven. "The Way Bush Sees the World." *Washington Post*, 17 February 2002, p. BI.

Natsios, Andrew. US AID Administrator, "Statement Before the Senate Foreign Relations Committee, April 25, 2001." www.usaid.gov/press.

———. "Statement Regarding Food Aid for North Korea, June 7, 2002." www.usaid.gov/press.

Newhouse, John. "The Missile Defense Debate." *Foreign Affairs*, July/August 2001, 97-109.

Olson, Elizabeth. "Bush Warns of Arms Threat, Citing North Korea and Iraq." *Washington Post*, 25 January 2002.

Perry, William. "Testimony Before the Senate Foreign Relations Committee, Subcommittee on East Asian and Pacific Affairs." Washington, D.C., 12 October 1999.

Powell, Colin, Secretary of State. "Confirmation Hearing—Remarks to the Senate Foreign Relations Committee." www.state.gov, 17 January 2001.

———. "Remarks at the Asia Society Annual Dinner, New York City." www.state.gov, 10 June 2002.

———. "Interview on ABC's This Week with George Stephanopoulos, December 29, 2002." www.state.gov/secretary.

Quinones, C. Kenneth. "The American NGO Experience in North Korea." *Proceedings of the Academy of Korean Studies First World Conference*, July 2002.

———. "Beyond Collapse—Continuity and Change in North Korea." *International Journal of Korean Unification Studies*, January 2003.

———. "Clinton Administration's Contingency Planning for the North Korea Nuclear Crisis." *Sekai*, no. 712, April 2003 (in Japanese).

———. "Dualism in the Bush Administration's Policy Toward North Korea." *Asian Perspective*, April 2003.

———. "Japan's Engagement of the Democratic People's Republic of Korea, 1990–2000." *International Journal of Korean Unification Studies* 9, no. 1(2000)

———. "Kim Jong Il's 'Strong and Great Nation' Campaign and the U.S. 'Imperialist Threat.'" *Proceedings of the Asia-Pacific Center for Security Studies Conference on Information Technology in North Korea*, forthcoming.

Roth, Stanley, State Assistant Secretary of State for East Asia and Pacific Affairs. "U.S. Policy Toward Asia: Where We've Been, Where We Need to Go—Remarks to the Asia Society." www.state.gov, 11 January 2001.

Sanger, David. "Administration Divided Over North Korea." *New York Times*, 21 April 2003, p. A15.

——. "Bush Aides Say Tough Tone Put Foes on Notice." *New York Times*, 31 January 2002.

——. "North Korea Says It Now Posses Nuclear Arsenal." *New York Times*, 25 April 2003, p. A1.

Slavin, Barbara. "Expectations Low for U.S.-North Korea Meeting." *USA Today*, 21 April 2003, p. 9A.

Solomon, Richard. "Pursuing U.S. Objectives in Asia and the Pacific, Statement Before the Senate Foreign Relations Committee, March 31, 1992." *US Department of State Dispatch*, 6 April 1992, p. 272.

Struck, Doug, and Bradley Graham. "U.S., Asian Allies Face Tough Choices." *Washington Post*, 25 April 2003, p. A18.

Van Diepen, Vann H., Director, State Office of Chemical Biological and Missile Non-proliferation. "Testimony Before the Senate Governmental Affairs Committee Subcommittee on International Security, Proliferation and Federal Services, Washington, D.C., July 29, 2002." www.state.gov/t/np.

Wolf, John, Assistant Secretary of State for Non-proliferation. "U.S. Approaches to Non-proliferation, Remarks to the 12th Annual International Arms Control Conference, April 19, 2002." Sandia National Laboratories, Albuquerque, New Mexico, www.state.gov/t/np.

Wolfowitz, Paul, Deputy Secretary of Defense. "DoD News Briefing, April 18, 2002." www.kison.org.

Woodward, Bob. "Ten Days in September—Inside the War Cabinet." *Washington Post*, 31 January 2002, Section B1.

Websites

www.china.org.cn/english/international
The official website of the People's Republic of China provides extensive links to China's government ministries. The foreign ministry's site maintains a comprehensive archive of official policy statements and press conference transcripts.

www.cnn.com
This is a good commercial source for news on daily developments from around the world.

www.InterAction.org
This is the website for InterAction, the umbrella organization for U.S. private voluntary organizations (PVO) involved in international humanitarian work. The organization North Korea Working Group maintains current materials about the North Korean food and refugee situations.

www.korea.net
The Republic of Korea (South Korea) maintains an excellent website that provides links to English-language materials about all aspects of Korea, south and north, including foreign policy, the economy, history, and culture. There are links to all of South Korea's English language newspapers.

www.korea-np.co.jp/pk
The Association of Korean Residents in Japan (*Chosen soron*) maintains this website. Based in Tokyo, the site provides daily, North Korean government approved coverage of news from North Korea. The site also maintains archives regarding numerous topics about North Korea.

Here are several U.S. government websites that maintain archives of official statements about U.S. policy toward North Korea:

www.dod.gov

www.state.gov/p/eap

www.state.gov/r/pa/prs

www.state.gov/secretary

www.state.gov/t/us

www.usaid.gov/press

www.whitehouse.gov

Books

Acheson, Dean. *The Korean War.* New York: W.W. Norton & Company, 1971.

Albright, David. *ISIS Reports: Solving the North Korean Nuclear Puzzle.* Washington, D.C.: Institute for Science and International Security, 2000.

Appleman, Roy E. *Escaping the Trap, The US Army X Corps in Northeast Korea—1950*. College Station: Texas A&M University Press, 1990.

Asia-Pacific Center for Security Studies. *Asia Pacific Space and Missile Security Issues— Report from the Conference of the Asia-Pacific Center, February 15-17, 2000*. Honolulu: Asia-Pacific Center for Security Studies, 2000.

Asia Watch. *Human Rights in the Democratic People's Republic of Korea*. Minneapolis: Minnesota Lawyers International Human Rights Committee, 1988.

Bamford, James. *Body of Secrets*. New York: Anchor Books, 2001.

Bermudez, Joseph S. *Shield of the Great Leader—The Armed Forces of North Korea*. Sydney: Allen & Unwin, 2001.

Blair, Clay. *The Forgotten War*. New York: Time Books, 1987.

Catchpole, Brian. *The Korean War 1950–53*. New York: Carroll & Graf Publishers, Inc., 2000.

Central Intelligence Agency. "Estimate of North Korea Missile Force Trends." In *Department of Defense, Proliferation and Response*. Washington, D.C.: U.S. Government Printing Office, 2002.

Chen Jian. *China's Road to the Korean War*. New York: Columbia University Press, 1994.

Chung, Chin O. *Pyongyang Between Peking and Moscow*. Tuscaloosa: University of Alabama Press, 1978.

Cummings, Bruce. *Korea's Place in the Sun—A Modern History*. New York: W. W. Norton, 1997.

Defense Intelligence Agency. *North Korea: The Foundations for Military Strength— Update 1995*. Washington, D.C.: Department of Defense, 1995.

Department of State. *Foreign Relations of the United States, 1950, Volume VII, Korea*. Washington, D.C.: U.S. Government Printing Office, 1976.

———. *A Historical Summary of United States-Korean Relations, 1834–1962*. Washington, D.C.: U.S. Government Printing Office, 1962.

Do You Know About Korea? Questions and Answers. Pyongyang: Foreign Languages Publishing House, 1989.

Echoes of the Korean War. Pyongyang: Foreign Languages Publishing House, 1996.

Encyclopedia of Japanese History. Tokyo: Kodansha International, 1985.

International Friendship Exhibition. Pyongyang: Foreign Languages Publishing House, 1990.

Jong, Ri Gun. *Korea's Reunification—A Burning Question.* Pyongyang: Foreign Languages Publishing House, 1995.

Kim, Doug Joong. *Foreign Relations of Korea During Kim Il Sung's Last Days.* Seoul: Sejong Institute, 1994.

Kim Il Sung. *Reminiscences with the Century.* Pyongyang: Foreign Languages Publishing House, 1992.

Korea Overseas Information Service. *Facts About Korea.* Seoul: Samhwa Printing Company, 1997.

———. *A Handbook of Korea.* Seoul: Samhwa Printing Company, 1990.

Korea Tour. Pyongyang: Foreign Languages Publishing House, 1997.

Lee Chae-jin. *China and Korea—Dynamic Relations.* Palo Alto, Calif.: Hoover Institution, 1996.

Lee Chong-sik. *The Politics of Korean Nationalism.* Berkeley and Los Angeles: University of California Press, 1965.

Liem, Channing. *The Korean War—An Unanswered Question.* Pyongyang: Foreign Languages Publishing House, 1993.

Marshall, S. L. A. *The River and the Gauntlet.* New York: Time Inc., 1962.

McCune, George M. *Korea Today.* Cambridge: Harvard University Press, 1950.

Meade, E. Grant. *American Military Government in Korea.* New York: King's Crown Press, 1951.

Medeiros, Evan S. *Ballistic Missile Defense and Northeast Asian Security: Views from Washington, Beijing and Tokyo*. Monterey, Calif.: Stanley Foundation and Monterey Institute of International Studies, 2001.

Moltz, James Clay, and Alexandre Mansourov, eds. *The North Korean Nuclear Program*. New York: Routledge, 2000.

Naewoe Press. *A Handbook on North Korea*. Seoul: Naewoe Press, 1998.

Natsios, Andrew. *The Great North Korean Famine*. Washington, D.C.: U.S. Institute of Peace Press, 2001.

Oberdorfer, Donald. *The Two Koreas*. Reading, Mass.: Addison Wesley, 1998.

Palmer, Spencer. *Korean-American Relations: Volume II The Period of Growing Influence 1887–1895*. Berkeley and Los Angeles: University of California Press, 1963.

Pang, Hwan Ju. *Korean Review*. Pyongyang: Foreign Languages Publishing House, 1987.

Panorama of Korea. Pyongyang: Foreign Languages Publishing House, 1999.

Pyongyang Review. Pyongyang: Foreign Languages Publishing House, 1995.

Quinones, C. Kenneth. "The Korean Peninsula—Preserve the Past or Move Toward Reconciliation." In *Managing Change on the Korean Peninsula*, edited by Han Sung-joo, 123-143. Seoul: Seoul Press, 1998. pp. 123-143.

———. "North Korea: from Containment to Engagement." In *North Korea After Kim Il Sung*, edited by Dae-sook Suh and Chae-jin Lee, 101–22. London: Lynne Reinner, 1998.

———. "South Korea's Approaches to North Korea—A Glacial Process." In *Korean Security Dynamics in Transition*, edited by Kyung-ae Park. 19–48. New York: Palgrave, 2001.

Ridgway, Matthew B. *The Korean War*. New York: Da Capo Press, 1967.

Ryo, Sung Chol. *Korea—The 38th Parallel North*. Pyongyang: Foreign Languages Publishing House, 1995.

Savada, Andrea M. *North Korea—A Country Study.* Washington, D.C.: U.S. Government Printing Office, 1994.

Sigal, Leon V. *Disarming Strangers.* Princeton, N.J.: Princeton University Press, 1998.

A Sightseeing Guide to Korea. Pyongyang: Foreign Languages Publishing House, 1991.

Sokolski, Henry. *Planning for a Peaceful Korea.* Carlisle, Pa.: Strategic Studies Institute, 2001.

Suh, Dae-sook. *Kim Il Sung—The North Korean Leader.* New York: Columbia University Press, 1988.

Tangun—Founder-King of Korea. Pyongyang: Foreign Languages Publishing House, 1994.

U.S. Government. *National Strategy to Combat Weapons of Mass Destruction.* Washington, D.C.: U.S. Government Printing Office, 2002.

U.S. Imperialists Started the Korean War. Pyongyang: Foreign Languages Publishing House, 1993.

Wagner, Edward. *Korea Old and New—A History.* Seoul: Ilchokak, 1990.

Wagner, Edward, trans. *Lee Ki-baik's New History of Korea.* Cambridge: Harvard University Press, 1984.

Weintraub, Stanley. *MacArthur's War.* New York: Simon & Schuster, 2001.

Whiting, Allen S. *China Crosses the Yalu.* Palo Alto: Stanford University Press, 1960.

Woodward, Bob. *Bush at War.* New York: Simon & Schuster, 2002.

Yang, Sung Chul. *The North and South Korean Political Systems, a Comparative Analysis.* Seoul: Hollym, 1999.

Yi, Pangja. *The World is One.* Seoul: Taewon Publishing Company, 1973.

Glossary

abducted Japanese   The Japanese government long maintained that North Korean agents had kidnapped several Japanese citizens. North Korea adamantly denied this until September 2002 when North Korean leader Kim Jong Il admitted, and apologized for, his government's abduction of Japanese citizens. The number of persons kidnapped remains a mystery. The Japanese people subsequently became enraged when they learned that some of the victims had died of unexplained causes in North Korea while still young. This aroused suspicions that they had been executed or tortured to death. Further normalization of bilateral relations must await resolution of this emotionally charged issue.

Aegis   *See* theater missile defense.

Agreed Framework   The first-ever diplomatic agreement between the United States and North Korea, signed in 1994. North Korea agreed to freeze its nuclear program in exchange for two nuclear light-water reactors, an annual supply of heavy fuel oil until the reactors went into operation, and further diplomatic talks aimed at the normalization of relations. See Appendix B for the Agreed Framework's full text.

axe murders   Killing of two U.S. Army officers by North Korean soldiers in the Joint Security Area (see entry) of the DMZ (see entry) on August 18, 1976. Tensions in Northeast Asia escalated to the brink of war. North Korean leader Kim Il Sung's signed expression of regret defused the situation. The incident's name refers to the North Koreans use of an axe handle to beat one the of the U.S. officers to death. This axe is on display in a museum on the north side of the JSA.

Axis of Evil   A phrase President George W. Bush used in his 2002 State of the Union speech to describe Iran, Iraq, and North Korea because they are authoritarian regimes that threaten peace with their weapons of mass destruction. *See also* weapons of mass destruction.

Beijing   The capital of China, the People's Republic of (see entry).

Beijing Channel   The first and only authorized diplomatic channel of communication between Washington and Pyongyang, set up in 1989 and in operation until 1993, when it was replaced by the New York Channel. The Beijing Channel consisted of the exchange of diplomatic notes between officials from the United States and North Korean embassies in Beijing, China.

chemical and biological weapons (CBW)   These weapons encompass a variety of lethal chemical gases and bacteria. They are one component of weapons of mass destruction (WMD).

China, People's Republic of (PRC)   Korea's neighbor to the west. From ancient protector to wartime ally to modern economic supporter, China has maintained a strong interest in Korea. China currently is North Korea's largest trading partner and leading provider of economic aid.

China, Republic of (ROC)   Governs the island of Taiwan and claims to be the legitimate government of all of China. The PRC claims Taiwan is a province of China.

Cho Myong-nok (also spelled Jo Myong Rok)   North Korea's top-ranking general and the vice chairman of the National Defense Commission (see entry). Vice Marshal Cho visited Washington, D.C., in October 1999 as Kim Jong Il's envoy and called on President Clinton at the White House, the first meeting between a North Korea official and the U.S. president.

Chosen soron   The Japanese name for the Association of Korean Residents in Japan. (The Korean name is *Choson chongnyon*.) Established in 1955 to protect members from Japanese prejudice against Koreans, North Korea's Workers' Party pumped money into the organization. Since 1998, its membership has shrunk to about 55,000 and ties with North Korea slackened.

Choson Reservoir (Chongjin Reservoir)   A large lake in northeast North Korea that became a famous battleground during the Korean War. A combined UN force of U.S. marines, U.S. army soldiers, and South Korean troops clashed with superior numbers of Chinese troops during bitterly cold weather at the end of November 1950. The UN forces fought their way out of the Chinese encirclement to safety and retreat back to South Korea.

CIA   The U.S. Central Intelligence Agency, which is responsible for the collection of intelligence material and development of intelligence assessments for the U.S. government's top-ranking foreign policy makers.

CINCUNC   Commander in Chief, United Nations Command.

CPV   Chinese People's Volunteers.

Dear Leader   The unofficial title that was reserved for Kim Il Sung's son Kim Jong Il before he inherited his father's place as North Korea's leader and became the new Great Leader (see entry).

Demilitarized Zone   Created when the Korean War Armistice ended hostilities in 1953. The opposing armies pulled back from one another, creating a three-kilometer wide no-man's land across the waist of the Korean Peninsula, creating the DMZ. It has become the *de facto* border between North and South Korea, as well as a sanctuary for rare animals and birds.

Democratic People's Republic of Korea (DPRK)   This is the official name for North Korea. Established on September 9, 1948, this government rules the northern half of the Korean Peninsula. The DPRK became a member of the United Nations in 1991, together with the Republic of Korea (South Korea). Kim Il Sung founded the DPRK and his son Kim Jong Il succeeded him in 1994 after his father's death. North Korea has an estimated population of about 23 million people, and a GDP in 2002 of about US $22 billion. Its army ranks fifth in the world and is equipped with ballistic missiles and chemical and biological weapons, and it is developing a nuclear arsenal.

DIA   The abbreviation for the U.S. Defense Intelligence Agency, which is responsible for the collection and assessment of military-related intelligence data regarding the United States's adversaries, present and future.

DMZ   *See* Demilitarized Zone.

DPRK   Democratic People's Republic of Korea, the official name for North Korea.

East Sea (Sea of Japan)   Koreans prefer to refer to the sea off the east coast of the Korean Peninsula as the East Sea. Imperial Japan (1968–1945) named it the Sea of Japan, as it appears on most modern maps.

five megawatt (e) reactor   The formal designation of the primary nuclear reactor at North Korea's Yongbyon Nuclear Research Center. The *five megawatt* refers to the amount of electricity (e) the reactor can produce when in operation. The reactor's design is based on Soviet technology that dates from the 1950s and relies on graphite to moderate (control) the nuclear reaction. About 8,000 uranium rods fuel the reactor. North Korea claimed early in 2003 that it had refueled and restarted the reactor. *See also* spent fuel rods and Yongbyon Nuclear Research Center.

Gauntlet *See* Kaechon.

Great Leader The unofficial title the North Korean people apply to their leaders, the deceased Kim Il Sung and his son and current leader, Kim Jong Il.

HEU *See* highly enriched uranium.

highly enriched uranium (HEU) One of two basic ingredients needed to produce a nuclear explosion. The other is plutonium. HEU is uranium in which the percentage of uranium 235 has been increased above its naturally occurring level (less than 1 percent) to more than 20 percent. North Korea informed the United States in October 2002 that it had initiated an HEU program, in disregard of its several internal pledges not to do so.

Hwasong 5/6 This is the North Korean name for its reverse-engineered version of a Soviet-designed Scud C ballistic missile. Based on Germany's World War II V-2 rocket, this missile has a single-stage, liquid-fuel engine with a 500 kilometer (300 mile) range carrying a 770 kilogram (three quarter ton) payload.

IAEA *See* International Atomic Energy Agency.

Inchon South Korea's major west coast port, located about 25 miles west of Seoul. During the Korean War, UN commander Douglas MacArthur, ignoring Inchon extreme tides, ordered his forces to land there. North Korean resistance in South Korea crumpled, allowing UN forces to rapidly push the North Korean army northward almost to the Chinese border.

International Atomic Energy Agency (IAEA) The United Nation's agency responsible for conducting inspections at NPT (see entry) member nations nuclear facilities. Its headquarters are in Vienna, Austria. In 1993, North Korea discontinued its membership in the IAEA.

JAL hijacking incident Japan Airlines hijacking incident. *See* Japanese Red Army (JRA).

Japan This island nation, east of the Korean Peninsula, long has been Korea's nemesis. Fearing that a foreign power would occupy the weak Korean kingdom at the end of the nineteenth century, Japan annexed Korea into its growing empire. Japan's relations with South Korea were normalized in 1965, but relations with North Korea remain estranged. Nevertheless, Japan is a major trading partner of both Koreas.

Japan Self Defense Forces (JSDF)   Refers to the army, navy, and air force that Japan maintains to defend itself. Japan's constitution, written by the U.S. occupation government that ruled Japan from the end of World War II (1945) to 1953, bars Japan from maintaining a regular armed force. Units of the JSDF are not allowed to be deploy abroad, except as approved by Japan's legislature, in a defense capacity, or as members of a UN peacekeeping force or on a humanitarian mission.

Japanese Red Army (JRA)   Formed about 1970 by Japanese radical communists as an international terrorist group after they separated from the Japanese Communist League-Red Army faction. The JRA was also known as the Anti-imperialist International Brigade (AIIB), the Nippon Sekigun, Nihon Sekigun, the Holy War Brigade, and the Anti-War Democratic Front. The JRA conducted the 1972 massacre inside the terminal at Israel's Lod Airport, hijacked two civilian airliners, one to Pyongyang (the so-called JAL Hijacking Incident), and is suspected of having planted a bomb in a USO club in Naples, Italy, that killed five people, including a U.S. servicewoman. Pyongyang has provided safe haven to four JRA members since they hijacked a JAL airliner to North Korea in 1970.

Jo Myong Rok   *See* Cho Myong-nok.

Joint Declaration on the Denuclearization of the Korean Peninsula of 1992   A joint promise by the two Koreas not to develop, possess, or use nuclear weapons. *See* Appendix B for the text.

Joint Security Area (JSA)   The neutral zone inside the DMZ where representatives of the UN Command (UNC, see entry) and Korean People's Army (see entry) hold meetings concerning implementation of the Korean War Armistice. The JSA is located near the former village of Panmunjom toward the western end of the DMZ. Tourists from both sides are allowed to visit the JSA.

JRA   *See* Japanese Red Army.

JSA   *See* Joint Security Area.

JSDF   *See* Japan Self Defense Forces.

juche   This is the Korean name for Kim Il Sung's interpretation of Marxism-Leninism. Juche is usually translated as "self reliance." The ideology rejects Marx's universalism and instead embraces Korean nationalism. Kim also rejected Marx's theory that economic forces are the prime mover of history. Instead, he designated man as history's prime mover. Kim also preferred a rigid, highly stratified social order to Marx's egalitarianism. But Kim subscribed to Lenin's theory of imperialism, which essentially alleged that economic greed propelled powerful nations to exploit and colonize smaller, weak nations.

Kaechon   The modern name for the city known as Kunuri during the Korean War. In December 1950, it is the site of one of the most disastrous defeats in the annals of the U.S. Army. As the UN column began its retreat south out of Kunuri, it encountered the Gauntlet. This was the American nickname for the stretch of narrow road where Chinese and North Korean forces ambushed the retreating column of tanks, trucks, and troops.

KAL 858 incident   Occurred on November 29, 1987, when a bomb aboard Korean Airlines flight 858 exploded off the coast of Burma (Myanmar), killing 115 persons aboard. The bomb had been hidden in a radio two North Korean agents had placed on the plane prior to getting off at the next stop. One of the agents, Kim Hyon-hui, was subsequently caught. At first she claimed to be a Japanese citizen and was carrying a Japanese passport. Later her Japanese language teacher in North Korea was identified as one of several Japanese citizens that North Korean agents had abducted. *See also* abducted Japanese.

Kang Sok Ju (Kang Sok-chu)   North Korea's First Vice Minister of Foreign Affairs who negotiated the Agreed Framework (see entry). North Korea's leaders Kim Il Sung and Kim Jong Il respect his views regarding policy toward the United States.

KCNA   *See* Korean Central News Agency.

Kim Dae-jung (Kim Dae Jung)   The popularly elected president of South Korea from 1998 to 2002. He formulated and pursued sunshine diplomacy (see entry) toward North Korea, which set the stage for the first ever North-South Korea summit in June 2000. For this he won the Nobel Peace Prize. His hopes of North-South reconciliation remain more a dream than a reality.

Kim Gye Gwan (or **Kim Kye-gwan**; 1937–)   One of North Korea's vice ministers of foreign affairs. He usually appears as North Korea's chief negotiator during talks with the United States. A career diplomat, he speaks fluent French and broken English and has traveled extensively around the world.

Kim Il Sung (1912–1994)   The founder of North Korea. Kim was a communist guerilla prior to World War II. He was eventually selected by the Soviets to be their proxy in North Korea. After taking power, Kim deftly played the Soviets and Chinese off each other to develop North Korea and his own hold on power. The initiator of the Korean War, Kim managed to portray North Korea as victor in that conflict, and his own role as defender of the North Korean people. Kim developed a uniquely Korean version of Marxism, called juche. Kim Il Sung is still revered as the Great Leader in North Korea, and his son, Kim Jong Il (see entry) is careful to maintain Kim Il Sung on a literal and figurative pedestal, deriving legitimacy for his own regime by association. *See also* juche.

Kim Jong Il (1942–)   The son of North Korea's founder Kim Il Sung. When Kim Il Sung died in July 1994, he succeeded his father as North Korea's ruler. Kim Jong Il is informally referred to as the Great or Dear Leader. His formal titles are Supreme Commander, Chairman of the KWP, and Chairman of the NDC.

Kim Jong Nam (1973–)   Kim Jong Il's first-born son who attempted to enter Japan in 2001 using a counterfeit passport.

Kim Jong Suk (1919–1949)   The name of Kim Il Sung's wife and the mother of North Korean leader Kim Jong Il.

Kim Yong-nam (1925–)   North Korea's prime minister and former foreign minister who is one of North Korean leader Kim Jong Il's closet advisers.

kimchi   Name for a type of Korean side dish. To qualify as *kimchi*, the dish must be spicy hot, contain scallions and garlic, be salty and smelly, and be made from chopped cabbage, radishes, cucumbers, or other green leafy vegetables.

Koguryo   *See* Three Kingdoms.

Kojong (1852–1919)   The reign title of the second to last Yi Choson monarch, the husband of Queen Min (see entry) and father of Sunjong. He attempted, unsuccessfully, to preserve Korea's independence by balancing one foreign power against another. Ultimately, the Japanese forced him in 1907 to abdicate in favor of his son.

Korean Central News Agency (KCNA)   The North Korean government controlled ageny for the distribution of all officially approved mass media news.

Korean Peninsula   The landmass where North and South Korea are located. It is situated between China and Japan and flanked by the East Sea and the West Sea.

Korean Peninsula Energy Development Organization (KEDO)   This agency was created as a result of the Agreed Framework between the United States and North Korea, to provide peaceful nuclear energy to North Korea. KEDO continues to build two nuclear light-water reactors in North Korea.

Korean People's Army (KPA)   Refers to North Korea's estimated one million personnel army. It is the fifth largest land force in the world behind the People's Republic of China, the United States, Russia, and India. Backing it are about 7.4 million reservists, ballistic missiles, and an arsenal of chemical and biological weapons. The army may already, or soon will, have nuclear weapons.

Korean War   Conducted from June 1950 to July 1953. North Korea attacked South Korea, hoping to unite the nations under the Kim Il Sung regime. The United States and South Korea (with other UN forces) eventually drove the North Koreans back to the border with China. China then attacked across the North Korean border, forcing a general UN retreat. The fighting finally stabilized along the 38th parallel (the pre-war boundary), and an armistice was reached. The current border between the two Koreas follows the front line as it was at the time of the armistice.

Korean Workers' Party (KWP)   The official name of North Korea's three million member communist party. North Korea's leader Kim Jong Il is the KWP's chairman.

Koryo   The name of the dynasty that ruled Korea from 935 to 1392. Its first capital was in Pyongyang.

KPA   *See* Korean People's Army.

Kumjangni   The name of the North Korean village near a site that the U.S. intelligence community suspected might be a secret nuclear facility. After these suspicions leaked to the U.S. press in August 1998, the United States demanded and eventually was able to inspect the site, but it proved to be only an empty cavern in a mountainside.

Kunuri   *See* Kaechon.

KWP   *See* Korean Workers' Party.

MAC   Military Armistice Commission.

MDL   Military Demarcation Line.

Ministry of Public Security   Directs the national police and civil defense forces in North Korea. It shares political monitoring of the population with the SSA. *See also* State Security Agency.

Missile Moratorium   The common title used for North Korea's promises, first made in September 1999, not to test long-range ballistic missiles. North Korea reaffirmed this promises in September 2002, but in December 2002 threatened to discontinue it.

National Defense Commission (NDC)   The peak of power in North Korea. Kim Jong Il chairs the NDC. Its membership consists of his closest advisers on political and military affairs.

National Intelligence Estimates   Contain the U.S. intelligence community's best estimate of an adversary's capabilities and intentions.

National Security Agency (NSA)   The U.S. government intelligence organization for the interception of electronic transmissions around the world, and the breaking of codes.

New York Channel   Replaced the Beijing Channel in 1993 as the primary channel of diplomatic communication between the United States and North Korea. Communication is conducted via telephone and fax, as well as occasional face-to-face meetings, usually in New York. *See also* Beijing Channel.

NIE *See* National Intelligence Estimates.

NKPA North Korean People's Army.

NLL *See* Northern Limit Line.

NNRC Neutral Nations Repatriation Commission.

NNSC Neutral Nations Supervisory Commission.

Nodong North Korea's name for its medium range, single stage liquid fuel rocket deployed by North Korea. The missile has a maximum range of about 1,500 kilometer (780 miles) carrying a 1,000-kilogram (one ton) payload.

Nodong Shinmun The Korean name of North Korea's leading daily newspaper. Members of the KWP (see entry) and the general public read it to obtain official guidance about national policy matters. Translated into English, the name means "Labor Daily News."

North Korea *See* Democratic People's Republic of Korea.

Northern Limit Line (NLL) In 1953, shortly after the Korean War Armistice had been signed, the United Nations Command, at the behest of South Korea, unilaterally established this line in the West Sea. The NLL divided rich fishing grounds into those accessible to South Korea and those accessible to North Korea. The line, however, disregards North Korea's 12-mile territorial waters and remains the cause of naval clashes between the two Koreas.

North-South Basic Agreement The common Korean reference for the 1992 North-South Agreement on Nonaggression, etc. See the North-South Agreement on Nonaggression, Economic Cooperation and Exchanges of 1992.

North-South Korea Joint Statement of 1972 The first joint statement by the two Koreas. Issued on July 4, 1972, it became a cornerstone of reconciliation efforts between them. See Appendix B for the text.

NPT *See* Treaty on the Non-proliferation of Nuclear Weapons.

NSA *See* National Security Agency.

Nyongbyon *See* Yongbyon.

Panmunjom *See* Joint Security Area.

plutonium *See* spent fuel rods.

PRC *See* China, People's Republic of.

***Pueblo* incident**   Took place on January 23, 1968, when North Korean navy patrol boats fired upon and seized the USS *Pueblo*, a U.S. Navy electronic intercept ship collecting intelligence material for the National Security Agency (NSA; see entry). The ship was towed to the port of Wonsan and its crew imprisoned in Pyongyang. During their one year of imprisonment, many were severely beaten and tortured. Tensions between the United States and North Korea subsequently reached the brink of war. The situation was finally defused and the crew released only after a U.S. officer provided North Korean military officers a written apology. The Soviet Union and North Korea gained a treasure trove of knowledge about the U.S. intelligence capabilities, electronics intercept technology, and decoding skills. North Korea has preserved the U.S. ship as an American imperialist spy museum for young people and soldiers.

Pusan   South Korea's largest port city, located on the southeast tip of the Korean Peninsula.

Pusan Perimeter   The name given to the defensive line UN Forces established early in the Korean War to defend Pusan against the invading North Korean army. *See also* Korean War.

Pyongyang   The capital of North Korea. With a population of about three million, it is the largest city in the country, and the center for political power and main entry point to the country.

Queen Min (1842–1895)   The consort of King Kojong and mother of the Yi Choson dynasty's last monarch. Japanese advocates of Korea's modernization saw her as an obstacle to their plans. In 1895, Japanese soldiers assassinated her in her palace, dismembered her body, and burned it.

Rangoon bombing   Took place on October 9, 1983, in Rangoon, Burma (Myanmar) when North Korean agents exploded a bomb at a site South Korea's president was scheduled to visit. The bomb explored prior to his arrival and instead killed several members of his cabinet.

reprocessing   *See* spent fuel rods.

Republic of Korea (South Korea or ROK)   Established in 1948, the ROK governs the southern half of the Korean Peninsula. It has been a member of the United Nations since 1991. The ROK is a prosperous, technologically sophisticated nation of about 48 million people with a democratic government and a capitalistic economy. It is a close ally of the United States.

Rhee Syngman   *See* Syngman Rhee.

ROC   *See* China, Republic of.

ROK   *See* Republic of Korea.

Seoul   The capital of the Republic of Korea (South Korea). Approximately one quarter of South Korea's 48 million people live in the Seoul metropolitan area, making it a prime target for North Korea's 12,000 long-range artillery pieces, 50 ballistic missiles, and one million man army in the event of another Korean War. You can drive the 25 miles from downtown Seoul to the DMZ in about an hour.

South Korea   *See* Republic of Korea.

South-North Korea Agreement on Reconciliation, Non-aggression, and Exchanges and Cooperation of 1992   The first formal agreement signed between the two Koreas. The two sides agreed to co-exist peacefully, to respect one another's sovereignty and political systems, to cooperate economically, and to facilitate cultural and other exchanges. *See* Appendix B for the text.

South-North Liaison Office   Established in 1972 to facilitate communication between Seoul and Pyongyang via telephone fax. The office is located in the Joint Security Area at Panmunjom inside the DMZ (see entry). Unfortunately, the connection is usually disconnected whenever tensions between the two Koreas intensify. *See also* Joint Security Area.

spent fuel rods   The 8,000 highly radioactive nuclear fuel rods that North Korea removed from its five megawatt (e) nuclear reactor at the Yongbyon Nuclear Research Center in May 1994. Under the Agreed Framework, these rods were placed in long-term storage under constant IAEA monitoring. North Korea in December 2002 expelled the IAEA monitors and early in 2003 claimed it had begun to reprocess these rods. Reprocessing is the chemical process of extracting plutonium (the core element of a nuclear weapon) from the uranium in these rods. When all 8.000 rods have been reprocessed, they would yield sufficient plutonium to make six to eight nuclear weapons, depending on size and explosive power. North Korea repeatedly claimed early in 2003 that it had reprocessed these rods to extract their plutonium. *See also* Agreed Framework, five megawatt (e) nuclear reactor, and Yongbyon Nuclear Research Center.

State Security Agency (SSA)   North Korea's secret police. They are responsible for monitoring citizen's behavior, to ensure that all live and work in accordance with the Ten Principles of North Korean society. *See* Chapter 12 for more information.

Sunjong (1874–1926)   Yi Chosun (1392–1910) Korea's last monarch; he reigned from 1907 to 1910. The son of King Kojong and Queen Min, he received the crown when his father abdicated, under pressure from Japan, in 1907. After Korea's 1910 annexation, the Japanese arranged his marriage to a Japanese princess and housed the couple in Tokyo. The Japanese had believed she would not be able to bear children, thus ending the challenge of a hereditary Korean monarchy. However, the couple did have a daughter. The young princess eventually married and had a son who was educated in the United States and who married an American woman. The family lived a reclusive life in the United States. No claimants to the Yi Chosun throne survive.

sunshine diplomacy   The nickname for President Kim Dae-jung's strategy of engaging North Korea diplomatically and economically. His effort was viewed as projecting warmth toward the frigid North in the hope of getting the North to warm its attitude toward the South. South Korean businessmen were urged to invest in the North and humanitarian organizations to send food and medical aid. Most South Koreans, despite sunshine diplomacy's subsequent uneven record, still prefer it to previous strategies.

Supreme Commander   One of the official positions held by North Korea's leader. This title refers to Kim Jong Il's role as the commander of the North Korean People's Army (KPA). Kim Jong Il's other official titles are Chairman of the National Defense Commission (NDC) and Chairman of the Korean Workers' Party (KWP).

Supreme People's Assembly (SPA)   The DPRK's 687-member legislature that annually rubber stamps the national budget. The legal term of office is five years. Suffrage is universal beginning at age 17, but elections are not held regularly.

Syngman Rhee (Korean spelling Yi Sung-man, 1875–1965)   The first president of the Republic of Korea (ROK, South Korea) who ruled 1948–1960. An early advocate of Korea's modernization, he migrated to Hawaii, obtained a Ph.D. at Princeton University, and became a leading figure in the Korean independence movement between World War I and the end of World War II. An ardent anticommunist, he refused to sign the Korean War Armistice. His corrupt reelection in 1960 sparked the so-called Student Rebellion, which ended his rule. He fled to the United States where he died in exile.

Taechon   The name of the town near the construction site of what could become North Korea's largest nuclear reactor, the 200 megawatt Taechon nuclear reactor. Work at the site was suspended in 1994 under the terms of the Agreed Framework, but early in 2003, North Korea claimed it had resumed construction of this older design, graphite moderated reactor.

Taepodong I* and *II   The North Korean designations for a multistage ballistic missile with a projected range of 8,000 kilometers (4,800 miles) carrying a 1,000 kilogram (one ton) conventional warhead. North Korea has test-fired the missile only once, in 1998. Hoping to place a satellite in orbit, the launch was a failure, but it enraged the Japanese people because the missile had flown over Japanese airspace.

Taft-Katsura Accord   Refers to the informal agreement dated July 27, 1905, between U.S. Secretary of War William Howard Taft (later president) and Japan's diplomatic envoy Count Katsura. In it, the United States agreed not to interfere in Japan's sphere of influence in Korea, and Japan promised to do likewise regarding the United States colonization of the Philippine Islands. President Teddy Roosevelt confirmed the accord. All Koreans see it as a symbol of superpower treachery, particularly that of the United States and Japan regarding Korea's loss of independence in 1910.

Tangun   The name of Korea's legendary founder whom many Koreans believe established Korea's first dynasty in 2333 B.C.E. According to legend, Tangun's father was a bird deity and his mother a bear. He is said to have been born on *Paektu-san* (White Head Mountain).

theater missile defense (TMD)   The antiballistic missile system jointly developed and deployed by the United States and Japan. It combines over-the-horizon Aegis radar with Patriot PAC-3 short-range antiballistic missiles.

38th parallel   Designated at the end of World War II in 1945 as the temporary border between the U.S. occupied southern half of the Korean Peninsula and the northern, which the Soviet Union was to occupy. The two then allies were to have disarmed the Imperial Japanese Army within their respective zones. As U.S.-Soviet and South-North Korea rivalries intensified, the line became the political boundary between the two Koreas. It was replaced by the DMZ at the end of the Korean War.

Three Kingdoms   Ruled the Korean Peninsula from 57 B.C.E. to 935 C.E. They were Koguryo in the north, Paekche in the southwest, and Shilla in the southeast. Korea's unique culture developed at this time. Buddhism flourished and Korean scholars carried it and China's writing system and Confucian teachings to Japan. North Korean leader Kim Il Sung greatly admired Koguryo's founder.

TMD   *See* theater missile defense.

Treaty on the Non-proliferation of Nuclear Weapons (NPT)   The cornerstone of the international effort to halt the proliferation of nuclear weapons. The world's key nuclear powers (the United States, Russia, and United Kingdom) formulated the treaty and put it into effect in 1970. The NPT created the International Atomic Energy Agency (IAEA) as the UN agency responsible for the treaty's implementation via a system of safeguards agreements between the IAEA and member nations. Some 158 countries are a party to the NPT, but North Korea withdrew from the treaty in January 2003. *See also* International Atomic Energy Agency.

UNC   United Nations Command.

USFK   United States Forces Korea.

USS *General Sherman*   A merchant ship chartered by an American Protestant missionary who sought in 1866 open Korea to commerce. When he sailed up the Taedong River almost to Pyongyang, Koreans blocked the ship's passage and set it ablaze. All hands perished. North Korea's founder Kim Il Sung claimed his grandfather participated in this event. The United States retaliated in 1871 when U.S. gunboats and marines destroyed fortresses that guarded the Han River entrance to Seoul.

USS *Pueblo*   *See Pueblo* incident.

weapons of mass destruction (WMD)   A category of weapons designed to kill large numbers of people. They encompass chemical and biological weapons (CBW), nuclear weapons, and ballistic missiles. North Korea has a significant number of ballistic missiles, and the U.S. intelligence community believes it has the capability to produce and deliver CBW. North Korean officials have claimed their country has developed nuclear weapons.

West Sea   The Korean name for the sea between the Korean Peninsula's West Coast and northeast China. This sea is generally known as the Yellow Sea, named for the yellow dust blown into the sea from the Gobi desert.

Yi Choson   The Korean dynasty that ruled Korea from 1392 to 1910. Founded by a general, the monarchy refined the Chinese centralized bureaucracy and a system of civil and military service examinations while continuing the Korean preference for a powerful hereditary nobility and a stratified society based on heredity.

Yongbyon (spelled Nyongbyon in North Korea)   A small city and the center of silk production in northwest North Korea that is located 100 miles due north of Pyongyang. It is near the site of North Korea's Yongbyon Nuclear Research Center.

Yongbyon Nuclear Research Center   North Korea's primary nuclear facility. The five megawatt (e) nuclear reactor is located here, together with the nuclear spent fuel rods storage facility, reprocessing plant (the North Koreans prefer to call it a radiochemical laboratory), nuclear fuel fabrication plant, nuclear waste storage facilities, and a high explosives research institute. Construction of a 50 megawatt nuclear reactor near the center was scheduled for completion in 1996, but Agreed Framework froze the work. North Korea claimed early in 2003 that it had resumed construction of this reactor. A second much larger 200 megawatt nuclear reactor was under construction about 10 miles northwest of the research center near the town of Taechon. North Korea has also claimed it has resumed construction at this site early in 2003.
See also Agreed Framework, five megawatt (e) nuclear reactor, and spent fuel rods.

Index

Numbers

1905 Treaty of Portsmouth, 87

A

Acheson, Dean, 120
ADB (Asian Development Bank), 267, 312
Ae, Kim Song (Kim Il Sung second wife), 156
Aegis, 292
Agreed Framework of 1994, 6, 251-252
    beginnings, 251-252
    components of agreement, 255-256
    demise, 258
    future revisions, 336
    helicopter crash, 257
    Kim Il Sung's death, 254-255
    negotiations, 253
    Perry Report, 257
    President Jimmy Carter's dialogue, 254
    semi-war alert, 253-254
    suspended withdrawal, 253
air force, war readiness, 283-284
Albright, Madeleine, 258
American Trading Company, 86
    Usan, 126
Amnok River, 34
ancestry, 49-50
Ancient Choson, 51
Anti-Terrorism and Arms Export
    Amendments, 311
Arch of Triumph, 172, 184
aristocracy, 157-158

armistice negotiations, Korean War, 128-129
Arms Export Control Act, 267
army, 12-13
    monitoring, 276
        data gathering, 277
        intelligence reports, 278
        National Intelligence Estimate,
            278-279
        surveillance choices, 276-277
    size, 19-20
arsenal, missile range, 22-23
ASEAN (Association of South East Asian
    Nations), 186
Asian Development Bank (ADB), 267, 312
Association of Korean Residents in Japan,
    241
Association of South East Asian Nations
    (ASEAN), 186
attire, status symbol, 152-154
axis of evil, 6-7

B

back benchers, war readiness, 283
ballistic missiles, 294
    exports, 297
    Hwasong scud, 295
    Nodong, 296
    Taepodong, 296-297
    technology genealogy, 294-295
Beijing, diplomatic negotiations, 15
Beijing Channel, 249
Berlin Airlift, 120
Berlin Conference, 101
Biological and Toxin Weapons Convention
    (BWC), 301

books, education, 169
borders, 34-35
brainwashing, 165-166
Brilliant Exploits, 107
Buddhism
    culture, 54-55
    government controlled, 38
bureaucracy, Chinese legacy, 65
Bush, President George H. W.
    Korean nuclear weapons threat, 250-251
    negotiations to reduce weapons, 6
Bush, President George W.
    offer for disarming nuclear weapons,
        14-15
    shift in policy, 6-7
    U.S. stalemate with Korea, 336-337
        China's request, 337
        dialogue, 338
        escalated negotiations, 339
        HEU program, 338-339
        Korea's requirements for weapons dis-
            mantling, 337
        Six Party Talks, 339-340
        U.S. requirements to Korea, 337-338
BWC (Biological and Toxin Weapons
    Convention), 301

C

cabinets, political system, 146
Caine, Michael, 127
Cairo Declaration, 98-100
Carter, President Jimmy, negotiations with
    Korea, 254
Catholicism, 80-81
CBW (chemical and biological weapons),
    301-302
CCP (Chinese Communist Party), 125
Central Identification Laboratory, Hawaii
    (CILHI), 126
Central Intelligence Agency (CIA), 21
CFC (Combined Forces Command), 129

Ch'ongchon River, 35
Chang, David, 249
Chang-ho, An, 104
Changwang Health Complex, 184
chemical and biological weapons (CBW),
    301-302
Chilbo Mountains, 33
China
    balanced relations with two Koreas, 208
        crossing borders, 210
        increased trade with South Korea, 209
        investments, 209-210
        trade terms, 208-209
    emergence from, 54
        Buddhism, 54-55
        Confucius, 57
        contemporary society, 56
        history seen as power, 57
        individualism, 55
        social hierarchy, 56
        spreading faith, 55
    entrance in Korean War, 125-126
        armistice negotiations, 128-129
        battle at Kunuri, 126-128
        estimated deaths, 131
        firing of MacArthur, 128
        Korean War Armistice, 129-131
    European threat, 79-80
        Catholicism, 80-81
        France, 82
        Germany, 81
        Korean view of China opium move-
            ment, 80
        opium dealers, 80
        United States, 81-82
    Korea's alliance with, 203
        blood-bond, 205-206
    legacy
        early dynasties, 61-62
        emulating luxuries, 71
        foreigners, 71-73
        job competition, 66

Korean advance away from, 67
Koryo kings, 62-65
manufacturing, 70
Marxism, 60-61
noble pedigree, 67-68
regionalism, 69-70
role of women, 68
social pyramid, 70
Sung, Kim Il, preferences, 60
number of North Korean refugees, 27
reaction to Korean nuclear weapons, 214
multilateral talks, 215-216
public reaction, 214-215
request for peace with U.S., 337
rivalry with Japan over Korea, 84
shift in relations, 210
common ground, 213
courting Kim Jong Il, 212
crude oil trade, 211
first nuclear crisis, 211
food aid, 211
friendship reaffirmation, 212-213
Korea withdrawal from NPT, 209-210
refugees, 213-214
up and down diplomacy, 206-208
World Order, 78-79
Chinese Communist Party (CCP), 125
Chinese World Order, 78
Chol, Chong, 157
Chol-chu, Kim, 156
Chondoist Chongu Party, 145
Chong-nam, Kim
birth, 157
heir apparent, 157
Chong-suk, Kim (Kim Il Sung's wife), 113,
155-156
Chongryu Restaurant, 184
Chosen soron, 47, 234-235
Christianity, government controlled, 38
Chung-gun, An, 92, 104
Chung-hee, Park, assassination attempt,
308-309

Churchill, Winston, 98
CIA (Central Intelligence Agency), 21
CILHI (Central Identification Laboratory,
Hawaii), 126
CINCUNC (commander in chief of the UN
command), 122
climate, 33
Clinton, President Bill
Agreed Framework, 6, 251-252
beginnings, 251-252
components of agreement, 255-256
demise, 258
helicopter crash, 257
Kim Il Sung's death, 254-255
negotiations, 253
Perry Report, 257
President Jimmy Carter's dialogue, 254
semi-war alert, 253-254
suspended withdrawal, 253
Korea relations, 248
clothing, status symbol, 152-154
coal, 35
Cold War, ending, 331-332
Il, Kim Jong, regime survival, 333-334
nuclear weapons possession, 333
collectivism, 142
Combined Forces Command (CFC), 129
comfort women issue, 313
Japan's response, 314
judgment of Japan, 314
sanctions, 315
commander in chief of the UN command
(CINCUNC), 122
Committee for Afro-Asian Solidarity, 161
Committee for Solidarity with the World's
People, 161
Committee for the Peaceful Reunification of
the Fatherland, 160
Communist Manifesto, The, 46
Confucianism, historical record, 107
Confucius, 57
teaching in children's early years, 165

Convention of Tientsin Between China and Japan, 85
copper, 36
Coup d'Etat of 1884, 85-86
crude oil, shortage, 180
cruise missiles, 294
Cultural Reform Period, 95-97
culture, Buddhism, 54
currency, 40
curriculum, education, 168

D

Dark Period, 95
Demilitarized Zone (DMZ), 11
defense against military, 285
    attacks to South Korea, 285
    deterrence, 285-286
    North Korea's façade of military, 286-287
defense first policy, economy, 176-177
    gains made during Cold War, 177-178
Defense Intelligence Agency (DIA), 21
democracy, current political view, 143-144
Democratic Front for the Reunification of the Fatherland, 160
Democratic Lawyers Association, 160
Democratic People's Republic of Korea (DPRK), 4, 116
Democratic Youth League, 160
Department of Energy, 21
DIA (Defense Intelligence Agency), 21
Diamond Mountain, tourism, 269
Diet, 233
DMZ (Demilitarized Zone), 11
    opening, 269
Doo-hwan, Chun, 223
Down-with-Imperialism Union, 107
DPRK (Democratic People's Republic of Korea), 4, 116
driving, 153
dynasties
    Koryo, 61-62
    Yi Choson, 61-62

E

economic sanctions
    impact, 268
    North Korea terrorist nation, 311-312
    opposition, 267-268
    option for reunification, 266-267
    terrorism, 315
economy, 39-40
    currency, 40
    defense first policy, 176-177
        gains made during Cold War, 177-178
    downfall, 178-179
        crude oil shock, 180
        environmental disasters, 181
        farm machines, 181-182
        fertilizers, 180-181
        food production, 184-185
        irrigation, 181
        massive construction projects, 183-184
        Pyongyang bunker building, 184
        Soviet Union, 179-180
        sport facilities, 183
        surge in construction, 182-183
        trade decline, 185
    GDP, 40-41
    industries, 41
    positive trends, 185-187
    weapons of mass destruction dilemma, 187
education, 165-166
    curriculum, 168
    early Confucius teachings, 165
    graduation, 171
    higher education, 169-170
    historical sites, 171-173
    Kim Il Sung University, 170
    KWP control, 167
    labor, 171
    media governing, 174
    military training, 170
    mind-molding, 166-167
    special education, 167
    textbooks, 169

Eisenhower, President Dwight D., election, 128

employment, examination system, 66

Engels, Friedrich, 60
Communist Manifesto, The, 46

Enlightenment Party, 85

espionage, Korean Airline flight 858, 306-307

ethnic groups, population, 38

Europeans
threat, 79-80
Catholicism, 80-81
France, 82
Germany, 81
Korean view of China opium movement, 80
opium dealers, 80
United States, 81-82
viewed as foreigners, 72-73

examination system, 66
noble pedigree, 67-68

exchanges, 271

Export Administration Acts, 267

F

farms
machines, 181-182
society status, 154
versus city life, 152

fertilizers, economic problems, 180-181

FETZ (Rajin/Sonbong Free Economic and Trade Zone), 237

field-trips, historical sites, 171-173

food
economic downfall, 184-185
struggle to get, 25-27

Forced Assimilation, 95-97

Foreign Operations Appropriations, 312

foreigners, 71, 77-78
European threat, 79-80
Catholicism, 80-81
France, 82
Germany, 81
opium dealers, 80
United States, 81-82
Europeans, 72-73
Japan
pirate-traders, 72
show of force in Korea, 83
Mongols, 72
obstructing outside influence, 325-326
victim of great powers, 83-84
China-Japan rivalry over Korea, 84
Coup d'Etat of 1884, 85-86
military mutiny of 1882, 84
Protectorate Treaty of 1905, 87
Russo-Japanese War, 87
Sino-Japanese War of 1894–1995, 86-87
Treaty of Chemulpo, 84-85
unequal treaties, 85
United States return, 86

France, 82

French plunder, 82

fuel rods, 21

future, 341
ending Cold War, 331-332
Il, Kim Jong, 333-334
nuclear weapons possession, 333
stalemate, 336-337
China's request, 337
dialogue, 338
escalated negotiations, 339
HEU program, 338-339
Korea's requirements for weapons dismantling, 337
Six Party Talks, 339-340
U.S. requirements to Korea, 337-338

United States dilemma, 334-335
  hard landing, 335
  living with danger, 336
  revised Agreed Framework, 336
  soft landing, 335
futures, North and South Korea reconciliation, 272

G

Gallucci, Robert, 251
GDP (gross domestic product), 40-41
gender, society status, 151
General Federation of the Unions of Literature and Art of Korea, 160
geography, Korean Peninsula, 31-33
Germany, movement to Korea, 81
gold, 36
Gorbachev, Mikhail, 195
government, 145
  divisions, 38
  leadership, 39
  representatives, 147
  structure, 39
graduation, continuing education, 171
Grand Monument on Mansu Hill, 172
Grand People's Study Hall, 183
Grew, Joseph, 99
gross domestic product (GDP), 40-41

H

Han, 51
Hankuk, 47-48
hard currency, trade of weapons for, 7-10
  father and son duo, 8-9
  proliferation security initiative, 8
hard landings, 335
Hee, Park Chung, 222-223
helicopters, military readiness, 283
HEU (highly enriched uranium), 300-301

higher education, 169-170
highly enriched uranium (HEU), 300-301
Hirobumi, Ito, 91-92
  assassination, 104
history, 45-46
  Buddhism, culture, 54
  China legacy
    early dynasties, 61-62
    emulating luxuries, 71
    foreigners, 71-73
    job competition, 66
    Korean advance away from, 67
    Koryo kings, 62-65
    manufacturing, 70
    Marxism, 60-61
    noble pedigree, 67-68
    regionalism, 69-70
    role of women, 68
    social pyramid, 70
    Sung, Kim Il, preferences, 60
  emergence as nation, 50
  emergence from China, 54
    Buddhism, 54-55
    Confucius, 57
    contemporary society, 56
    history seen as power, 57
    individualism, 55
    social hierarchy, 56
    spreading faith, 55
  Europe's threat, 79-80
    Catholicism, 80-81
    France, 82
    Germany, 81
    Korean view of China opium movement, 80
    opium dealers, 80
    United States, 81-82
  historical sites, 171-173
  Japan
    erasing Korean independence, 94-97
    prelude to annexation of Korea, 90-92
    show of force, 83

Treaty of Annexation, 92-94
World War II effects on Korea, 97-101
Koguryo, 51-52
    legacy, 52
    Sung, Kim Il, 52-53
Korean struggle for independence,
    104-105
    Ku, Kim, 106
    Syngman, Rhee, 105
    Tong-hwi, Lee, 106-108
Korean War
    never-ending, 118-120
    pre-war activities, 120-125
    start of war, 125-131
Shilla, 53
Soviet Union occupation, 113-114
    division of Korea, 115-116
    Korean Cold War, 114-115
Sung, Kim Il, early years, 108-113
    ancestry, 108-110
    return to Pyongyang, 114
victim of foreign powers, 83-84
    China-Japan rivalry over Korea, 84
    Coup d'Etat of 1884, 85-86
    military mutiny of 1882, 84
    Protectorate Treaty of 1905, 87
    Russo-Japanese War, 87
    Sino-Japanese War of 1894–1995,
      86-87
    Treaty of Chemulpo, 84-85
    unequal treaties, 85
    United States return, 86
    Yi Choson, gradual change, 76-79
Hon-yong, Pak, 114
Hui, Kim Hyon, 313
human rights
    continuity versus change, 328-329
    North Korean view, 318
    obligations versus rights, 318-319
      legal tyranny, 319-320
      push for change, 322-323
      repair versus revamp, 324
      soft versus hard landings, 323

      survival struggle, 321-322
      Western concepts, 320-321
    obstructing outside influence, 324
      following ancestors, 324-325
      foreigners, 325-326
      migrants, 327-328
      monitoring flow of refugees, 327
      refugees, 326-327
humanitarian aid, 271
Hwasong, scud, 295
Hwasong 6, 22-23
Hye-kyong, Kim, 157
Hye-nim, Song, 156
Hyon-hui, Kim, terrorist, 306
Hyong-jik, Kim, 108-109
Hyong-sil, Kim, 156
Hyong-sop, Yang, 156

I

IAEA (International Atomic Energy Agency),
    14, 198
Il, Kim Jong, 5-9
    birth, 113
    clinging to past, 334
    confessions of kidnapping Japanese citi-
      zens, 315
    continuity versus change, 328-329
    desire for regime survival, 333-334
    despair over father's death, 9-10
    family, 156-157
    military matters, 12-13
    obstructing outside influence, 324
      following ancestors, 324-325
      foreigners, 325-326
      migrants, 327-328
      monitoring flow of refugees, 327
      refugees, 326-327
    personal relationships, 10
    personality, 11
      manipulator, 11-12
      technology fascination, 12

power development, 6
   axis of evil, 6-7
   breaking of promises, 7
   weapons negotiation, 6
public image, 10
regime, 27-29
U.S. stalemate with Korea, 336-337
   China's request, 337
   dialogue, 338
   escalated negotiations, 339
   HEU program, 338-339
   Korea's requirements for weapons dismantling, 337
   Six Party Talks, 339-340
   U.S. requirements to Korea, 337-338
   wealth, 10-11
Il-chon, Hong, 157
IMF (International Monetary Fund), 267, 312
Imjin River, 35
Imperial Japan, 158-159
independence, 104-105
   Ku, Kim, 106
   Syngman, Rhee, 105
   Tong-hwi, Lee, 106-108
individualism, 55, 319
industries, 41
intelligence reports, Korean military, 278
International Atomic Energy Agency (IAEA), 14, 198
International Monetary Fund (IMF), 267, 312
international terrorism, North Korea's support, 23-25
investment, inter-Korean, 270
iron ore, 35
irrigation, economic downfall, 181

J

JAL (Japan Airlines), 307
Japan
   comfort women issue, 313
      judgment of Japan, 314
      response from Japan, 314
      sanctions, 315
   erasing Korean independence, 94-95
      Cultural Reform Period, 96-97
      Dark Period, 95
      Forced Assimilation, 97
      March 1 Movement, 95-96
   issues with North Korea, 235
      bilateral normalization declaration, 235-236
      continued dialogues, 236-237
      demands for compensation, 238
      nuclear crisis, 238
      Rajin/Sonbong Free Economic and Trade Zone, 237
      Tumen River Development Project, 236-237
   kidnapping of citizens, 312
      Il, Kim Jong, confessions, 315
      language teachers, 313
      normalization talks, 313
   North Korean relations, 232
      attempts at dialogue, 232-233
      Chosen soron, 234-235
      Four Dragon competition, 233
   pirate-traders, 72
   prelude to annexation of Korea, 90
      iron fist rule, 91-92
      Righteous Armies, 92
      United States complacency, 90-91
   rivalry with China over Korea, 84
   second round normalization talks, 239-240
      Japan outrage at missile launch, 241-242
      Japanese spouses, 239

summits, 242-243
Taepodong ballistic missile, 240
unresolved issues, 243-244
show of force in Korea, 83
Treaty of Annexation, 92-93
citizenship benefits, 93
fortress against Russia, 94
land ownership, 93
new economy, 94
poverty of Korea, 94
World War II, 97-98
Allied powers trusteeship of Korea, 99-100
Cairo Declaration, 98
doubts of Korean independence, 99
Korea divided, 100-101
Potsdam Conference, 100
Yalta Summit, 98
Japan Airlines (JAL), 307
Japan's Self-Defense Forces (JSDF), 291-292
Japanese Red Army (JRA), 23, 307
JCS (Joint Chiefs of Staff), 21
Jenkins, Private Charles R., 24, 243
jobs, examination system, 66
Joint Chiefs of Staff (JCS), 21
Joint Declaration on the Denuclearization of the Korean Peninsula, 226
Jong, Kim Il, son Kim Chong-nam 157
Jordan, Michael, 111
Journalists Union, 160
JRA (Japanese Red Army), 23, 307
JSDF (Japan's Self-Defense Forces), 291-292
juche, 140-143
obligations versus rights, 318-319
legal tyranny, 319-320
push for change, 322-323
repair versus revamp, 324
soft versus hard landings, 323
survival struggle, 321-322
Western concepts, 320-321
Juche Tower, 184
judiciary, 145-147
Jung, Kim Dae, 218, 223, 227

K

Kaechon, 126
Kai-shek, Generalissimo Chiang, 98, 104-106, 120, 125
KAL (Korean Airline), 306
Kanemaru, Shin, 233
Kaya, 50-51
KEDO (Korea Peninsula Energy Development Organization), 179
Kim Chaek University of Technology, 169
Kim Hyong-jik College of Education, 157
Kim Il Sung Higher Party School, 169
Kim Il Sung Reminiscences, 106
Kim Il Sung Socialist Youth League, 160
Kim Il Sung University, 169-170
Kim-song, Chang, 156
Kimchaek University, 170
kimchi, 176
Kimichi, 50
kingdoms, emergence of nation, 50
Koguryo, 50-52
legacy, 52
Sung, Kim Il, 52-53
Koizumi, Junichiro, 242, 315
Kojong, 81
Korea, naming scheme, 9
Korea Peninsula Energy Development Organization (KEDO), 179
Korean Airline (KAL), 306
Korean Airline flight 858
terrorist act, 306-307
Korean Communist Party, 114
Korean General Federation of Trade Unions, 160
Korean Independence Movement, 99
Korean Peninsula, 13, 18, 31-33
Korean people, view of Korea, 46-47
ancestry, 49-50
name changes, 47-48
Tangun, 48-49

Korean People's Army (KPA), 19-20
Korean People's Socialist Party, 106
Korean Revolution Museum, 172
Korean Traders Association (KOTRA), 185
Korean War
    never-ending, 118-120
    post war efforts
        juche, 140-142
        rebuilding, 137-138
        reinterpretation of Marxism, 139
        secretive society, 136-137
        serving the great, 139-140
    pre-war activities, 120
        armies line-up, 121
        Kim Sung Il invades South Korea, 121-122
        KPA on edge of victory, 123-124
        MacArthur, General Douglas, 125
    start of war, 125-126
        armistice negotiations, 128-129
        battle at Kunuri, 126-128
        estimated deaths, 131
        Korean War Armistice, 129-131
        MacArthur replaced, 128
Korean War Armistice, 4, 118, 129-131
Korean Workers' Party (KWP), 39, 144
    education, 166-167
Koryo
    celadon, 70
    early dynasties, 61-62
    kings, 62-63
        bureaucracy, 65
        land ownership, 64-65
        mandate of heaven, 63-64
Koryo Communist Party, 106
KOTRA (Korean Traders Association), 185
KPA (Korean People's Army), 19-20, 39
Ku, Kim, 104-106
Kumgang Mountains, 34
Kumsusan Mausoleum, 173
Kunuri, Korean War battle, 126-128
Kuryong River, 35

Kwang-sop, Kim, 156
Kwangju Incident, 223
Kwangju Student Resistance Movement, 97
KWP (Korean Workers' Party), 39, 144
    education, 166-167
Kyong-hui, Kim (Kim Il Sung's daughter), 113, 155
Kyong-jin, 156

L

labor education, 171
language, population, 38
leadership, 39
Lenin, Vladimir
    influence on Kim Il Sung, 76
    juche thought, 143
Li, Colonel, 119
Lianjiang, 111
life expectancy, population, 37
limestone, 35
luxuries, 71

M

MAC (Military Armistice Commission), 130
MacArthur, General Douglas, 100, 118
    CINCUNC, 129
    Korean War, 125-126, 131
        armistice negotiations, 128-129
        battle at Kunuri, 126-128
        firing of MacArthur, 128
        Korean War Armistice, 129-131
        pre-war activities, 125
    view of communism in Korea, 119
magnetite, 35
males, society status, 151
Man-sik, Cho, 114
manganese, 36
Mangyongdae, 172

Mangyongdae Children's Palace, 183
Mangyongdae Revolutionary School, 169
manipulating reality, 164
    armed personnel fiction, 164-165
    early Confucius teachings, 165
Mansudae Assembly Hall, 184
March 1 Movement, 95-96
Marx, Karl, 60
    Communist Manifesto, The, 46
Marxism, 60-61
    post Korean War reinterpretation, 139
mechanized units, 19-20
media, governing, 174
Memories of the Three Kingdoms, 48
migrants, 327-328
military, 12-13
    army size, 19-20
    defense against, 285
        attacks to South Korea, 285
        deterrence, 285-286
        façade of military, 286-287
    monitoring, 276
        data gathering, 277
        intelligence reports, 278
        National Intelligence Estimate,
          278-279
        surveillance choices, 276-277
    mutiny of 1882, 84
    objectives, 279
        armed reunification, 280
        defensive change, 280
        revised national priorities, 281
        technological superiority, 281
    training, 170
    war readiness, 282
        air power, 283-284
        back benchers, 283
        communication advances, 284
        helicopters, 283
        mechanized ground forces, 282
        navy, 284
        Special Operations Forces, 282-283

Military Armistice Commission (MAC), 130
Ministry of Public Security (MPS), 161
Minjuuiwon, 106
missiles
    range, 22-23
    talks, 298
Molotov, V. M., 99
Mongols, 72
monitoring North Korea, 276
    data gathering, 277
    intelligence reports, 278
    National Intelligence Estimate, 278-279
    surveillance choices, 276-277
monsoons, 177
MPS (Ministry of Public Security), 161
multilateral conference, Russia, 201
multilateral talks, 15-16
Murphy, Admiral Dan, 249
mutiny, military mutiny of 1882, 84
Myohyang Mountains, 34
Myohyang-Pyongyang Expressway, 36

N

names
    Korea name changes, 47-48
    married name for women, 108
NAN (nonaligned nations), 193
National Defense Commission (NDC),
  145-146
National Intelligence Estimate (NIE), 21,
  278-279
National Peace Committee, 160
National Security Agency (NSA), 21
National Security Council (NSC), 21
National Security Law, 221
natural resources, 35-36
nature, economic devastation, 176-177
navy, war readiness, 284
NDC (National Defense Commission),
  145-146

nepotism, 155-156
Neutral Nations Repatriation Commission (NNRC), 129
Neutral Nations Supervisory Commission (NNSC), 130
New People's Association, 106
news, governing, 174
nickel, 35
NIE (National Intelligence Estimate), 21, 278-279
NNRC (Neutral Nations Repatriation Commission), 129
NNSC (Neutral Nations Supervisory Commission), 130
nobility, luxuries, 71
noble pedigree, examination system, 67-68
Nodong, 22-23, 296
nonaligned nations (NAN), 193
nordpolitik strategy, 249
normalization talks, kidnapped Japanese citizens, 313
North Korea
    army size, 19-20
    current relationship with United States, 4
        North Korea's true threat, 5
        war versus peace, 4-5
    location, 17-19
    nuclear weapons, do they have them, 21-22
    threat to peace, 13
        Beijing talks, 15
        building of nuclear arsenal, 14
        Bush's blackmail, 14-15
        multilateral talks, 15-16
        news of nuclear weapons program, 14
    trade for hard currency, 7-10
        father and son duo, 8-9
        proliferation security initiative, 8
    view of United States, 6
        axis of evil, 6-7
        breaking of promises, 7
        weapons negotiations, 6

North Korean People's Army (KPA), 39
North-South Joint Communiqué, 223
NPT (Treaty on the Non-proliferation of Nuclear Weapons), 14
NSA (National Security Agency), 21
NSC (National Security Council), 21
nuclear power plants, 270
nuclear umbrella, 281
nuclear war, threat of, 13
    Beijing talks, 15
    building of nuclear arsenal, 14
    Bush's blackmail, 14-15
    multilateral talks, 15-16
    news of nuclear weapons program, 14
nuclear weapons, 298-299
    beginning of nuclear program, 299
    highly enriched uranium, 300-301
    Korea relationship with Russia, 201
    Korean effort to build, 201-202
    plutonium extraction, 300

O-P

oil shortage, 180
Olympics, Seoul, 224
organized worship, ban, 38
Oriental Development Company, 93
Overland Trade Agreement with Russia, 85

PAC-3, 292
Paekche, 50-51
Paektu-san Mountains, 34
Pan-sok, Kang, 108
Pang-ja, Yi, 91
Panmunjom, 130
Parhae, 51
People's Republic of China (PRC), 120-125
    North Korea relations, 206-207, 212
Perry Report, 257
Perry, William, 257

pirate-traders, Japanese, 72
plunder, 82
plutonium program, 300
police state, 164-165
political parties, 39
political system, 142
    cabinet, 146
    current self image, 142-143
    democratic view, 143-144
    government, 145
    judiciary, 147
    Korean Workers' Party, 144
    National Defense Commission, 145-146
    succession hereditary, 145
    Supreme People's Assembly, 146
    token parties, 145
politics
    Marxism, 60-61
    Sung, Kim Il preferences, 60
population, 37-38
Potsdam Conference, 100-101
Potsdam Proclamation, 101
power
    society pyramid, 155
        Chong-nam, Kim, 157
        Imperial Japan, 158-159
        Kim Jong family, 156-157
        nepotism, 155-156
        new aristocracy, 157-158
        political organizations, 160-161
        Soviet Union similarities, 159
PRC (People's Republic of China), 125
    North Korea relations, 206-207, 212
private voluntary organizations (PVO), 137
production, 39-40
    currency, 40
    GDP, 40-41
    industries, 41
proliferation security initiative (PSI), 8
Protectorate Treaty of 1905, 87
PSI (proliferation security initiative), 8

publications
    Communist Manifesto, The, 46
    governing, 174
    Kim Il Sung Reminiscences, 106
pukhan saram, 48
purchasing power parity method, 41
Pusan Perimeter, 124
Putin, Vladimir, 199
    multilateral conference, 201
    nuclear weapons, 201
    redefining Korea relationship, 200
PVO (private voluntary organizations), 137
Pyong-il, 156
Pyongyang, 4
Pyongyang Central Youth Hall, 184
Pyongyang Circus, 184
Pyongyang Communist University, 169
Pyongyang Maternity Hospital, 184
Pyongyang University, 169
Pyongyang-Nampo Expressway, 36
Pyongyang-Wonsan Expressway, 36

Q-R

Queen Min, assassination, 92
Quinones, Dr. C. Kenneth, author, 19

railroads, linking South and North Korea, 270
Rajin/Sonbong Free Economic and Trade Zone (FETZ), 237
Rangoon, terrorist murders, 310-311
Reagan, President Ronald, Korea nuclear threat, 249-250
Reconciliation Agreement, 270-271
reeducation, 165-166
refugees, 326-327
    monitoring flow, 327
    number in China, 27
regionalism, 69-70
religion, 38

Republic of China (ROC), 125
Republic of Korea (ROK), 4, 115
reunification, 262
    military forcing, 280
    options for
        economic sanctions, 266-267
        impact of sanctions, 268
        peaceful co-existence, 268
        political system collapse, 265-266
        positive dialogue, 269-271
        regime change, 264-265
        renewed dreams of reunification,
            268-269
        sanction opposition, 267-268
        war, 262-263
Reunification Highway, 36
reverse engineering, 295
Revolutionary Martyrs Cemetery on Mt.
    Taesong, 173
revolutionary sites, 171-173
Rhee, Dr. Syngman, 99, 104, 115, 120
Righteous Armies, 92
rivers, 34-35
ROC (Republic of China), 125
ROK (Republic of Korea), 4, 115
Rok, Jo Myong, 258
Roosevelt, President Franklin D., Cairo
    Declaration, 98
Roosevelt, President Theodore, 1905 Treaty
    of Portsmouth, 87
Russia. *See also* Soviet Union
    Koreas need for, 195
        altered security in Northeast Asia, 197
        Moscow relationship cools, 198-199
        relationship devastations, 195-196
    North Korea relations, 194-198
    Northeast Asia ambitions, 192
        Korea taking from Stalin, 193-195
        Korean guerillas, 192-193
        protection against United States, 193
    view on Korean nuclear weapons, 201-202

Vladimir Putin, 199
    multilateral conference, 201
    nuclear weapons, 201
    redefining Korea relationship, 200
Russo-Japanese War, 87

S

Samgukyusa, 48
San Francisco conference, 101
Scud C, 22
Scud D, 22
self sufficiency in food, 26
Seoul, attempted assassinations, 307
Shilla, 50-53
silver, 36
Sin'ganhoe, 97
Sin-suk, Kim, 156
Sino-Japanese War of 1894–1895, 86-87
Sino-Soviet dispute, 138
Sirhak, 77
Six Party Talks, future, 339-340
Social Democratic Party, 145
social pyramids, 70
society
    keeping order
        attire status symbol, 152-154
        city versus farm, 152
        farmers, 154
        gender status, 151
        rank privileges, 151
        Sung, Kim Il, ten conduct rules, 150
        transportation, 154-155
    Ministry of Public Security, 161
    pyramid of power, 155
        Chong-nam, Kim, 157
        Il, Kim Jong, family, 156-157
        Imperial Japan, 158-159
        nepotism, 155-156
        new aristocracy, 157-158

political organizations, 160-161
Soviet Union similarities, 159
State Security Agency, 161
SOF (Special Operations Forces), 282-283
soft landings, 335
Sok-ju, Kang, 251
Sol-song, Kim, 157
Song-t'aek, Chang, 155
South Korea
dialogue, 222
attempt at reconciliation, 222-223
Olympics in Seoul, 224
return to rivalry, 223
reversals of prosperity, 224-225
Seoul, 223
end of Cold War dialogue, 225-226
closer to agreement with U.S., 226-227
four party talks, 227
nuclear crisis, 226
estrangement, 218
confrontation, 220
contact by citizens, 221
deter aggression, 219-220
intense competition, 219
mutual distrust, 219
threat to each other, 220-221
future prospects for reconciliation, 272
sunshine diplomacy, 227-229
South-North Korea Agreement on
Reconciliation, Non-aggression, and
Exchanges and Cooperation, 226
South-North Liaison Office at Panmunjom,
269
Soviet Union. See also Russia
Korean economic downfall, 179-180
Koreas need for, 195
altered security in Northeast Asia, 197
Moscow relationship cools, 198-199
relationship devastations, 195-196
North Korea relations, 194, 198
occupation of North Korea, 113-114
division of Korea, 115-116
Korean Cold War, 114-115
Sung, Kim Il, return to Pyongyang, 114
Sung, Kim Il, retreat to, 112-113

SPA (Supreme People's Assembly), 39, 146
special education, 167
Special Operations Forces (SOF), 282-283
Stalin, Josef, 98
starvation, food struggle, 25-27
State Administrative Council, 145
State Department Bureau of Intelligence and
Research (State INR), 21
State INR (State Department Bureau of
Intelligence and Research), 21
State Security Agency, 161
streams, 34-35
Students Committee, 161
Sunchon Vinalon Complex, 179
Sung, Kim Il, 8-9
climb to power, 45-46
death, 9-10, 254-255
early years, 108
ancestry, 108-110
communist education, 111
fathers anti-Japanese influence,
109-110
joining guerilla groups, 111-112
march home, 110-111
retreat to Soviet Union, 112-113
Soviet Union life, 113
Koguryo, 52-53
Marxism, 60-61
need for Soviet Union, 195
altered security in Northeast Asia, 197
Moscow relationship cools, 198-199
relationship devastations, 195-196
politics, 142
cabinet, 146
democratic view, 143-144
government, 145
judiciary, 147
Korean Workers' Party, 144
National Defense Commission,
145-146
preferences, 60
self image, 142-143

succession hereditary, 145
Supreme People's Assembly, 146
token parties, 145
post Korean War efforts
juche, 140-142
rebuilding, 137-138
reinterpretation of Marxism, 139
secretive society, 136-137
serving the great, 139-140
pre-Korean war activities, 120
return to Pyongyang, 114
rise to power, 107
ten conduct rules, 150
Sung,Kim Il, 5
Sung-il, Kim, terrorist, 306
Sunjong, 91
sunshine diplomacy, 227-229
Supreme People's Assembly SPA), 39,
145-146
Syngman, Rhee, 105

T

Taedong River, 35
Taepodong, 296-297
Taepodong, 22-23
Taepodong II, 23
Taewon'gun, 81
Taft, President William Howard, 90
Taft-Katsura Accord, 90-91
Tam, Ho, 156
Tangun, 48-49
teachers, kidnapping, 313
television, governing, 174
terrain, 33-34
terrorism
attempted assassinations, 307
capture of USS *Pueblo*, 308
chronology, 309
comfort women issue, 313
Japan's response, 314
judgment of Japan, 314
sanctions, 315

JRA hijacking to Pyongyang, 307
kidnapping Japanese citizens, 312
Il, Kim Jong, confessions, 315
language teachers, 313
normalization talks, 313
killing of American officers, 309-310
Korean Airline flight 858, 306
covert espionage, 306-307
North Korea
public renunciation, 316
support, 23-25
terrorism nation, 311-312
Park Chung-hee assassination attempt,
308-309
Rangoon murders, 310-311
textbooks, education, 169
Theater Missile Defense System (TMD),
241, 292
Three Kingdoms, 51
TMD (Theater Missile Defense System),
241
Tomb of King Tongmyong, 171
Tomb of Tangun, 171
Ton-uk, Kang, 109
Tong-hwi, Lee, 104-108
Tonghak Rebellion, 106
Tongil-ro Highway, 36
trade
decline, 185
inter-Korean, 270
train transportation, 36
training, military, 170
transportation, 36
society status, 154-155
travel, to North Korea, 29
Treaty of Annexation, 89-93
citizenship benefits, 93
erasing Korean independence, 94-95
Cultural Reform Period, 96-97
Dark Period, 95
Forced Assimilation, 97
March 1 Movement, 95-96

fortress against Russia, 94
land ownership, 93
new economy, 94
poverty of Korea, 94
Treaty of Chemulpo, 84-85
Treaty of Portsmouth, 90
Treaty on the Non-proliferation of Nuclear
Weapons (NPT), 14
Treaty with France, 85
Treaty with Germany, 85
Treaty with Great Britain, 85
Treaty with Italy, 85
Treaty with Russia, 85
Treaty with the United States, 85
Truman, President Harry S., 99
firing of MacArthur, 128
Tumen River Development Project, 34,
236-237
typhoons, 177
tyranny, legalized, 319-320

U

U.S. Export Administration Act, 311
U.S. Forces in Korea (USFK), 19, 129
U.S.-Japan Defense Guidelines, 240
U.S.-Japan Mutual Defense Treaty, 240
UN Development Program (UNDP), 236
UN Security Council, members, 122
UN Temporary Commission on Korea, 115
UNC (United Nations Command), 129
UNDP (United Nations Development
Program), 179
unequal treaties, 85
Ung-u, Kim, 108
UNHCR (United Nations High
Commissioner on Refugees), 27
Unified Shilla, 51
uniforms, status symbols, 152-154
United Nations Command (UNC), 129

United Nations Development Program
(UNDP), 179
United Nations High Commissioner on
Refugees (UNHCR), 27
United States
Agreed Framework, 251-252
beginnings, 251-252
components of agreement, 255-256
demise, 258
helicopter crash, 257
Kim Il Sung's death, 254-255
negotiations, 253
Perry Report, 257
President Jimmy Carter's dialogue, 254
semi-war alert, 253-254
suspended withdrawal, 253
complacency of Japan annexation, 90-91
current relationship with North Korea, 4
North Korea's true threat, 5
war versus peace, 4-5
entrance in South Korea, 113-114
division of Korea, 115-116
Korean Cold War, 114-115
first appearance in Korea, 81-82
future dilemma, 334-335
hard landing, 335
living with danger, 336
revised Agreed Framework, 336
soft landing, 335
Korea relations
future prospects, 272
North and South reconciliation
prospects, 271
reunification possibilities, 262-271
Korean nuclear weapons threat, 246
Bush, President George H. W.,
250-251
Clinton administration, 248
containment, 248-249
international censure, 247-248
limited time negotiations, 248
Reagan administration, 249-250
threat to pull out of NPT, 246-247

Korean War, never-ending, 118-120
North Korea's view, 6
  axis of evil, 6-7
  breaking of promises, 7
  weapons negotiations, 6
relations stalemate, 336-337
  China's request, 337
  dialogue, 338
  escalated negotiations, 339
  HEU program, 338-339
  Korea's requirements for weapons dismantling, 337
  Six Party Talks, 339-340
  U.S. requirements to Korea, 337-338
retaliatory attack, 82
Unsan, 126
USFK (U.S. Forces Korea), 19, 129
USS *General Sherman*, 81-82
USS *Pueblo* capture by North Korea, 308

V–W–X

Versailles Peace Conference, 95
Victorious Fatherland Liberation War Museum, 173

Wan-yong, Yi, 92
war, option for reunification, 262-263
weapons of mass destruction (WMDs), 289-290
  ballistic missiles, 294
    exports, 297
    Hwasong scud, 295
    Nodong, 296
    Taepodong, 296-297
    technology genealogy, 294-295
  economic woes, 187
  missile talks, 298
  North Korea paranoia, 290
    China, 292
    deterring U.S., 293-294

Japan's Self-Defense Forces, 291-292
    options, 292-293
    Russia, 292
    South Korean threat, 291
    U.S. threat, 291
  nuclear weapons, 298-299
    beginning of nuclear program, 299
    highly enriched uranium, 300-301
    plutonium extraction, 300
  potential danger, 303
  targeted countries, 297-298
Wilson, President Woodrow, Fourteen Points, 95
Wisda, LTC Marty, 168, 310
WMDs (weapons of mass destruction), 289-290
  ballistic missiles, 294
    exports, 297
    Hwasong scud, 295
    Nodong, 296
    Taepodong, 296-297
    technology genealogy, 294-295
  missile talks, 298
  North Korea paranoia, 290
    China, 292
    deterring U.S., 293-294
    Japan's Self-Defense Forces, 291-292
    options, 292-293
    Russia, 292
    South Korean threat, 291
    U.S. threat, 291
  nuclear weapons, 298-299
    beginning of nuclear program, 299
    highly enriched uranium, 300-301
    plutonium extraction, 300
  potential danger, 303
  targeted countries, 297-298
women
  China legacy, role, 68
  comfort women issue, 313
    Japan's response, 314
    judgment of, 314
    sanctions, 315
  married name, 108
  society status, 151

Woo, Roe Tae, 225
World War II, 97-98
   Allied powers trusteeship of Korea,
    99-100
   Cairo Declaration, 98
   doubts of Korean independence, 99
   Korea divided, 100-101
   Potsdam Conference, 100
   Yalta Summit, 98

Y-Z

Yak-san Mountains, 34
yakuza, 234
Yalta Conference, 100
Yalta Summit, 98
Yalu River, 34
Yanbian, 51
yanggui, 71
Yeltsin, Boris, 198
Yi Choson
   early dynasties, 61-62
   gradual change, 76-77
      Chinese World Order, 78-79
      foreigners, 77-78
Yokota, Megumi, kidnapping, 312
Yonbyon, 51
Yong-chu, Kim, 156
Yong-hui, Ko, 157
Yong-il, 156
Yong-suk, Kim, 157
Yongbyon Nuclear Research Center, 20

Zedong, Mao, 120, 125
zinc, 35

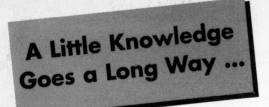
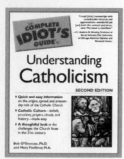

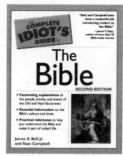